MICROPROCESSORS
FOR MEASUREMENT
AND CONTROL

MICROPROCESSORS FOR MEASUREMENT AND CONTROL

David M. Auslander and Paul Sagues

Osborne/McGraw-Hill
Berkeley, California

Published by
OSBORNE/McGraw-Hill
630 Bancroft Way
Berkeley, California 94710
U.S.A.

For information on translations and book distributors outside of the
U.S.A., please write OSBORNE/McGraw-Hill at the above address.

MICROPROCESSORS FOR MEASUREMENT AND CONTROL

234567890   DODO   898765432

ISBN 0-931988-57-8

PHOTO CREDITS: All photos by Harvey Schwartz except Figure 1.13
which is by Paul Sagues.

BOOK AND COVER DESIGN: Irene Imfeld

CONTENTS

To:
Grandma Rose and Grandma Stella
Victor and Janice

PREFACE

This text describes the role of microprocessors in the instrumentation and control of mechanical and process equipment. We approach our subject by means of case studies in order to introduce concepts which can be understood and applied at each stage of discussion as we build towards problems of increasing complexity. We assume that our readers have had no previous exposure to microprocessor hardware or software, or to machine or assembly language programming, but that they do have some experience with a scientific, high-level programming language.

Our case studies are not tied to any particular language or computer. Rather, we stress the importance of developing machine-independent problem solutions. We have, however, provided specific solutions to the case studies in appendices.

These are presented in either assembly language, FORTRAN, BASIC, Pascal, or C and cover the 8080/8085/Z-80 series of 8-bit processors and the PDP-11/LSI-11 series of 16-bit processors.

To describe program structures in the case studies, we introduce the use of transition diagrams, which we have found to be particularly convenient for control problems.

By presenting plans and specifications for prototype systems used in the case studies as well as documented, tested programs for specific, widely used computer systems, we hope to emphasize that practice is the main route to acquiring microprocessor system design skills. We suggest that the programs in the appendices be used as a starting point for exercises and laboratory projects. By proceeding through the series of studies leading to the final case study solution, the reader can develop a concrete understanding of the concepts discussed in the text and test the performance limits of the various programs. The case studies can then be extended by designing and implementing modifications and added functions for the programs. Readers who are following this procedure for the case studies in Chapters 3 through 7 should develop sufficient skill and confidence to initiate such a project and carry it through to completion.

Chapter 1 introduces the use of microprocessors in instrumentation and control through previews of all the case studies. In Chapter 2, we discuss information and power in the analog and digital portions of measurement and control systems. The first case study, on DC motor control and speed measurement, appears in Chapter 3. In this chapter, we show how the computer's digital I/O port can be used both to control the motor (with a pulse-width modulated signal) and to measure its speed (with a pulse-generating tachometer). We present all programming for this first case study in a high-level language, in order to be free to concentrate on two basic concepts: how to connect microprocessors to instruments and actuation equipment, and how to synchronize the computer with an external time source.

Chapter 4 uses a study of stepping motor control to introduce fundamental concepts of machine and assembly language programming. The chapter examines CPU architecture, memory organization, instruction coding, and the use of a debugger/monitor.

In Chapter 5, a temperature control case study is the vehicle for further exploration of programmed I/O. We discuss the use of a terminal and study programming techniques which permit the operator to interact with the control program without interfering with the control process itself. To illustrate basic methods of analog/digital and digital/analog conversion, we use an external, integrating-type A/D converter and a ladder network D/A converter.

Blending, a multivariable control problem, is the subject of Chapter 6. In this case study, we present the use of interrupts to coordinate the control program timing and the operator interaction through the console terminal. Standard plug-in modules are used for A/D and D/A conversion. By the end of Chapter 6, most of the major addressing modes and a large part of the instruction set will have been introduced.

In Chapter 7, software techniques discussed earlier are integrated into a study of data acquisition and real-time graphic display for an automated weighing system. We design an interrupt processor which illustrates the multi-task nature of the data acquisition and display program. To simplify the data analysis programming without losing the flexibility required for effective interrupt handling, we use a combination of high-level and assembly language programming.

In contrast to Chapters 3 through 7, Chapters 8 and 9 emphasize the hardware and system design aspects of microprocessor systems. Stepping motor control is revisited in Chapter 8 to illustrate the use of a microprocessor as a direct replacement for hardwired digital logic. Instead of using a separate logic circuit to control the stepping motor's windings, we perform this function using microprocessor software. The application is the control of a radial-arm digital plotter. We also examine the design trade-offs associated with the plotter's drawing speed, resolution, and line quality.

Chapter 9 covers the complete design cycle for a stand-alone, single-board system for use in production machinery. In this case study, the computer controls a cut-off machine for producing discrete lengths of product from a continuously-produced material. The study includes initial controller conceptualization and design, processor selection, programming, development systems for in-circuit emulation, and final controller implementation.

The equipment which we use in all the case studies is easy to construct. Even without this equipment, however, the major benefits of doing the case studies and subsequent modifications can be realized with nothing more than standard laboratory equipment such as oscilloscopes, signal generators, and operational amplifiers. In the same vein, any computer, from the most simple to the most elaborate, may be used to follow through on the case studies. At the minimum, the computer system should have a parallel, input and output port with access to an interrupt line. Standard, laboratory-type analog/digital and digital/analog converters are useful, but not essential.

While the authors have thoroughly tested each case study, neither they nor the Publisher will accept any responsibility for any damage to any person, equipment or property resulting from case study work.

ACKNOWLEDGEMENTS

We owe debts of gratitude to many people. Chief among them are: our editor, Vivian Auslander, whose skills were applied to the extent of nearly rewriting the entire book; Dee Davis, Al Shaw, Bob Cesarello and Rod Ramos, who were responsible for the design, construction and maintenance of much of the equipment used for our case studies; students in Mechanical Engineering at the University of California, Berkeley, and in Mechanical and Aerospace Engineering at Princeton University, who put all our work to the test.

The University of California provided the environment and resources that allowed us to conceive of and carry out this work. The manuscript was prepared on several computers, and typeset by Osborne/McGraw-Hill from our disks. The National Food Processors Association of Berkeley, California and MDB Systems, Inc. of Orange, California provided services and equipment which made manuscript preparation easier.

Chapter 1

MICROPROCESSORS AS COMPONENTS IN ENGINEERING SYSTEMS

Flexibility is a key to increased productivity and energy efficiency in mechanical and process systems. Microprocessors and minicomputers provide the built-in intelligence which engineering systems must have in order to respond with maximum speed and efficiency to diverse and changing demands. Computers are the most cost-effective solution for achieving functional flexibility, because they are inherently flexible: they can be reprogrammed without making any physical changes in the system of which they are a component, facilitating modifications, upgrades, even eleventh-hour fixes, at minimum cost.

This book explores the techniques for designing mechanical and process equipment which includes real-time computer systems. We use the term *real-time* to define computational systems which must carry out predetermined tasks at regular intervals, as well as respond to external events occurring at unpredictable times.

To understand the design of real-time control and instrumentation systems, one must know the ways by which a computer can be connected to external equipment, and the kinds of program instructions that affect this interaction. To provide this information, we present the techniques of real-time system design using a series of case studies, each of which examines the role of a mini- or microcomputer in a common control or instrumentation setting.

Each of the case studies includes descriptive material on the control and computer hardware necessary to achieve the objectives of that particular application, as well as on the programming techniques and

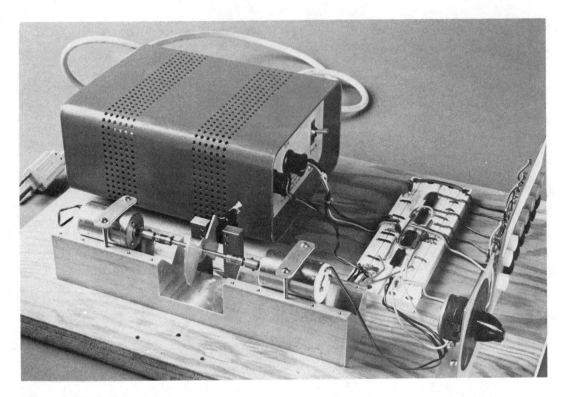

Figure 1.1: DC Motor Apparatus

program structures for the system software. All of the program descriptions emphasize the structure and logical relationships of the various program elements, independent of the particular computer hardware or programming language used. Solutions for specific computers, languages, and processors may be found in the appendices.

Below, we describe the systems that will appear in the case studies and introduce the range of applications for microprocessors in instrumentation and control.

DC MOTOR SPEED MEASUREMENT AND CONTROL

DC motors can be used either as speed or position control elements in mechanical systems. This case study investigates one method of solving the interfacing problem between a control computer and a DC motor, when motor speed is the variable to be controlled.

The most natural control signal for a motor is a continuously variable voltage or current; however, the most natural input or output signal for a computer is one that is quantized to two levels, either on or off. Our study examines how to use pulse-width modulation on the command signal to achieve continuous control of the motor's speed, even though the command signal has only on and off values.

A photograph of the apparatus used for this case study appears in Figure 1.1, and a pulse-width modulated signal with constant frequency and a varied on-time to off-time ratio appears in Figure 1.2. Figure 1.3 shows a response curve for the system pictured in Figure 1.1. The motor speed goes to zero at a duty cycle below about 50 percent because the power supply controller provides braking during the off part of the cycle.

Measuring the motor's speed presents a challenge similar to that of controlling it. The motor can run at any speed, and conventional tachometers produce a voltage that is proportional to speed. As we have seen, however, it is easiest for a computer to read a two-state signal. We solve this interface problem by using a tachometer that produces a pulse-frequency modulated signal. Such a signal has a pulse of constant (usually short) duration, while the period between pulses varies. In the pulse-generating tachometer used, the pulse frequency is proportional to motor speed. The computer determines the speed either by measuring the time between pulses—to ascertain the motor period—or by recording the number of pulses in a fixed time—to calculate speed directly. The pulses are generated optically, as shown in Figure 1.4.

USE OF A STEPPING MOTOR FOR MECHANICAL POSITIONING

Another approach to the computer-motor interface problem is to use a motor with characteristics that make it more adaptable to computer control. A synchronous motor like a stepping motor is particularly well suited for this purpose, because it can be controlled by power amplifiers that need only respond to logic (two-state) signals, which are easily generated by a computer. A stepping motor has coils that can be excited in proper sequence by on-off signals, causing it to move through a predictable sequence of positions, taking one step each time the excitation changes states. As long as it isn't overloaded, it will hold a fixed position until an excitation change causes it

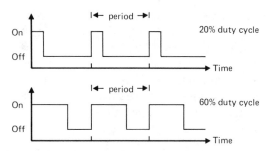

Figure 1.2: Pulse-Width Modulation

to take another step. The size of the step is determined by the motor's geometry. Since the position of the motor can always be predicted from its excitation sequence, it needs no position-measuring instrument in normal operation. The stepping motor's major disadvantages are limited speed, compared to DC servo-motors of similar capacity, and a high level of vibration, caused by the uneven motion of the motor as it is stepped.

In this case study, the computer has a control task that is even more simple than the one described above, because of the type of controller used. The apparatus in Figure 1.5 is a stepping motor with an inertial load and a control box that contains the power amplifiers, plus a hard-wired logic circuit that accepts simplified command signals from the computer. One of the lines connecting the computer to the control is

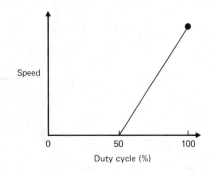

Figure 1.3: Speed/Duty-Cycle Characteristic for DC Motor

used to fix the direction of rotation. The other is the pulse-input line. Every time a pulse is received on the pulse-input line, the control circuit sequences the coil excitation so that the motor will take one step in the direction indicated by the direction-control signal. The computer generates the pulse by turning the appropriate line on, then off. The width of the pulse is not critical.

TEMPERATURE CONTROL

Considering the number of home heating systems in operation today, temperature control systems must be the most common man-made feedback control systems in existence. In this case study, we look at the problem of controlling the temperature of a liquid bath, Figure 1.6. Heat

can be added to the liquid with an electric resistance immersion heater. The rate of heat addition is equal to the power dissipated in the resistor, which is roughly proportional to the square of the voltage applied across the heater. The temperature is measured with a temperature-sensitive semiconductor which has an output voltage proportional to temperature. We wish to use a microprocessor to implement a feedback control scheme that can hold the temperature at some desired value.

In the case studies highlighted above, we discussed solving the interface problem between the continuously variable quantities on the mechanical side of the system and the quantized variables on the computer side by modifying the control and

Figure 1.4: Pulse-Generating Tachometer

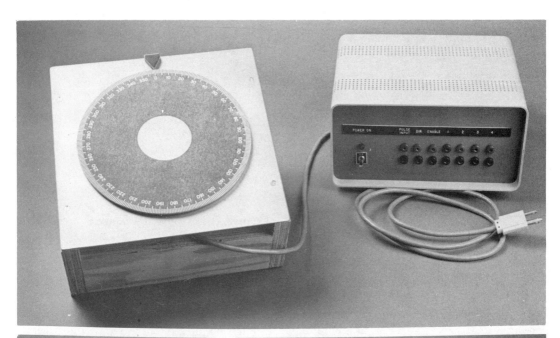

Figure 1.5: Stepping Motor System

measuring elements. In the DC motor case, we described the use of modulated signals; in the stepping motor case we used a control element capable of responding directly to logic signals. Our temperature control study brings the interface closer to the computer side of the system by introducing analog-to-digital and digital-to-analog converters. These are devices that are capable of conversion back and forth between continuous (analog) voltages and numbers stored in the computer. Thus, using a digital-to-analog converter (DAC or D/A) the computer can convert a number to a voltage. The voltage then goes to a power amplifier to run the heater. To close the loop, the temperature sensor produces a voltage proportional to the liquid temperature. This is converted to a digital number by the analog-to-digital converter (ADC or A/D). A program in the computer uses that information to calculate

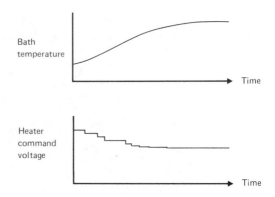

Figure 1.7: Response to Change in Temperature Set Point

the next command signal for the heater.

A typical response curve for a change in temperature appears in Figure 1.7. The abruptness of the changes in command voltage is indicative of the limited precision of the DAC used in the system.

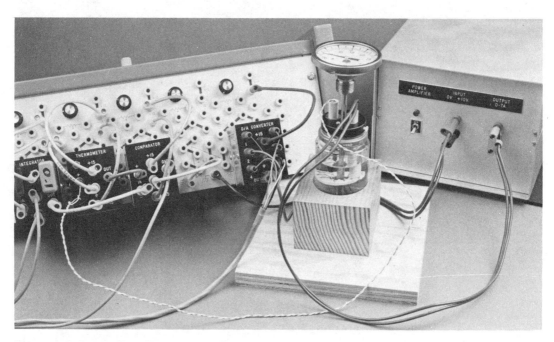

Figure 1.6: Liquid Bath Temperature Control

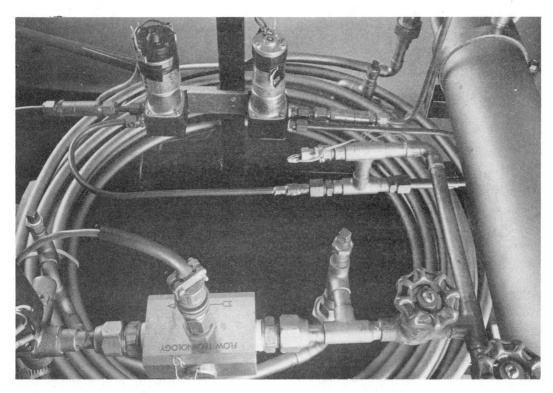

Figure 1.8: Blending System

BLENDING

Many industrial processes require the blending of two or more streams of material on a continuous basis. As a laboratory prototype of a blending process, we use the system shown in Figure 1.8, which blends hot and cold water using the two pumps. The flow rate and temperature of the stream are measured downstream of the mixing point. The control objective is to maintain both the flow rate and temperature at desired values. DACs and ADCs interface the computer to the blending system, and a simple multi-variable control algorithm computes the pump command signals on the basis of the flow rate and temperature measurements. Typical response curves may be found in Figure 1.9.

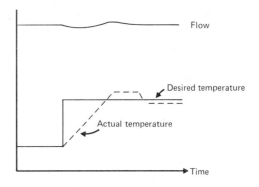

Figure 1.9: Response of Blending System to Change in Desired Temperature

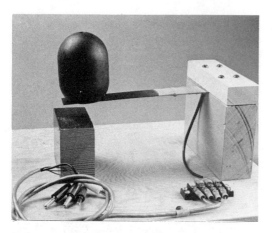

Figure 1.10: Weighing System

AUTOMATED WEIGHING

In this case study, we leave the domain of process control to examine automated production. A common task in the production of discrete items is to weigh them at one or more stages of the production process. By using computer-controlled weighing, a variety of functions can be combined with the determination of the weight, including communication with a plant supervisory computer.

Figure 1.10 shows the computer-controlled scale. Displays are provided for the weight of the item currently on the scale and the weight distribution of the most recently produced items.

In operation, the computer automatically detects the presence of the item to be weighed; it digitally filters the signal from the scale and allows it to settle, then displays the weight on the read-out and updates the distribution of weights on the graphic display. The item is then removed, either on the basis of time or on a signal from the computer indicating that the weighing is complete, and the cycle repeats. If necessary, the computer could also give an actuating signal to sort the item by weight.

The dual display gives the operator both short and long term information about the status of the machinery or raw material feed upstream of the scale. The weight display alerts the operator to major malfunctions or changes in feed properties, short of total failure, while more subtle changes—of the sort requiring adjustments to machines—appear as shifts in the distribution.

Information transmitted from the weighing-control computer to the plant supervisory computer can be used to optimize plant operation, for diagnostic purposes, or to compile management information. Information flowing in the other direction, from the supervisory computer to the weighing-control computer, can be used to change internal parameters, or even logic, in the weighing-control computer, so that it can adapt to changes in the characteristics of items being produced.

RADIAL-ARM PEN PLOTTER

Commercially available pen plotters use linear X-Y motion to move the pen, with one actuation motor controlling the X motion and another controlling Y motion. As shown in Figure 1.11, we have chosen to use a mechanism in which one motor controls radial motion and the other controls angular motion. This mechanism is easier to build than an X-Y mechanism, but the computation required is much greater. Recent tremendous reductions in computation costs make our approach cost-effective.

Because we use stepping motors to drive both axes in this case study, we have the opportunity to investigate the operation of these widely used components much more thoroughly than we did in the earlier stepping motor case study. In particular, we

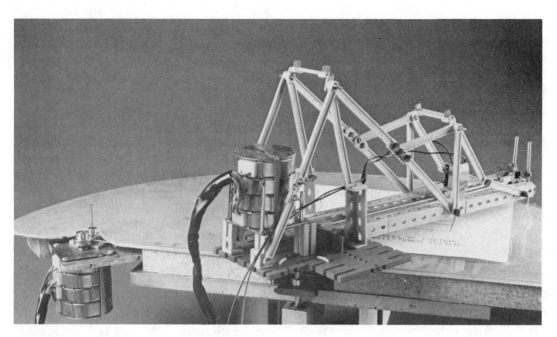

Figure 1.11: Radial-Arm Plotter

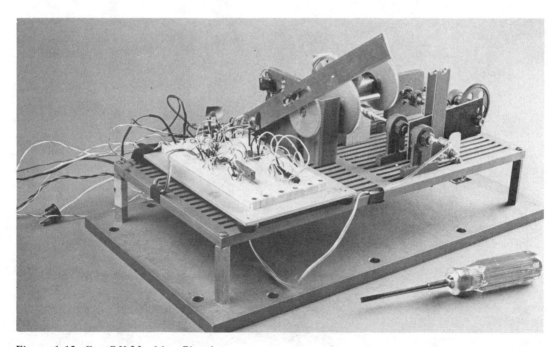

Figure 1.12: Cut-Off Machine Simulator

examine how to use software instead of a hardwired logic circuit to sequence the excitation of the motor's windings, and we explore how to achieve smoother, faster, and more precise stepping motor operation.

A MICROPROCESSOR CONTROLLER FOR A CUT-OFF MACHINE

In our final case study, we examine the entire design cycle for a typical microprocessor-based controller, as applied to a manufacturing process used to produce a continuous length of material. The microprocessor system controls the machine that cuts the material into predetermined lengths.

The design cycle begins with the definition of the task, specification of a program structure to meet the operating requirements, and specification of the types of interfaces required in order for the microprocessor to read the transducer signals from the machine and produce the correct actuation signals. We examine the design sequence, discussing in particular the advantages of designing the machine to be controlled at the same time as the microprocessor system which will control it. Next, we use a general-purpose *development* system to debug the first version of the program. To test the program, we use a mechanical simulator of the actual cut-off machine, as shown in Figure 1.12. Depending on the circumstances, simulators can be anything from the machine itself to a purely software simulation. After debugging and refining the program, we have enough information available to begin the design of a special purpose microprocessor system prototype tailored to our application. The cut-off machine appears in Figure 1.13.

Figure 1.13:
Cut-Off
Machine

Chapter 2

INFORMATION
AND POWER

This chapter introduces concepts and terminology common to virtually all microprocessor instrumentation and control. Microprocessors are connected to the outside world electrically. Electrical signals are characterized by a pair of variables: voltage and current. The product of these two varables describes the power transmitted. For computation and control, the important characteristics of an electrical signal are its information and power. Information is usually vested in one or the other of the voltage-current pair: usually, but by no means always, in the voltage. The power-handling capability of an electrical signal can be expressed three different ways: in units of power, in terms of the complementary variable (the one which is not carrying information), and as impedance (a quantity with units of voltage divided by current).

Information in microprocessor systems is characterized as *analog* or *digital*. Analog information is non-quantized; that is, the resolution associated with an analog signal allows for the recognition of one of an infinite number of possible values at any instant, except for the limitations imposed by noise. Digital signals, on the other hand, are in almost all cases quantized to contain only two possible values.

ANALOG SIGNALS

The most important characteristic of an analog signal is its power level. The power level is typically expressed in terms of voltage and current, or as one of the signal variables plus some form of power specification. With the exception of power supplies, all analog signals contain both information and power. These signals are divided into two classes: those valued for their power, and those valued for their information.

Power signals are used for actuation and can cover a wide variety of voltages and currents. They can be referenced to an earth ground, or they can *float* (voltage measured from wire to wire). Information signals come in three general levels: high level signals of an order of magnitude of one volt or more, produced, for example, by amplifiers or other signal conditioning equipment; low level signals of the order of millivolts, produced by such instruments as thermocouples; and ultra-low level signals in microvolts that are typical of crystal-based instruments. The information-class signal equivalent of a floating signal is called a *differential* signal. The algebraic average of the two differential signal lines is called the *common-mode voltage*. Differing ground levels at different points in a system can lead to so-called ground loops, which can wreak havoc in measurement systems, particularly if long wires are involved.

In information-class signals, the information flow is unidirectional: from a sender (or driver) to a receiver. The power flow is almost always in the same direction. The power capability requirement in such systems is often expressed in terms of impedance. The impedance describes the incremental change in voltage as a result of a change in current. Use of an impedance specification usually implies that the voltage is the information-carrying variable. It takes two impedances to specify the power characteristics of a sender-receiver pair. The sender's output impedance tells how much power the sender can provide. A very low output impedance implies large power output capability, since even relatively large changes in current will not affect the (information-carrying) voltage. The receiver's input impedance expresses how much power the receiver requires to process the signal. A very high input impedance implies low processing power requirements, because significant changes in the voltage do not cause significant changes in the receiver's demands for current.

To match senders and receivers properly, it is important to remember that physical systems are limited by the speed with which they can respond. The temporal characteristics of signals can thus be as important as their power requirements. These characteristics are commonly described in terms of spectral or frequency content. Spectral characteristics are relatively easy to measure, and frequency analysis of component behavior is usually easier to obtain than transient analysis. Since the frequency characteristics of non-periodic signals are not always well defined, it might be preferable to use other measures, such as rise time or pulse width to define temporal characteristics.

CODING OF ANALOG INFORMATION

Information is typically vested in one of the signal variables, but there are many means of coding that information. The simplest most common method is to code the information by the signal level: voltage or current. An alternative method is to modulate (modify) some form of carrier signal. This might be done to better match the characteristics of a transfer medium (as with radio frequency signals) or to reduce sensitivity to noise; it might be necessary because an instrument produces such a signal or because an actuator requires the modulated signal. The oldest form of modulated signal uses a sinusoid as the carrier. The most common modulation techniques are amplitude (AM) and frequency (FM) modulation.

DIGITAL SIGNALS

Digital signals are nearly always quantized into two values. These values may be called zero and one, on and off, true and false, or any complementary pair. Information is usually carried in a signal's voltage. The relation between voltage and the digital signal's value is specified by the circuit designer: *positive true*, if a higher, more positive voltage represents the true state, and *negative true*, if a lower, or more negative voltage represents the true state.

The voltage levels which determine the digital signal's state are dictated by the choice of logic family or type. Table 2.1 surveys the major logic families and lists their high and low voltage ranges. Note that a signal within one of the given ranges is defined, while a signal between the high and low states is undefined and could be interpreted as either high or low. Undefined states are discussed below.

TIMING OF DIGITAL SIGNALS

Because a digital signal passes through an undefined region when changing from true to false or false to true, much of digital design involves delineating a signal's state as clearly as possible.

Two general solutions to the undefined signal problem are commonly used. One is to avoid ambiguous outputs by designing a circuit which controls the order in which signals change. Circuits designed this way are *asynchronous*. A second solution is to specify the times during which the signal outputs should be considered valid.

To understand the problem of an undefined signal and the two solutions we have indicated, consider the following analogy:

You are driving your car in search of gas at the lowest price. You pass several stations with signs reading, *$1.20*. Suddenly, you see a person on a ladder in front of a sign that reads, *$1.25*. His hand is on the 2. Has he just raised the price, or is he going to replace the *2* with a *1*? While he is tinkering with the sign, the price is undefined. You cannot predict what price you will be charged if you drive into the station.

To remove the ambiguity of updating the gas station sign, we could create a rule specifying that each digit in the price—regardless of whether or not it needs changing—should be removed, starting from the right, until none that needs changing remains. Then the correct numbers should be installed, beginning at the left. The price would be considered defined if two numbers to the right of the decimal point were visible. Alternately, using a temporal solution, we could say that the price on the sign is valid except when a person is on the ladder working on the sign. In electronic circuits, this strategy requires the use of an independent signal which indicates periods of transition and periods of validity. This signal, commonly called a *clock*, is usually periodic. Clocked circuits, utilizing *synchronous* design practices, are applied

Logic Family	Minimum High Level Output Voltage (Voh)	Maximum Low Level Output Voltage (Vol)
TTL (Transistor-Transistor Logic)	2.4V	0.4V
CMOS (Complementary Metal Oxide on Silicon) (10V Supply)	9.0V	1.0V
CMOS (5V Supply)	4.5V	0.5V
DTL (Transistor-Diode Logic)	2.4V	0.4V
ECL (Emitter-Coupled Logic) (25C)	−0.96V	−1.62V

Table 2.1: Typical Output Thresholds

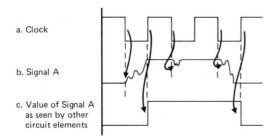

a. Clock

b. Signal A

c. Value of Signal A
as seen by other
circuit elements

Figure 2.1: Synchronization Using a Clock

extensively in microprocessor systems to coordinate signals in different portions of the machine. Although asynchronous design techniques may be used within circuits on a single integrated circuit, synchronous design prevails between integrated circuits.

Figure 2.1 is a *timing diagram* which shows how a clock affects *signal A*. Signal A is constrained while the clock is high. When the clock's falling edge occurs, the signal is allowed to change. Because signal A results from a logical combination of other signals, it displays irregular transitions which may cause serious problems in asynchronous circuits. The clock masks out the confusing transitions and indicates the times during which signal A is stable and valid. The rising edge of the clock tells other circuit elements that the wire carrying signal A is valid and represents the true state of the signal. The arrows in Figure 2.1 indicate cause and effect relationships.

DIGITAL COMMUNCATION PROTOCOL

Serial Communication

We have examined the nature of digital signals. How may we use them to transfer information? One of the first digital electric protocols, the Morse code, sends information in *serial* fashion: depressing a switch causes the voltage on a signal wire to change. One or more key depressions represent a character, and one or more characters represent a word. Serial communication is used extensively in microprocessor systems. Most keyboards and printers send and receive serially.

Timing is of critical importance in serial communication. Consider the case in which we are listening to a Morse code transmission and hear four *dits*. Did we just hear four *E's* or one *S* and one *E*, or one *H*, or one of the other possibilities? The answer is dependent upon the temporal spacing between individual bits. Humans have a remarkable ability to generate and interpret the relative spacing between bits, characters, and words. Electronic circuits which send and receive serially use a similar strategy.

Two types of serial transmission are commonly used. In *asynchronous* serial transmission, each character is sent in a packet of equally spaced bits. Spacing between the characters is arbitrary. Several packet formats are used, but a common one is shown in Figure 2.2. In this example, the transition of the serial signal to a low value indicates the start of a packet. The receiver synchronizes on this first edge since correct resolution will depend upon knowing the time at which to sample the signal. A seven-bit character follows. The character codes commonly used, at least in computer peripheral equipment, are the seven-bit American Standard Code for Information Interchange, known as ASCII, or IBM's eight-bit Extended Binary-Coded Decimal Interchange Code, known as EBCDIC. An error check bit, called a parity bit is often included with the character. The message transmitter sets the parity bit such that the number of ones in the packet is either always even or always odd. The receiver may check the packet and detect some single-bit errors. Finally, a stop bit, which signals the end of a packet, is sent.

One drawback of asynchronous serial protocol is that roughly 30 percent of the packet is timing information. If one is able to accept a considerable increase in equipment complexity, then the more effective *synchronous* serial transmission may be used. This protocol requires that the sender and receiver be constantly in synchrony to allow characters to follow with no space between. Error checking may be done on blocks of characters rather than on individual characters. Constant synchrony implies that, during periods when no information is being transmitted, special idle characters must be sent to avoid loss of synchronization. Synchronous protocol is commonly used in long distance, high speed data transmission.

Parallel Communication

One advantage of serial transmission is that only one conductor (and perhaps a signal common) is required to send a character. If we are willing to pay the price to provide one conductor for each bit of a character, we can eliminate the logic required to serialize and increase the rate of transmission by a factor of seven or more. Such a strategy is used in *parallel communication* protocol. Most information flow within a microprocessor system takes place in parallel. For example, in an eight-bit processor, the memory is organized as an array

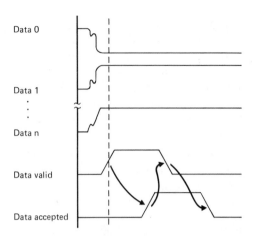

Figure 2.3: Parallel Interface Handshake Logic

which is eight bits wide. When a memory location is accessed, eight bits are transferred simultaneously. Such transfers are coordinated by the system clock. (The system clock is a periodic signal that is the primary source of synchronization within the system.)

Sometimes parallel transfers are performed with the aid of *handshake* signals. This is especially true of devices external to the microprocessor. Figure 2.3 shows a typical parallel data transfer using handshake logic. The transmitting device controls the *data valid* signal which indicates to the receiver that the signal lines carrying the data are stable. The receiver reads the data and then raises its *data accepted* signal to inform the sender that the transaction is complete.

Figure 2.2: Typical Serial Packet Format

Tri-state Logic

When we stated that digital signals are quantized into two values (true and false), we were ignoring a possible third state, the high impedance third state. The significance and usefulness of this state will become clear when we discuss buses in Chapter 9. For now, we will only mention that some circuit elements permit inactive transmitters to assume a high impedance state and effectively remove themselves from the circuit so that conductors may be shared.

NOISE AND NOISE SOURCES

The advent of standard integrated circuit logic families has to a large degree reduced the amount of electrical engineering which a control system designer must perform. But anyone working with digital systems should be aware of the sources and effects of undesired signal transitions, commonly called *noise*. Noise may be generated within the microprocessor system or—especially in a hostile process environment—received from outside.

Noise may be generated internally if the printed circuit board is laid out improperly or if the timing requirements of logic circuits are misunderstood. Improper layout may lead to low noise margins, caused by mismatching logic types, overloading outputs, or switching circuits in such a way that they inject unwanted, unanticipated information into the power supply signal. In addition, ringing at the ends of unterminated conductors or crosstalk between conductors can introduce undesirable level transitions. Timing problems which generate noise often stem from the failure to use good synchronous design practices. A detailed treatment of these topics may be found in many design and application books.

Outside noise can originate from the switching of inductive loads and be coupled through the microprocessor's power supply. Arc welders, motor brushes and other sources emit radio frequency noise which may be received by microprocessor cables and wires. To prevent these noise sources from degrading the microprocessor's performance, any wiring in the process environment should be shielded and grounded at one point (preferably where the signals are processed); ground loops should be avoided or broken with some form of optical or electrical isolation; and the microprocessor's power supply should be adequately designed and fed with a low impedance AC source.

Chapter 3

DC MOTOR CONTROL
AND TESTING

Mechanical designs which incorporate electric motors frequently require that the motor shaft speed be controlled. The speed of an electric motor connected to a constant load can usually be changed by varying its power signal. Synchronous AC motors are most sensitive to changes in power line frequency, although the speed of some induction motors can be varied by altering the voltage by phase control. Speed control of DC motors is more straightforward, since most DC motors respond to changes in voltage. In Chapter 5, we will show how a microprocessor can produce discrete voltage levels which, with proper amplification, may be used to control the speed of a DC motor. Since digital computers naturally produce digital signals, we will examine a method for varying the speed of a DC motor using only a digital actuation signal. We will describe a method for measuring the velocity of a motor and describe a strategy for automated mapping of the relationship between the actuation signal and the motor's speed.

MODULATED DIGITAL SIGNALS

Intuition tells us that if we rapidly toggle the power switch of a DC motor, the motor will turn at less than its maximum speed. We could vary the amount of time the switch is on with respect to the time the switch is off. *Pulse width modulation* (PWM) is the name given to this method. Figure 3.1 shows four pulse trains with a constant frequency but different *duty cycles*. A signal with a 50 percent duty cycle is a familiar, symmetrical square wave. The area under each pulse train is a measure of power. Power increases with duty cycle.

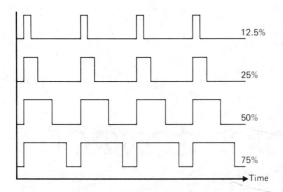

Figure 3.1: Pulse Width Modulation. Four Pulse Trains of Constant Frequency but Different Duty Cycles

Figure 3.1: Pulse Width Modulation. Four Pulse Trains of Constant Frequency but Different Duty Cycles

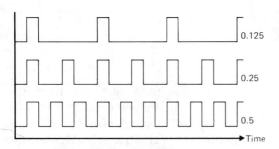

Figure 3.2: Pulse Frequency Modulation. Three Pulse Trains of Constant Pulse Width but Different Pulse Frequency

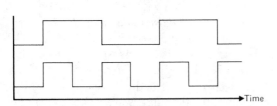

Figure 3.3: Two Pulse Trains With Equivalent Duty Cycles (50%) but Different Frequencies

Instead of varying the duty cycle of a digital signal, we could alter the frequency of fixed-sized pulses. This strategy is called *pulse frequency modulation* (PFM). Figure 3.2 shows three pulse trains, each made up of equal area pulses. We see that power is a function of pulse frequency for fixed width pulses.

We have implied that motor speed is a function of the area under a given pulse train. Consider Figure 3.3, which shows two pulse trains with equal duty cycles but different pulse frequencies. Although the power in each ideal signal is the same, the motor's dynamics create different motor speeds. We will examine graphically the relationship between pulse frequency and speed for constant duty cycle.

THE SYSTEM

Figure 3.4 depicts the motor test apparatus. The operator initiates test sequences from the computer terminal. Two parallel output bits and two parallel input bits are connected to the computer. One output bit is connected to an actuator which can drive the small permanent magnet DC motor. The motor shaft is connected to a load (in this case, it is another DC motor shunted by a variable resistance) and a tachometer.

The tachometer shaft turns a disk whose alternate quadrants have been removed. A photo diode/photo transistor pair detects the passage of the disk's quadrants, producing two electrical pulses per revolution of the shaft. A computer may be used to deduce the speed of the motor by detecting and counting the tachometer pulses, but there is a caveat associated with this strategy. If the computer does not sample the parallel input fast enough, it can miss pulses (see Figure 3.5).

A simple solution to the missed pulse

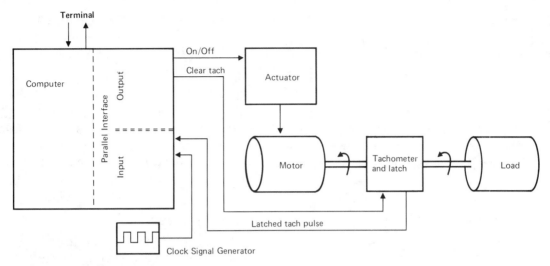

Figure 3.4: Motor Control and Test System

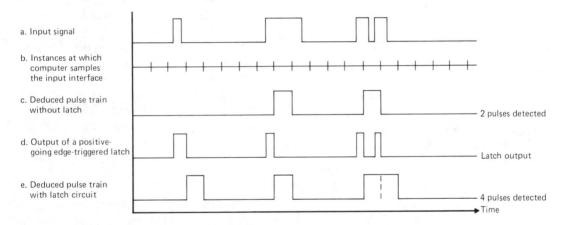

Figure 3.5: The General Problem of Pulse Detection

problem is to build a latch circuit which *remembers* the fact that a pulse has occurred. Latches are an important circuit-building block used as one form of memory in every digital computer. Figure 3.6 is a timing diagram which shows how the latch is set and reset. Recall that the arrows show cause and effect relationships. Figure 3.5 shows

that the latch helps the computer detect the non-uniform pulses it missed when sampling the unlatched circuit.

TELLING TIME

We have examined all the building blocks of our motor testing apparatus except one, the clock. In order to produce the pulse

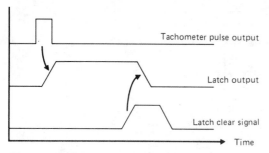

Figure 3.6: Setting and Clearing a Latch

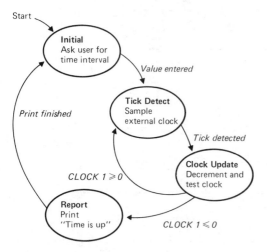

Figure 3.7: Transition Diagram for Time-telling Program

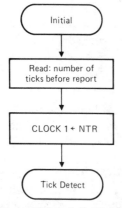

Figure 3.8: Flow of Module Initial for Time-telling Program

width modulated motor actuation signal and to determine the frequency of the tachometer pulses, we must time the formation of pulses and the spacing between pulses. A clock serves this purpose. You will recall that clocks are digital signals which often have a 50 percent duty cycle. In order to time events, we must have access to a value which represents the number of clock cycles or *ticks* which have elapsed. Our program will update a variable which represents the number of ticks detected.

THE PROGRAM

The key to success in solving real-time control problems is designing and selecting the necessary software and hardware without ever losing sight of one's final goal. Hardware should be chosen, all components tested, and all signal characteristics verified in terms of the project's overall aim. Despite the temptation to begin writing programs early on, designers should make it a critical priority to understand their entire project before writing any program code. Within this essential overall framework, it is easiest to structure solutions to real-time control problems in modular form, constructing programs in segments which interconnect, rather than attempting to design an entire program at once. Breaking the problem into modules facilitates debugging, eases program maintenance, and increases program reliability. In our case study, for example, we will break the design task into three sections: describing and flowcharting the time-telling routine, adding the velocity determination algorithm, and finally, inserting the motor speed control section. The finished program will ask the user to enter values for the length of the test, the frequency with which samples are taken, and the motor actuation pulse frequency and duty cycle. The test will then begin; the motor will start; and motor velocity will be reported to the terminal. When the test period ends, the motor will stop.

We will discuss the computer shown in Figure 3.4 in detail when we examine microprocessor architecture in Chapter 4. For the purposes of this case study, we will assume that our readers have had programming experience in a high level language such as FORTRAN, BASIC, C, or Pascal, and that they understand flowcharts.

The language we will employ has one capability which may be unfamiliar. In order to actuate the motor, clear the tachometer latch, and read the tachometer and clock, the language will possess two instructions commonly called PEEK and POKE or IN and OUT or GET and PUT. These instructions permit us to write to or read from a parallel interface connected to our motor system.

Time Telling Program

Figure 3.7 is a *transition diagram* showing four modules and their mutual relationships. Each circle represents a *state* during which the nature of the task does not change. Each arrow represents a transition between states. As each specific condition is fulfilled, the program advances to the next state. Sometimes the value of a program variable will determine the subsequent state. For example, in Figure 3.7 the state following Clock Update can be either Tick Detect or Report. The variable CLOCK1 determines the correct transition. States are not subroutines. Although subroutines may be used within states, the states themselves don't return. Branch instructions (goto, next, case, etc.) implement state transitions. The program described in Figure 3.7 will start by asking the user to enter the number of ticks of the clock which are to elapse before a report should be made

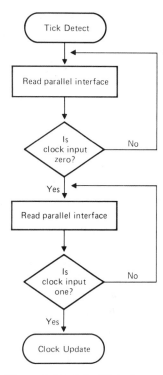

Figure 3.9: Flow of Module Tick Detect for Time-telling Program

(Figure 3.8). The report is a message printed or displayed by the terminal which says, "Time is up."

Figure 3.9 is a flowchart for the tick-detect module. The flowchart contains two conditional branches, both based upon the value of the external clock. The two-branch design causes the program to wait for a low-to-high transition of the clock. The frequency of the clock will be made low enough so that the program begins looking for a transition before the transition takes place. If the program were to use a single branch—and merely check to see that the clock is high—then two or more subsequent passages through the tick-detect module could "detect" the same clock pulse.

After detecting a tick, the module

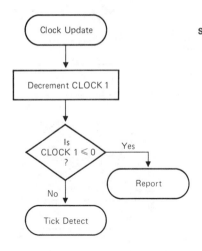

Figure 3.10: Flow of Module Clock Update for Time-telling Program

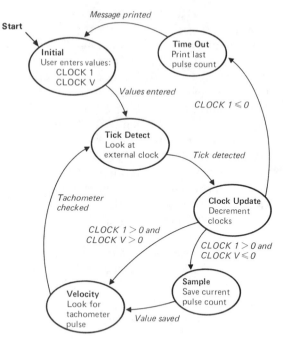

Figure 3.12: Transition Diagram for Velocity Test Program

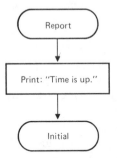

Figure 3.11: Flow of Module Report for Time-telling Program

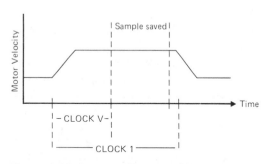

Figure 3.13: Relative Temporal Magnitudes of Clocks CLOCK1 and CLOCKV Compared to Motor Velocity

Clock Update (Figure 3.10) decrements (i.e., reduces by one) the user-entered value for the number of ticks which are to elapse. If this value is not zero, the tick-detect module awaits the next tick. If the number of ticks *is* zero, the Report module (Figure 3.11) prints or displays "Time is up," and the program starts over again.

Velocity Determination Program

If we assume that the motor is turning at constant speed, then the algorithm shown in Figure 3.12 will count the number of tachometer pulses occurring during a fixed period of time. The algorithm will accumulate a value of tachometer pulses/n-ticks. The motor velocity in revolutions per minute may be found by multiplying this value by the rate of n-tick (n-tick/min) and the number of revolutions per pulse (0.5). In order to guarantee that the motor speed is constant, we have designed the algorithm to sample the motor speed repetitively, but to report only the last sample taken. If we simply started the motor and counted the tachometer pulses for the length of our former time-out variable CLOCK1, the count would then include the acceleration phase. Figure 3.13 shows the relationship between the time-out clock CLOCK1 and the velocity clock CLOCKV.

Every time the program detects a tick of the external clock, it reduces both clock variables CLOCKV and CLOCK1 by one (see Figure 3.12). If neither clock is zero, the program looks for the tachometer input pulse. If it detects a pulse, it increases the value NUMPULSE by one and clears the tachometer pulse latch. If CLOCKV is reduced to zero in Clock Update, then state SAMPLE saves the current value of NUM-PULSE in a variable called LASTPULSE. Finally, if the clock CLOCK1 is zero, the program enters state Time Out and prints the last value of the number of pulses, LASTPULSE. It then reenters state Initial.

The Initial state (Figure 3.14) asks the user for the length of the test and the sampling interval. The program accepts the length of the test (the number of clock ticks which will elapse before the program enters the time-out state) from the terminal and copies it to a variable called CLOCK1. It

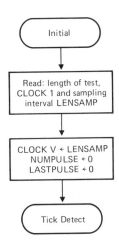

Figure 3.14: Initial Module for Velocity Test Program

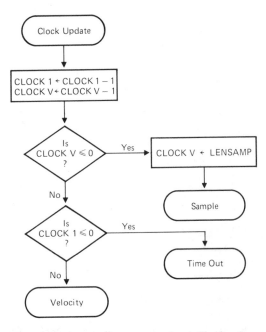

Figure 3.15: Flow of Module Clock Update for Velocity Test Program

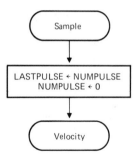

Figure 3.16: Flow of Module Sample for Velocity Test Program

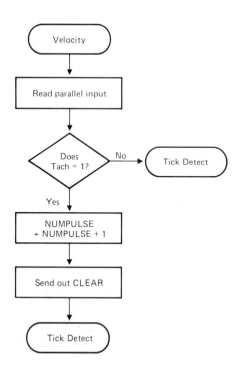

Figure 3.17: Flow of Module Velocity for Velocity Test Program

then accepts the sampling interval (the number of clock ticks to occur before the tachometer pulse count is saved) and copies it to two variables. The first variable, LENSAMP, will remain unchanged and will be used to reset the second variable, CLOCKV, which will be counted down by Clock Update. The program next initializes to zero the variable which contains the number of tachometer pulses, NUMPULSE, and the variable for the last sampled number of pulses, LASTPULSE.

State Tick Detect is unchanged from our time-telling program. In Figure 3.15, the flow of state Clock Update has been modified slightly to include the second clock CLOCKV. When this clock is decremented to zero, it is reset with the variable LENSAMP. State SAMPLE (Figure 3.16) copies the variable NUMPULSE into the variable LASTPULSE and resets the current tachometer pulse count to zero.

Although the logic of the flowchart depicted in Figure 3.17 appears straightforward, two related problems exist. Recall that the parallel input interface has attached two signal lines. The external clock *and* the tachometer pulse line are connected to the same interface (Figure 3.4). How are we to know which of the signals is high or low? If the tachometer were connected to the least significant bit position and the clock to the next least significant bit (Figure 3.18a), we would know that the value of 1 read from the interface would indicate that the tachometer pulse line is high and the external clock signal, low. Similarly, a 2 would imply that the clock is high and the tachometer signal, low. With a 2-bit interface, the number of combinations is only $2^2 = 4$, but with a common 16-bit interface, the number of combinations is $2^{16} = 65,536$. Clearly, we must not generate a flowchart with 65,536 branches! We wish to

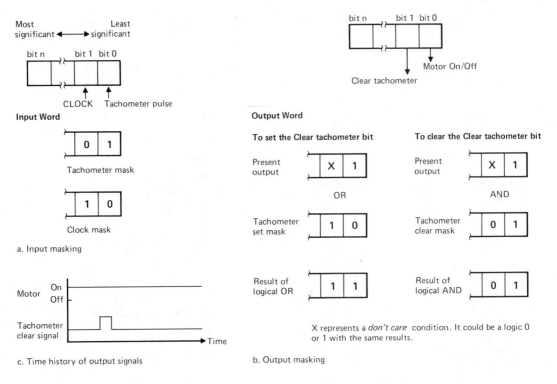

Figure 3.18: Masking a Parallel Interface Word

ignore all signals except the one in which we are interested. This ignoring operation is called *masking*. The value of the parallel interface is read and then logically AND-ed with a mask word which has the appropriate bit (or bits in some cases) set. Our mask for the tachometer pulse would be 1, and the mask for the external clock, 2. The value 2 is used since the parallel interface word is viewed as a binary number: 10_2 is 2. (Number systems will be covered more thoroughly in Chapter 4.)

We also use a masking operation to set or clear bits selectively on a parallel output interface. If, for example, we wished to clear the tachometer latch without affecting the bit which controls the motor power, we would logically OR the current motor status

with a mask word which has the tachometer clear bit set (Figure 3.18*b*). Likewise, to clear the tachometer clear bit, we would logically AND the current motor status with the tachometer clear mask. To output a clear pulse on the tachometer clear signal line, we would perform these two operations in succession: first OR-ing to produce a 1, then AND-ing to reset to 0. Figure 3.18*c* shows the values of both signals through the two logical operations. The reader is encouraged to verify that the state of the motor signal is unchanged if it is initially zero. The concept of masking may be extended to words of any width, with any combination of bits set or cleared. This important topic will be re-examined in Chapter 4.

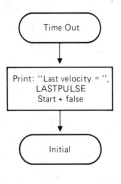

Figure 3.19: Flow of Module Time Out for Velocity Test Program

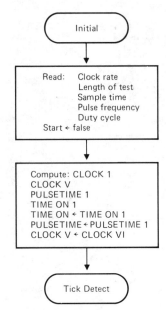

Figure 3.21: Flow of Initial Module for Motor Control and Test Program

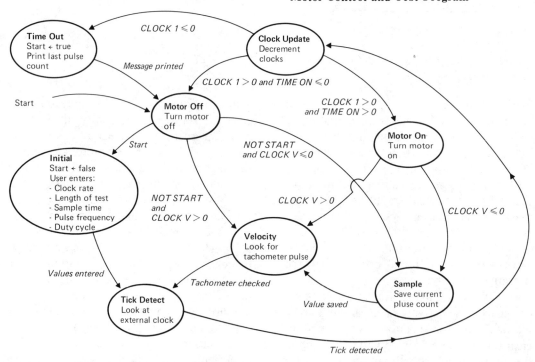

Figure 3.20: Transition Diagram for Motor Test and Control Program

Having explored masking, we can now understand Figure 3.17, in which a conditional branch asks, "Is the tachometer input set?" If the result of the mask operation is true, we deduce that it is set and proceed to increment the value of the current number of tachometer pulses. We must clear the tachometer pulse signal using the method we just discussed.

Figure 3.19 shows that, in state Time Out, the program sends the last complete count of tachometer pulses to the terminal, completing the motor test, and reenters the state Initial. The motor speed could be manually adjusted and the test re-run to determine another velocity, but we want to examine pulsed actuation. Let us look at the final transition diagram for this chapter.

Motor Control and Test Program

Figure 3.20 describes the automated test algorithm. Note that the two new states have been added. The program entry point is now the state Motor Off, to ensure that the motor will not be spinning wildly (at maximum speed) while the user enters test parameters. Regardless of the state of other variables, the program will enter the state Initial next, since the value START is true. As we see here, a major benefit of the transition diagram approach to real-time program development is that it makes it possible for the designer to isolate controlling variables at different parts of the program.

The state Initial (Figure 3.21) asks the user for five values: the length of the test, the sampling interval, the frequency of the acutation pulse, and the duty cycle of the actuation pulse. Instead of entering values as ticks of the clock, as we did in the earlier programs, the user enters the frequency of the external clock. The program then multiplies entered time intervals by the clock frequency to yield ticks (ticks/s × s = ticks).

The clock variables are calculated in state Initial, rather than after each sampling instance, since mathematical routines could delay the program sufficiently to miss tachometer pulses.

The Clock Update state (Figure 3.22) functions as before, except that four clock variables are now decremented. In addition to the test length and sampling interval clocks, a clock called PULSETIME

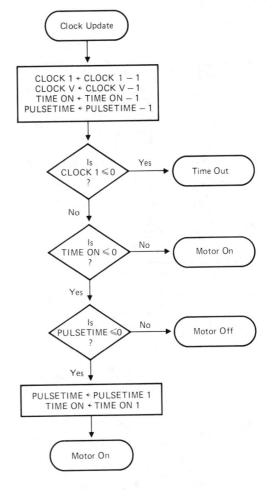

Figure 3.22: Flow of Clock Update Module for Motor Test and Control Program

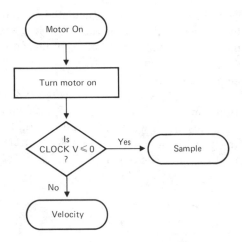

Figure 3.23a: Flow of Motor On Module for Test and Control Program

measures (in ticks) the period of the motor actuation pulse, while the clock TIMEON represents the number of ticks that the motor is on during the pulse period. Thus, if PULSETIME = 2 × TIMEON, the duty cycle of the actuation signal is 50 percent. Clock Update exists to Time Out at the end of the test period, as it did in the velocity program. However, if CLOCK1 is greater than zero, Clock Update exits to either Motor On or Motor Off based upon the value TIMEON. The tachometer is sampled as before. Figure 3.23 shows the motor control routines which branch to the sampling routines.

Motor Controller Details

The configuration of the photo diode/ photo transistor pairs is shown in Figure 3.24. Two pairs are used so that direction of rotation can also be detected, although that feature is not needed for this case study. The circuit diagram for the tachometer

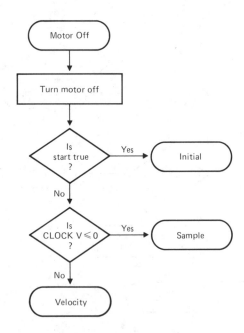

Figure 3.23b: Flow of Module Motor Off for Motor Test and Control Program

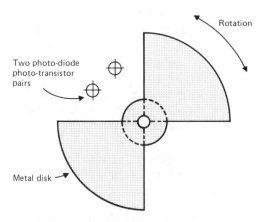

Figure 3.24: Tachometer Disk Showing Location of Photo-Diode/Photo-Transistor Pairs Which are Occluded by Disk. Use of Two Pairs Allows Determination of Direction of Rotation.

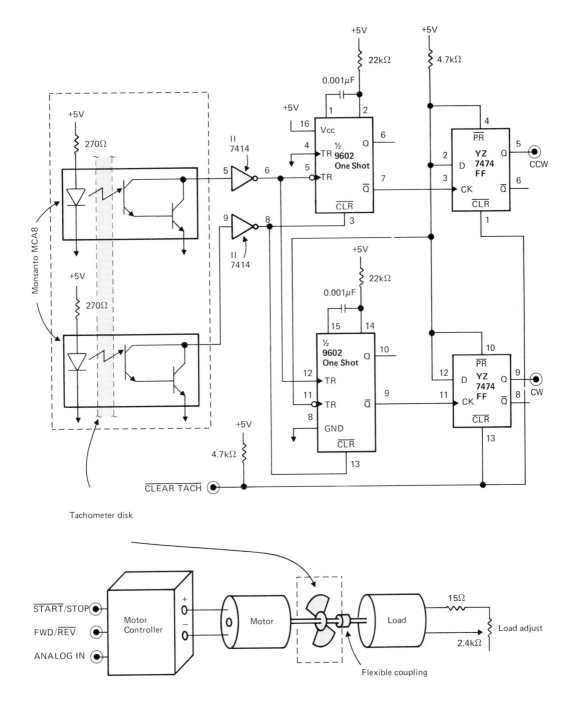

Figure 3.25: DC Motor Tachometer Detail with Pulse-Conditioning Circuit and Latch

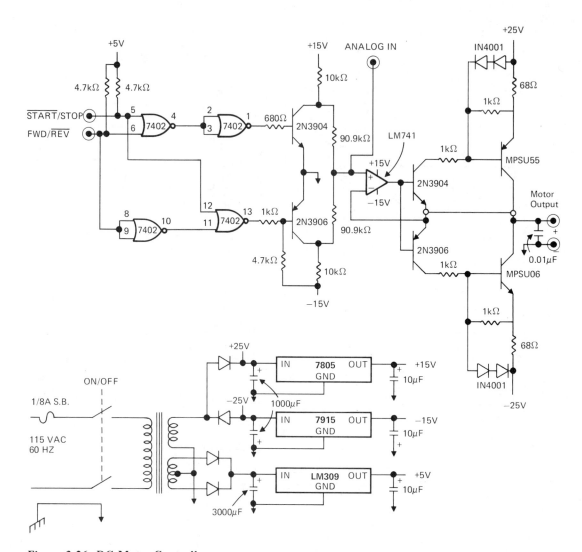

Figure 3.26: DC Motor Controller

pulse conditioning system is in Figure 3.25. The output pulse train appears at the terminal marked CW or at the one marked CCW, depending on the direction of rotation. The power control circuit is shown in Figure 3.26. An analog input is also supplied for projects requiring speed control with a variable voltage.

PROJECTS

1. The time-telling program may be run even if you do not have a DC motor and motor-driving amplifier. Run the program and determine the maximum clock frequency your time-telling program can tolerate before it misses ticks. What happens when ticks are missed? What happens when you change the duty cycle of the clock? What clock duty cycle allows greatest time-telling speed? If the duty cycle of the greatest clock rate is not 50 percent, can you explain why?

2. Modify your time-telling program. Does changing the order in which the modules are written affect maximum attainable clock frequency?

3. Modify your time-telling program. Assume you wish to limit the maximum number of ticks which the user may specify. Try two strategies: **a.** add a state Limit to be entered after each tick of the clock is detected which limits the number of times that the clock is updated, and **b.** add the state Limit which is entered after state Initial and which checks the user's entry against a fixed maximum and limits it. What is the maximum usable clock rate in either case? What general rules can you infer concerning strategies in increasing real-time program execution speed?

4. If you have more than one high-level language available or two brands of the same language, try writing the time-telling program in each. Does maximum attainable clock speed vary? If your high-level language interpreter or compiler allows options such as *inhibit error message generation,* see if such changes affect maximum clocking rate. (Always debug the program before inhibiting useful diagnostics.)

5. If your high-level language allows specification of both integers and reals (or floating point), compare execution speeds with each type. Do you expect a difference? Did you find a difference?

6. Demonstrate the usefulness of the tachometer latch circuit by running the velocity test program without a latch. What is the effect?

7. Investigate the effect of increasing the length of the tachometer pulse in order to overcome the limitations encountered in Project 6. The pulse-stretching solution is not considered good design practice. Why?

8. Modify the motor test program. Cause the program to run the motor until the speed settles. When the speed has settled, stop the test and print or display the speed. One method of determining settling would be to add a state perhaps called Settle which is entered after Sample. State Settle must manipulate some variable which causes the test to stop or continue after Clock Update.

9. Modify the motor test program. Close the speed control loop statically, that is, cause the motor to run at a user-defined speed. After sampling the speed, cause the program to update the pulse duty cycle to allow the motor speed to approach the user-entered speed goal. The program should terminate when the desired pulse width is found, and should display the pulse width. If the speed cannot be attained, the program should inform the user.

10. Explore the limitations of your computer and high-level language by closing the speed control loop dynamically; that is, modify the motor test program to vary the motor actuation pulse duty cycle *during the test* in order to approach a desired speed. Discuss real-time limitations.

Chapter 4

POSITION CONTROL WITH A STEPPING MOTOR

One of the most common mechanical control problems is accurate positioning. The two major components of positioning systems are the actuator and the sensor. The various requirements of the control task affect the costs of these two components in different ways. Actuator cost tends to depend most heavily on power requirements, while the cost of the sensor is most sensitive to accuracy and precision requirements. For low power applications, where the cost of the sensing system can be a major factor, stepping motor actuators have been widely applied because of their ability to do accurate positioning without using any position measurement sensors. They have also proved attractive because they are easily controlled by microprocessors. In this chapter we will examine the techniques that could be used to program a small stand-alone microprocessor to control a stepping motor.

STEPPING MOTORS FOR NO-FEEDBACK POSITION CONTROL

A typical stepping motor configuration is shown in Figure 4.1. Whenever the motor receives a pulse on the pulse input line, it will take one step in the direction determined by the signal present on the direction control line. As long as the load stays within the specifications of the motor used, each pulse will cause the motor to take one and only one fixed angular step. The reliability—in terms of the size of the step and the fact that it actually will be taken—is such that as long as the initial position is known, the final position can be accurately determined by summing the number of steps taken (with appropriate direction sign).

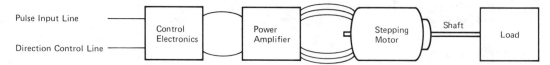

Figure 4.1: Schematic of Stepping Motor System

This case study will assume that the control electronics have been supplied and that only pulses and direction signals must be generated to run the motor. Circuit schematics for the control electronics and the motor model number appear at the end of this chapter. The problem of controlling stepping motors when no control electronics are used is discussed in Chapter 8. Principles of stepping motor operation can be found in handbooks published by stepping motor manufacturers.

DEDICATED MICROPROCESSOR CONTROLLERS

Computer applications for controlling stepping motors often call for a microprocessor to be buried within some other piece of equipment and used only for the task of stepping motor control. The computer responds to signals generated elsewhere in the equipment, but is usually not directly accessible from outside. The advent of microprocessors has made this kind of application economically feasible, since they make it possible to buy only as much computing power as is needed for the task at hand. Some typical applications of a dedicated microprocessor to stepping motor control are found in valve controllers, plotters, and positioning control components in an automobile engine.

Storing the Program

In a general purpose computing system of the sort we used in Chapter 3, it is

expected that many different programs will be run on the system at different times. Magnetic disks or tapes are usually used for convenient loading of these programs into the computer's memory. In contrast, from the time the dedicated microprocessor is installed to the time the equipment of which it is a part is scrapped, it usually runs only one program, which is rarely, if ever, changed. Magnetic tapes or disks are not needed (fortunately, because their relative cost would be prohibitive). Instead, programs are most usually stored in permanent memory called *read-only memory* (ROM). Once information is stored in ROM it is maintained, regardless of whether or not power is present, and is extremely difficult to erase or change. ROM contrasts with read-write memory, popularly called RAM, an acronym for *random-access memory.** In general purpose computers, all of the main memory is RAM. In dedicated microprocessor systems, only enough RAM memory is provided to meet calculation needs.

Development

High-level languages, as used in Chapter 2, are convenient and efficient for developing and debugging programs; however, they tend to generate actual com-

---

* This acronym makes no sense, since ROM is just as random access as RAM! However, the name RAM is so commonly used that we will use it also.

puter code that is not very efficient, either with respect to speed of operation or to the amount of memory required to run the program. In addition, the constraints of the language may limit access to the computer's complete repertoire of functions. Either situation generally leads to more or costlier hardware. In contrast, programming in assembly language usually takes more time and effort, but if skillfully done, can result in a more efficient product. For economic and functional reasons, current practice for dedicated microprocessors is to use a language that is computer-specific. In situations where the program developed for the dedicated microprocessor will be used in many units—millions in automobile engines, for example—the extra programming cost of using assembly language is more than repaid by savings in hardware costs. As new languages, such as Pascal, C, and PL/M, which make better use of a computer's functional capabilities, come into use for microprocessors, high-level, machine-independent language programming is becoming more economical.

In the next section, we will use the most primitive form of programming language, machine language, to solve a stepping motor control problem. Doing so would not ordinarily be wise, except in the simplest of applications; however, here it will permit us to explore the fundamental operation of a microprocessor.

CONTROLLING DIGITAL OUTPUTS

The Parallel Interface

The first step in creating a pulse to drive the stepping motor is turning the output line on. We will now examine how the computer's *central processing unit* (CPU) and its parallel interface interact to accomplish this. The interface used between the computer and the control electronics of the stepping motor system is the same as the interface used in the speed control system of Chapter 3. It is an interface that has some number of digital input lines and, usually, the same number of digital output lines. Each of these lines can be used for independent control functions, but internally, they must usually be manipulated in units of 8 or 16 by the computer program. Masking techniques must thus be used in order for the program to treat each of the lines as functionally independent.

Instructions

The central processing unit (CPU) of a computer can be thought of as a device that is wired to perform certain functions in response to commands that it receives, much as the processor in a calculator adds when the + key is pushed. In a computer, the CPU receives its commands from instructions stored in its memory. Information in the memory is represented as series of binary digits, called bits, and is accessible in groups of bits called *words* or *bytes*. One or more of these memory words constitute an instruction to the CPU. The instruction must contain information concerning the operation the CPU is to perform as well as the data (operand) on which it is to operate.

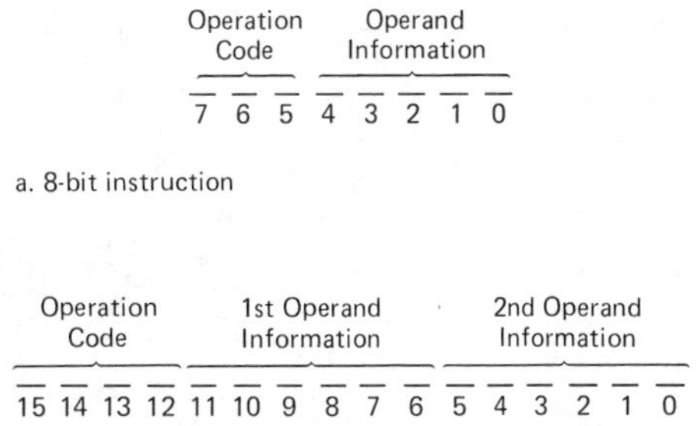

Operation Code	Operand Information
7 6 5	4 3 2 1 0

a. 8-bit instruction

Operation Code	1st Operand Information	2nd Operand Information
15 14 13 12	11 10 9 8 7	6 5 4 3 2 1 0

b. 16-bit instruction

Figure 4.2: Sample Instruction Formats

Most mini- and microcomputers use memories organized into words of either 8, 16, or 32 bits. (The term byte refers to 8 bits; it thus refers to half of a 16-bit word and is used interchangeably with the word ''word'' for computers with 8-bit words). Some possible instruction formats appear in Figure 4.2. The division between operation and operand information in an instruction is not necessarily the same for all instructions in a computer's instruction set. The numbers under the bit positions in Figure 4.2 are for convenience in identifying the portions of the word. They could be numbered either from right to left, as shown, or from left to right. In almost all computers, the counting starts from zero rather than from one.

Any particular instruction is a collection of binary digits. Using 0 and 1 for the binary digits, an 8-bit instruction could be something like 10010111. This form of writing instructions must ultimately be used in order for the CPU to respond to a command, but it is so awkward to use that programmers use a mnemonic shorthand called *assembly format*. Although the exact format varies, a typical format is:

LOC: OPERATION OPERAND(S)   ;Comments

LOC is a symbolic name for the place in memory at which this instruction is stored. The *comments* field is program documentation and has no effect on how the computer actually interprets the instruction.

A program is a sequence of instructions stored in the computer's memory. The memory is organized so that its words are accessed by a numerical index called an *address*. The CPU executes instructions in the order in which they are stored, unless it encounters an instruction that explicitly changes that order. Therefore, when the CPU finishes executing an instruction, it will normally look in the memory location having an address one higher than the address at which the current instruction ends. To do this, it uses an internal *register* called the *program counter* (PC). The CPU's internal registers are very fast memory units that are used for its control or processing tasks. The program counter is a register which keeps track of the location from which the next instruction will come. Figure 4.3 illustrates this. Memory cells, shown as boxes, are identified by the addresses shown to their left in binary. If the CPU were currently executing an instruction that occupied memory words 11010 and 11011, the program counter would contain the next higher memory address, 11100, which identifies the next instruction to be executed. After completing the current instruction, the CPU brings in the instruction at which

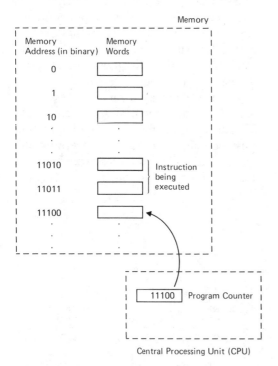

Figure 4.3: Keeping Track of the Next Instruction

the program counter is pointing for interpretation and execution.

There are three major types of instructions: copy instructions, data manipulation instructions, and instructions that change the instruction sequence. To access the digital control port, we have to use copy type instructions.

Accessing the Control Port

Copy instructions read data from some place in the computer and write the information some place else. We use the term "copy" for these types of instructions rather than the more commonly used "move," because, in almost all cases, the original source of information is not disturbed and the information is duplicated at the destination. Operating the stepping motor requires information to be controlled on two of the digital output lines. To simplify the control for the moment, we will assume that the direction control line is being set from some external source. Since we will then only be using one line of the output port and ignoring the others, the information required to turn the pulse line on will always be the same: a binary word with zeroes everywhere, except for the bit position corresponding to the pulse line, which has a one. For constant information such as this, the most convenient form of copy instruction to use is one that includes the information to be copied within the instruction itself. This is an *immediate mode* instruction. The operation of an instruction that copies immediate data to a CPU register is shown in Figure 4.4. In addition to the program counter, the CPU has a number of other registers, including some that are known as general purpose registers.

The general purpose registers are the scratchpad memory of the CPU, and are used for high-speed data manipulation

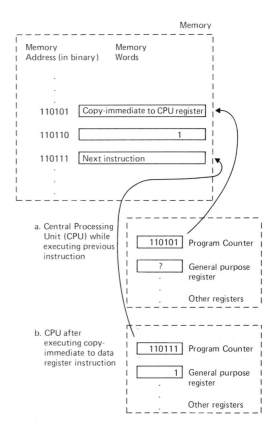

Figure 4.4: Instruction Sequence for Copy-Immediate

operations. In many computers, it is also necessary to pass information through a general purpose register to access an input or output port. In Figure 4.4, the copy-immediate instruction occupies memory locations 110101 and 110110. The first word of the instruction specifies the nature of the operation and indicates that "immediate" data is to be copied to a particular CPU general purpose register. The data to be copied is in the second memory location of the instruction. Part *a* of the figure shows the state of the CPU before the copy-immediate instruction is executed. The program counter is pointing to 110101, which

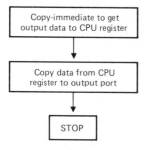

Figure 4.5: Flowchart to Turn Control Bit On or Off

is the address of the copy-immediate instruction, the instruction that will be executed next. There is some information in the general purpose register (?), but it is of no interest to us at this point. Part *b* of the figure shows the state of the CPU after the copy-immediate instruction has been executed. The general purpose register contains a binary 1 which will turn on bit 0 (the bit at the extreme right, using the numbering system of Figure 4.2) of the output port when it is copied there.

The program counter points to the instruction following the copy which is about to be executed. Most computer manufacturers would call this instruction a *move* or a *load* instruction. Finally, the information must be copied to the output port. Another copy-type instruction is used for this operation. This copy instruction must specify that information is to be copied from the CPU register to the output port. The instruction sequence, shown in flowchart form in Figure 4.5, will turn on the output line attached to the pulse input of the stepping motor controller. The STOP instruction will cause the CPU to turn off, that is, to stop executing instructions. Actual instruction sequences in assembly format for various computers are given in the Appendix. Running this program will test whether or not the instructions as coded

are correct and whether or not the output port is correctly wired.

RUNNING THE OUTPUT PORT TEST PROGRAM

To run a program using machine language, we must be able to translate the program from the assembly format in which we wrote it to the binary instruction codes to which the CPU will respond. Furthermore, we have to get the instructions into the computer's memory, start the CPU in such a way that the first instruction it executes is the first instruction of our program, and verify that the program is performing as anticipated.

Binary Instruction Codes for Output Port Test

Computer reference manuals provide instruction formats, operation codes for all of the instructions, and information on how to construct the operand portion of an instruction. Even computer manufacturers do not like to write instruction codes in binary! Instead they take advantage of the very simple conversions that can be made from binary to any number system in which the base is an integer power of two. The two number systems that are used for this purpose are base 8 (octal) and base 16 (hexadecimal or *hex* for short). For conversion from binary to octal, the binary digits are grouped in three's. Three digit binary numbers can form the numbers from 0 (000) to 7 (111), which are the digits that are used in a base 8 number system. Thus, as shown in the "octal" columns in Figure 4.6, the binary digits are grouped in three's to form octal digits. If the number of binary digits is not an even multiple of three, the usual convention is to group from the right so that the extra bits are at the left. In the 8-bit example in Figure 4.6, the digit at the extreme right comes from the three binary digits 100 to yield an octal 4. Since the group at the extreme left contains only two binary digits, only the octal numbers 0,1,2, or 3 can be in that position. To convert back from octal to binary, all we must do is write down the binary equivalent for each octal digit and then put the binary numbers together in groups of three. If the binary word being converted were an instruction, the operation code and operand information might be broken up as shown in Figure 4.6. (This is the same breakdown used in Figure 4.2.) Notice that the divisions of the parts of the instruction do not necessarily correspond with the divisions that result from converting the number to octal.

In the 8-bit word, for example, the 3-bit operation code straddles parts of two octal digits, and the 5-bit operand occupies all of the digit on the extreme right, but only part of the middle octal digit. To interpret the operation codes in the manufacturer's reference manual, it is necessary to refer first to the bit assignments and then to the octal operation code. For the 8-bit instruction shown, the operation code would be shown as 34 octal, indicating that the two binary digits at the extreme left are 11 (octal 3) and that bit 5 of the instruction is a 1. Because the operation code only occupies bit 5 of the middle octal digit, the second octal digit for operation codes in this format would be either a 4, to indicate that bit 5 is a 1, or a 0, to indicate that bit 5 is a 0. Likewise, the operand portion of that instruction would be written as 24. When the operation code of 34 is put together with the operand code of 24, the middle octal digit must be formed by sum-

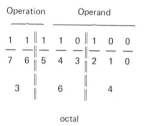

a. Conversion of 8-bit instructions to hex and octal

b. Conversion of 16-bit instructions to hex and octal

Figure 4.6: Hex and Octal Instruction Coding

ming the second digit of the operation code and the first digit of the operand code to get 364. The 16-bit instruction in the example poses no such problem, because the octal boundaries and instruction code boundaries coincide.

Almost all of the popular mini- and microcomputers use 8-, 16-, or 32-bit words. None of these word sizes divides evenly into three's, but all of them divide evenly into four's. Grouping the binary digits four at a time gives the numbers from 0 to 15, which are digits of a base 16 (hexadecimal) number system. A hexadecimal number system requires 16 unique digits. We can get 10 of them from the decimal system, 0 to 9, but six more are needed. We will use the first six letters of the alphabet. Counting from 0 to 15 in hexadecimal thus becomes: 0,1,2,3,4,5,6,7,8,9, A,B,C,D,E,F. Once we grow accustomed to using A,B, etc., the conversions to and from hex work in the same manner as the octal conversion.

At the same time that we construct the instruction codes by translating the assembly format instructions into octal or hex, we must also select the region in memory which the program is to occupy. For a very short program like this one, the selection is not difficult: a convenient starting address such as 100 or 1000 is usually used. (Most computer systems reserve certain parts of memory, particularly the low-numbered memory locations, for special functions. These regions must not be used indiscriminately.)

To avoid any ambiguity about the number system base in which we are working, we will follow the convention that numbers intended to be in the decimal system be written without any special notation, numbers intended to be in hexadecimal will be followed by an H, and numbers intended to be in octal will be followed by a Q. Numbers in the binary system will be followed by the letter B. Thus, 100H would mean 100 interpreted as a hex number, 100Q would be in octal, 100 would be decimal, and 100B would be a binary number. When we use assembly format, we will follow the conventions established by the computer manufacturer.

Loading and Running the Program with a Monitor

In the past, the most common practice for running machine language programs in a computer was by means of a control panel consisting of switches, for binary inputs to the computer, and lights, for binary outputs. These marvelously instructive, if inefficient, control panels have given way to control programs called *monitors* or *debuggers,* which communicate with us by means of a terminal. By typing commands on the keyboard, we can write information into the computer's memory, examine the contents of memory locations, examine or change CPU registers, and start the CPU running. Some monitors also include features which allow us to enter operation codes in mnemonic form, rather than in hex or octal.

Writing (or loading) a program into memory, then, involves typing the appropriate monitor command, identifying the address at which the information is to be written, and typing the instruction in either octal or hex. To verify that no typing errors have been made, the monitor is used to examine the memory locations where the program has been loaded. To run the program, we type the monitor command that activates the CPU. This command must include the memory address at which the program starts, so that the program counter can be set to that address before the CPU begins to run.

Program Verification

Program verification requires tremendous ingenuity. It challenges you to become your own worst enemy, drawing up adverse situations and input combinations to which the computer could be subjected—even those that seem rationally, but not physically impossible—then predicting what the program should do and testing it to see how it actually behaves. The order of this process is important, and the temptation to ignore or rationalize almost any result is powerful. To ensure against unanticipated consequences, it is extremely useful to have someone else verify your programs if at all possible.

The most obvious verification of our simple, three instruction program (that includes the STOP) is to examine the output line with a voltmeter, an oscilloscope, or a light attached to the output line. But is this sufficient? Since the output line is digital, it can have only one of two values. If we merely examined the output line, or ran the program to test it without first predicting its behavior, we would have only a 50 percent chance of finding an error. This problem can be virtually eliminated by modifying the program.

Orderly Stopping: Returning to the Monitor

Stopping a program by executing a HALT instruction works, but does not provide sufficient information about internal program results. Instead of stopping the CPU with a HALT, it is preferable to return to the monitor, so that memory locations or CPU registers can be examined, particularly if final results are incorrect. One way to do this is to use the *breakpoint* facility, if the monitor has one. Another is to substitute for the HALT (or STOP) at the end of the program a change-of-sequence instruction

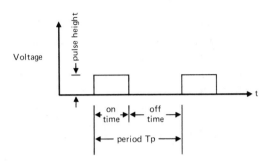

Figure 4.7: Pulse Train

that causes the next instruction executed to be the beginning of the monitor. (Recall that the monitor itself is just another program that resides in memory.) Computer manufacturers usually list instructions that change the program sequence as a separate category called *branch* or *jump* instructions.

PULSE TRAIN GENERATION

A pulse train is a sequence of pulses as defined in Figure 4.7. The pulses are described by a period—the time from the beginning of one pulse to the beginning of the next one—a pulse height, an on-time, and an off-time. For a digital output line, the pulse height is determined by the nature of the digital components; 0 to 5 volt transitions are common. The ratio of on-time to period is the aspect ratio of the pulse. For stepping motor control, the on-time is usually very much shorter than the off-time.

The program logic for the generation of a pulse train with a fixed number of pulses is shown in Figure 4.8. If we design the program for external direction control, the programs developed in the previous section can be used to turn the output line on and off. We examine below how to program the waits that are used to establish the pulse on-and-off times.

Timed Waits

The easiest way to produce a wait is to give the computer a benign, but predictable task like counting. The counting loop of Figure 4.9a serves as a simple wait. Each of the three blocks in the flow chart represents

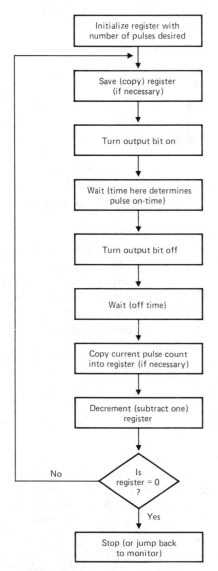

Figure 4.8: Flowchart for Pulse Train Generation Module

a different type of instruction. The first block can be implemented with the copy-immediate to a CPU register instruction that we have already used. The number put into the register represents the number of times we want the program to go through the loop. The bigger this number is, the longer the wait will be. The second block is a data manipulation instruction. As a result of executing the decrement instruction, the number in the register is reduced by one, or decremented. The third block is a change-of-sequence instruction, but unlike the change-of-sequence instruction used earlier, the change in this case is conditional.

In early minicomputers, conditional change-of-sequence instructions tested the status of a particular CPU register. This was easy to do, since most of the early minicomputers only had one or two CPU registers. As the number of CPU registers proliferated, this method became unworkable, and *condition* or *status codes* were introduced. Condition codes are really one-bit CPU registers that are set or cleared as instructions are executed. Typically, condition codes will be set if the result of executing an instruction is zero, negative, or has caused some kind of overflow (an overflow is a result that exceeds the capacity of the word size). Each instruction affects certain of the condition codes in specific ways. These effects are contained in the CPU reference manual.

To return to the wait loop, we are concerned with a test for zero vs. not-zero. In computers that use the condition code method, the decrement instruction will set the condition code for zero (which is usually called Z) if the result is zero, and will clear Z (i.e., set Z to zero) if the result is not zero. The conditional change-of-sequence instruction tests the Z bit and changes the sequence of instructions if the test result is

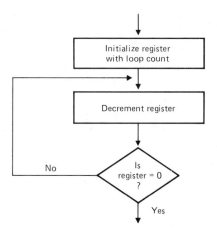

a. Wait loop

Figure 4.9: Wait Loops

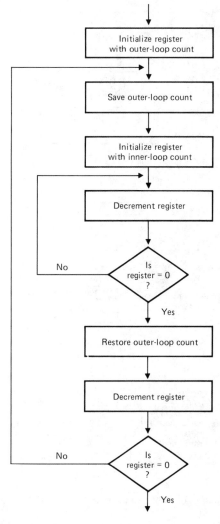

b. Nested wait loop

affirmative; it goes on to the next instruction if the test result is negative. The conditional change-of-sequence instruction needed in this case would usually be called branch-on-nonzero or jump-on-nonzero, corresponding to the branch-back arrow in the flow chart for the *no* result.

How long a wait can this method achieve? The wait loop contains two instructions: the decrement and the conditional branch. Execution time for these instructions could run from two to twenty microseconds in typical mini- and microcomputers. Taking a total execution time for the loop as ten microseconds, with a computer that can do 16-bit arithmetic directly, the largest loop index that can be used is $2^{16} - 1 = 65,535$. Multiplying by 10 microseconds gives a total maximum wait time of about 0.6 second. With computers that do 8-bit arithmetic, the maximum wait time is based on a maximum loop index of $2^8 - 1 = 255$, for a maximum wait time of about 2.5 milliseconds. If a modest increase in the wait time is needed (i.e., a factor of two to ten), the execution time of the loop can be increased by padding it with do-nothing instructions. The classic do-nothing instruction that most computers have is NOP, *no-operation*. For much larger increases in wait time, nested loops can be used, as shown in Figure 4.9*b*. For 16-bit arithmetic, the wait time can be increased by a factor of 65,535 this way. Any number

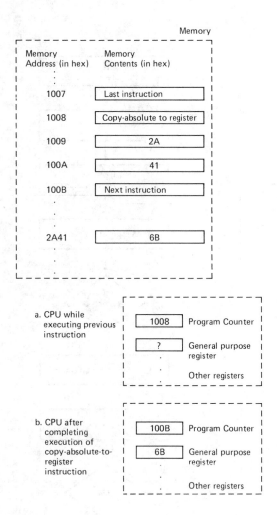

Figure 4.10: Copy-Absolute Instruction

complementary restore are implemented with copy instructions. If other CPU registers are available for storing information but not for arithmetic operations, a register-to-register copy can be made. If no other CPU register is available, the information must be stored in memory. The copy-immediate instruction that we used earlier will not work here, because the information being copied is changing constantly. The copy-absolute instruction will do what we need. In *absolute mode,* the instruction specifies the address of the data to be copied, rather than the data itself. A copy-absolute-to-register instruction for a computer with 8-bit memory words is shown in Figure 4.10. Almost all 8-bit computers allow for memory addresses that use 16 bits, facilitating direct addressing of memories of up to 65,536 8-bit words, or bytes, as they would be called in this case. Using only 8-bit addresses would limit the number of accessible memory locations to 256, which is too small to be practical for all but the simplest applications.

A copy-absolute instruction appears in Figure 4.10 in memory location 1008H. The address of the data follows in the next two bytes, giving a total of three bytes for the instruction. The address must be two bytes long to allow for the full 16-bit address. The CPU designer decides which of the two following bytes is the high-order portion of the address and which is the low-order portion. In this case, we have assumed that the high-order portion comes first. The address at which the data will be found is, therefore, 2A41H, and the data currently stored there is 6BH. The effect of the instruction is to copy the data (6BH) from the address (2A41H) to a CPU register. The instruction for copying from the CPU register back to memory is constructed in exactly the same way.

of such loops can be nested to achieve extremely long wait times.

The flowchart for the nested loop also addresses the problem of saving the outer loop count while the inner loop is executing. Whether or not this operation is needed depends on the number of general purpose CPU registers available and how they may be accessed. The save operation and the

Running the Stepping Motor

The same instructions that were used to complete the wait loop are all we need to complete the pulse train generation program of Figure 4.8. We next code the program in assembly format from the flowchart and translate it into instruction codes, preparatory to loading and running the program with a monitor. To verify the program, we first observe the program output with an oscilloscope. We also predict the pulse train parameters and then check to see that they vary appropriately, as we change the data in the program that controls them. We must also verify the total number of pulses generated. With this done, we can connect the stepping motor and examine the effects of the pulse train parameters on its operation, paying special attention to the pulse period and the on-time. To see if any steps have been missed, we check the distance the motor has moved against the number of pulses in the pulse train.

DIRECTION CONTROL

To control the stepping motor's direction, it is necessary to control two independent output lines on the same output port. This involves a modification of the instructions that were used to turn the output line on and off, since we had assumed, you will recall, that only one line of the output port was in use. A method similar to that used in Chapter 3 must be devised to control the output lines independently. To control the value of a single line, it is necessary to know the values of all of the other lines, unless the computer being used includes instructions to do single-bit manipulation. The value to be copied to the output port is a word with as many bits as the output port has. All of the bits of that word are set to zero, except the bit corresponding to the line being controlled. That bit is set to the desired output value. For example, using the numbering system of Figure 4.2, if we want to set bit 4 of an 8-bit output port to a value of 1, we construct a data word with the value 00010000B, which is equal to 10H. By using logical OR, this data word can be combined with the current value of the output port in such a way that only the desired bit is affected. This operation is shown in Figure 4.11a. If the value at the output port is accessible, it can be copied directly to a CPU

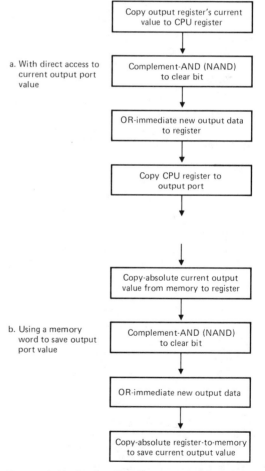

a. With direct access to current output port value

- Copy output register's current value to CPU register
- Complement-AND (NAND) to clear bit
- OR-immediate new output data to register
- Copy CPU register to output port

b. Using a memory word to save output port value

- Copy-absolute current output value from memory to register
- Complement-AND (NAND) to clear bit
- OR-immediate new output data
- Copy-absolute register-to-memory to save current output value

Figure 4.11: Instruction Sequence with Direction Control

register. Then an OR-immediate-to-register instruction can be used to create the composite output word. The OR-immediate instruction works like the copy-immediate instruction already discussed, except that the immediate data is OR-ed with the current contents of the register. It does not replace the current contents, as it would for the copy instruction. Next, the composite output word is copied to the output port. If the current value at the output port is not accessible, the modified sequence in Figure 4.11b can be used. In that case, a memory word is used to keep track of what has been written to the output port. Copy-absolute instructions are used to access the memory image of the output port.

These new output instruction sequences should be substituted for the old instructions in the program just written to control the stepping motor. If no new instructions are added to set the direction, the direction will be controlled by whatever value the direction line of the output port takes when the computer's power is turned on. If the output port value is being saved in

memory, the direction will reflect the value that the memory location had when the program began. Aside from the unpredictability of the direction, the program should behave identically.

A considerable simplification of the programming task can be made by taking advantage of the fact that the wait module appears three times in the program, twice in the pulse train generation module, and one additional time to control how long the motor pauses before returning to its original position. Once we have developed the code for a basic wait loop, we can copy it directly into all three places. Because each of the wait modules will probably have a different waiting time, we copy only the part of the module that begins after the desired loop count has been set in the register. Use of text substitution of this sort is a common and useful part of programming practice. The text substituted for a symbolic label— in this case, the instructions that form the wait module for the symbolic name "wait"—is called a macro. The new program can now be run and tested.

PULSE TIMING CONTROL USING AN EXTERNAL CLOCK

Pulse timing based on wait loops has the advantage of simplicity, but has two major disadvantages: the amount of time consumed in the wait loop depends on the speed with which the particular computer executes instructions, leading to re-calibration problems every time there is an equipment change; in addition, the CPU is occupied in counting almost all the time. As soon as the CPU time occupied by the noncounting part of the program becomes significant, the calibration job becomes even more difficult, because the pulse timing parameters will then also depend on the amount of CPU time that other program

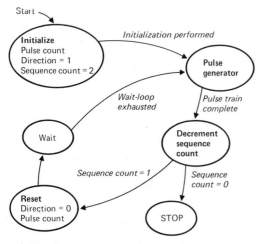

Figure 4.12: Stepping Motor Control Program

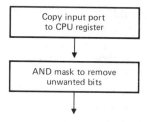

Figure 4.13: Reading a Digital Input Port

segments are absorbing. These problems can be avoided by using an external clock for timing, as was done to measure the velocity of the DC motor in Chapter 3. A much greater percentage of CPU time will then be available for useful computation, and the overall timing will be controlled by the external clock frequency rather than the operating speed of the computer.

The clock signal can be brought into the computer on one line of a digital input port. You will recall that the computer deals with the port as an n-bit unit, but that each of the bits represents an independent function. The solution to this dilemma is to use the logical AND as a masking function (see Figure 4.13). The mask word has zeroes in all bit positions except the one being examined, which has a 1. When the mask word is AND-ed with the input word from the digital input port, the result is zero in all of the bit positions corresponding to those where there is a zero in the mask word. The position that contains a 1 will contain whatever is in that bit position in the input word. For example, if the clock input is on bit zero, the mask word for an 8-bit processor will be 00000001B, which is equal to 1. When AND-ed with the input word, bit zero will contain the input value on that line, and bits 2 to 7 will be zero. The presence or absence of a signal from the clock can be determined after AND-ing by using a conditional instruction that checks the Z bit.

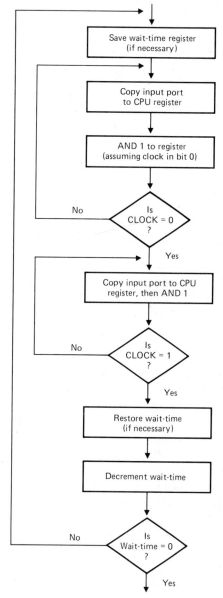

Figure 4.14: Wait Macro Using Clock for Timing

The logic for a new wait macro appears in Figure 4.14. Like the previous wait macro, the program expects to find the wait time in a CPU register when it starts. After

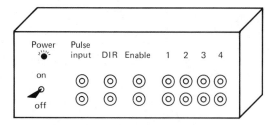

a. Front panel

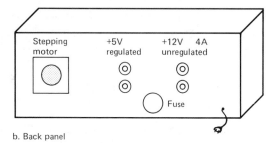

b. Back panel

Figure 4.15: Stepping Motor Controller

saving the wait-time loop count, the program waits until the clock input is zero, then waits for it to become one again to count one clock pulse. (This logic is identical to the time module used in Chapter 3.) No new instructions are needed for coding this wait macro. After loading the program, the user should verify it, beginning once again with the oscilloscope test, to see that the pulses are being generated properly.

CONTROL ELECTRONICS CIRCUITS AND SPECIFICATIONS

Stepping Motor Controller Details

Figures 4.15a and 4.15b show, respectively, the front and back of the chassis boxes which contain the circuits of Figure 4.15c. Figure 4.15a shows 14 receptacles into which standard plugs may be inserted. The pulse and direction inputs are described in this chapter, while the other 10 inputs, which are described fully in Chapter 8, allow us to bypass the circuit which generates the stepping motor actuation sequence. The motor with which we experiment plugs into the back panel of our controller.

The circuit of Figure 4.15c contains a supply to provide motor power as well as a voltage regulator to produce power for several logic circuits. The selector (74157) will connect signals on pins 3, 6, 10, and 13 to pins 4, 7, 9 and 12 respectively, if the enable input is not connected. In this mode, the logic circuit comprising the two 7486's and two 7474's will generate the proper motor actuation sequence in response to the direction and pulse inputs. In Chapter 8, we will ground the enable input in order that the computer may directly generate the actuation sequence. The power transistors at the right of Figure 4.15c amplify the logic level signals in order to drive the motor.

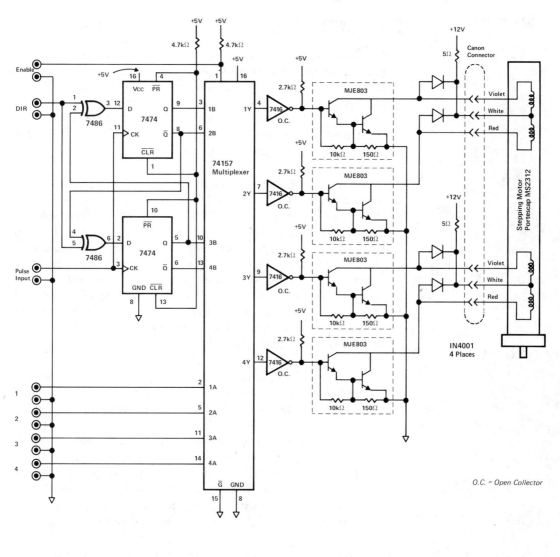

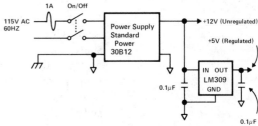

Figure 4.15c: Stepping Motor Controller, Circuit Level Realization

PROJECTS

Some of these projects do not require a stepping motor.

1. Using Figure 4.8 as a model, load and run a pulse train generation program. Design your first version to produce pulses endlessly so that you can observe the pulse train with an oscilloscope or frequency counter. What is the highest frequency that your program can generate? Utilizing a single loop decrement, test, and branch structure, what is the lowest frequency pulse train your program can generate?

2. Write a nested loop timed wait program (see Figure 4.9) which produces a 10 Hz pulse train. Insert a number of no-operation (NOP) instructions into one of your program loops in order to deduce the speed at which your computer executes a NOP. Does your calculation agree with the computer manufacturer's specification? Examine your computer's instruction set, and select an instruction which requires a large number of machine cycles to execute. Replace the NOPs with an equal number of these instructions. Is the resulting pulse train frequency what you predicted? Why do you think your slow instruction takes more time to execute than a NOP?

3. Use your pulse train program to cause a stepping motor to step. Start with a low frequency pulse train of 10 Hz or less. How many steps produce one revolution of the motor shaft?

4. Investigate the highest frequency pulse train that will cause your stepping motor to start rotating. Begin with an unloaded motor. At this critical frequency, what do you suspect is happening? Try to make the stalled motor rotate by giving it a twist. Sketch a graph which shows the qualitative relationship between motor torque (ordinate) and pulse train frequency (abscissa).

5. A simple method of measuring the torque of a small stepping motor employs a spring scale and a length of cord connected to the scale. One end of the string is wound neatly around the motor shaft to make frictional contact (as a hawser about a capstan). The motor is then run. As the frictional load increases, the scale will roughly measure torque. A good reference is the scale reading when the motor stalls. Plot the relation between motor torque at stall (ordinate) and pulse train frequency (abscissa).

6. Write a program which allows you to enter (using the monitor), at run time, the number of *revolutions* (not steps) which the motor is to rotate and the number of *seconds* which are to elapse before the motor moves. Use an external clock if you wish.

7. Modify the program of Project 6 to allow specification of the direction which the motor is to turn, and make the delay be the length of time to elapse before the motor reverses and travels back to its starting point (see Figure 4.12).

8. Connect a small switch such that its state may be read at a parallel input port. Devise a simple mechanism which allows the motor to rotate and actuate the switch. Write a program which drives the motor until this simple limit switch is sensed.

9. After performing Project 8, add a second limit switch such that your motor has a high and low limit. Write a program which allows the motor to begin at any point and find each limit and then rotate to a point halfway between the limits. (Hint: In base ten, how do you divide by ten?)

Chapter 5

TEMPERATURE CONTROL

Computer control systems, regardless of complexity, have similar overall structures. This case study examines a simple but typical computer system for controlling the temperature of a liquid (see Figure 5.1).

Because temperature is an important variable in so many processes, there are many different kinds of instruments for measuring temperature and a wide variety of actuation devices for adding energy to or removing energy from systems. Almost all of the instruments available for measuring temperature produce their output in the form of an analog signal, and actuators usually require analog signals to control their power output. To interface with this equipment, computers need *analog-to-digital* (A/D) and *digital-to-analog* (D/A) converters. This is illustrated in Figure 5.2.

In our system, the A/D and D/A converters are connected to the computer through parallel ports. We heat the liquid with an electric heater controlled by a power amplifier and measure the temperature with a solid state sensor. We will read the temperature sensor and control the heater using converters made from operational amplifiers and digitally controlled switches. A schematic of our complete system appears in Figure 5.3. We will do our programming in machine language in order to make full use of the CPU's capabilities, but instead of constructing our codes manually from the assembly format instructions, we will lighten our task by using a computer program called an *assembler*. The assembler maintains CPU specificity while keeping track of operation codes and memory addresses in symbolic form.

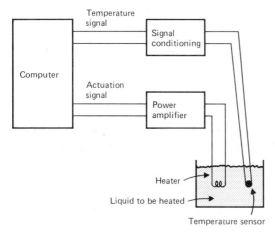

Figure 5.1: Thermal Control System

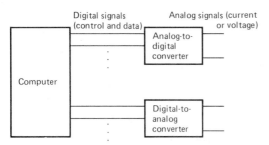

Figure 5.2: Analog/Digital Interaction

Figure 5.3: Complete Computer Control System

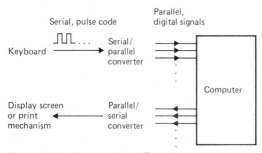

Figure 5.4: Connecting a Terminal to a Computer

ACCESSING THE TERMINAL

We will develop our control program in four stages: terminal I/O, the D/A converter, the A/D converter, and the control logic, beginning with the terminal, so that it can be used in the programs written to test the operation of the A/D and D/A converters.

Figure 5.4 shows the most typical method of connecting a terminal to a computer. A terminal consists of a keyboard and a printer, or display. Although the keyboard and the display may be housed in a single unit, they are distinct components and must be programmed separately. Terminals are connected to computers via a single transmission path. This ensures maximum flexibility for locating terminals at any distance from the computer, but it also means that information must be sent in serial form, usually asynchronously (see Chapter 2, Digital Communication Protocol). The computer's terminal interface converts the information from serial to parallel form, so that the computer can use it. The device within the interface that does the actual serial/parallel conversion is usually a universal asynchronous receiver-transmitter (UART). The electrical characteristics of the serial transmission path usually follow one of three standards: the 20 mA current loop, the Electronic Industries Association (EIA) RS-232-C, or the newer RS-422-A and RS-423-A, which include RS-232-C as a subset.

The computer stores the information it receives from the terminal in the form of binary digits which are coded to correspond with the characters on the keyboard and the characters displayed or printed. The code is a matter of convention. The code used most frequently for mini- and microcomputer serial information is seven bit ASCII. Table 5.1 presents this code in decimal, octal, and

Character	Octal	Decimal	Hexadecimal	Character	Octal	Decimal	Hexadecimal	Character	Octal	Decimal	Hexadecimal
NUL	000	000	00	0	060	048	30	`	140	096	60
SOH	001	001	01	1	061	049	31	a	141	097	61
STX	002	002	02	2	062	050	32	b	142	098	62
ETX	003	003	03	3	063	051	33	c	143	099	63
EOT	004	004	04	4	064	052	34	d	144	100	64
ENQ	005	005	05	5	065	053	35	e	145	101	65
ACK	006	006	06	6	066	054	36	f	146	102	66
BEL	007	007	07	7	067	055	37	g	147	103	67
BS	010	008	08	8	070	056	38	h	150	104	68
HT	011	009	09	9	071	057	39	i	151	105	69
LF	012	010	0A	:	072	058	3A	j	152	106	6A
VT	013	011	0B	;	073	059	3B	k	153	107	6B
FF	014	012	0C	<	074	060	3C	l	154	108	6C
CR	015	013	0D	=	075	061	3D	m	155	109	6D
SO	016	014	0E	>	076	062	3E	n	156	110	6E
SI	017	015	0F	?	077	063	3F	o	157	111	6F
DLE	020	016	10	@	100	064	40	p	160	112	70
DC1	021	017	11	A	101	065	41	q	161	113	71
DC2	022	018	12	B	102	066	42	r	162	114	72
DC3	023	019	13	C	103	067	43	s	163	115	73
DC4	024	020	14	D	104	168	44	t	164	116	74
NAK	025	021	15	E	105	069	45	u	165	117	75
SYN	026	022	16	F	106	070	46	v	166	118	76
ETB	027	023	17	G	107	071	47	w	167	119	77
CAN	030	024	18	H	110	072	48	x	170	120	78
EM	031	025	19	I	111	073	49	y	171	121	79
SUB	032	026	1A	J	112	074	4A	z	172	122	7A
ESC	033	027	1B	K	113	075	4B	{	173	123	7B
FS	034	028	1C	L	114	076	4C	¦	174	124	7C
GS	035	029	1D	M	115	077	4D	}	175	125	7D
RS	036	030	1E	N	116	078	4E	~	176	126	7E
US	037	031	1F	O	117	079	4F	DEL	177	127	7F
SP	040	032	20	P	120	080	50				
!	041	033	21	Q	121	081	51				
''	042	034	22	R	122	082	52				
#	043	035	23	S	123	083	53				
$	044	036	24	T	124	084	54				
%	045	037	25	U	125	085	55				
&	046	038	26	V	126	086	56				
'	047	039	27	W	127	087	57				
(	050	040	28	X	130	088	58				
)	051	041	29	Y	131	089	59				
*	052	042	2A	Z	132	090	5A				
+	053	043	2B	[	133	091	5B				
,	054	044	2C	\	134	092	5C				
−	055	045	2D	]	135	093	5D				
.	056	046	2E	∧	136	094	5E				
/	057	047	2F	—	137	095	5F				

Abbreviations for Control Characters

NUL	null, or all zeros	HT	horizontal tabulation	DC2	device control 2
SOH	start of heading	LF	line feed	DC3	device control 3
STX	start of text	VT	vertical tabulation	DC4	device control 4
ETX	end of text	FF	form feed	NAK	negative acknowledge
EOT	end of transmission	CR	carriage return	SYN	synchronous idle
ENQ	enquiry	SO	shift out	ETB	end of transmission block
ACK	acknowledge	SI	shift in	CAN	cancel
BEL	bell	DLE	data link escape	EM	end of medium
BS	backspace	DC1	device control 1		

SUB	substitute
ESC	escape
FS	file separator
GS	group separator
RS	record separator
US	unit separator
SP	space
DEL	delete

Table 5.1: 7-Bit ASCII Code

hex. An eighth bit, which can be used as a parity bit for error detection, is often appended to the seven bit code. Most often, ASCII devices transmit eight bits of information whether the parity bit is in use or not. The parity bit must be masked off before the character is interpreted.

Controlling Data Transfer

Because terminals vary widely in speed and are always much slower than the computer, a mechanism must be built into

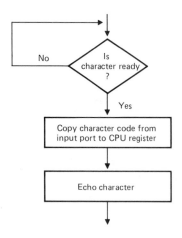

a. Reading a character from a terminal

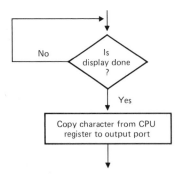

b. Printing a character on the terminal

Figure 5.5: Program for a Terminal

the interface to control data transfer so as to avoid loss of information. Since data transfers are made one character at a time, information loss can occur if the computer tries to send a character to the terminal before the display of the previous character has been completed, or if the terminal sends a character to the computer before the computer has examined the previous character. Two one-bit registers called *flags,* located in the interface, are used for this purpose. One of the signals indicates that the interface has received a character from the terminal which is ready to be read. The other indicates that the display has completed processing a character. Logic circuits in the interface clear the *character-ready* flag after the computer program has read the character, and the circuits clear the *display-done* flag after a new character has been sent. Figure 5.5 shows the program logic necessary to achieve the transfer.

When the program enters a state in which it expects information from the terminal, it must query the character-ready flag, repeating the query until the flag indicates that the character may be read. When the program is about to transmit a character to the terminal, it must repeatedly query the display-done flag until the flag indicates that the character may be sent. The display-done flag assures that no information will be lost by too rapid transmission from the computer to the terminal; however, in this form of input/output (I/O) transfer, the programmer must take care that the program examines the character-ready flag often enough so that it doesn't miss any characters. Serial transmission rates are expressed in bits/sec, with a named unit called *baud rate.* Since asynchronous ASCII packets usually contain 10 bits (seven for the character code, one for parity, one start bit, and one stop bit), their character rate is one-tenth of the baud rate. Commonly used terminal transmission rates range from 110 baud to 19,200 baud.

The Echo Character box in the read-character flowchart (Figure 5.5*a*) reflects the logical separation of the keyboard and the display. One of the consequences of this separation is that a character will only appear on the display if the computer transmits it back to the terminal after receiving it. One complication in character echoing is that returning the carriage to the beginning of the line and feeding the paper up one line are two separate processes. To avoid typing a carriage return and a linefeed character at the end of every line, it is normal programming practice to have the computer echo both the carriage return and the linefeed, whenever it receives a carriage return.

An interesting and easy project that vividly demonstrates keyboard/display separation appears in Figure 5.6. Since the program increments the character code by one before echoing the character, a user typing an A at the terminal will see a B echoed.

Running the Program

The terminal test programs should be written in assembly format, just as the stepping motor programs were. Instead of hand-translating them into machine language, we enter them into a computer file using an editor (a program that accepts commands at the terminal for the insertion and manipulation of text). The assembler which translates the file into machine language will also check for syntax errors in the assembly format version of the program (the *source* program). To produce an actual memory image version of the program in binary, ready for loading into the computer's memory, we need one additional step, called *linking* or *loading*. In the early

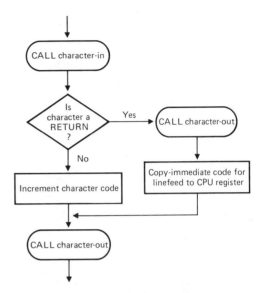

Figure 5.6: Program for Shifted Echo

stages of program development, a monitor is usually loaded into memory along with the program to assist in debugging. In addition to the features described in Chapter 4, most monitors make it possible for the user to interrupt the program at a specific memory location in order to examine how the program is functioning. This very valuable debugging aid, known as a *breakpoint,* enables the user to check intermediate results, to verify correct operation of portions of the program, or to isolate portions that contain errors.

Debugging the terminal test programs will be more difficult if the user's program to control the terminal interferes with the operating system's connection to the terminal or with the debugging monitor's use of the terminal.

Subroutines

The character-in and character-out functions are shown as *subroutines* in Figure 5.6. Subroutines are an extremely convenient way to implement frequently used

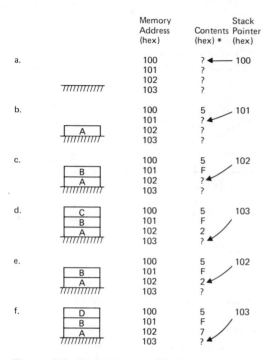

	Memory Address (hex)	Stack Contents (hex) *	Pointer (hex)
a.	100	? ⟵	100
	101	?	
	102	?	
	103	?	
b.	100	5	101
	101	? ⟵	
	102	?	
	103	?	
c.	100	5	102
	101	F	
	102	? ⟵	
	103	?	
d.	100	5	103
	101	F	
	102	2	
	103	? ⟵	
e.	100	5	102
	101	F	
	102	2 ⟵	
	103	?	
f.	100	5	103
	101	F	
	102	7	
	103	? ⟵	

Figure 5.7: Operation of a Stack

functions. Unlike the macro discussed in the last chapter, the actual machine code to implement the subroutine's function appears only once in memory; after *calling* the subroutine, the main program relinquishes control to it for the time that it performs its function. The main program must make a record of the location from which it has called the subroutine, so that it can take over again on the instruction following the call instruction when the subroutine has completed its task. The trade-off between using a macro and using a subroutine is that a macro requires more memory, because the actual code is reproduced at every place in the program where the function is performed, whereas a subroutine requires less memory but more computing time, because of the extra CPU time needed to execute the CALL and RETURN instructions.

The difference between a subroutine CALL instruction and other change-of-sequence instructions is the need to save a return address. Most computers provide instructions in their CPU instruction sets for saving return addresses on a *stack*. A stack is a means of storing information in such a way that only the piece of information written most recently is immediately accessible. It is analogous to a physical stack of items, with only the item at the top immediately available. A CPU register, the *stack pointer,* keeps track of which item of information is currently on top of the stack. Each time a new item is added to the stack (PUSHed), the stack pointer is automatically incremented to point to the next free memory location (see Figure 5.7*). Initially, the stack is empty, and the stack pointer's value is 100H, the first location allocated to the stack. In the analogous physical stack shown in the lefthand column of the figure, no items are yet present. When item A, with a value of 5, is PUSHed onto the stack, the value 5 is written into memory location 100H, and the stack pointer is incremented to 101H. In the physical analog, item A is placed in the position reserved for the pile of blocks. Items B (0FH) and C (2) are added to the stack, with similar results. Note that the most recently added item, C, is the one immediately available (this is the last-in, first-out format, LIFO). Between steps (d) and (e), the top item, C (2), has been removed (POPped) from the stack. A and B still remain, and B is now at the top of the stack. When a new item, D (7), is PUSHed onto the stack, the configuration (f) results.

In a subroutine CALL, the return address, which is the current value of the

---

* The ?'s in Figure 5.7 indicates *don't care* contents.

program counter, is automatically PUSHed onto a stack as shown in Figure 5.8. The CPU then copies the subroutine's starting address into the program counter, and the subroutine takes over. When it reaches the RETURN instruction, it POPs the stack to the program counter, and the main program resumes control. Because the CALL instruction does not save the CPU's general purpose registers, care must be taken to avoid losing the information they contain. In the sequence shown in Figure 5.8, the subroutine saves the information from the registers it will be using by PUSHing it onto the stack before taking any other action. Just before returning, it POPs the saved information to the registers. The registers and the stack may be manipulated this way to pass information (arguments) to a subroutine and to transmit subroutine results back to the calling program.

The stack structure is ideal for saving subroutine returns, because subroutines can be nested to any level, as long as the number of subroutine return addresses saved doesn't exceed the amount of memory allocated to the stack. The last-in first-out arrangement assures that the return address available is the one for the most recently called subroutine, which is the subroutine that will need a return address first. When using stacks, it is important to balance PUSHes and POPs, much as parentheses must be balanced in arithmetic; otherwise, unpredictable results will occur.

DIGITAL-TO-ANALOG CONVERSION

A simple, 6-bit digital-to-analog converter is shown in Figure 5.9. Each of the double-throw, digitally controlled switches changes the input impedance to the operational amplifier in such a way that operating them one at a time produces output voltages that change by a factor of two. This gives us

just the pattern that is needed to convert a binary number to an equivalent voltage. By combining this operational amplifier circuit with a computer's parallel port, we make it possible for a program to control an analog voltage. In order to demonstrate the working principles of a D/A converter, we have chosen to use external components to build ours (and will do the same for the A/D converter). In most computer control systems, the D/A and A/D converters are integrated with a parallel interface, making it difficult to observe how they operate.

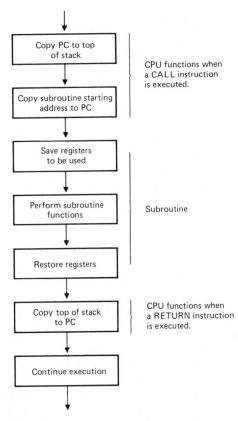

Figure 5.8: Sequence of Events in Using a Subroutine

Figure 5.10 is a D/A test program in which the user types the number to be converted (in decimal) at the terminal. The converted value may then be checked with a voltmeter to verify that the converter is operating properly. Since this converter has only six bits corresponding to the numbers 0 to 63, two characters are all the user must type to test all possible combinations. The program shown in Figure 5.11 will read the user's test command using the following conventions:

1. the first two characters typed on a line are the command number; subsequent characters will be ignored.

2. numbers less than 10 must include the leading zero, i.e., 07 for 7.

3. no action will be taken until a carriage return has been typed.

4. if numbers greater than 63 are typed, only the lower-order six bits will be used.

5. typing errors—for example, typing a non-numeric character—will not be detected and will produce strange but predictable results.

Conversion from decimal to binary is straightforward. If we use (CHAR1) to indicate the equivalent numerical value of the character in memory location CHAR1, the binary value corresponding to the number typed is

$$\text{BINVAL} = 1010B \times (\text{CHAR 1}) + (\text{CHAR 2})$$

where $1010B = 10$. To do this, however, we must be able to instruct the CPU to multiply. If the computer has a multiply instruction, it can be used; however, many computers, particularly microcomputers, do not have multiply instructions and must use subroutines instead. Binary multiplication algorithms are based on the manual method of multiplying two numbers. This method makes use of partial products obtained by successively multiplying the multiplicand by each digit of the multiplier. As the partial products are produced, they are written down in positions that are successively shifted one position further to the left for each partial product. This procedure is shown below for the product of 1101B times 1001B.

```
      1 1 0 1
  X   1 0 0 1
      1 1 0 1
    0 0 0 0
  0 0 0 0
1 1 0 1
1 1 1 0 1 0 1
```

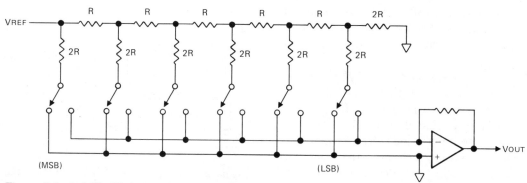

(MSB)   **(LSB)**

Figure 5.9: A 6-Bit Digital-to-Analog Converter

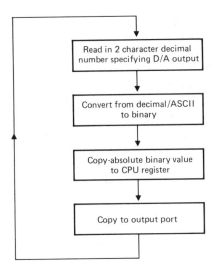

Figure 5.10: D/A Test Program

The binary multiplication procedure is much simpler than decimal multiplication in one major respect: the complete multiplication table is 0X0=0, 0X1=0, 1X1=1. If the digit of the multiplier being used to get a partial product is a 1, the multiplicand is just copied into the right position to form a partial product. If the digit is a zero, a row of zeroes is used for the partial product. One feature of multiplication that causes added complexity in finite precision machines, like computers, is that the result of multiplying two n-digit numbers together is a product that can have up to 2n significant digits. Registers and/or memory locations must be used in pairs to contain this double precision product. A subroutine to perform binary multiplication is shown in Figure 5.12. The shifting required to line up the partial products properly is implemented with the left-shift instruction, illustrated in Figure 5.13. In executing a left shift, the bit at the extreme left is shifted into the Carry (C) bit of the condition code register. The position at the extreme right is filled with a zero.

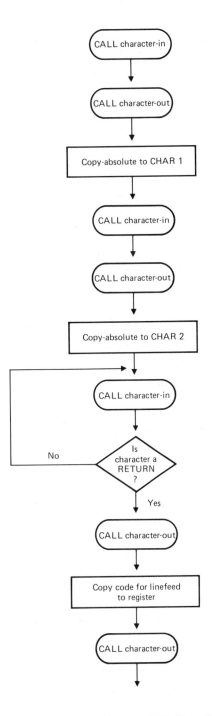

Figure 5.11: Reading the D/A Test Command

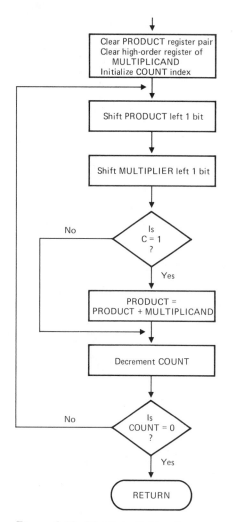

Figure 5.12: Multiply Subroutine

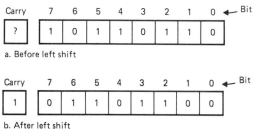

a. Before left shift

b. After left shift

Figure 5.13: Left Shift Operation

ANALOG-TO-DIGITAL CONVERSION

The integrating analog-to-digital converter shown in Figure 5.14 is a simplified version of the A/D converters used in most digital voltmeters. It works by integrating a reference voltage to produce a voltage ramp with known voltage-time characteristics. The output of the integrator, V1, goes to a *comparator,* where it is compared to the unknown voltage. When the magnitude of voltage V1 crosses the unknown voltage, VTEST, the comparator output changes abruptly. The time from opening the reset switch to the change in comparator output is proportional to the unknown voltage. A subroutine to control this type of A/D converter is shown in Figure 5.15. After setting an output bit of the parallel port to open the reset switch, the program begins a counting loop to time the period until the comparator switches. The precision of this A/D conversion depends on the amount of time available for counting as well as on the stability and quality of the operational amplifier components. For example, we estimated that the timed loop program in Chapter 4 would take about 2.5 ms to n ake 256 passes. The loop in Figure 5.15 wo ild take a bit longer, because of the added instructions to read the input port and check for overflow. The convert-time for eight bit precision, that is, one part in 256 error for a full-scale input, is thus around 3 ms or longer for this kind of A/D converter.

The terminal can be used to run an A/D test program, as shown in Figure 5.16. Using conventions similar to those used in the D/A test program, the user starts the A/D conversion process by typing GO and a carriage return. When the conversion is complete, the computer will have a binary value in its memory corresponding to the value of the voltage. The binary number must be converted to decimal digits and then to ASCII for printing. Conversion from binary numbers to decimal digits requires successively dividing the number by 10 (decimal) and saving the remainders, as shown in Figure 5.17. This produces decimal digits in sequence, beginning with the lowest-order digit. As the digits are produced, they must be saved, so that they can be printed later on in the normal highest-to-lowest order. To convert decimal digits to ASCII character code, the program adds the code for the character zero (indicated by the notation "0") to each of the digit values. The program continues this conversion process until it obtains a quotient of zero, or as in the case presented here, until it has proceeded through a predetermined number of steps covering the maximum possible number of digits.

To complete the A/D test program, we must implement the binary-to-decimal conversion algorithm by adding a subroutine for division. Like the multiplication algorithm, the division algorithm follows the pattern of manual long division. Again, to understand the operation, we must carefully examine the precision (number of bits) of each of the operands and the results (see Figure 5.18). We will assume

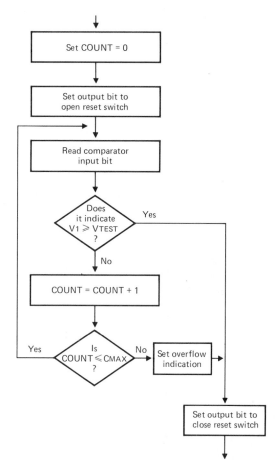

Figure 5.15: A/D Converter Subroutine

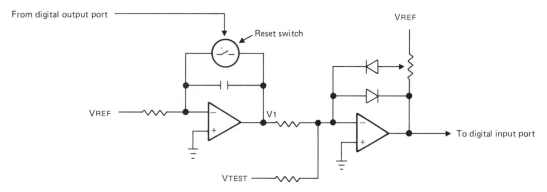

Figure 5.14: Integrating Analog-to-Digital Converter

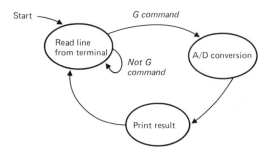

Figure 5.16: A/D Test and Calibration Program

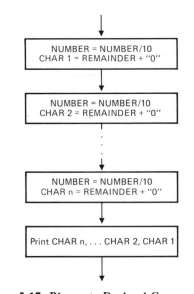

Figure 5.17: Binary to Decimal Conversion

that the dividend is a double-precision number, with a higher-order part and lower-order part occupying a pair of memory locations or registers. In this version of the algorithm, the divisor, quotient, and remainder will all be single-precision numbers. In order to represent the quotient as a single-precision quantity, the divisor must be greater than the higher-order part of the dividend. This condition can be checked

before entering the divide part of the subroutine, if desired, and an error bit set to indicate overflow if the divisor is not greater than the high-order part of the dividend. The rest of the logic exactly parallels the manual process for a 4-bit processor, as illustrated in Figure 5.19. We have crossed out the leading zero of the quotient to indicate that it is always zero (you will recall that the divisor must be greater than the high-order part of the dividend). The other crossed-out zeros represent bits that are lost when the dividend is shifted left. Our A/D test program can now be run to calibrate the converter.

DISCRETE-TIME, FEEDBACK CONTROL

Sampling

The most important distinction between a digital and an analog control system is that the digital computer system does not have continuous information about the variables it is measuring; rather, it must sample them at discrete instants. A serious characteristic of this discrete sampling procedure is that the longer the interval between samples (sample time) becomes, the more information is lost. Figure 5.20 shows a continuous sinusoidal signal and signals produced from sampling it at different intervals. Signals produced by sampling the original signal at intervals no greater than half the period of the sinusoid represent the frequency and amplitude of the original signal accurately, as long as the sampling record is long enough. However, once the sampling time exceeds half the period, the amplitude information about the original signal remains, but the frequency information is lost. The rule that the sample time must be less than half the highest frequency is the Shannon, or Nyquist, sampling rule. Note how sample time affects the frequency of the signals produced from the original signal: those with long sample times have much lower frequencies than the original. This effect, known as *aliasing,* has two consequences for computer control system design. It means that the sampling frequency must always be more than twice the highest spectral component we expect the system to have in response to input or disturbance variables. It also means that digital control systems are more sensitive to high frequency instrument noise than are analog systems.

It is common to expect some noise from instruments and signal conditioning equipment in control systems that has a frequency spectrum far above the spectrum of the control and process output signals. Normal analog equipment usually contains enough natural low-pass filtering that, at modest noise levels, the high frequency noise does not significantly affect the control process. As shown above, however, in computer control systems where the signal must be sampled, this noise will appear in the sampled signal at full amplitude and reduced frequency, because the sampling process does not affect the amplitude characteristics of the signal. The frequency reduction can bring the noise signal into the same frequency band as the process information, making it impossible to filter. The only solution, if such problems exist, is to insert analog filters ahead of the A/D converter to remove high frequency noise or to sample fast enough so that digital filtering techniques can be applied.

The Control Algorithm

The control system itself follows the traditional feedback control structure (see Figure 5.21). The dashed box represents the computer's function. The devices which read or generate signals are indicated at the

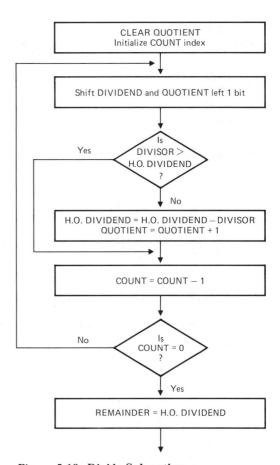

Figure 5.18: Divide Subroutine

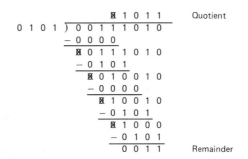

Figure 5.19: Binary Long Division

points where the signal lines cross the dashed lines. The operator's terminal generates the reference signal, r; the A/D converter produces the temperature measurement, y; and the D/A converter puts out the heater control signal, m.

The control algorithm used is proportional control, with the manipulated variable m, computed according to m = Ke + C, as shown. C is a nominal output value that sets the heater output to the approximate value required in order to obtain the operating point desired. The term Ke corrects the heater power based on the measured temperature. Since integer arithmetic must be used to compute the product Ke, the computational part of the control program must make allowance for the restrictions imposed

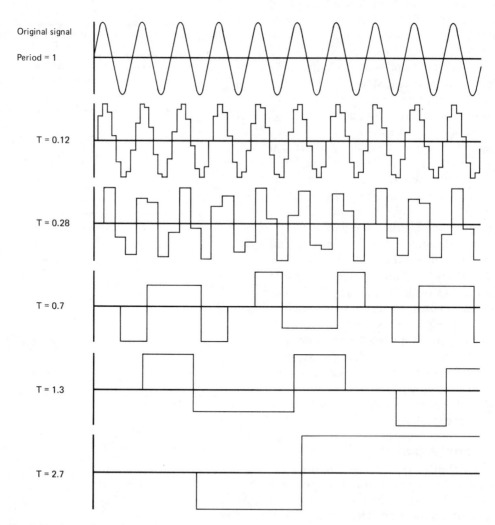

Figure 5.20: Time Data Sampling

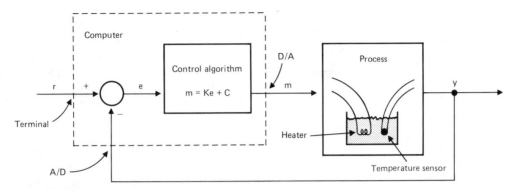

Figure 5.21: Control System Structure

by the multiply and divide subroutines and by the nature of integers, the precision of which is a function of their value. If we were to set the control gain, K, to a value near one, only the values 0,1, or 2 could be represented as integers. Furthermore, there are no possible values of K, other than zero, which are less than one. To avoid these problems and improve precision, we will represent K as the quotient of two integers, KNUM/KDEN, and accept the added computing time required for a division and a multiplication. The order of computation used is (KNUM*e)/KDEN. This avoids any truncation in the division operation and takes advantage of the fact that the double-precision product of the multiplication can immediately become the double-precision dividend required by the divide subroutine.

Finally, we note that the numerical value of the error, e, can be either positive or negative, and that we have not established any convention for representing signed numbers.

An n-bit word can only represent 2^n unique numbers. If signed numbers are used, some method must be devised to divide the set into positive and negative numbers. The most common method is 2's complement notation. The positive num-

bers are those from zero (which is considered positive) through the number that has a zero in the bit at the extreme left and ones in all other bits. For an 8-bit word size, for example, the positives would be 0,1,10B,11B,100B, ..., 01111111B. The negative numbers are the set obtained by counting backwards from zero (which is not included in the negatives), starting with the number that is all ones (designated as -1) and continuing through the number which has a one in the bit at the extreme left and zeros elsewhere. That number is the negative number with the largest possible magnitude. For an 8-bit word size, the negative numbers are 11111111B (-1), 11111110B (-2), 11111101B (-3), 11111100B (-4), ... 10000000B (-128). The negate operation involves two steps: 1. take the bit-by-bit complement of the number to be negated (that is, exchange all zeros for ones and all ones for zeros), and 2. add 1 to the result. For example, the 2's complement negative of the 4-bit number 0101B is formed by taking the bit-by-bit complement to get 1010B, then adding 1 to get the result 1011B. Although the bit at the extreme left is not a sign bit *per se,* it is equal to 1 in all negative numbers.

Neither our divide nor our multiply

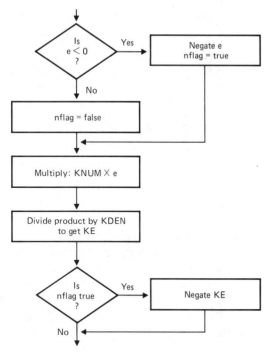

Figure 5.22: Computing KE

subroutines can handle signed numbers. For this case study, however, we will constrain KNUM and KDEN to be positive, so that only the error, e, can be negative. The flowchart in Figure 5.22 presents a procedure for obtaining the signed result, (KNUM*e)/KDEN, which is called KE on the flowchart.

The overall logic for the control program appears in the transition diagram of Figure 5.23. We meet the requirement that process control be maintained while the program is communicating with the operator by executing the terminal-in module every clock tick to check for characters from the terminal. To meet timing requirements, the external clock frequency must be high enough so that two characters cannot be typed in the duration of a single tick (about ten characters per second is the maximum typing rate for a human typist). On the other hand, to ensure that no clock pulses are missed, they must last longer than any

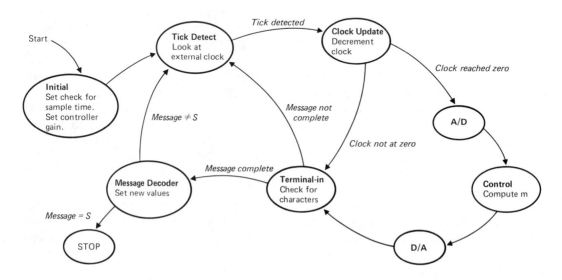

Figure 5.23: Control Program

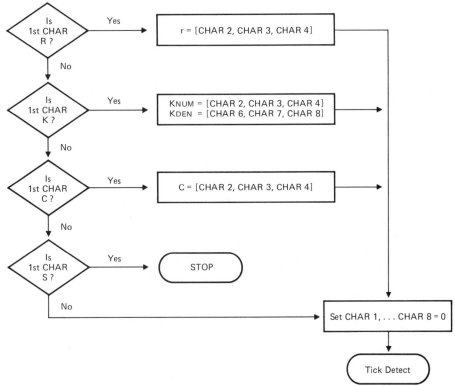

Figure 5.24: Message Decoder

computational path that starts from and returns to tick-detect. The longest path is clock-update, A/D, Control, D/A, terminal-in, message-decoder. If these requirements are in conflict, or if the tick duration is too long for the control task, more efficient programs must be written, a faster CPU must be used, or some compromise in performance must be made.

Operator Interaction

The protocol which the operator follows to communicate with the control program while it is controlling the process is a generalization of the terminal interaction used on the D/A and A/D test programs. Each line the operator types starts with a single character command, followed by one or two 3-digit decimal numbers. If two numbers are typed, they are separated by a comma. The appropriate command characters are R, to set a new setpoint, K, to put in new values for KNUM and KDEN, C, to enter a new value for C, and S, to stop the program. The program converts these numeric characters to binary and stores the results (see Figure 5.24). If it receives a command character that is not valid, it ignores the whole message. As in the previous examples, the program will not consider the message complete until it receives a carriage return.

To determine where to put each typed character, the terminal-in module initializes

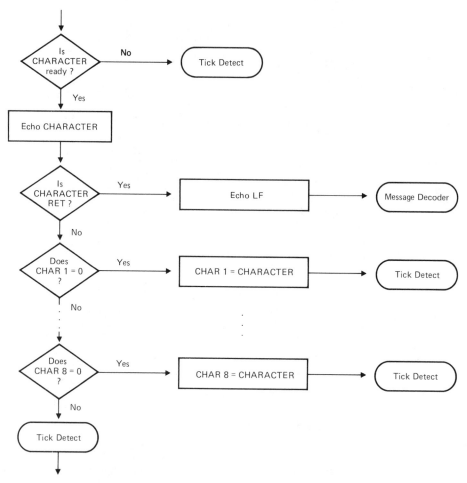

Figure 5.25: Terminal-In Module

to zero the memory locations for the eight characters that comprise the longest possible message (this corresponds to the ASCII code for the NULL character). When Terminal-in receives a character, it puts it in the next zero character location it can find (see Figure 5.25). If all the character positions are nonzero, terminal-in ignores the character. If it receives a RETURN, it transfers control to the message-decoder module. When this module has completed its interpretation of the message, it resets all

of the character positions to zero. A typical response to a setpoint step change (change in r) is shown in Figure 5.26.

Details of Temperature Control System

The temperature control system is implemented with a series of modules, one for each of the major functions. The user interface for the integrator module is shown in Figure 5.27. It is designed to be used with an external power supply providing a regu-

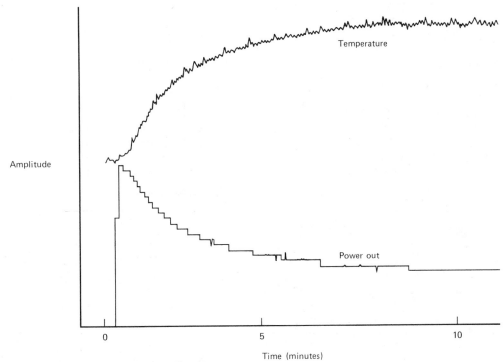

Figure 5.26: Temperature Control Results

lated +15 V input. The circuit functional diagram is in Figure 5.28, and the actual circuit relization is in Figure 5.29. Figures 5.30, 5.31, and 5.32 give the same information for the D/A module. To provide the signal to the computer indicating that the magnitude of the integrated reference voltage has crossed the unknown voltage, a comparator is required. An operational amplifier implementation of a comparator that has a TTL compatible output is shown in Figure 5.33. The set-up for the heater and temperature sensor are shown in Figure 5.34 and the user interface for the heater amplifier is shown in Figure 5.35.

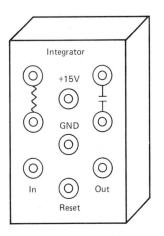

Figure 5.27: Integrator Module, Outside of Box

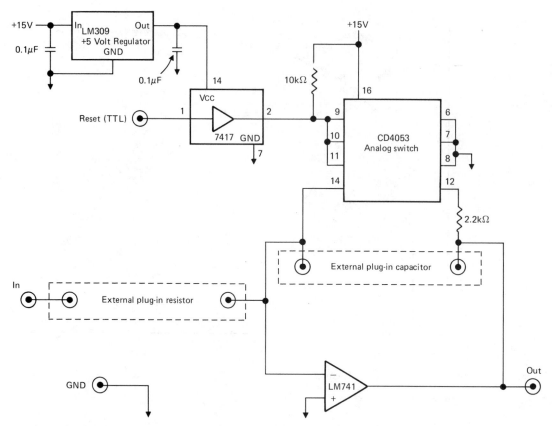

Figure 5.29: Integrator Module, Circuit-Level Realization

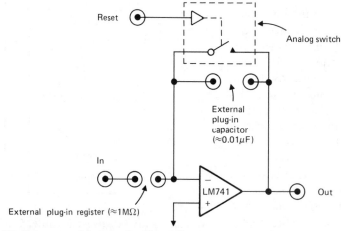

Figure 5.28: Integrator Module, Inside of Box

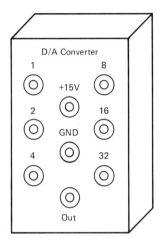

Figure 5.30: D/A Module, Outside of Box

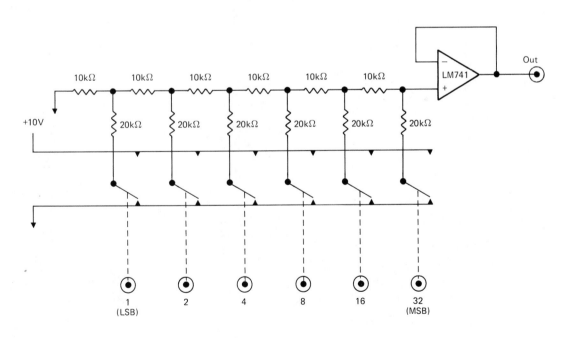

TTL Inputs

Figure 5.31: D/A Module, Inside of Box

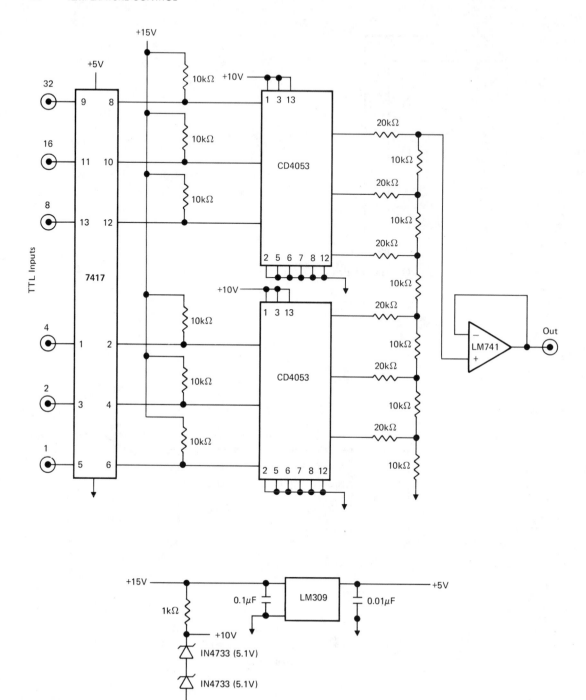

Figure 5.32: D/A Module, Circuit-Level Realization

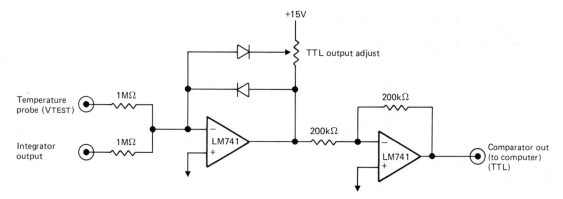

Figure 5.33: Typical Comparator Realization Using Laboratory Operational Amplifier Manifold and Components. Output is TTL.

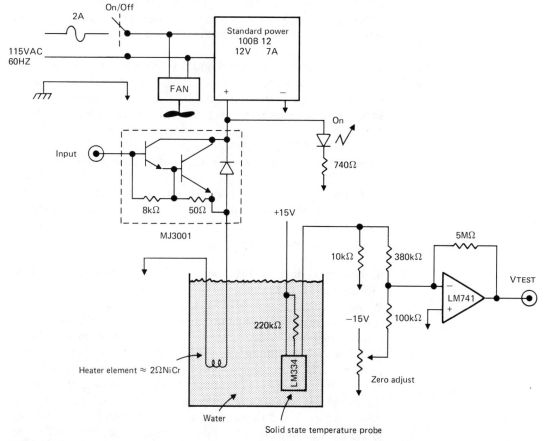

Figure 5.34: The Temperature Control System Showing Elements for Adding Heat and Measuring Temperature

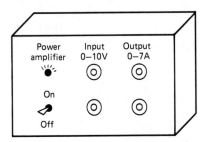

Figure 5.35: Heater Power Amplifier Enclosure

PROJECTS

1. Experiment with terminal input and output. Write a routine that places a space between each character displayed so that a user who types "the" will see "t h e" displayed. If your terminal has upper- and lower-case characters, transform all upper-case typed characters to lower case before displaying them.

2. Investigate multiplication and division overflow. What is the largest 8-bit, unsigned number? How many bits are required to store the square of this number? If this product is divided by the smallest positive integer, can it be represented by an 8-bit number? Use the answers to these questions to help you formulate the values of KNUM*e which will cause an overflow using your computer. What is a division overflow, and when can one occur?

3. Calibrate your D/A converter. Do you expect that the D/A design employed will produce an output that is linearly proportional to the value of the digital input? Plot digital input value (ordinate) vs. output voltage.

4. The integrating A/D you build can be quite precise if you scale the integrator time constant to your computer counting loop. Write and debug your A/D subroutine. In order to perform the scaling, arrange the comparator input so that it continuously indicates "integrator is below Vtest." The A/D routine will always overflow in this configuration. Write a program which repetitively calls the A/D subroutine such that it runs continuously and does not wait for an initiation command. With an oscilloscope, examine the integrator output. The integrator output should be a sawtooth wave. Adjust the RC constant of the integrator such that the integrator saturates (reaches its maximum value) just prior to the A/D subroutine overflow. Can you explain how this tuning improves precision?

5. Calibrate your A/D converter using a digital voltmeter. Plot the result of your calibration. Is the relationship between applied voltage and the digital A/D output linear? Should it be?

The remaining projects all begin with the assumption that your temperature control system functions.

6. Make your controller less of a black box. Add a command which allows you to interrogate the value of internal variables. Allow for the display of error, setpoint, and controller output.

7. Your controller utilizes pure proportional control action which means that if you have adjusted C in the term Ke + C so that there exists no steady-state error, then changing the heat transfer rate of the system (for example, by applying forced convective cooling to the system) will result in a steady-state offset error. You may eliminate the steady-state error by adding integral control using as a control algorithm

$$m = K_p e(k) + \sum_{j=0}^{k} K_i e(j).$$

Devise a simple strategy for implementing the I-action and discuss your results.

8. Often in industrial batch processes the temperature of a vessel must follow a predefined profile. Modify your program so that the setpoint varies in some predetermined fashion as a function of time. Plot the setpoint, controller output, and temperature.

9. Your controller assumes that the temperature system is linear. That is, 2(Ke) should produce twice the heat output as Ke. But it doesn't because heat input to the water is roughly proportional to the square of the voltage. *Linearize* the control output of the D/A by using a table look-up to *square* the controller output variable m.

10. The form of user input to the controller could be more flexible and forgiving. After using the input scheme outlined in the text, modify the input portion to allow **a.** the user to leave leading zeros off entered values, **b.** correction of typing errors, and **c.** use of an arbitrary number of spaces to separate entered values.

Chapter 6

CONTROL OF
A BLENDING PROCESS

The system we will study next demonstrates the natural application of microprocessor technology and control theory to continuous stream blending. Our object will be to manipulate streams to achieve a desired mixture and flow. Because we will be controlling more than one value, we will be dealing with a multi-variable control problem. Figure 6.1 shows how two inputs, AH and AC, control the flow rates of two pumps handling hot and cold water. The controlled variables, flow and temperature, are measured with a flowmeter and temperature probe. Since a change in either input will cause a change in both flow and temperature, the two inputs are said to be *coupled*. (The situation is exactly analogous to the adjustment of one's shower temperature and flow.)

In order to be able to change temperature without affecting flow, we will describe a digital control algorithm which will make it possible to decouple the flow and temperature setpoints to some degree. We will describe the hardware required to implement this algorithm and develop the software for it in a step by step manner. To complete the study, we will describe a small laboratory blending system and test the control strategy for it. The controller's performance will be monitored through the console terminal.

DESCRIPTION OF THE SYSTEM

In Chapter 5 (Figure 5.3) we described the basic computer control elements which are common to digital control systems. The arrangement of these elements for this case study is shown in Figure 6.2. The portion of the system functioning

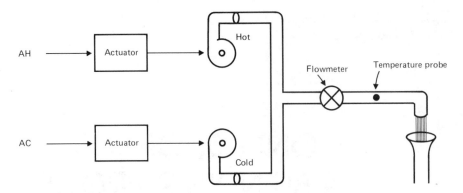

Figure 6.1: The Control Object

as the controller is enclosed within a dotted line. The controller's two analog outputs actuate the two pumps. The analog values of the controlled variables, flow and temperature, are inputs to the controller. As in previous case studies, an external clock regulates sampling times.

The operator plays a key role in this system. Interacting with the computer through the terminal, the operator will start and stop the pumps, specify temperature or flow rate setpoints and controller gains, and request a list of controller variables to evaluate the quality of control.

In its function as a controller, the computer will perform many tasks. It will accept commands from the operator, print messages to the operator, measure flow and temperature periodically, calculate appropriate actuation values, and update the actuation outputs.

INTERRUPTS

The programs we have designed thus far have all taken into account the speed at which computers perform tasks. We have been careful to write transition diagrams which do not linger in one state and thereby miss a critical event. For this system, in theory, we could program the computer to check the port which holds commands from the operator frequently enough to ensure that none would be lost. In theory, we could write the program so that no activity would last longer than one real-time clock tick. Practically speaking, however, if a computer is to respond to a real-time event within a predictable length of time, some method must exist to alter program flow. Most microprocessors made today offer a *hardware* solution to this software problem: an *interrupt cycle* incorporated into the basic machine cycle. As its name implies, the interrupt cycle makes it possible to suspend the current sequence of instructions in order to execute a series of instructions of more time-critical importance.

We described the basic processor cycle in Chapter 4. In the simplest machine cycle, the CPU fetches the instruction to which the program counter points and executes it. The cycle then repeats. The flowchart in Figure 6.3 depicts the orderly implementation of the interrupt cycle. It is important to note that an interrupt can only occur *after* the instruction in which it is recognized has been completed. Even in the simplest system, interrupts can be disabled. In the interrupt cycle, the contents of the program counter are stored (often on a stack), and the address of the first instruction of the interrupt program is copied into the program counter. In order to avoid re-entering the interrupt cycle immediately, the CPU must be able to clear or ignore the current interrupt request. In Figure 6.3, further interrupts are disabled.

Microprocessors typically implement an enhanced version of the flowchart in Figure 6.3. Consider, for example, the case in which any one of one hundred devices may request service by interrupting the processor. In the scheme of Figure 6.3, we must assume that the single interrupt routine *polls,* or interrogates, each of the one hundred devices to determine which one requested service. To avoid polling, a common approach is to build a hardware device which loads the program counter with the interrupting device's interrupt service *vector.* The vector is the address of the start of an interrupt routine specifically written to service the interrupting device. Vectored interrupts eliminate, or at least reduce, time-consuming polling. The price paid for this more efficient performance is an increase in complexity.

Before proceeding with our control program, we must point out that interrupt routines have a reputation for being difficult

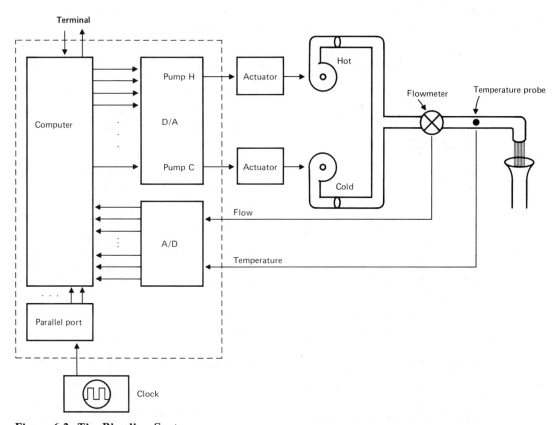

Figure 6.2: The Blending System

to program. These difficulties probably arise from overlooking the cardinal rule of interrupt programming: *an interrupt routine must preserve the state of the machine.*

Let us consider the case in which the main program contains the instructions

    COMPARE A,B
    BRANCH-IF-ZERO   LOC.

If an interrupt occurs while the compare instruction is being executed, the program will enter the interrupt routine after completing the compare instruction. If the interrupt routine alters the zero condition flag, then when the main program resumes, it will execute the branch-if-zero instruction in the opposite manner of that intended. To avoid such errors, the designer must take care to preserve the state of the machine by saving (storing) the condition flags (carry, zero, overflow, etc.), any registers used, and any intermediate results which occupy memory space which the interrupt routine uses. If subroutines or parts of the main routine share code with interrupt routines, the designer must make the shared code *reentrant,* that is, designed so that it can be partially executed by one routine and then fully executed by an interrupting routine.

In our control program, we will incorporate three interrupt routines. The first will be executed whenever the operator types a character. The second will be executed whenever one character has been sent and the next is awaiting printing. The third will be invoked at every tick of the external real-time clock. We will present simple test programs for each of these devices.

TEST PROGRAMS

Main Program

The flowchart shown in Figure 6.4 is the skeleton of the program which will perform the blending control task. We assume that, when the main program is loaded into

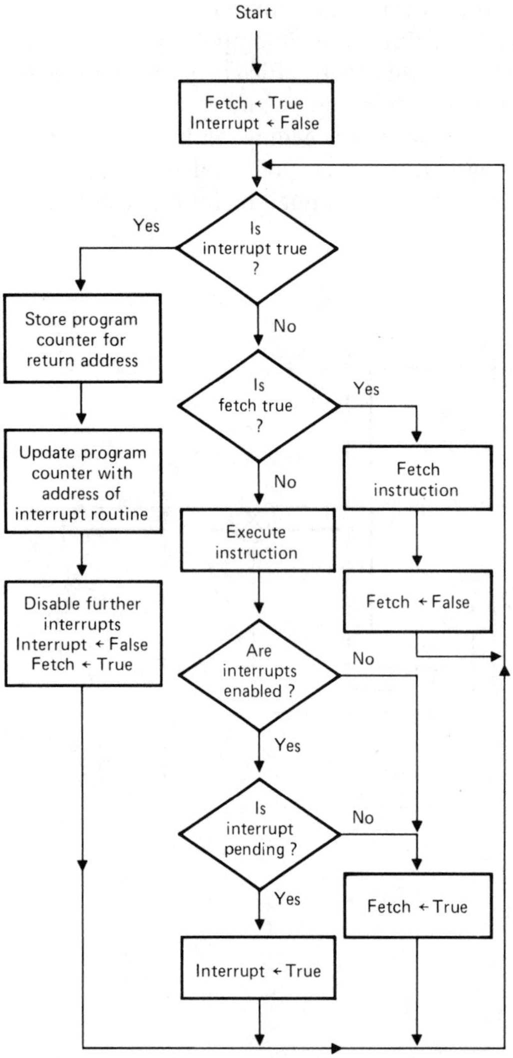

Figure 6.3: Flowchart of a Typical Interrupt Cycle

memory, its first task is to disable any active interrupts. It then repeatedly interrogates the operator's terminal input for the character G. When it detects the go command, it echoes G and then zeros one or more registers which the interrupt routine will use. Next, it performs any initialization required by the interrupt routine. For example, after setting the counters to appropriate values, the program might place interrupt vectors in memory and enable interrupts. The main program, which is now interruptable, proceeds to test continuously the registers which it earlier zeroed, in order to ascertain whether or not the state of the machine is being properly preserved. If it finds that any register previously zeroed has become non-zero, it halts the CPU.

Clock Interrupt Program

We will test two components of our system with a clock interrupt program that simulates the portion of the control program which samples the flow and temperature signals, computes the pump actuation signals, and writes them to the two D/A channels (see Figure 6.5). After preserving the machine state, the interrupt program decrements a counter and copies the value to a digital-to-analog converter (D/A). When it finds that the counter has reached zero, it resets it to a predetermined value. It then restores the machine state by executing a return from interrupt instruction, which restores the program counter to its pre-interrupt value so that the main program can take over. This program can be verified by connecting an oscilloscope to the D/A output. The programmer should observe a sawtooth waveform with an amplitude which is a function of the count reset value. The wave's frequency should be a function of both the count reset value and the interrupting clock frequency.

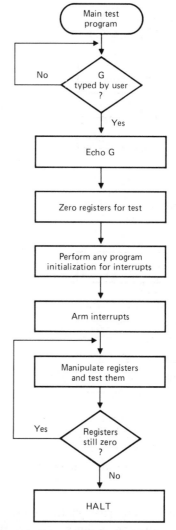

Figure 6.4: Flow of Main Test Program

Terminal Input Interrupt Program Using Indirect Addressing

In Chapter 5 we used absolute mode addressing to store characters. We will now examine *indirect addressing,* a mode which makes it possible to store characters in sequence with greater efficiency and flexibility. In the indirect mode, one memory

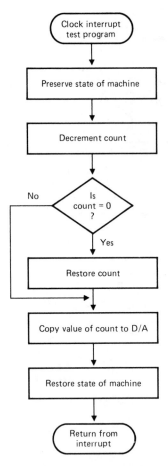

Figure 6.5: Flow of Clock Interrupt Test Program

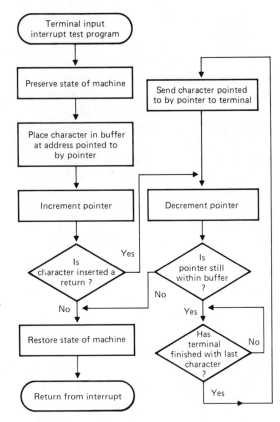

Figure 6.6: Flow of Terminal Input Interrupt Test Program

location or register is designated as a *pointer,* which contains the address of a memory location. The algorithm for storing characters in this mode is: 1. initialize a memory location or a register to contain the address of the position where the first character will be stored 2. insert a character at that address 3. increase the value of the pointer by one address 4. repeat 2 and 3 until finished. The memory space containing the characters is usually called a *buffer.*

The terminal input test program shown in Figure 6.6 begins by preserving the machine's state. The program places characters in the buffer using indirect addressing until it encounters a RETURN (carriage return). Note that the program does not echo characters to the terminal as they are keyed in. Rather, after receiving a RETURN, it sends the contents of the entire buffer back to the terminal in reverse order, using the skip logic described in Chapter 5. When the pointer to the buffer no longer points within the buffer (the program determines this by testing the pointer's value with respect to the address of the start of the buffer), the program exits.

Terminal Output Interrupt Test Program

Sending a buffer full of characters to a terminal can take a relatively long time. For example, it takes roughly two seconds to send 60 characters at 300 baud (a common serial rate for a printing terminal). But the amount of CPU time required to move that group of characters to the serial port is on the order of a few hundred microseconds. An interrupt routine, triggered when the terminal is ready for the next character, permits the CPU to execute useful code during the relatively long transmission time. The interrupt program outlined in Figure 6.7 sends one character, increments the pointer, and then examines the next character to send. If the character is an ASCII null (i.e., not a printing character) the routine deduces that the entire buffer has been sent and completes its function. Many alternate strategies are used to implement this common operation. Instead of looking for a null character, for example, the interrupt program could examine a memory location for the number of characters currently in the buffer, decrement the number, and test for zero.

THE CONTROL ALGORITHM

We will design the controller following the strategy we discussed in Chapter 5. In Figure 6.8, both variables, flow and temperature, have their own controllers to produce the manipulated variables for temperature and flow (MF and MT). We decouple the variables by summing MF and MT to produce the hot water pump actuation signal, MH, and by taking the difference, MF-MT to produce the cold water pump actuation signal. We will use proportional plus integral (PI) action controllers in order to reduce the offset error present in proportional controllers. The discrete-time velocity algorithm is described by

$$M(n) - M(n-1) = \Delta M(n) = KC * [(E(n) - E(n-1)) + ((T/TI)*E(n))] ,$$

where T is the sampling period. If we let the error at time n be

$$E(n) = R(n) - C(n)$$

where $R(n)$ is the setpoint at time n and $C(n)$ is the controlled variable at time n, then the expression for the change in the manipulated variable at time n becomes

$$\Delta MT(n) = KTP*(CT(n-1) - CT(n)) + KTI*(RT(n) - CT(n))$$

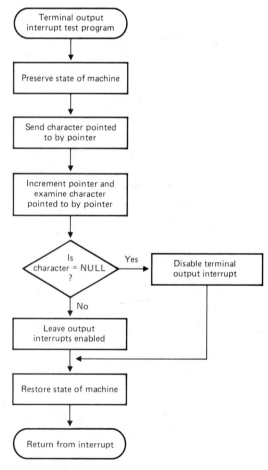

Figure 6.7: Flow of Terminal Output Interrupt Test Program

for the manipulated temperature and

$$\Delta MF(n) =$$
$$KFP*(CF(n-1) - CF(n)) + KFI*(RF(n) - CF(n))$$

for the manipulated flow. KTP, KTI, KFP, and KFI are the proportional and integral gains for flow and temperature. As in Chapter 5, we will enter the gains and store them as integer numerators and denominators to allow representation of values near one. The motor actuation signals are sums and differences of the flow and temperature manipulated variables. That is, the hot water pump actuation signal at time n will be $MH(n) = MH(n-1) + [\Delta MF(n) + \Delta MT(n)]$,

and the cold water pump actuation signal at time n will be

$$MC(n) = MC(n-1) + [\Delta MR(n) - \Delta MT(n)].$$

THE BLENDING CONTROL PROGRAM

The three interrupt routines described above simplify our transition diagrams considerably. The effect of the interrupt structure is to break what would have been a complex transition diagram into four separate but interconnected parts. The only

diagram which we will show is the clock interrupt routine (Figure 6.9). At every tick of the real-time clock, the routine samples the controller inputs, computes new outputs, and copies the computed values to a D/A. The control program will recognize the following commands:

- G activates the clock interrupt routine and the controller.
- S shuts off the pumps and disables clock interrupts.
- T followed by up to three digits updates the temperature setpoint.
- F sets the flow setpoint to the entered value.
- L requests a list of the current values of important variables.
- KFP and KTP update the proportional gains.*
- KFI and KTI update the integral gains.*
- E causes a return to the monitor.

---

* The operator enters the numerators and denominators of the gains on one line, separated by a comma, e.g., "KTI10000,1211."

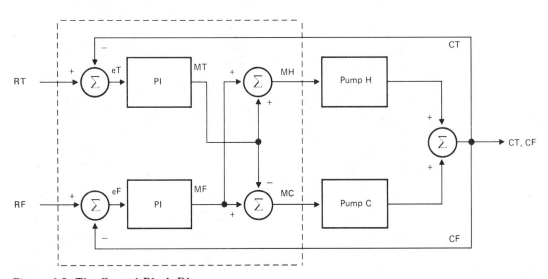

Figure 6.8: The Control Block Diagram

If our program functioned with one buffer to handle incoming characters, it would have to process the buffer before the operator typed the first character of the next command. If the program failed to process the buffer in time, the newly typed character would replace the first character of the previous command, producing unpredictable results. Although our program could probably interpret the buffer before the next character could possibly be typed, we have opted for a safer strategy: maintaining two input buffers. Each of these buffers is associated with a memory location which represents its status: vacant, busy or ready. A vacant buffer becomes busy after the last character has been placed in the other buffer. After receiving this last character (a RETURN in our case) the other buffer is ready to be processed. At the same time, the vacant buffer becomes busy. When the ready buffer has been processed, it becomes vacant. This strategy is easy to implement. It is not terribly general, but it hints at the methods which are used by commercially available operating systems to queue numbers of input/output buffer packets. Since L is the only command which generates terminal output, we need only one output character buffer.

Terminal Input Interrupt Program

Since to err is human, we have designed the interrupt program which accepts the operator's typed commands to recognize two error correction codes, delete and control-U. In response to a typed delete (sometimes called a rubout) the program deletes the last typed chracter from the buffer and echoes it to the console. In response to a control-U (entered by holding down the control key and typing a U) it deletes the entire current buffer (see flowchart, Figure 6.10).

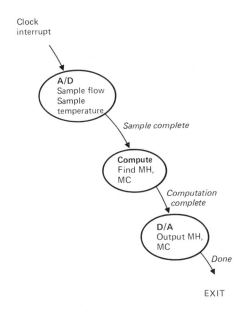

Figure 6.9: Clock Interrupt Transition Diagram

Our program also anticipates that the terminal may have set the parity bit of the character being typed. Since the program must compare characters with immediate-mode operands whose parity bit is clear, it removes any parity bits from incoming characters before echoing them to the terminal and storing them in the busy buffer. When the routine detects a RETURN, it sets the variable LFED to true, which causes the terminal output routine to send a linefeed. To activate the terminal output routine, the program enables its interrupt. It echoes the entered buffer. It marks the busy buffer ready, flags the vacant buffer as being busy, restores the machine state, and exits.

Terminal Output Interrupt Program

The terminal output program shown in Figure 6.11 has two functions. If LFED is true, we know that a linefeed is to be sent,

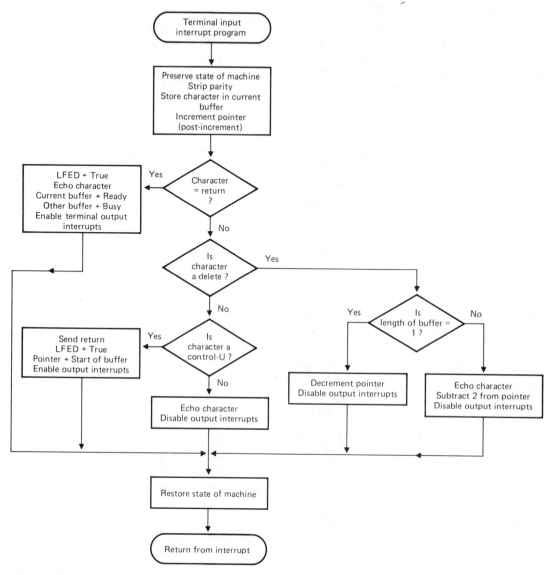

Figure 6.10: Flow of Terminal Input Interrupt Program

since the previous character sent was a RETURN. Since a linefeed may be the last character in the buffer, the program checks the output buffer status. If it finds that the status is ready, it leaves the terminal output interrupts enabled. Otherwise, it disables them. The program's second function is to empty the output buffer. It keeps track of the current buffer position with a pointer. If it finds a RETURN, it sends it, and then sets the flag LFED, which signals the need for a linefeed. Note that the program always leaves interrupts enabled when emptying the buffer.

Clock Interrupt Program

As we have discussed, the clock interrupt routine saves the machine state and samples the analog values of temperature and flow. It performs this function with the help of an electronic selector switch, a *multiplexer,* connected to the A/D converter. On command from the interrupt program, the multiplexer connects the A/D converter to the input *channels,* first to flow, then to temperature. After sampling and converting both values, the program computes the changes in the manipulated variables. Since we use arithmetic subroutines in both the foreground (interrupt) and background (main) programs, we must either verify that the routines are reentrant or use entirely separate multiply and divide subroutines to avoid affecting a calculation that the interrupted routine may have been performing at the time of the clock interrupt. Failure to ensure independence can lead to a class of errors which seem to occur at random and which surface only when the

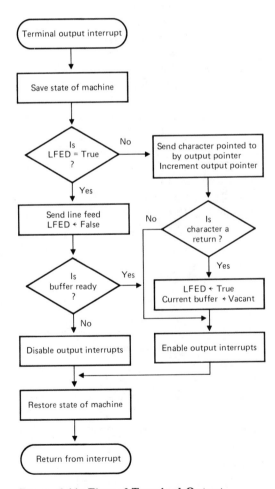

Figure 6.11: Flow of Terminal Output Interrupt Program

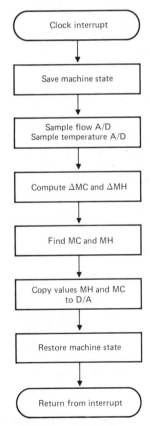

Figure 6.12: Flow of Clock Interrupt Program

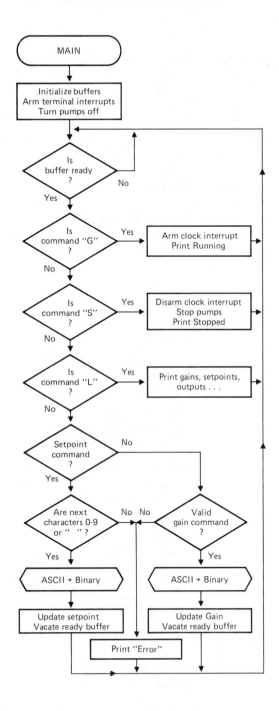

Figure 6.13: Flow of Main (Non-Interrupt) Program

two routines attempt to share each other's data—a conflict that could well escape normal verification procedures. Finally, after finding the actual pump actuation signals, copying them to their respective D/A's, and restoring the machine state, the clock interrupt routine exists.

Main Program

As we see in Figure 6.13, the role of the main blending control program is to arm and disarm interrupt routines and to interpret and act upon messages from the operator. The main program does not deal with the terminal directly. Instead it checks the buffer status flags. If it detects a ready, it examines the buffer. If it finds that the buffer does not conform to the required format, it prints "Error" and takes no further action. If it accepts the buffer, the main program responds by changing gains or setpoints, enabling or disabling interrupts, or listing the current values for gains, setpoints, and outputs.

The actual components used in the blending system are shown in Figure 6.14.

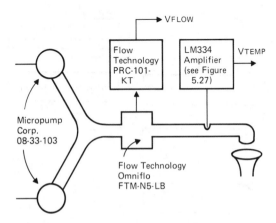

Figure 6.14: Blending System Details

PROJECTS

1. Learn more about pointer manipulation by modifying the terminal input interrupt test program of Figure 6.6. Why is it particularly easy to echo the buffer in reverse order? Modify the program so that the buffer is echoed in the order typed. Examining Figure 6.7 may help.

2. The pointer used in indirect addressing must be limited in the values it can assume. Consider the program of Figure 6.6. What is likely to happen if the user types more characters than the programmer anticipated? Modify your version such that **a.** each character is echoed as typed and **b.** after a RETURN is typed, a linefeed is sent and then the whole buffer printed. If the number of characters typed exceeds the size of the buffer, the program should print a warning message. In any event, the program should not allow the indirect addressing mechanism to modify memory outside of the buffer.

3. The program of Figure 6.6 utilizes skip logic to print the buffer contents. About how much time must the CPU spend in this printing loop if 80 characters are to be sent to a 300 baud terminal? Modify your functioning program so that the buffer is printed by an interrupt routine. For your computer, about how much time must the CPU spend processing the 80 character buffer?

4. After you have succeeded in observing a sawtooth wave produced by the routine of Figure 6.5, modify it to produce a triangular wave. Try to approximate a sine wave.

5. Why do we say that the flow control variables are coupled? How does the controller described in Figure 6.8 achieve the decoupling?

The following problems will aid in making the control system functional.

6. Examine the scaling of your analog and digital values. What voltage does the flow meter produce when both pumps are stopped? What digital value does the A/D produce with this input voltage? Run both pumps at maximum flow rate. What analog voltage and digital values do you find? What is the range of digital values? With what precision does the range of digital values allow you to resolve the flow? What is limiting the flow measurement precision?

7. Turn on only the cold water pump. After the system has stabilized, what analog and digital values to you observe? With only the hot water pump operating, what analog voltage and digital value do you find? What is the measurement precision?

8. Verify that your clock interrupt program is designed to scale the A/D values of temperature and flow into unsigned integers ranging from zero (for lowest temperature and flow to $(2^n) - 1$ where n is the number of bits of your A/D.

9. Verify that your clock interrupt program actuates the pumps in such a way that the lowest possible result of the controller calculation produces the lowest possible pump speeds, and the largest possible manipulated variable results in the highest pump speeds.

10. Run your control program. Set the integrator gains to zero by entering a numerator of zero and a denominator of one. If you have not determined time constants of the temperature and flow systems, choose a proportional gain of one, and start the pumps. Concentrate on temperature first. Making frequent use of the L list command, adjust the proportional gains to obtain stable temperature output. Once you have achieved stability in temperature and flow, slowly increase the integrator gains to reduce offset error. Graph the system response to a setpoint change.

Chapter 7

AUTOMATIC WEIGHING

It is often necessary to weigh items produced in a manufacturing, filling, or packaging process for such purposes as classification, quality control, or feedback control. In order for such a production system to operate efficiently, local controllers should be designed to accept commands from a central supervisory control system and to exchange information with it. The local system should be able to keep the supervisory system informed about production status, provide ongoing production statistics, and reconfigure itself on command, as raw material feed or product specifications change. Figure 7.1 is a schematic of a weighing station in a production line. For this case study, we wish to design a microprocessor that can control the scale and provide statistical information on the items being produced.

SYSTEM SPECIFICATIONS

Our scale is a beam and a strain gauge which measures the deflection of the beam (see Figure 7.2). Using a DC bridge and an amplifier, the strain gauge produces an analog voltage that is proportional to beam deflection. Figure 7.3 depicts a typical output for sudden loading. (The ringing is due to beam vibration.) We will assume that all of the items to be weighed are of the same nominal weight. The microprocessor must detect the presence of each item on the scale, filter the signal coming from the strain gauge, wait for the signal to settle, determine the item's weight, and display it on a light-emitting diode (LED) display. Simultaneously, it must keep track of the weight distribution of a predetermined number of items, and display this distribution graphically on a CRT screen. The dis-

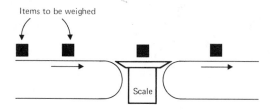

Figure 7.1: Weighing Continuously Produced Items

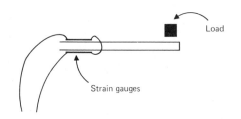

Figure 7.2: Laboratory Version of Scale

tribution display gives the operator an instant picture of how the process or machine is behaving and provides an early warning when adjustments are required (see Figure 7.4).

The program for this job requires three interrupt-driven, high priority tasks: one to get the data from the strain gauge, another to refresh the CRT display, and the third to transmit messages to and receive them from the supervisory system. The data processing tasks run in the background to perform the data filtering, determine when items are put on and taken off the scale, compute the distribution, control the LED display, scale the distribution data for graphic display, and interpret messages. We will write the interrupt-driven tasks in assembly language in order to maximize their execution speed and to perform functions

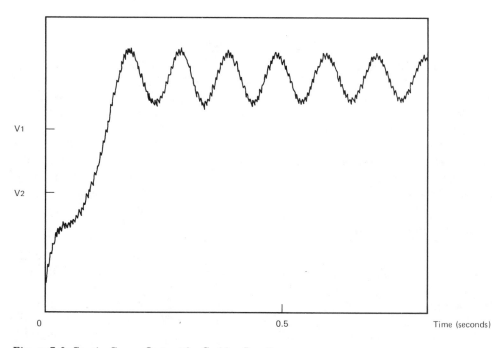

Figure 7.3: Strain Gauge Output for Sudden Loading

such as register saving with maximum efficiency. The background tasks can be programmed much more easily in a high-level language. Using both languages in combination increases programming efficiency; however, doing so successfully depends on having a compiler or interpreter which can generate code that runs fast enough to meet the time constraints, and does not require more memory than is economically feasible.

WEIGHING ALGORITHMS

Because the items to be weighed are all approximately the same weight, we can assign threshold voltages that define when an item is on and off the scale (see Figure 7.3). It is not sufficient to use a single threshold because the signal from the scale oscillates too wildly and could contain noise. If a single threshold were used, the

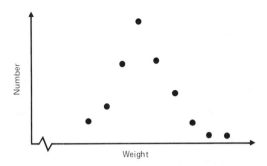

Figure 7.4: Distribution of Item Weights

signal could cross it several times in the time that it takes to weigh a single item or part. We will use two thresholds and consider that an item is on the scale when the voltage exceeds V1 and off, when the voltage drops below V2. Just as with a household bathroom scale, we must allow each weight reading to settle. One method

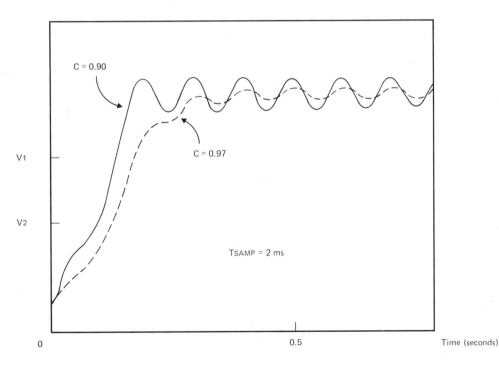

Figure 7.5: Filtered Scale Output

for doing this is to average a set of the most recent values of the scale output. The test for settling is that all the members of the set fall within some tolerance of their average value. It is important to choose the settling sample time carefully: if the sample interval is too short with respect to the response time of the scale, successive readings will have nearly the same value, falsely implying that the signal has settled.

We can speed up the weighing process by filtering the data before applying the settling criterion. The simplest digital filtering algorithm, the exponentially weighted past algorithm, is equivalent to an analog (continuous time) first-order filter or to an electrical R-C filter. The current output, $Y(k)$, is computed from the most recent output value, $Y(k-1)$, and the current scale reading, $V(k)$, by the formula, $Y(k)=C*Y(k-1)+(1-C)*V(k)$. Figure 7.5 shows the output signal of Figure 7.3 after it has been filtered in this manner. It is important to choose a value for the filter constant, C, that will expedite determination of the weight. For small values of C, only the most recent past is weighted heavily enough to effect the output significantly. A value that is too small, therefore, has little or no effect on the output. As C increases, more and more of the past is included. Consequently, choosing too large a value for C actually increases the settling time.

The logic for the background program appears in Figure 7.6. Transitions are defined in terms of the variables POS, DR, MC, and PC. Communication with the interrupt routine takes place in the data-wait module, which checks to see if new data is ready for processing. When new data becomes available, control is passed to the filter module, which computes the filtered output signal and updates the array contain-

ing past values. If the filter finds that no part is currently on the scale (POS=false), it passes control to the the check-upper module, which compares the filtered output to the upper threshold. If check-upper finds that the output is less than the upper threshold (i.e., no change in POS), it sets DR to false and returns control to the data-wait module. If check-upper detects a new part on the scale, it passes control to the new-part-setup module which initializes appropriate variables and arrays and sets the variable MC to false, indicating that a measurement is in progress but not yet complete. New-part-setup then returns control to data-wait through DR=false. If the filter module finds a part on the scale, it completes its computing and updating and transfers control to the check-lower module, which compares the filtered output to the lower threshold to see if the part has been removed from the scale. The transitions from check-lower depend upon the values of both POS and MC. A direct transition to data-wait through DR=false occurs if a part which has been weighed has not yet been removed from the scale (POS and MC both true). If a spurious signal has crossed the upper threshold and been received, even though no part is actually on the scale, or if a part is removed from the scale prematurely, this same direct transition occurs (POS and MC both false). The remaining two paths for leaving the check-lower module are normal conditions. If a part is on the scale but has not yet been weighed (POS true and MC false), the check-settling module does a calculation to determine if the weighing has been completed. If the measurement is not complete (MC still false), it transfers control to data-wait. If the measurement is complete (MC true), the weighing-complete module displays the result on the console terminal and

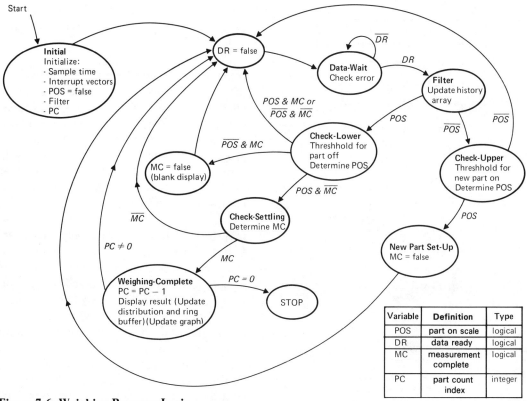

Figure 7.6: Weighing Program Logic

Variable	Definition	Type
POS	part on scale	logical
DR	data ready	logical
MC	measurement complete	logical
PC	part count index	integer

returns to data-wait, unless PC=0, indicating that it should stop. Finally, if a part which has been weighed has just been removed from the scale, the transition path from check-lower will have POS false and MC true. In that case, check-lower transfers control to data-wait via a module that sets MC to false, indicating that the system is now ready to make a new measurement.

The settling algorithm requires access to the most recent filtered readings. A simple way to provide such access is by *percolating* values through an array, with a sequence of statements of the form OLDEST = A(N); A(N) = A(N−1); A(N−1) = A(N−2); ... A(2) = A(1); A(1) = NEWEST. This works well for small n's, but for large values of N it

requires a considerable amount of computing time. A more efficient method is the use of a *ring buffer*. This method is illustrated in Figure 7.7a. In this scheme, data are not moved at all; a pointer to the memory location containing the oldest data is incremented as the oldest data are removed for processing and new data take their place. The continuity of the ring is maintained by testing M against MMAX each time M is incremented. If M is beyond the bounds of the array, it is reset to 1. The logical variable FIRST allows a test to be made to determine if the ring buffer contains full historical information. This can be important during the transient period after the start-up of a program when the buffer is being filled for

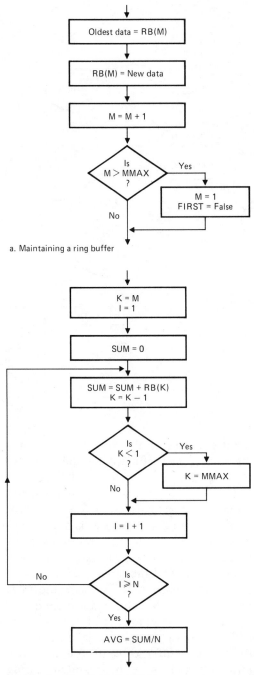

a. Maintaining a ring buffer

b. Averaging the n most recent points

Figure 7.7: Using a Ring Buffer

the first time. The logic for finding the average of the n most recent points appears in Figure 7.7*b*.

The program in Figure 7.6 requires a companion interrupt routine to provide it with data. The signal that new data is available is the variable DR, which is set to true in the interrupt routine when it generates new data and set to false in the main weighing program to indicate that the processing is complete for that data. The only interrupt used for the first trial version of the program—that from the clock—spaces the samples evenly. The clock interrupt routine may be found in Figure 7.8. A counter, COUNT, specifies how many ticks of the clock correspond to a sample interval. If sampling is to take place (COUNT=0), the routine checks the data-ready flag (the word *flag* is often used for logical variables) to see if it is still true. If it is, indicating that the data processing is not yet complete, the routine sets an error flag. The remedies for this error are either to take samples less frequently or to increase the computing efficiency of the main program. If the data-ready flag is not true, the interrupt program samples the scale output voltage via the A/D converter, sets the data-ready flag true, restores the registers, and executes a return-from-interrupt instruction.

Since the interrupt routine is written in assembly language and the main routine is written in a high-level language, some method is necessary for communicating between them. Selecting an appropriate method depends heavily on the implementation details of the high-level language; however, two likely approaches are putting the data to be communicated (DR and scale output voltage in this case) in an area that can be accessed by both routines or calling an assembly language subroutine that returns the desired information.

DISTRIBUTION OF PART WEIGHTS

A graphical display of the weight distribution of the parts produced most recently gives the operator immediate feedback on the operation of the process machinery. For a discrete set of values of the variable w, $w(i)$, $i=1,m$, the distribution is a function that expresses the number of occurences of $w(i)$ for each of a set of zones defined over a given range of values for w.

This can be expressed as:

d(w) = [Number of values of w(i) satisfying
w-dw/2 $<$ w + dw/2] /dw

The scaling factor that divides the entire expression, dw, is normally included in the formula for the distribution so that the numerical values of the distribution, $d(w)$, do not change in range as the value of dw changes. In our case, it will not be necessary to divide by dw, because, once we have chosen its discretizing interval, it will not change.

To maintain the information necessary to compute the distribution, we must have access to the m most recently measured parts. A ring buffer of the sort described earlier can be used for that purpose. Two methods for the actual calculation of the distribution are shown in *a* and *b* of Figure 7.9. The first method uses more computing time because the program must recompute the entire distribution each time it updates the ring buffer. In the second method, the contribution of the oldest value is subtracted from the distribution and the contribution of the newest value is added. This method is more streamlined, but it is less reliable, because computational errors go uncorrected until the process begins again from scratch the next time the computer is restarted.

GRAPHIC DISPLAY OF THE DISTRIBUTION

We will use a laboratory-type oscilloscope to create a display consisting of a set of points corresponding to the distribution and a second set of points corresponding to the axis. Because our oscilloscope won't maintain images on its screen, we will have to run the graphic display routine at least 20 times per second, in order to avoid flicker. Normally, refreshed displays of data

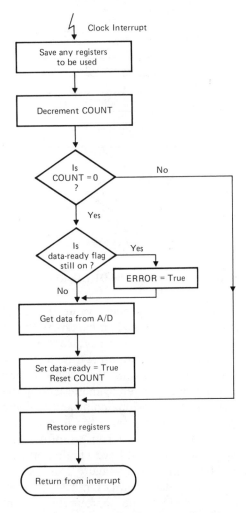

Figure 7.8: Clock Interrupt Service Routine

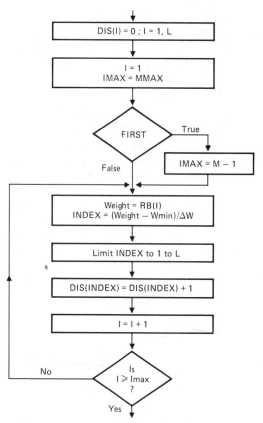

a. Computing entire distribution each time
L is number of points in distribution

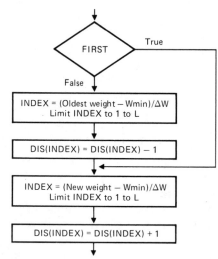

b. Update method of computing distribution

Figure 7.9: Computing the Distribution

points require the x and y values for all of the points to be stored in memory. With our display, however, we can save considerable storage and some computing time by taking advantage of the fact that the x value for any point can be computed by incrementing the x value of the previous point and that the axis y values are the same for all points.

Because it must run so often, the graphics routine must have a higher priority than the main routine (Figure 7.6). On the other hand, data samples must be taken from the scale at the appropriate time in order for the filtering algorithm to work cor-

rectly. The clock interrupt routine shown in Figure 7.10 places the graphics midway in priority between the sampling routine and the main program by enabling the interrupt before entering the graphics portion of the routine. This makes it possible for clock interrupts and data sampling to occur while the graph is being refreshed and ensures that the main routine will not run until the current refresh cycle is finished. The graph-flag is true while the refresh is running. If, at the beginning of a refresh cycle, the program finds that the flag is still true, indicating that there has not been sufficient time to complete the previous refresh cycle, it sets the error flag, ERRORG, to true and terminates the refresh operation.

The graph drawing subroutine is shown in Figure 7.11. It assumes that the main (background) program has supplied it with an array of y values equally spaced in the x coordinate. The x values are artificially constructed so that the graph will spread across the whole width of the CRT screen. Within the point-plotting loop, the x and y values are sent to the digital-to-analog converters and then a signal is sent to the oscilloscope to intensify the beam so that the point appears on the screen. After a delay to allow time for the beam to build up its strength (the amount of time depends on the characteristics of the CRT), the program turns off the intensify signal so that no spurious traces appear due to the motion of the beam from point to point. In some cases, a delay might be required between sending the x,y values to the D/A and sending the intensify signal to allow the D/A converters to settle and to give the beam time to get to its destination. Since we need to provide a y=0 axis, we will repeat the point-plotting process using the same x value and a y=0. We increment X and decrement i to display the next point.

DISPLAYING THE WEIGHT FOR THE OPERATOR

Process operators can make important quality checks if they can see the weight of each part as it is weighed. If the computer controller does not have a terminal, a numeric display like that in a digital voltmeter is a simple and inexpensive way to let the operator know the weight of each part. A seven-segment LED display that could be used for this purpose is shown schematically in Figure 7.12a. Each of the seven segments can be either dark or

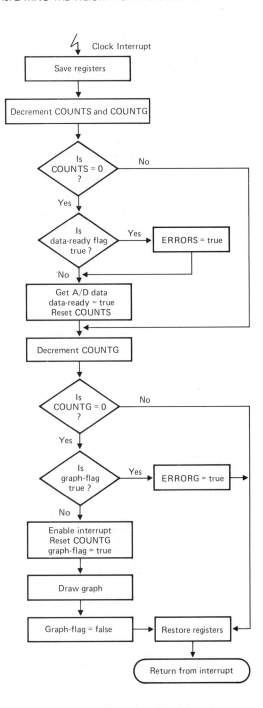

Figure 7.10: Clock Interrupt Routine with Graphics Refresh

lighted to form different numbers; for example, the lighted (crosshatched) segments in the sketch form a 2. To control the display directly, seven signals are needed, one for each segment. Alternately, decoder

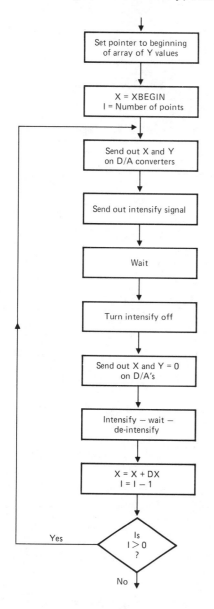

Figure 7.11: Graph-drawing Routine

chips that accept 4-bit binary-coded decimal (BCD) inputs are available (see Figure 7.12b). BCD code is widely used in instrument systems and calculators. In its usual form, it represents the decimal digits in natural binary, from 0000B for 0 to 1001B for 9. BCD coding is quite wasteful because only ten of the possible sixteen combinations in the 4-bit number are used, but it is extremely convenient in systems that must read or display decimal information.

The program to control a multi-digit display, Figure 7.13, is very similar to those used to produce numerical output for a terminal. The numbers must be broken into decimal digits by repeated divisions by ten. The remainder at each stage is the digit to be displayed. If no decoder is used, the code for which of the segments to turn on can be found from a table. Since the BCD code is the same as the binary representation of individual decimal digits, no further coding need be done if a decoder chip is used. The value can then be sent out on the output port associated with the digit just generated. Using distinct computer output ports is satisfactory for the display of a small number of digits (two or three, as in this problem), but if a larger number of digits is to be displayed, it is probably more effective to use some form of hardware multiplexer logic than large numbers of computer parallel output ports.

FINAL PROGRAM LOGIC

The overall program logic described in Figure 7.6 continues to apply, even when the distribution calculation, graphics, and LED weight display are added. As indicated by parenthetic entries in the module descriptions, the functions of two modules increase or change. The weighing-complete module gets most of the added burden. It must update the ring buffer containing the past weights, recompute the distribution, and update the graphics information. Instead of using the console terminal to display the result, it must use the LED display. The MC=false module also blanks the display. Since it only does so after a part has been removed from the scale, there is never any confusion about which part corresponds to the displayed weight. The actual graph drawing takes place in the revised clock-interrupt routine and graph-drawing routine shown in Figures 7.10 and 7.11.

COMMUNICATING WITH A SUPERVISORY COMPUTER

A production or processing system integrates a large number of activities to produce a desired result. In many cases, a supervisory computer coordinates the various parts of the system by monitoring and controlling the actions of many small computers doing local data acquisition or control tasks. The supervisory computer uses commands to the local systems to make changes in the process (e.g., a change from apples coming from one orchard to

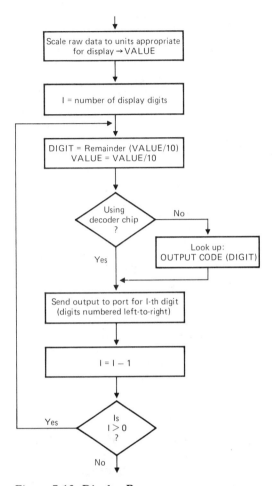

Figure 7.13: Display Program

those from another) or in the product itself (e.g., a change in apple size). It requests information from the local systems in order to:

- fine-tune or optimize the process
- detect malfunctions
- schedule maintenance
- gather management information
- audit the system (e.g., to keep track of valuable material or parts)
- implement adaptive control (e.g., to detect tool wear in a machine tool).

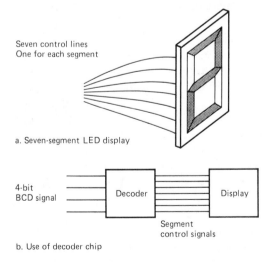

a. Seven-segment LED display

b. Use of decoder chip

Figure 7.12: LED Display

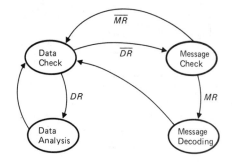

a. Priority-order background tasks

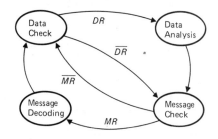

b. Equal priority background tasks

Figure 7.14: Scheduling Background Tasks

In our automated weighing system, two types of interactions might take place: 1. the supervisory computer could send commands to the weighing control computer giving new weighing parameters (threshold values, settling tolerances, etc.), 2. the supervisory computer could request information from the weighing computer about distribution results, average weights for some past interval, etc.

Program Structure

Adding the capability to communicate with a supervisory computer requires changes in both the foreground (interrupt) and background portions of the weighing control program. Because our supervisory and local computers will communicate serially, we must add interrupt service routines to the foreground portion of the program. These will be very similar to those used for terminal communications in the blending control system and should introduce little or no additional complexity, since they will not require much computing time.

At the background level, however, some major decisions must be made, because the need to interpret and process messages from the supervisory computer changes the character of the background program from single-task to multi-task. This change requires us to decide which background task to run at any given instant. To do this, we will use a simple scheduling algorithm based on the constraint that a background task must run to completion before any other background task begins (during the time the task is running, however, it can be interrupted by foreground tasks).

For systems with relatively few tasks, the scheduling rules can be built into the program structure so that no scheduling module is needed. Since this is the case for our system, the scheduler itself can run in the background. Our weighing program will have two background tasks, the data analysis task described in Figure 7.6, and the message processing task. Two programs, each with built-in scheduling, are shown in Figure 7.14. In Figure 7.14a, the data analysis task has higher priority than the message decoding task. Both the data-analysis and message-decoding modules return control to the data-check module when they are finished. If data-check finds that a data point is ready to be processed, it transfers control to the data-analysis module, even if a message is waiting to be processed. In Figure 7.14b, the two tasks have equal priority. When the data-analysis module completes its task, it passes control to the message-check module. If message-check finds that a message is ready it will pass control to the message-decoding module. The data-check module will take over again only after message-decoding has completed its task.

These structures can be generalized for any number of tasks, as shown in Figure 7.15. In *a,* the priority goes from task T1, which is our highest priority, to task T2, T3, etc. Whenever any task finishes running, it returns control to T1-check to see if T1 is ready to run again. Only if T1 is not ready will control pass to T2-check. Thus, a high priority task can run many times before a low priority task gets its first chance to run. In the equal priority method, Figure 7.15*b,* each task runs in turn. For our weighing program, we will use a priority scheduling algorithm which gives the message decoder lowest priority.

Before fixing the background structure, we need one more background task, which anticipates timing problems that could occur during parameter changes in the weighing program. For example, if the supervisory computer called for a parameter change while a part was on the scale, a weighing error could be made. To avoid this, we must buffer all parameter changes, that is, store the new values in a separate memory array until the supervisory computer sends out a RESET-PARAMETERS command. The complete background program structure appears in Figure 7.16. Note that the priority order is reset-parameter (highest), data-analysis, message-decoding.

Using a scheduling algorithm based on having background tasks run to completion greatly simplifies programming, but it also introduces some restrictions in the way that the background tasks must be constructed. For example, the running time for each task

must be short enough to satisfy the timing constraints of higher priority tasks. To meet such constraints, it might be necessary to break a task into several subtasks. If doing so still does not satisfy the time constraints, the run-to-completion constraint may have to be relaxed. This would complicate scheduling considerably, because a scheduler would have to be introduced as a foreground task. The scheduler would have to keep track of the status of each task, the restart information for interrupted background tasks, and the rules for deciding

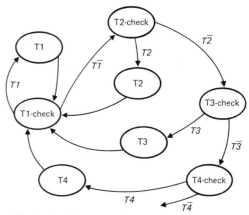

a. Priority scheduling

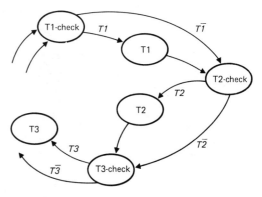

b. Equal priority scheduling

Figure 7.15: Scheduling Structures

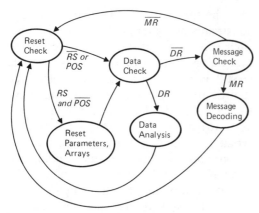

Figure 7.16: Priority Scheduler with Reset Module

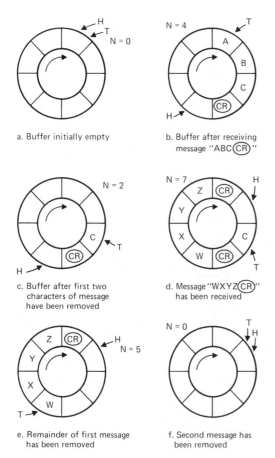

a. Buffer initially empty

b. Buffer after receiving message "ABC(CR)"

c. Buffer after first two characters of message have been removed

d. Message "WXYZ(CR)" has been received

e. Remainder of first message has been removed

f. Second message has been removed

Figure 7.17: Ring Buffer for Characters

which task is to run at any given time. It would normally have to run every time an interrupt is received. In addition, all system library subroutines shared by background tasks would have to provide for reentry.

Character Handling

A basic function of the foreground program is to receive and buffer characters, while the background program processes them. The ring buffer structure shown in Figure 7.17 can be used to buffer characters which have been received but not yet processed. The ring buffer is a generalization of the double-buffering described in Chapter 6. Its major advantage is that it can buffer an unrestricted number of messages, as long as the total number of characters being buffered fits in the array. Although it requires more computation time than does double-buffering, it is particularly useful in situations where messages are not all the same length. The ring buffer can be thought of as a memory array constructed in a circular manner. It is associated with an H (head) pointer, which moves around the array just ahead of the character string and with a T (tail) pointer, which moves around the array indicating the end of the string. A variable N keeps track of the number of characters currently in the buffer. The buffer puts the characters it receives into the locations indicated by H, which then moves to the next available cell in the buffer. For example, if an empty buffer (Figure 7.17a) received the message ABC followed by a carriage return (CR), it would look as pictured in 7.17b. The T pointer is the indicator for character removal. It points to the oldest character in the buffer. Characters are processed in the order in which they are received. As each character is removed, T moves on. Figure 7.17c shows the buffer after the A and B have been removed for

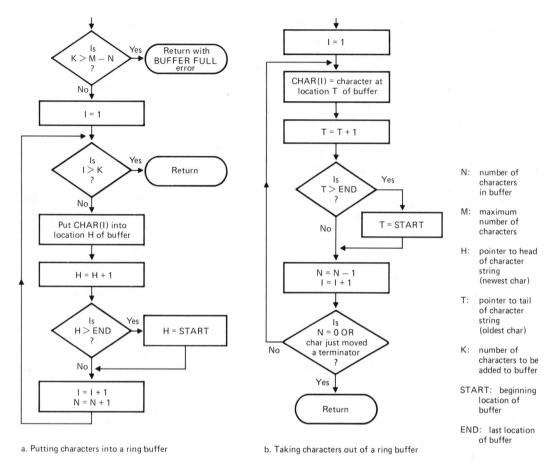

a. Putting characters into a ring buffer

b. Taking characters out of a ring buffer

Figure 7.18: Servicing a Ring Buffer for Characters

processing. In *d,* a new message has been received, but no further processing has taken place; H has moved, but T has not. In *e,* the first message has been processed. In *f,* all processing has been completed, and the buffer is again empty.

Since memory is not constructed in rings, some processing must be done in order to create a ring buffer. The algorithms for putting characters into a ring buffer and removing them are shown in Figure 7.18; the interrupt service routines to implement the ring buffer appear in Figure 7.19. The input interrupt service routine, Figure

7.19*a* must include a message-ready test, since it sets the message-ready (MR) variable which was introduced in the state diagram of Figure 7.16.

In order to include the appropriate test in the interrupt service routine, we must establish what constitutes a message. Depending on the nature of the information being transmitted, a message can be a single character, a single line, or a string of characters terminated by some special code to indicate end-of-message. In this case, the information fits neatly into the single line format, so the interrupt routine includes a test to see if the character being processed is a return (CR); if it is, the routine sets message-ready to true. The input routine also tests to see if there is sufficient room in the buffer for the incoming character. If there is not enough room, it sets an error indicator to true.

Two situations can exhaust the buffer's storage capacity. In one case, enough CPU processing time is generally available to process all of the incoming message, but a burst of characters arrives at a time when the background program can-

not process them fast enough to leave room in the buffer. This problem can usually be solved by making the buffer larger. In the second case, the average rate at which incoming characters arrive might be too fast for processing in the amount of CPU time available to the message-decoding module. This problem may be solved by redesigning the programs to accomodate message processing needs, or by using a faster CPU.

The output interrupt service routine must continually ascertain whether the buffer is empty so that it can disable the out-

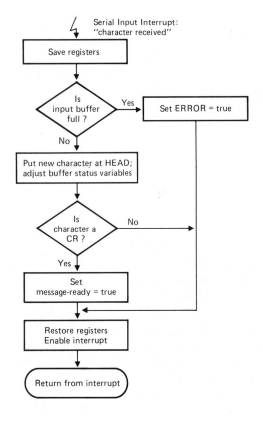

a. Serial input interrupt routine

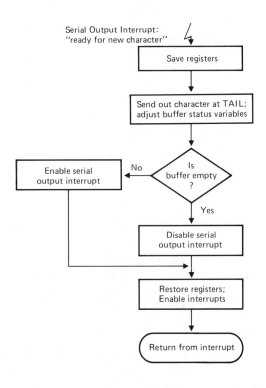

b. Serial output interrupt service routine

Figure 7.19: Serial Line Interrupt Routines

put interrupt when no more characters are available for transmission. The output buffer must be filled by another subroutine which is part of the background. When any of the background modules have information to send, they call the output routine to put those characters into the buffer. If the output routine finds the buffer empty, it must enable the output interrupt routine. In Figure 7.20, no special check need be made for an empty buffer, because the output interrupt is always enabled. This method of operation presumes that the computer being used has *maskable* interrupts, that is, interrupts for various devices can be enabled or disabled selectively. If this is not the case, the output service routine should clear the character-ready flag whenever it detects an empty buffer. The background output routine must then send out a character to start the interrupts again.

Message Processing

The messages which the supervisory computer sends to the weighing-control computer are relatively simple and can be processed with algorithms very similar to those used in preceding case studies. For example, to set a new value for the upper threshold, the supervisory computer would send the message TU=new value. To ask the weighing computer for the current distribution of weights, the supervisory computer would send TD. Despite this simplicity, we must take into account that an industrial environment tends to be very noisy. Our message processing algorithms and the protocols we use for constructing and transmitting messages must anticipate that errors may occur in the transmission of information. To do this, we will need a simple error-checking protocol, based on the following rules for the supervisory and local computer:

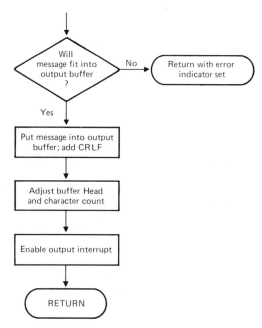

Figure 7.20: Output Subroutine

1. The local computer never initiates a transaction.
2. The supervisory computer will never send a new command until all the actions associated with the previous command have been completed.
3. All messages will be checked for validity. Messages found to be invalid will be re-transmitted. (For the purpose of this study, we will assume that all characters transmitted are received, even though errors might occur in the transmission process.)

Messages will be checked for validity two ways. First, the syntax of the message must be correct. The command must be a valid one, and the numbers, if any, must be valid numbers. Although this test will catch many transmission errors, the nature of the ASCII character set is such that many errors can still get through. For example, a one-bit error in the ASCII code for a number could well result in the code for another number. To check the validity of information further, we will add a *checksum* to all messages. To compute a checksum, we sum the ASCII codes of all the characters in the message (often in a fixed precision modulo format) and append the sum to the message. When the program receives the message, it performs the summation again and checks it against the checksum that was transmitted with the message. Any discrepancy indicates a transmission error.

A typical example of an interchange between the supervisory computer and the local control computer is a request from the supervisory computer for production statistics. The general logic for processing such a message is shown in Figure 7.21. As we see in the central portion of that flow diagram, the program checks the message's checksum for validity. If the checksum is valid, control ends up at the *decode command* block, where the command itself is checked for validity. If the command passes the validity test, the program sends an acknowledge message back to the supervisory computer.

To avoid having many acknowledge and not-acknowledge messages pile up, we do not use the checksum method to determine acknowledge or not-acknowledge validity. Instead, we use a message format with a high enough degree of redundancy to ensure a very high probability of successful transmission. The acknowledge format is a string of consecutive A's. It is decoded at the other end by applying the test that if an acknowledge is expected and the message contains more than a certain number of A's, it is an acknowledge (more than a certain number of N's is a not-acknowledge). After the acknowledge message has been sent (that is, the string of characters has been sent to the output routine), the local pro-

gram assembles the information requested by *message pending* buffer. It does not transmit the data, however, since doing so would constitute an unsolicited message. We avoid unsolicited messages in this system because the supervisory computer must service many local computers at once. It has therefore a higher probability of missing characters than the local computers. When the supervisory computer receives the acknowledge message, it sends out the "send" command, which must include a checksum. After the local computer decodes and validates the send, it transmits the requested data. When the supervisory computer receives the data successfully, it responds with an acknowledge, which triggers the local computer to clear the message pending buffer.

Errors can occur at several points in this sequence, but they will be corrected. If, for example, the original message from the supervisory computer has a transmission error, the local computer's checksum will not match. The local computer will then send out the not-acknowledge message, a string of N's. On receiving the not-acknowledge, the supervisory computer will send the message again. If the data sent by the local computer to the supervisory computer in response to the send command has any transmission errors, the supervisory computer detects this through its checksum calculation and sends back a not-acknowledge. Since the local computer continues to maintain the message in its message pending buffer, it will respond by sending the data out once again.

The validity protocol we have explored here is simple and effective; however, situations can arise that will cause erroneous results. For example, if the end-of-message character (a return in this case) is garbled, whichever computer is receiving

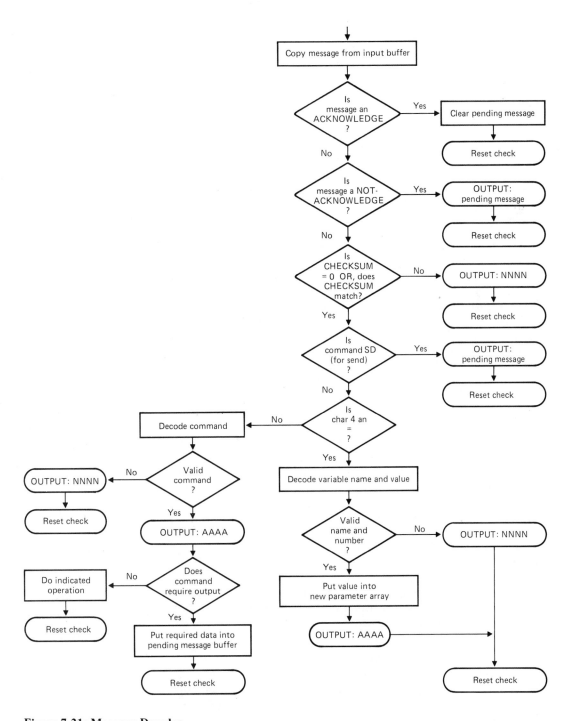

Figure 7.21: Message Decoder

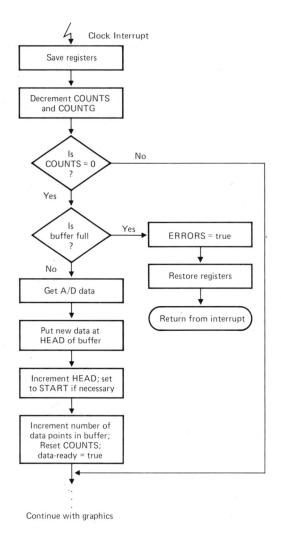

Figure 7.22: Modified Clock Interrupt Routine

the message will continue to wait for the end of message, causing a complete communication breakdown. Another communication breakdown will occur if one of the computers gets out of synchronization with the other. For example, if the local computer receives a send or a not-acknowledge message at a time when there is nothing in the pending message buffer, it will not respond. More complex protocols can be devised to protect against these and other situations; for example, a timer can be used to terminate a message after some maximum time has elapsed or another message can be added in the acknowledge/ not-acknowledge series for resynchronizing. The complexity (and thus the cost) of the protocol to be used must be balanced against the probability of various types of errors occurring and the associated downtime and restart costs.

PERFORMANCE IMPROVEMENT

Most real-time programs reach a point at which it is necessary or desirable to improve system performance. The two most common needs are for faster computation speed to meet real-time constraints or for more memory. Although it is theoretically possible to change to a faster processor or to one that can address more memory — particularly if the performance needs are identified and anticipated at the design stage — it may not be practical to do so: a substantial software commitment to a processor which does not have a faster version may already have been made; the economics might not allow for a different processor; or it may be desirable to maintain compatibility with units that have already been manufactured. In such cases, any improvements in performance must come from redesigning the system's programs. We explore this approach with our program.

The computing capability of our program is limited considerably by the run-to-completion rule we established for the background segments. This constraint means, for example, that the message-decoding module can run no longer than the sampling interval for data from the scale. It is limited to this amount of time because, once a sample has been taken, the data-analysis module must run before the next sample is taken; otherwise, an error is indicated and data are lost. This computing limitation could be overcome by using a background scheduling algorithm that allowed background modules to interrupt each other, but doing so would require additional computing overhead to run the more complex scheduler. An easier solution would be to segment the message-decoding module so that no single segment violated the time constraint. This approach, though effective, would be awkward to program because the foreground, real-time constraints would have to be considered every time the background, low priority program was modified. Additionally, foreground-

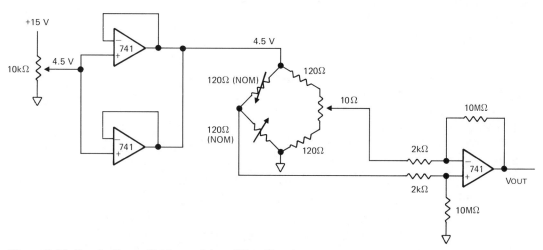

Figure 7.23: Strain Gauge Bridge and Amplifier Circuit

operating parameters, such as sample intervals, would become constrained by the background.

We can improve computation time more smoothly by exploiting the storage capabilities of our processing system: unlike a feedback control system, it has no intrinsic need to process sampled data points immediately. It can store several points and process them whenever the data-analysis module runs, as long as the processing delay is short in comparison to the amount of time each part remains on the scale. Figure 7.22 shows a modification to the clock interrupt routine that will accomplish this. A ring buffer is set up to store sampled data points. As long as there are points in the buffer, the data-ready flag is set. The error flag is set only if the buffer is full at the time a new point is sampled. With this modification, the low priority background task is no longer bound by a strict real-time constraint on its running time, the potential for CPU utilization improves, and less interaction is needed between the background and foreground sections of the program.

LABORATORY SCALE REALIZATION

The laboratory version of the automated weighing machine is built out of a piece of spring steel with strain gauges to measure its deflection. A simple bridge circuit to amplify the strain gauge signal is shown in Figure 7.23. The circuit has more drift than would be acceptable in an industrial environment, but works well in the lab. The configuration of the strain gauges is shown in Figure 7.24.

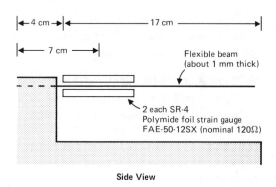

Side View

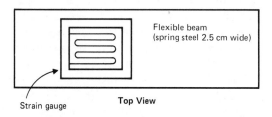

Top View

Figure 7.24: Scale and Strain Gauge Detail

PROJECTS

1. Assemble your scale using Figure 7.23 as a guide for producing the analog weight signal. The bridge is the heart of this circuit. Two sides of the bridge are formed by the upper and lower strain gauges. The other two are fixed resistors which determine the zero point of the unloaded scale. Figure 7.23 is intended to be realized on an operational amplifier breadboard often found in instrumentation and control laboratories, thus explaining the unorthodox voltage source at the left of the figure. Adjust the voltage source to the highest value possible noting the current or power dissipation specifications of your strain gauge. The bridge amplifier shown at the right of Figure 7.23 achieves a gain of 5000. Select the gain of your amplifier such that the signal Vout is scaled closely with your A/D. What voltage range can your A/D measure? Into how many bits does your A/D resolve this range? What values can Vout assume if you place a heavy weight on the scale? (Include the mechanical ringing.) With what precision can your A/D measure the weight?

2. Examine the weighing programs in the appendix and implement the logic of Figure 7.6 on your computer. First, debug the clock interrupt routine by causing it to print a character on the console every 100 clock ticks. Next, debug the communication link between foreground and background by causing the foreground routine to set a flag every 100 clock ticks. The background routine should wait for the flag and then clear it and print a character. At this point, you are ready to run the weighing program.

3. Before modifying the digital filter algorithm, you must understand how it functions. Write a short program or use a calculator to tabulate the filer output $Y(k)$ given that $C = 0.9$, $Y(0) = 0$, and $V(k) = 1$.

4. Measure the settling time of your scale. That is, lightly drop a weight on the scale and time the program's response. Repeat and average. Change the filter constant C. Visualize the role of C by plotting about 10 values of C vs. the resulting average settling time.

5. The text stated that the upper limit of the digital filter constant C occurs where too much of the past is included in the filtered output (see Figure 7.5). Modify the filter algorithm such that $Y(k)$ is set to V1 after the first sample is taken in which $V(k)$ is greater than V1. What is the goal? What is the result?

6. The scale described in the text is only lightly damped. Explore the effect of mechanical damping by designing a simple frictional damper. What type of friction does your damper employ? What is the effect of the damper on the scale's zero point? On measuring precision? If you were asked to produce a production prototype, how would you recommend increasing weighing speed?

7. Assume that your scale is to be used in a continuous production setting and that a heavy penalty is assessed on the producer of underweight items. Modify Figure 7.6 and then your program so that the operator is notified when an underweight item is placed on the scale.

8. Increase the usefulness of your scale by calibrating it so that the output is in grams. Is the analog bridge voltage linear with weight? If not, how can you linearize it?

9. Modify your program such that—after a "production run" of n items—a report is generated which shows the mean weight, the median, and the standard deviation for all items within acceptable limits. A list of all unacceptable items with item number should be listed separately.

10. You know that your lightly damped system acts as a spring-mass system (see Figure 7.3). The filter algorithm described in the text does not take explicit advantage of this oscillatory behavior. Design a digital filter which, to some extent, exploits the periodic nature of the scale output in order to increase weighing rate.

Chapter 8

A POLAR PLOTTER

In earlier chapters, we introduced how microprocessors function and examined in some detail the methods by which they may be interfaced with mechanical and process equipment. In these final chapters, we wish to use this information as the basis for a broader exploration of system design. The case study in this chapter typifies a design process in which the designer chooses to break with traditional approaches in order to design a system which exploits the computational ability and the favorable price/performance ratio of a microprocessor.

The device we will design is a *pen plotter* which will be capable of drawing a line between two points. The line will be the primitive element with which graphs can be made, curves approximated, and lettering generated. The completed system will consist of a mechanism to hold a pen and paper,

actuators to move the mechanism, a microprocessor to control the actuators, and software to generate the vectors.

STATE OF THE ART

Our design strategy begins with a survey of plotters which are commercially available. Two types of pen plotters are in common use today: those which move the pen in two dimensions and those which move the pen in one dimension and the paper in the other. Flat-bed (x-y) plotters use a pen which rides on a gantry mounted on one or two roller ways. The gantry moves over a flat bed to which the paper is attached. In order for the pen to draw in two dimensions, a way is fitted on the moving gantry. The plotter also includes a mechanism for lifting the pen.

The other common plotter is a *drum*

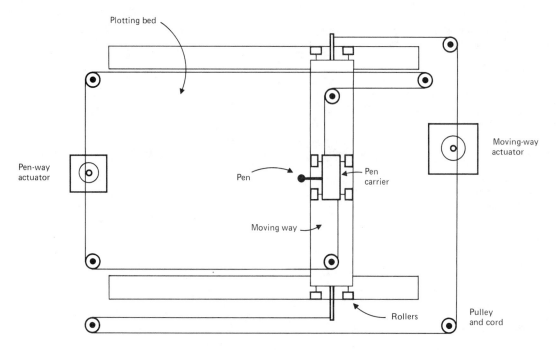

Figure 8.1: Stylized View of an X-Y Flatbed Pen-Plotter and Actuators

plotter, so called because the paper is mounted on a rotating drum, while the pen rides on a stationary way.

Flat bed plotters are usually driven by either of two types of actuation systems. One system has an actuator mounted on the base of the plotter to move the gantry and another mounted on the gantry to move the pen. This design, while mechanically simple, makes it difficult to achieve high speed performance, because of the inertia of the actuator mounted on the gantry. The second typical system for flat-bed plotters uses pulleys and cords to move the gantries (see Figure 8.1). The pulleys and cords are driven by two actuators mounted on the plotter base. This design overcomes the inertia problem but is more complex mechanically.

Drum plotters simplify the pen drive considerably, but they require a drum

actuator which is larger and often more costly than those needed for flat-bed plotters.

A POLAR SOLUTION

For our plotter design, we will seek to combine the best features of plotters that are commercially available: low inertia, so that we can improve speed or decrease actuator cost, and mechanical simplicity. We will incorporate a microprocessor into the design to provide support for any computational complexity that may result.

The mechanism we design, a *polar plotter,* will move a pen in two dimensions. It will consist of a boom driven by an actuation motor mounted on the base of the plotter. The boom will sweep an arc. The pen will ride on a way mounted on the boom (see Figure 8.2). This approach will eliminate the need for one set of machined ways. Additionally, it will reduce the problem endemic to the flat bed plotter—that of actuating the second gantry—because the pen actuation motor may be mounted at the origin without significantly increasing the inertia of the plot arm (see Figure 8.4). Since our plotter will operate with polar coordinates, we will use a microprocessor to transform the points which the user specifies in Cartesian coordinates.

Any point in the Cartesian plane described by (x,y) may be represented by the polar coordinates (r, θ), where r is the radius from the polar ordinate and θ is the angle which the radius makes with the reference radius (see Figure 8.3).

The transformation of Cartesian to polar coordinates may be described as

$$r = \sqrt{x^2 + y^2}$$

and

$$\theta = \arcsin(y/r)$$

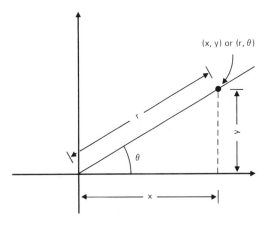

Figure 8.3: Cartesian and Polar Coordinates

ACTUATOR CHARACTERISTICS

All plotters require actuators with similar characteristics. Most plotters are driven by rotary electric motors. A myriad of motor designs exist, but one major distinction can be made: the motor may be either *synchronous* or *asynchronous*. Although asynchronous motors have several attractive qualities, such as good power to weight ratios and jerk-free operation, they have one negative characteristic which makes them suitable only for costly systems. In order to be accurately positioned, asynchronous motors require feedback. By contrast, synchronous motors may be operated open loop (see Figure 8.5). The angular displacement of a synchronous motor is correlated to the actuating power signal. Electric plug-in clocks, for example, are typically driven by a synchronous induction motor which follows the AC line frequency. Such a motor is designed to rotate a fixed angle for each cycle of the AC line.

THE STEPPING MOTOR

Because a stepping motor is synchronous, it is well-suited to our plotter application. Stepping motor coils are usually

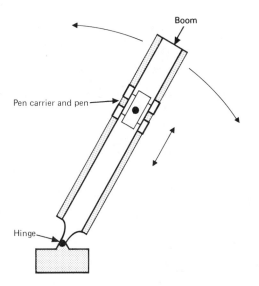

Figure 8.2: Stylized Polar Pen-Plotter

excited by direct current rather than by alternating current. Inside the "black box" stepping motor controller which we used in Chapter 4 is a circuit which applies direct current to combinations of motor coils in such a manner that the rotor advances from one stable position to another each time the step input is toggled. We will first examine how a stepping motor responds to the patterned actuation of the coils and then propose two methods for generating the sequence of actuations.

Figure 8.6 depicts an idealized stepping motor. The four poles may be magnetized by sending a current through one of the two coils on each pole. Poles 1 and 2 are of opposite polarity, as are poles 3 and 4. Each pole-pair has two coils, wound in opposite directions, so that a unipolar voltage source may be used. The same effect could be achieved with a single coil by using a bipolar (positive and negative) power supply and permitting current to flow in either direction through the coils. The double-wound pole is called a *bifilar winding*. We will assume that current flowing through coil A, but not B, will cause pole 1 to be magnetized south and pole 2 north. The opposite will occur if current flows through B and not A. Likewise, current flowing in coil C and not D will cause pole 3 to be south and pole 4 to be north. The rotor is a permanent magnet designed so that each of the teeth has a south sense. If an imbalance exists between the magnetic field of the rotor and the net magnetic field of the

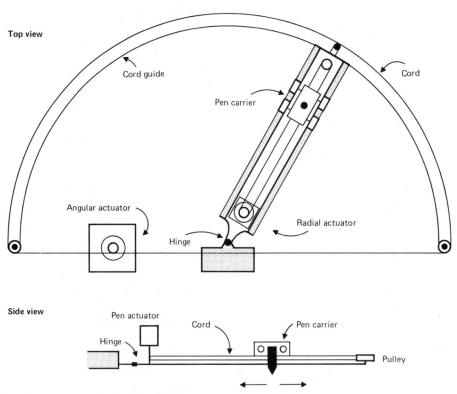

Figure 8.4: Actuating the Polar Pen-Plotter

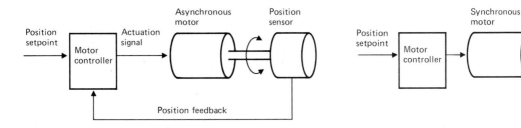

a. Closed loop control of an asynchronous motor

b. Open loop control of a synchronous motor

Figure 8.5: Synchronous and Asynchronous Motor Positioning

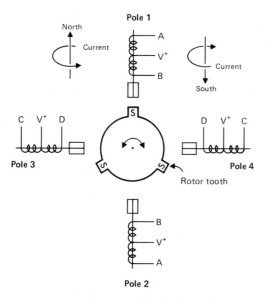

Figure 8.6: Idealized 4-phase, Bifilar-wound, Permanent Magnet Stepping Motor

coils, the motor will rotate. Because the number of rotor teeth is not equal to the number of poles, changing the polarity of one set of poles will always result in a torque on the rotor.

To verify that the coil excitation sequence given in Table 8.1 actually causes the shaft to rotate 30 degrees for each step in the sequence, we strongly suggest that the reader trace the rotor, cut it out, and lay it on Figure 8.6. Then, for each excitation change, move the rotor to its nearest stable equilibrium point.

Table 8.2 differs from table 8.1 in only one respect. Inserted between each *full-step*

Counterclockwise	Coil				Pole				Clockwise
	A	B	C	D	1	2	3	4	
	On	Off	On	Off	S	N	S	N	
	On	Off	Off	On	S	N	N	S	
	Off	On	Off	On	N	S	N	S	
	Off	On	On	Off	N	S	S	N	

Table 8.1: Full-Step Actuation Sequence

Counterclockwise	Coil				Pole				Clockwise
	A	B	C	D	1	2	3	4	
	On	Off	On	Off	S	N	S	N	
	On	Off	Off	Off	S	N	Off	Off	
	On	Off	Off	On	S	N	N	S	
	Off	Off	Off	On	Off	Off	N	S	
	Off	On	Off	On	N	S	N	S	
	Off	On	Off	Off	N	S	Off	Off	
	Off	On	On	Off	N	S	S	N	
	Off	Off	On	Off	Off	Off	S	N	

Table 8.2: Half-Step Actuation Sequence

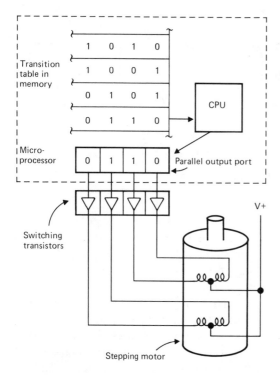

Figure 8.7: Programmed Logic Generation of Stepping Motor Excitation Sequence

is a step in which only one of the two poles is energized. This sequence causes the rotor to *half-step* or move 15 degrees. Half-stepping doubles the precision with which the rotor may be positioned and increases the number of points on the plotting bed to which the pen can be moved. Decreasing step size in this manner increases the quality of the finished plot. The price paid for the quality gain is a reduction of available torque to roughly 70 percent of the full-step torque.

GENERATING THE EXCITATION SEQUENCE

The black box which we showed schematically in Chapter 4 in Figure 4.15c contains a *sequential logic circuit* designed to

produce a 4-phase *excitation sequence.* By connecting the four signal lines—one for each set of coils—to a parallel output port, we can use a microprocessor instead of a sequential logic circuit to generate the sequence. An easy way to accomplish this is to store in memory a table of words, each of which is the pattern for one stable rotor position. Indexing through the table by ascending addresses causes the motor to step in one direction. Indexing through the table by descending addresses causes the motor to step in the opposite direction (see Figure 8.7).

TIMING AND RAMPING

Figure 8.8 shows how a programmed sequential logic generator rotates the stepping motor. A microprocessor can execute this algorithm in about 25 microseconds, which is much faster than the motor can step. We can determine the maximum rate at which the motor can be stepped as follows: the rotor and the motor-load are inertial masses which must be accelerated. Because the torque of the magnetic field is relatively constant, motor step rat is most severely limited when the rotor i stationary. Once the motor is rotating, however, we can *ramp* the step rate in order to bring the motor to maximum speed. Figure 8.9 shows a three level ramp designed to permit the motor to reach a given angular velocity under maximum load before its stepping rate is increased. The ramping profile is tailored for worst case load because the motor is open-loop.

MICRO-STEPPING

Another step-size refinement that will further enhance the quality of our finished plot is *micro-stepping.* Consider the case in which the stepping motor of Figure 8.6 is in a stable position, with coils A and C energized. If we reduce the current in coil A, the rotor will move some distance. Figure 8.10 shows the qualitative relationship between the current in coil A and the resulting rotor position. We emphasize that this relationship is qualitative and show no scaling for the rotor position because the function which maps current to rotor position is determined by the motor design and may well be non-linear.

One way to implement micro-stepping is with D/A converters (see Figure 8.11). Using one converter per coil, we can apply discrete currents to the four coils. The motor will micro-step through the resulting set of angles.

We can refine this approach by transferring the function of the four costly D/A converters to a microprocessor. We know that the force exerted on the stepping motor rotor is a function of the power delivered to the coils. We also recall that varying the duty cycle of a digital signal by either pulse width modulation or pulse frequency modulation changes the signal's power output. Modulated digital signals can therefore be substituted for the D/A converters.

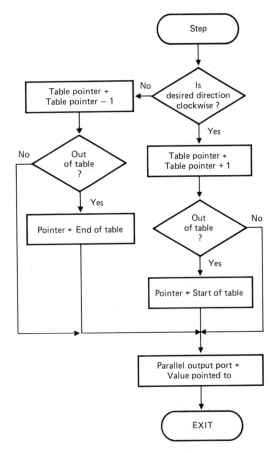

Figure 8.8: Flow of Programmed Logic Sequencer

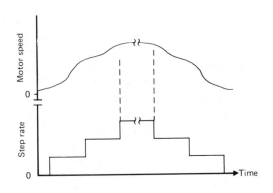

Figure 8.9: Ramping the Step Rate

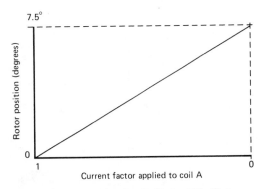

Figure 8.10: Qualitative Relationship Between Stepping Motor Coil Current and Rotor Position

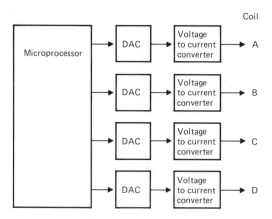

Figure 8.11: A Conceptual Solution to the Microstepping Requirement

THE SOFTWARE CHALLENGE

A successful polar plotter design requires both an effective mechanism and realistic software for vector generation. We will now write a subroutine which has as its parameters the starting and ending points of a vector. The subroutine will generate, in real time, the actuation signals required by the plotter's two 4-phase stepping motors. In order to place a realistic constraint upon our design, we will specify that our

algorithm must step one motor at a minimum rate of 100Hz.

Figure 8.12 shows how the polar coordinate system will map onto the Cartesian coordinates of the paper. The radius at $\theta = 0$ will bisect the plotting surface. In order to use the transformations presented earlier, the algorithm will rotate the Cartesian coordinate system 90 degrees and shift it by $1/\sqrt{2}$ times the maximum radius.

Because a stepping motor is only stable in a finite number of positions, the pen will trace a staircase vector (except in the special case where $\theta_1 = \theta_2$). Our goal is to develop an algorithm which will draw the best approximation possible to the desired vector. An ancillary goal is to have the algorithm do this *efficiently*.

The Brute Force Method

The brute force method is often a good starting point from which to move to a more efficient solution. Figure 8.13 shows the eight points to which the pen can possibly move from position P. The points can be reached by positive or negative angular steps, positive or negative radial steps, or combinations of angular and radial steps. We must select one of the eight points. The best point is the one whose distance to the ideal vector is the smallest. We find this distance by determining the equation of a line through the trial point which is perpendicular to the desired vector, then finding the intersection of the two lines, and finally finding the distance between the trial point and the intersection point (see Figure 8.14). The brute force algorithm requires us to solve for each of eight points

$$distance = \sqrt{(x_t - x_i)^2 + (y_t - y_i)^2}$$

where $x_i = (a/(a^2 + 1))(y_t + x_t/a - b)$

and $y_i = ax_i + b$

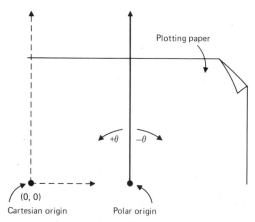

Figure 8.12: Location of the Cartesian Plotting Surface Relative to the Polar Origin

xt and yt are the coordinates of the trial point; a is the slope of the desired vector; and b is the y intercept of the desired vector. We will judge the performance of our algorithm by counting the number of calculations required to produce the eight distances. Table 8.3 lists the number of arithmetic operations required to select the point closest to the desired vector using the brute force algorithm. The column labeled *normalized computation time* is related to the number of machine cycles required to perform the calculation compared to some simple operation. Finding the sine of an angle, for example, requires more machine cycles than does adding two numbers.

A More Efficient Algorithm

A key goal of designers interested in modern microprocessor-based design is to create more effective systems by relating their knowledge of how microprocessors implement algorithms to their understanding of how mechanisms function. In our case, we can significantly increase computing speed by improving on the brute force algorithm described above without affecting plotting quality. We know, for instance, that the radial arm need only move in one angular direction in order to draw any vector. If the algorithm is designed to determine what this direction is, its search time for the best next point will be cut roughly in half. In addition, we may benefit from performing our point selection in polar coordinates, because neither the angular nor the radial step size varies with respect to pen position.

Figure 8.15 shows the trigonometric relationships which may be exploited for rapid point selection. If the present boom angle is not equal (that is, within delta theta) to the final angle, the boom takes an angular step. To determine whether radial steps are needed, the program compares the

present radial pen position with the radial distance to the desired vector (iri). iri is determined using the law of sines. The advantage to this method is that one of the angles is constant (alpha) and the other

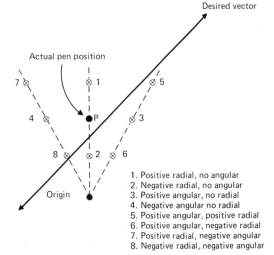

1. Positive radial, no angular
2. Negative radial, no angular
3. Positive angular, no radial
4. Negative angular no radial
5. Positive angular, positive radial
6. Positive angular, negative radial
7. Positive radial, negative angular
8. Negative radial, negative angular

Figure 8.13: Brute Force Algorithm Point Selection

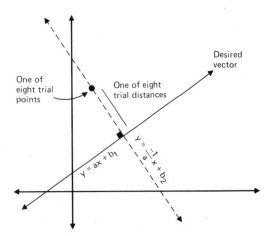

Figure 8.14: Brute Force Point Selection by Method of Intersecting Lines

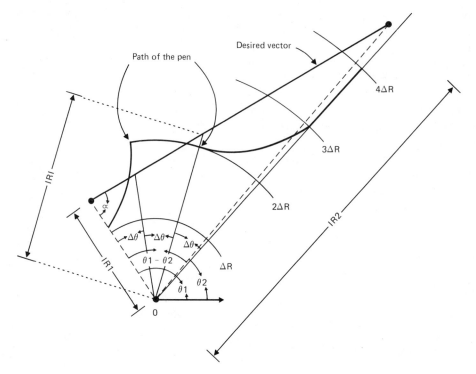

Figure 8.15: Exaggerated View of Dimensions Used in Polar Plotting Algorithm

Operation	Number of Operations	Normalized Computation Time (Integer Addition = 1)
Add	56	358
Subtract	24	154
Multiply	48	442
Divide	32	541
Sin/Cos	16	2350
Square	24	242
Square Root	8	220
Total Normalized Time 4307		

Table 8.3: Calculations Required to Select Next Point: Brute Force Algorithm

Operation	Number of Operations	Normalized Computation Time (Ingeter Addition = 1)
Add	1	6
Subtract	0	
Multiply	0	
Divide	1	17
Sin/Cos	1	147
Square	0	
Square Root	0	
Total Normalized Time 170		

Table 8.4: Calculations Required to Select Next Plot Point: Improved Algorithm

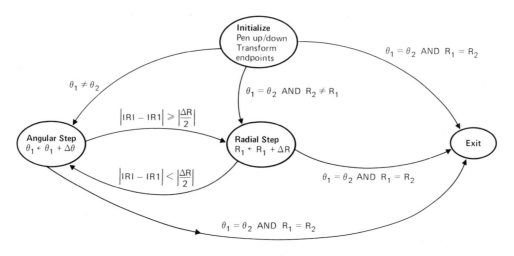

Figure 8.16: Transition Diagram of Polar Plotting Algorithm

increases or decreases by delta theta. In addition, one of the sides (ir1) is constant. As a result, we only have to determine the new angle

$$\theta_1 = \theta_2 \pm \Delta\theta$$

and

$$iri = c_1/\sin(\theta_1),$$

where c1 is a constant containing alpha and the value ir1. The program determines if a radial step is required by ascertaining whether the present radial position is within one-half of a radial step. (A transition diagram for the algorithm appears in Figure 8.16.) Table 8.4 lists the approximate number of calculations required to select the next plot point. We urge the reader to compare the number with those in Table 8.3. The reduced complexity of the algorithm can make the difference between a product which requires too much processor power to be cost-effective and one which can be marketed competitively.

REAL TIME SOFTWARE TIME CONSTRAINTS

Floating Point Arithmetic Operations

For ease of programming, we have used *floating point* numbers to develop our polar plotter algorithm. Floating point numbers, also known as real numbers, are values represented in scientific notation. Floating point operations generally require significantly more processor cycles to execute than do integer calculations. For example, the operation

$$0.5 \times 10^{-2} + 0.6 \times 10^{-3}$$

yields (after normalizing the two exponents and adding the mantissas):

$$0.5 \times 10^{-2} + 0.6 \times 10^{-3} =$$
$$5 \times 10^{-3} + 0.6 \times 10^{-3} = 5.6 \times 10^{-3}$$

Because of the complexity and expense of implementing operations like this, most microprocessor applications use integer arithmetic. Indeed, if we wished to take our laboratory prototype into commercial production, we would have to consider seriously changing to integer arithmetic.

Floating point number storage is determined to some degree by processor architecture. More generally, however, hardware and software designers determine the storage configuration by striking a compromise between the *range* of the numbers to be represented and the *precision* to which a given number may be represented. Figure 8.17 shows the range and precision of three simple number storage schemes.

Careful Scaling

One way to avoid floating point operations without losing accuracy is to use integer arithmetic, scaling all internal quantities to fit within the range of available integers. Consider, for example, the case in which we must multiply a series of integers ranging from zero to 1000 by a fraction ranging from zero to one to yield another integer. To ensure that the result of the multiplication doesn't overflow the capacity of the integer word, all of the variables need be carefully scaled. As we discussed in Chapters 5 and 6, we can represent the fraction as an integer numerator and an integer denominator and perform an integer multiplication followed by an integer divide. This problem is typical of control problems in which the controller gain might be a fraction less than one.

Integer arithmetic has such severe range and precision limitations that every operation must be scrutinized to avoid overflow or excessive round-off error. The reward for careful effort can be a significant increase in performance.

HIGH-LEVEL LANGUAGE CONSIDERATIONS

In Chapter 3 we used a high-level language so that readers who were as yet unfamiliar with microprocessor architecture could write a real time program. We emphasized the nature of the algorithm, not its implementation. We switched to assembly language programs in Chapter 4 in order to examine how a computer implements algorithms. By Chapter 6 (blending), the assembly language routines we were writing to multiply and divide integers were becoming so complex and tedious that we returned to the use of a high-level language in Chapter 7 (Automated Weighing). Our task in this chapter is to implement as quickly and inexpensively as possible a functioning prototype of a polar plotter. Because we cannot afford the time to write a library of floating point and trigonometric routines, we

Integer representation: 8-bit word

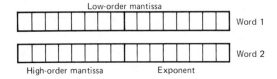

Range: −128 to 127
Precision: 1 part in 256

32-bit floating point representation:

Low-order mantissa

Word 1

Word 2

High-order mantissa   Exponent

Range: $-(1 - 2^{-23}) \times 2^{127}$ to $-(2^{-23}) \times 2^{-128}$

and: $2^{-23} \times 2^{-128}$ to $(1 - 2^{-23}) \times 2^{127}$

(Assuming normalization not required)

Or,

Range Base −10: -170×10^{36} to -350×10^{-48}

and: 350×10^{-48} to 170×10^{36}

Mantissa precision: 1 part in 2^{24}

Figure 8.17: Range and Precision of Two Storage Formats

will continue programming in a high-level language.

Traditionally, assembly language or languages similar to it have been used for instrumentation and control programming. In early control systems, hardware to software cost ratios were high. Many users who had designed relay-based systems easily adapted to Boolean logic assembly language-like programming. Many time-critical routines—especially foreground input/output routines—had to be coded in assembly language. The method by which these routines could be made compatible with high-level language programs was not always obvious. In all these cases, redesigning systems to take advantage of the newer, high-level languages has been slow. But momentum is growing. High-level languages have a tremendous potential for extensive use in all but high volume and high speed systems. How effectively they can be incorporated into real time systems depends on the designer's skill at transforming them for microprocessor use.

We summarize below the important advantages and disadvantages associated with using high-level languages for instrumentation and control programming.

Advantages

Succinct expression of algorithms. A significant feature of a well-designed high-level language is that it forces the user to express the algorithm in a clear and concise manner.

Program modification. Anyone who has read through pages of assembly listings will appreciate the fact that some programs cannot be modified. In contrast, the structure of programs written in a high-level language increases the probability that programs can be modified.

Complex arithmetic and logical expres-sions are evaluated. High-level languages effectively evaluate expressions which would be unmanageable to code in assembly language. Most high-level languages are supplied with extensive libraries of arithmetic and trigonometric functions, and some have matrix and imaginary number manipulation routines.

Machine independence. It is extremely valuable to be able to transfer programs from one machine to another in order to take advantage of continuing improvements in microprocessor design.

Error checking. Good compilers can detect errors in data type mismatch, some logic errors, and syntax errors. This error-checking capability increases programmer productivity.

Data structure support. High-level languages provide support for subscripted arrays and can do operations which maintain relationships within a program's data base.

File structure supported. Larger control systems commonly require access to mass storage devices. High-level languages—usually through operating system facilities—facilitate logical manipulation of widely varying physical devices.

Disadvantages

Speed and space restrictions. Some compilers generate programs that either require too much memory or run too slowly to be economically effective in microprocessor systems.

RAM/ROM conflicts. Small, dedicated control programs typically reside in ROM and use RAM scratchspace. In order for such programs to function, the compiler must be able to distinguish between these regions. Some do not.

Costly development systems are needed. While it is possible to develop machine

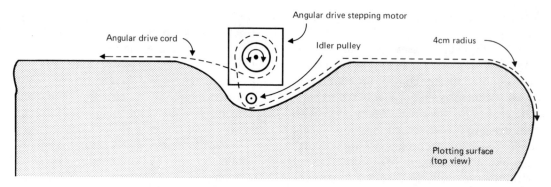

Figure 8.18: Angular Traction Drive Detail

language code directly on the target processor, working in high-level languages requires a disk-based development system.

Language cost. High-level languages require a compiler, which must often be purchased separately from the development system.

Foreground/background support. If one is to write foreground (interrupt-driven) routines in a high-level language, care must be taken to ensure that the routine preserves the machine state and that all library routines used by the foreground routine are re-entrant. Some compilers do not provide these features.

THE FINAL PROTOTYPE

The plotter which we designed is intended to be quickly and inexpensively built. We recommend the exercise of assembling a plotter but emphasize that our descriptions are only guidelines. Many of our engineering design choices were made out of expediency. The reader should work with available materials.

The plotting surface is made of acrylic plastic cut in the shape depicted in Figure 8.4. Around the circumference of the surface a groove is machined to contain the angular-drive cord. No pulleys are used. The braided nylon cord slides in the groove.

Figure 8.18 shows the traction mechanism used to move the cord. The pulley mounted on the angular-drive stepping motor should be as small as possible to reduce the boom's angular step size, but the pulley must be large enough to provide sufficient frictional force. Our prototype used a 13 mm diameter pulley with a rough surface. The idler pulley prevents cord tangling.

Figure 8.19 shows the key elements of the polar plotter. The boom and truss system was built using a high quality children's toy kit manufactured by Fischer Technik. The boom must be rigid enough to support the pen carrier. Since our boom was not made of a single piece of sufficient rigidity, the truss was employed. The radial-drive stepping motor is mounted so that the center of mass of the boom system falls roughly at the polar origin. The boom is attached to the angular-drive cord in a manner which reduces backlash.

The pen carrier, Figure 8.20, was conveniently built from a plastic Fischer Technik part which slides on two lengths of common 3/16 inch drill rod. A braided nylon cord simply wound around the shaft of the radial-drive stepping motor actuates the pen carrier. A lightweight solenoid was found which could be attached to a spring-loaded felt pen. When the solenoid is actu-

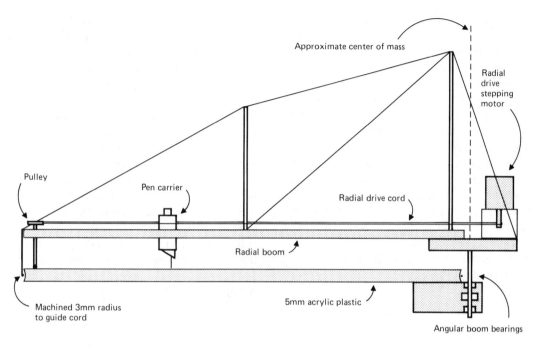

Figure 8.19: Stylized View of Prototype Polar Plotter Showing Important Elements (Not drawn to scale)

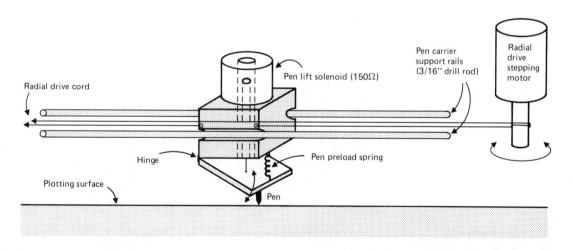

Figure 8.20: Radial Pen Drive Detail

ated by one bit of a parallel output port, the pen lifts. When the solenoid is turned off, the pen drops. Figure 8.21 shows a solenoid drive circuit which is capable of driving nearly any solenoid which the reader uses. (Check current and voltage limitations first.)

The plotter was first operated using a program which prompted the user for the Cartesian coordinates of two vector endpoints. This program was used to establish reference points on the plotting bed in order that the hardware boom position corresponded with the software boom position. Fascinating results occur if the two points do not agree. A reader with an interest in geometry should experiment.

Once the plotter was capable of drawing a vector, the polar plotter subroutine was incorporated into an existing graphic display program and the graph of Figure 8.22 was generated. Compare the graph drawn by our prototype plotter to that drawn by a commercial drum plotter (see Figure 8.23). Although the backlash resulting from the simple pen carrier design caused significant deformity of the letters, the polar plotter functioned rather well when commanded to draw long vectors. The goal of building a prototype is to demonstrate a concept well enough to justify continued effort. We have certainly shown that a novel mechanical design coupled with a microprocessor can generate interesting results!

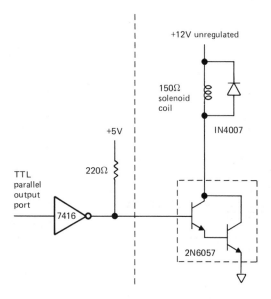

Figure 8.21: Pen-Lift Drive Circuit Capable of Driving a Wide Variety of Solenoids (the Transistor and Diode are Liberally Specified)

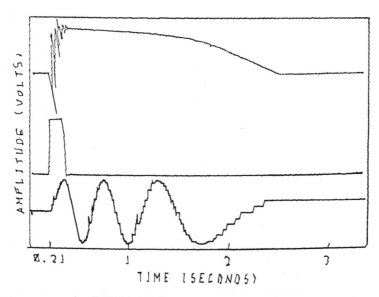

Figure 8.22: A Graph Drawn by the Polar Plotter

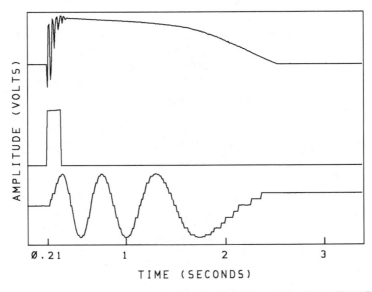

Figure 8.23: A Graph Drawn by a Commercial Drum Plotter

PROJECTS

1. Perform a series of timing tests in order to determine how quickly your computer executes various arithmetic operations. Write a small program which loops for several seconds or more before sending a bell to the terminal. Use a stopwatch for timing. You must subtract from the total time the amount required for your program to test the iteration count and branch. Write assembly language tests of integer addition and subtraction where both operands are fetched from memory. Write high-level language routines which time integer operations (if your language distinguishes) as well as all operations in Table 8.3.

2. Write a program which generates a 4-phase stepping motor actuation sequence on a parallel interface. Write both a half-step and full-step version. Introduce a large delay into the program and then observe the bit transitions with lights or an oscilloscope.

3. Connect a stepping motor controller to four bits of your computer's parallel output port. Run the program of Project 2 and verify that the motor turns. What is the magnitude of the angular full- and half-steps? What is the maximum stepping rate at which the motor will self-start?

4. Enter into your computer the vector-generating subroutine in the appendix. Call the subroutine with the program which prompts the user for vector endpoints. Even if you have not built a polar plotter, you should be able to determine if the algorithm is functioning properly by watching the stepping rates of the two motors. What is the effect of changing the variable which determines the angular step size?

5. Write a program which prompts the user for an arbitrary number of points, and then on command causes the stepping motors to "draw" the resulting shape.

6. What is the maximum rate at which the vector generation subroutine can generate the actuation sequence? Can your stepping motors step at this rate? How much time is required for the subroutine to setup for each new vector?

Chapter 9

AN AUTOMATED CUTTING MACHINE

The problem we will present in this chapter is similar to those of previous chapters; however, in contrast to the laboratory prototypes we designed in earlier case studies, our design here will be a functioning *industrial* prototype. The primary difference between the two is that our laboratory prototypes functioned with a disk-based computer system costing many thousands of dollars, while the industrial prototype will operate with a dedicated microprocessor costing a fraction of the price. Besides studying how a dedicated, single-board computer functions, we will look in some detail at how to use an interactive microprocessor development system to bring a dedicated processor into operation. In addition to developing the algorithm for the dedicated processor, we will examine a number of topics unique to functioning controllers, such as noise generation and noise immunity, reset characteristics, cost/reliability trade-offs, and considerations for the intended user or operator.

THE PROBLEM

A manufacturing company wishes to increase productivity while reducing employee exposure to a potentially carcinogenic material. The operation which the company wishes to replace is that of cutting a continuous length of braided material into discrete lengths by hand. Hand labor has been used up to now to minimize waste, to avoid material damage, and to eliminate extensive setup time, because only small numbers (hundreds to a few thousand) of the same length pieces need to be cut at one time.

The manufacturer, aware of these

restrictions but wishing to take a swipe at stagnant productivity, asks its design staff to build an automatic cutting machine that will:

- cut accurately,
- not waste material,
- reduce operator contact with the material,
- function in a production environment without an operator present,
- be cost effective,
- be easy to set up,
- be certifiable by a safety engineer.

Management allocates a budget that allows for about 100 hours of design time and 100 hours for fabrication, with the understanding that the design will not be optimized to the last cent because its cost will be amortized over only about 10 units.

The designers do not have sufficient time to perform many experiments or examine the theory of material cutting. Relying on experience and a bit of intuition, they perform a test and confirm that a radial, self-sharpening saw produces an excellent cut. They devise a scheme for feeding the material to the saw using a motor-driven roller mechanism and fabricate a mockup which confirms that a length of material can be fed underneath the saw and that the saw can be lowered, thus cutting the material. Figure 9.1 shows the mockup. At this point, the designers evaluate their progress and formalize their plans.

SEQUENTIAL LOGIC

Given the mechanism shown in Figure 9.1, one of the designers' major goals is to sequence the saw motor, the feed motor, and the cut-off motor in such a way that the machine functions as a cutter. The designers know that their machine will need some form of amplification in order to operate its saw and feed mechanisms, and that it will require some form of logic to achieve proper sequencing. They examine a few alternatives.

Relays

Figure 9.2a is a stylized view of an electro-mechanical relay. Magnetizing the coil pole causes a mechanical arm to open or close sets of contacts, which open or close the circuits. In the relay of Figure 9.2a, one set of contacts is open when the relay is not energized (normally open), while the second set is closed when the relay is not energized (normally closed). Figure 9.2b depicts the schematic elements of the relay of 9.2a. The circle marked *relay* represents the coil. The contacts labeled x and y are represented by parallel line figures. Note the distinction between normally open and normally closed.

Relays amplify signals, isolate input signals from output signals, and perform logic functions. So called *time-delay relays,* which are available commercially, are really hybrid circuits. A common relay amplifier is found in the automobile. In order to start the engine, something on the order of 200 amperes must flow through the starter motor. Instead of threading two massive wires through the dashboard to a 200 ampere key switch, automobile manufacturers use a power relay often situated directly on the starter. A relatively low power actuation signal from the ignition key closes the power relay. Power relays are commonly used in microprocessor systems to produce useful actuation signals from logic level signals.

We discuss relays as logic gates next and give an example of how the Boolean logic operators NOT, OR, and AND are implemented at the circuit level.

One of the classic exercises in Boolean logic is the design of the *majority voter cir-*

cuit, so named because its inputs are three pushbuttons to be pressed by three *voters.* The circuit is designed to determine if two of the three voters are holding down their buttons. In lieu of a formal solution, we will say that the circuit should indicate a true vote if buttons

(A and B) or (A and C) or (B and C)

are pressed. Using the operator + to represent OR and contiguity to represent AND,

the solution becomes

$$f(voter) = AB + AC + BC.$$

Figure 9.3*a* is a gate-level realization of the circuit. Figure 9.3*b* is a relay ladder diagram of the same circuit. The two supports of the ladder are power lines, while the rungs are circuits. We show no resistors because we are assuming that devices such as coils and lamps are power-limiting. If two or more pushbuttons, PBA, PBB, or PBC,

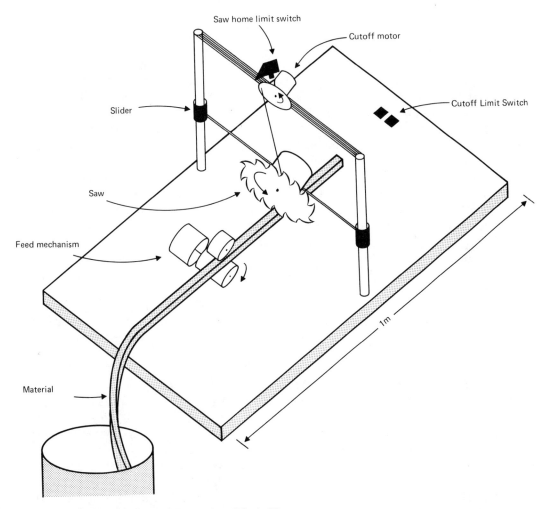

Saw home limit switch

Cutoff motor

Slider

Cutoff Limit Switch

Saw

Feed mechanism

Material

1m

Figure 9.1: Cutting Machine Mechanism Mock-Up

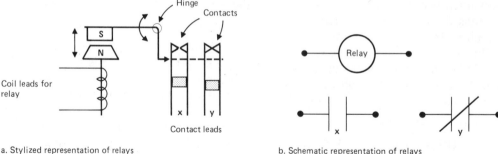

a. Stylized representation of relays   b. Schematic representation of relays

Figure 9.2: D.C. Relays: x Normally Open, y Normally Closed

are held down, the logic array of contacts will cause power to flow to illuminate the light and energize a *latch circuit* (not shown in Figure 9.3*a*). The latch continues to supply power to the light after one or more of the buttons have been released. This circuit which *remembers* the vote has a direct analog in solid state circuits and is one form of memory used in every digital computer. A *clear* pushbutton (PBCL) removes power from the latch and resets the voter circuit.

The designers contemplate using a relay-based sequential circuit to sequence the three motors of the cutting machine and draw a transition diagram to describe it (Figure 9.4). They define an *off* state, which may be entered at any time from any state by pressing *saw-off,* and design the *saw-on* state to allow the radial saw to attain operating speed before the cutting operation begins. Note that all three motors are off in the off state. Once the *start-cut* button is pressed, the feed/cut cycle begins. Only the *stop-cut* or saw-off buttons can cause the controller to exit this pattern.

Figure 9.5 is a relay ladder diagram for the cutting machine. The saw is started and stopped with pushbuttons. A latch keeps the system running when the saw-on button is released. This circuit, or a close relative, is used in virtually every motor starter in

industrial applications. Often, though, a thermal or overcurrent shut-off is placed in series with the stop button. Two limit switches provide feedback to the controller. The first limit, *home,* is closed when the saw is in the fully raised position. When the saw descends for a cut, the home limit switch opens. The second limit switch called *limit,* closes when the feed mechanism has delivered a desired length of material to the cutting position. The start-cut button initiates the feed/cut operation. Like the saw circuit, the cut circuit is latched by latch2. The motor which feeds the material (feed) and the motor which lowers the saw (cut) alternate, depending upon the states of the limit and home switches. The contact latch1 in series with the stop-cut pushbutton is designed to ensure that, if the saw is not running, the cutting and feeding operations will stop.

Programmed Logic

The designers recognize that their cutting machine transition diagram (Figure 9.4) is inadequate. They have made no provision for an operator's guard, which is necessary in order for a safety engineer to certify the cutter. The cutter will not operate unattended, since it will not stop when the desired number of pieces has been cut, nor does it reset automatically. The controller may not be easy to set up, as required, since it isn't possible to cut a single piece to check the length setting. Furthermore, if the machine jammed or the feeding material bypassed the feed limit switch, the material could be wasted and equipment damaged.

Their second attempt (see the transition diagram of Figure 9.6) includes a machine guard input which removes all power from the motor actuators. The new state, *not-ok,* can only exit when the guard is not violated. They add one register which the operator can set for the number of pieces he or she wishes to cut and a second, to keep track of the number of pieces cut. In order to simplify setup, they add an input labeled *single cycle.* When it is true, a single piece can be fed through and cut. The operator may measure the part and readjust the cutoff length before actuating cycle and turning it loose. In order to prevent catastrophic jams or overshoots, they incorporate timers for the feed and cut states which shut off all motors in case of a jam.

At this point in the process, the designers realize that it is still possible for them to do a relay or gate level design but that the task is quickly becoming more complex. A few "what if's" loom over their shoulders. What if the parts do not fall away from the cutting area as anticipated? They would have to add a part ejection device. What if management subsequently requested that several cutting machines be coupled to a supervisory computer for production control? Several registers and flag lines would have to be added. If this were 1950, the designers would have no choice but to use some combination of mechanical or electromechanical devices. In 1970, their attention would have focused on discrete and integrated solid state logic. Today, they

have a more flexible option. They decide to implement their transition diagram with a microprocessor.

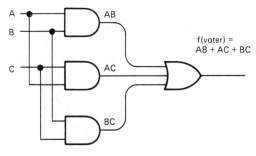

a. Logic gate realization

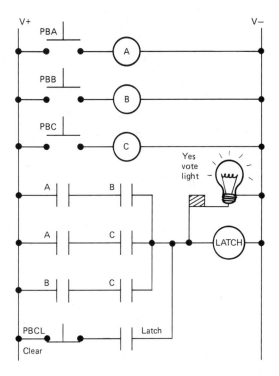

b. Relay ladder diagram

Figure 9.3: Majority Voter Circuit

THE DESIGN APPROACH

In the real world, there is no such thing as true top-down or bottom-up design. Creating the best design possible involves iterating between what is desired and what can be achieved with the time and resources available. To design a complete system one must understand the entire system, but this is difficult to do unless one knows how each of the system's components works. The cutting machine team decides upon a design methodology which is highly effective for learning about their system in detail. The designers will identify the key components of their system, simulate the operation of these components in hardware and software, test them, and only then link them together. If they have understood their problem, the pieces should interact properly.

With the overview of their cutting machine in mind, the designers begin selecting the sensors, actuators, and displays they will need in order to build a functioning laboratory mockup controlled by a disk-based laboratory computer. Once they have a functioning mockup, they will select a suitable single board computer for use with the development system. While the saw mechanism is being fabricated in the

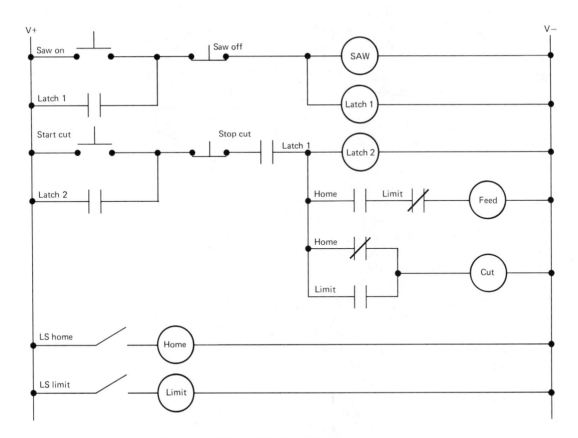

Figure 9.5: Relay Ladder Diagram of Simple Cutting Machine

machine tool facility, they will write a final version of the software for the single board computer. The cutting machine will be connected to both the single board computer and the development system for testing. After the production personnel have operated the machine and approved its performance, the design team will program the controller's read only memories and cut its umbilical cord to the development system.

Hardware Selection

The designers must specify four hardware elements which are related to, but not integral parts of, the microprocessor system: two limit switches, the motor actuators, the operator displays, and the operator entry device. Each of these four items is a key system component. Selection error could produce delays and redesign costs far in excess of the cost of the devices.

Limit Switches. The cutoff length detector must consistently signal that the material has been fed to the proper length. The feed motor is equipped with a brake which stops the feed well within the length tolerance of 0.4 mm (0.015 inch). The design team must devise a limit switch that is equally precise and can overcome two problems. First, the force required to trip the switch causes the fed material to buckle slightly, and this force varies, depending upon where the switch is contacted. Second, a light force switch can easily be jammed by dust from the saw or tripped by vibrations from the mechanism. The designers decide on a light beam which will be broken by the advancing material. In order to avoid false tripping by ambient light, they consider using a light transmitter which sends a modulated signal. The detector would then look for a difference in intensity rather than an absolute intensity. For reasons of availability and favorable technical

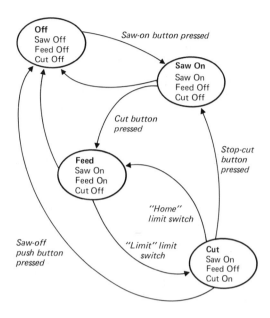

Figure 9.4: First Cutting Machine Transition Diagram

specifications, however, the designers choose an infrared transmitter and receiver which is oblivious to visible wavelengths.

The cam-actuated home limit switch does not have to trip at a precise position, but it is expected to have a life expectancy of many hundreds of thousands of cycles. The choice is a double-throw switch that is commercially available. The words switch or pushbutton should sound a warning tone in the ear of any electronic circuit designer, because they raise the spectre of *switch bounce.* Figure 9.7 shows what happens to a signal when the mass/spring system of the switch goes through a damped oscillation. The problem occurs because the microprocessor's response time is significantly shorter than the bounce time. For example, the processor can note that the switch has changed state and respond in perhaps 20 microseconds. When the switch bounces open a millisecond later, the processor

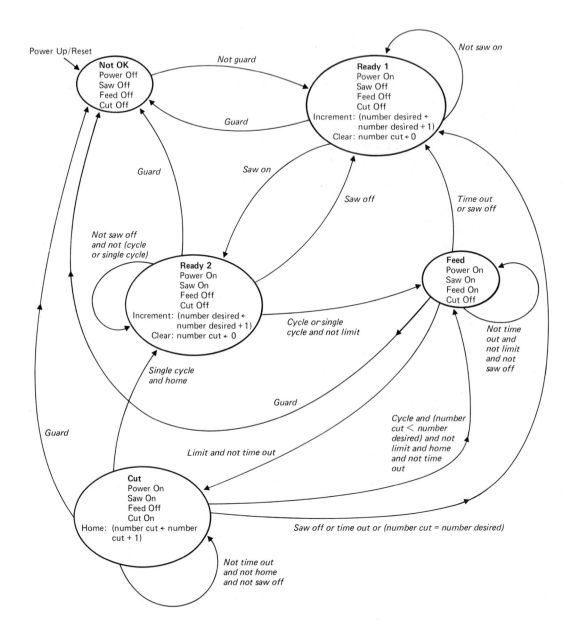

Figure 9.6: A More Realistic Transition Diagram

dutifully responds again. This process can repeat several times to the utter despair of the careful software designer who thought the "logic" was correct.

Switch bounce is not terminal if diagnosed early. As with many problems, it has both hardware and software solutions. Some switches are specifically designed for minimum bounce; relying on them, however, poses potential problems for part servicing and replacement. Dedicated integrated circuits designed to strobe arrays of keys (such as terminal keyboards) and debounce them are also available. A more general hardware solution to switch bounce appears in Figure 9.8. This approach is extremely effective, although it requires a double-throw switch and a latch. Another approach using a single-throw switch and a one-shot is not reliable.

Software solutions tend to be less expensive than hardware solutions. Figure 9.9 is a simple software debounce routine. Note that the processor will "hang" in this routine until a closure occurs. Often, a more sophisticated approach is required. For example, the processor could use a system timer, or a regularly scheduled foreground routine could be assigned the task of determining switch states.

Motor Actuators. The least expensive motor actuators possible for the cutting machine are electromechanical relays, but the design staff decides against them since they would be subjected to considerable wear; the feed and cut motors cycle on and off each time a part is cut.

To maximize the lifetime of the motor actuators, the designers specify a *solid state relay* which incorporates a triac (a semiconductor AC switch) and isolation circuits to isolate the triac from the microprocessor's power supply. The relay will provide for overvoltage suppression and heat dissipa-

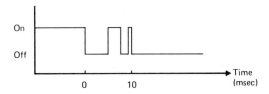

Figure 9.7: Switch Bounce

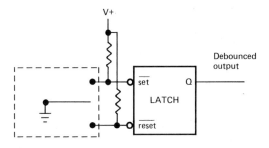

Figure 9.8: One Hardware Switch Debounce Technique

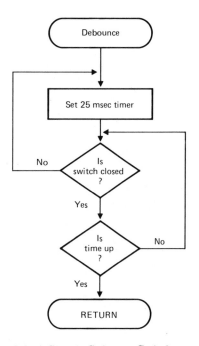

Figure 9.9: A Simple Software Switch Debounce Algorithm

tion and will be certified for safety, easing the task of complying with electrical safety codes.

Operator Displays. One of the many justifications for using a microprocessor in the cutting machine is that the controller can maintain a count of the number of pieces to be cut. The operator will have to enter this number and will wish to periodically check how many pieces have been cut. A count display such as the 7-segment display introduced in Chapter 7 would be a reasonable choice. But the designers, concerned about possible machine failures, look one step beyond the count display requirements. Suppose that the saw jammed or the material overshot the cutoff length detector, or the guard came ajar. It would be essential to display a message which would alert the operator. It would also be useful to

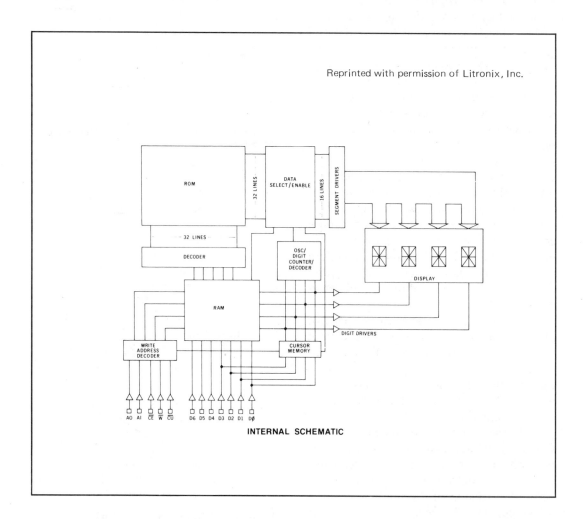

Reprinted with permission of Litronix, Inc.

Figure 9.10: Low Processor Overhead Alphanumeric Display

implement machine diagnostics so that the operator could test the limit switches, and diagnose an internal fault, or help with normal operation. The microprocessor can provide numerical prompts which the user can look up in a manual, or it can access an *alphanumeric display* to produce the message directly. (We use the term display to refer to single character or several character devices, not to cathode ray tubes, which are larger, multi-line devices.) The designers chose an alphanumeric display.

Alphanumeric displays have had a history of being prohibitively expensive for small systems. But volume production has brought the prices of several display types down to a level that is reasonable for most instrumentation and control applications. Regardless of the display technology used, a series of segments must be specified to represent the character. In Chapter 7, we showed how either a decoder integrated circuit or a memory-based table could be used to select the pattern of segments which represent a number. Alphanumeric displays may be approached the same way.

A recent trend has been toward alphanumeric displays which contain a dedicated integrated circuit designed to free the processor from all but the most basic I/O operation. The block diagram of one display shown in Figure 9.10 contains a writable memory into which the processor places an ASCII character. The character's address corresponds to its position in the display. The integrated circuit refreshes the displays by decoding the ASCII characters stored in the memory and energizing the individual segments. By performing such a complex function, the integrated circuit keeps the part count—a rough measure of probable reliability and cost—to a bare minimum.

Operator Input Devices. The designers have now specified all the hardware which

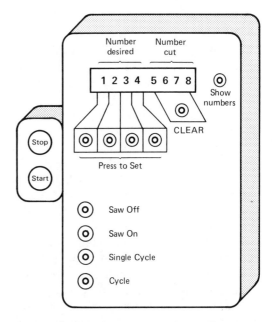

Figure 9.11: Designer's Front Panel Sketch of Cutting Machine

the microprocessor will use to interact with the outside world except for the operator input devices. The configuration of the operator controls in a sense determines the personality of the machine and the likelihood that it will be a tool, not an adversary. The microprocessor possesses an immense degree of flexibility with respect to the form of operator input which may be used. Designers may employ toggle switches, push buttons, keypads, thumbwheels, potentiometers, joysticks, or even tracker balls. One switch or button may act to change the function of other buttons, thus reducing both the number of controls which an operator must deal with and reducing the number of I/O ports required.

In consultation with operations personnel, the designers begin sketching some possible front panel configurations. They consider first a *menu selection* scheme, a

CRT display of a list of options or blanks with a movable arrow pointing to a member of the list. Menu selection has been applied with dramatic success to devices with reputations for being difficult to operate, such as logic state analyzers. The staff decides, however, that it is unnecessarily complicated for their machine.

They think next about a keypad, because it permits numeric values to be entered rapidly, but they decide that such a grouping of buttons might be too intimidating. Instead, they opt for the simple graphic front panel shown in Figure 9.11. The appendage at the left is included to meet the electrical code of the city in which the controller will operate. (Note that the design in Figure 9.11 is not presented as endorsed by any code.) The stop and start buttons connect to a standard motor starter which removes all AC power from the machine. This configuration helps to isolate the noise associated with the AC line from the logic level signals of the microprocessor inside the controller enclosure.

Operation Simulation

The cutting machine is now well defined, but, before committing themselves to fabricating a full-scale mechanism and selecting the microprocessor, the designers wish to convince themselves that they have defined all the controller inputs and outputs and that their algorithm will, in fact, sequence the cutter. They decide to spend a few hours building a small model which will have all the important characteristics of the full-scale device.

A vital element of the simulation process is determining what constitutes an appropriate simplification of the system. The designers decide that small DC motors like those introduced in Chapter 2 will represent the AC motors of the cutting machine. They feel that the dynamic characteristics of the limit sensors are very important and procure the actual photo-diode/photo-transistor pair which they intend to use in the production version of the machine. They use a simple switch to represent the operator guard. Instead of wiring all the pushbuttons, they assign a keyboard key to each button. The ASCII character S will represent saw-on, O will stand for saw-off, etc..

Figure 9.12 depicts the simple model. Gear trains have been used to reduce the speed of the little DC motors and thereby better approximate the dynamic behavior of the cutter. Since the sawing operation has already been tested on a full-scale apparatus, this model merely pokes a metal strip through the photo detector. An electrical breadboard amplifies the low-level photo-transistor output and introduces hysteresis to reduce noise when the light beam is occluded.

The designers fire up their model, and it operates! It behaves erratically at first, but smooths out as soon as they debounce the home limit switch in the software. Their success boosts their confidence and bodes well for organizational politics. A functioning model vividly conveys what is otherwise cloaked in technical jargon. It *will* work.

FINAL STAGES: THE DEDICATED CONTROLLER

A Single Board Computer

While the machine shop is fabricating the cutting machine, the designers must either select or build a small microprocessor which will carry out the functions of their expensive laboratory computer. *Single board computers,* or printed circuit boards which contain most of the elements of a computer system, are built either for general purpose

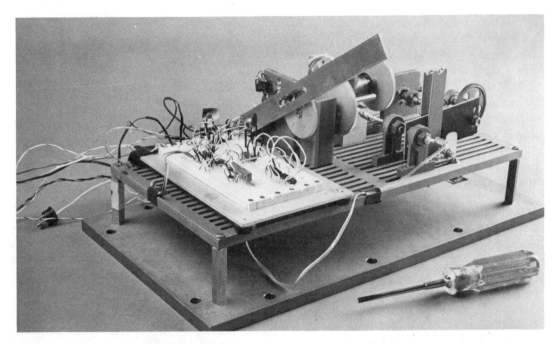

Figure 9.12: The Cutting Machine Model

use or to meet specific needs. End users, for example, may collect a well-defined group of integrated circuits to perform a specific control task. For example, an automobile manufacturer could design a single board skid-control computer which contains a processor, ROM, RAM, and timers on one integrated circuit, an analog-to-digital converter to measure brake line pressure, parallel input ports to detect axle and wheel rotation, and a digital output port to relieve brake line pressure. A personal computer manufacturer, on the other hand, might design a single card computer to provide serial communication with a console, a disk drive controller, and an interface with other printed circuit boards which perform specific functions. For example, the manufacturer might want a single card computer containing a CPU and 16 Kbytes of RAM to communicate with a board contain-

ing additional RAM or with one that includes an A/D converter.

Figure 9.13 is a schematic of a single board computer—an 8080A system—capable of performing all the functions the designers have specified for their cutting machine. Although more modern processors are available, we have chosen to describe an 8080A system because its circuitry illustrates particularly well how the various components of a single board system interrelate. Each rectangle in the figure is an integrated circuit package with pin numbers as shown. All power signals appear at the top of the rectangles, all inputs at the left, and all outputs at the right. For clarity, we show the data bus (the collection of data lines) compressed into one line, and we have not drawn the address bus. Signal names terminated by a slash (/) or written under a bar are true when at a *low* voltage.

The clock divider/driver (8224) generates the microprocessor clock by dividing the 18.000 MHz crystal to produce a two phase clock signal with a frequency of 2.00 MHz. It also handles system reset on power up or external reset. The RC circuit supplying the RESIN/ input is designed to introduce a delay until power supply signals have stabilized. The clock generator also produces a synchronizing signal STSTB/ specifically designed to allow the system controller chip (8228) to maintain synchrony with the 8080A. The 8228 controller interprets information from the microprocessor's data bus and generates the memory and I/O read/write signals which control ROM, RAM, and parallel I/O circuits.

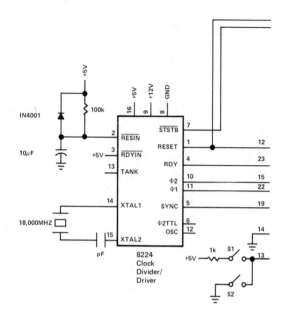

In the simple system of Figure 9.13, the only task the designer must perform besides connecting the standard chip set is to *decode* the combinations of control and address signals to enable memory and I/O chips at the proper time. For example, one parallel output port (8212) is selected if address line A6 is true (high) and I/O write (IOWR/) is true (low). If an output instruction which specifies an address of 40_{16} is executed, the 8212 will respond. In fact, the 8212 will respond to all 128 output instructions which specify an address with bit A6 set to true. This address-mapping method wastes I/O address space, but the waste is not significant, since only two I/O devices exist in the entire computer. In a similar manner, the select line of the bidirectional I/O port (8255) becomes true (low) if address bit A5 is high AND I/O read OR I/O write is true. The inputs RD/, WR/, A0, and A1 allow the 8255 to decode and respond to I/O read or write instructions to ports 20_{16}, 21_{16}, 22_{16}, and 23_{16} (as well as all others with address bits 0,1, and 5 set).

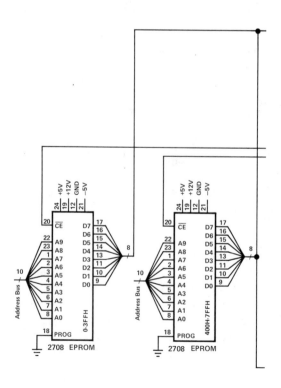

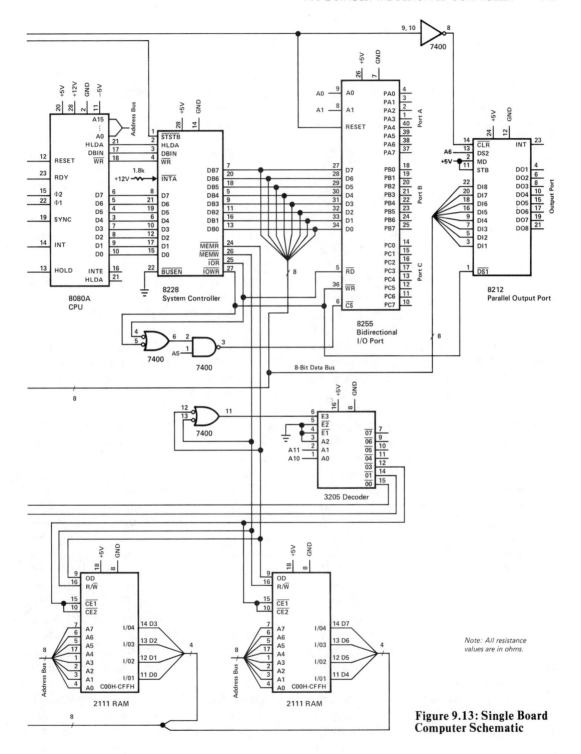

Figure 9.13: Single Board Computer Schematic

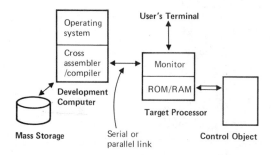

Figure 9.14: Down-loading Development System

A decoder (3205) maps the memory. The 3205 will make one of its outputs true (low) if two enable intputs (E1/ and E2/) are low and one is high (E3). The decoder inputs (A0, A1, or A2) determine which output will be true (low). In Figure 9.13, the 3205 is enabled when either memory read (MEMR/) or memory write (MEMW/) is true (low). The outputs of the 3205 decoder connect to the chip enable (CE/) inputs of the ROM or RAM chips. The EPROMs (2708) need no other enables to function, but the RAMs must know whether a read or write is to be performed. Since the two 2111 RAMs are 256-bit by 4-bit memories, two parallel chips produce byte-wide storage. The memory read and write signals (MEMR/ and MEMW/) enable the RAM output (via output disable, OD) and determine when read or write cycles occur.

A single 7400 (four NAND gates) provides the logic functions to select the memory integrated circuits (memory read OR memory write), select the 8255 parallel input/output device (I/O read or write AND address bit A5 true), and invert one reset signal for the 8212.

Since the designers have limited time and minimal production needs, they elect to buy a single board computer with the ROM,

RAM, I/O ports and other features they need, rather than build one.

Microprocessor Development Systems

With their single board computer now in hand, the designers could theoretically fabricate the front panel, place their program in programmable read only memory (PROM), plug in the PROMs, and turn everything on. But the probability is exceedingly high that the system would not function and that it would be very difficult to determine what their black box was doing. Instead, they will use a *microprocessor development system* connected to the processor which will actually operate in the controller. Among the systems they can use are two which we describe below.

Downloading Development System. Downloading is a method of program development which does not require that the development system and target processor be similar in any respect. Figure 9.14 is a block diagram of a downloading development system. The target processor must have two I/O ports dedicated to the development process; it must contain a simple monitor and small development program in ROM; and it must have enough RAM to store the program. These needs add to the cost of implementing the downloading approach. The user employs a monitor to execute a small download program which provides access to the development computer. The downloading program relays information between the user's terminal and the development computer. Inside the development computer, an operating system, file structure, text editor, and development programs are at the user's disposal. One of the development programs is a *cross assembler* or *cross compiler*. Cross assemblers and cross compilers are programs which generate object code for a computer with a *different* instruction set. The host processor *downloads,* or transmits, the output of the cross assembler or cross compiler to the target processor, where it is loaded into the target processor's RAM memory. Before the target computer executes this program, its monitor generally gives control of the target processor back to the user, who can install breakpoints, initialize registers, or perform any other monitor functions before running the program. When the user wants to modify the program, he or she can return to the relay mode, edit the source listing in the development computer, and start the process again. The entire process can be performed in well under a minute with moderate sized programs and a fast development computer.

Bus-interconnected Development System. Before we describe the second microprocessor development system—a bus-interconnected system—we must explore the rudiments of the structure called a *bus.* When one plugs a circuit

breaker into a breaker panel, the power supply device contacted is usually a bus bar. In a computer system, the bus provides information rather than power. In its most common implementation, a bus has only one sender at a time, but it may have many receivers. A *control bus,* which consists of a set of conductors, enforces a *protocol* which permits various devices to request and be granted use of the bus.

Figure 9.15 is an example of a simple bus structure. Attached to the bus is a bus controller (perhaps a CPU). A maximum of four *reading devices* and four *writing devices* are attached to each conductor of the bus, since there are only two address conductors for four combinations $(2^2=4)$. The devices may either be three bit memory words or three-bit parallel ports. In this figure, the controller is the only device permitted to drive the two-bit address bus or the one-bit control bus. The controller may drive or sense the data bus. For simplicity, each device may *either* drive or sense the data bus. Table 9.1 lists two typical *bus trans-*

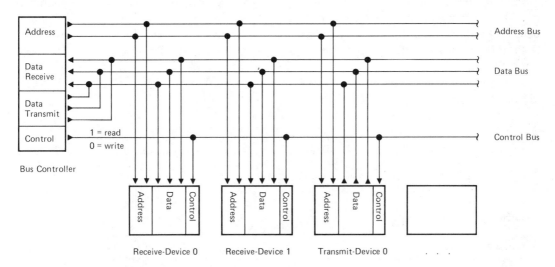

Figure 9.15: A Simple Bus Designed to Allow a Controller to Read from or Write to a Maximum of Four Devices

actions. In the first, the controller drives the address bus with the value 01B=1, indicating its desire to communicate with either Read Device One or Write Device One. The ambiguity is resolved when it drives the control bus with a 1 to signify that it wishes to read the value held by Device One. Device One senses the bus state "recognizes" through a Boolean solution to the combinations, and "responds" by driving the data bus with its value. The second transaction of Table 9.1 is a write operation.

In a properly designed system, devices connected by a set of buses can resolve their role in the activity of the system by sensing the state of the bus. As long as one is careful, one need not require that buses of one computer be separate from the buses of a second computer.

To construct a bus-interconnection development system, one connects the address and data buses and selected control lines of the target and development system computers (taking care, of course, to consider the hardware consequences of modifying speed-critical computer components). To avoid having the two CPUs compete for the same bus, a simple approach is to disable the target CPU by placing it in a hold state.

Interconnecting buses makes it possible for a program running in the develop-ment system to access I/O devices in the target processor system. Unlike the downloading system in which we added two I/O ports and additional ROM and RAM, the only hardware price associated with the bus interconnect system is that of providing a connection for appropriate bus lines. The bus-interconnection method is, therefore, quite attractive for simple, low cost systems. So-called *in-circuit emulation devices* operate on a principle similar to the bus-interconnection method. They are somewhat more flexible vis-a-vis processor architecture, but quite expensive.

To avoid damaging system components when connecting two processors, there must be no conflict in input port addresses. Another requirement for direct connection of buses may be that the target and the host processors run at the same speed. For example, if one writes a timed loop delay routine (e.g., load a register and count it to zero) for an 8 MHz development system, and then places the program in ROM to be used by a 2 MHz target processor, the resulting delay will be longer by a factor of four (assuming no other hardware ramifications). Finally, one must consider the interrupt response of the development system, since many control programs cannot effectively run without an interrupt structure.

	State of the Bus						Implication	Device Response
	control	data 2	data 1	data 0	address 1	address 2		
Transaction 1	1	0	1	0	0	1	Controller desires to read the value held by device 1	Device 1 transmits (drives) data bus with its value (010 = 2) as long as control is 1 (read)
Transaction 2	0	1	0	1	1	0	Controller desires to write the value (101 = 5) to device 2	Device 2 accepts the value (101 = 5) by sensing the data bus

Table 9.1: Two Transactions on the Bus Depicted in Figure 9.15

Since a bus-interconnect system facilitates using a simple single board computer, such as the one the designers have selected for the cutting machine, they will use this system in the final stage of their design process.

The Emulation Process

The cutting machine arrives from the machine shop, and the designers connect it to the development system and target processor. Beginning with a program they used to exercise the model cutter, they operate the real cutting machine and then use small, individual test programs to test the operation of the push buttons, display, limit switches, and actuators.

Once the controller operates properly, they ask those who will be using it to operate the machine and critique its performance. This vital interaction resolves any operator misunderstandings and assists the designers in making software changes.

As their last step, they program the read-only memories in the single board computer and launch it into independent operation. The microprocessor-based cutting machine is ready for production.

APPENDICES

The appendices contain programs which implement the designs presented in the case studies. They also include discussions of instruction sets and other machine-specific characteristics that have been utilized in writing the programs. Each section of the appendix contains all of the material related to a particular computer family.

In order to provide a case study that can be solved without any prior knowledge of machine or assembly language, we present the DC motor control problem in BASIC, Pascal, FORTRAN, and C. We provide only one sample version of each of these languages, because they vary only slightly from one computer to another and can be modified as needed.

Machine language, processor architecture, and instruction sets are introduced with the stepping motor programs and are further developed with the temperature and blending control systems. The discussion of the instruction sets is intended to complement the material found in processor or assembly language manuals for specific computers.

Interrupts are first discussed in connection with the blending control programs and are used in all subsequent programs. Interrupt procedures relevant to each of the specific computers and programming techniques to make use of interrupts are described in detail.

The automated weighing system and polar plotter programs use a mixture of high-level and assembly language. Since the limitations of the high-level languages generally determine how much assembly language coding is needed, the aim in these cases is to minimize the amount of assembly language without compromising the system's functional goals. The manner in which assembly and high-level languages are linked depends on the particular compiler or interpreters being used. The examples presented illustrate a variety of common linking techniques. No programs in BASIC are presented for these systems, because most BASICs do not have a fast enough computing speed.

APPENDIX A—8080/8085/Z80

DC MOTOR CONTROL PROGRAMS IN BASIC
A1   Time-Telling Program in BASIC
A2   Velocity Test Program in BASIC
A3   Motor Test Program in BASIC

DC MOTOR CONTROL PROGRAMS IN PASCAL
A4   Time-Telling Program in Pascal
A5   Velocity Test Program in Pascal
A6   Motor Test Program in Pascal

DC MOTOR CONTROL PROGRAMS IN C
A7   Time-Telling Program in C
A8   Velocity Test Program in C
A9   Motor Test Program in C

STEPPING MOTOR PROGRAMS
A10   Instructions to Turn On Output Bit
A11   Program with Hexadecimal Codes
A12   Using a Debugging Aid to Enter and Run a Program
A13   Timed Loop Program Using a Memory Location and a Register
A14   Timed Loop Program Using Two Registers
A15   Pulse Train Program
A16   Move-Wait-Return Program Using Delay Loop
A17   Test Program for External Clock Timing
A18   Move-Wait-Return Program Using an External Clock

TEMPERATURE CONTROL PROGRAMS
A19   Read Keyboard and Echo
A20   Print a Character
A21   Shifted Echo Program
A22   Multiply Subroutine and Test Program
A23   D/A Test Program
A24   A/D Test Program
A25   Divide Subroutine and Test Program
A26   A/D Calibration Program
A27   Temperature Control Program

BLENDING CONTROL PROGRAMS
A28   Clock Interrupt Test Program
A29   Terminal Input Interrupt Test Program
A30   Terminal Output Interrupt Test Program
A31   Blending Program

DC MOTOR CONTROL PROGRAMS IN BASIC

The BASIC version of the Time-Telling program is given in Listing A1. The four states for this program are defined by BASIC statement (line) numbers and identified in the listings with REMark statements giving the states' names. Transitions from one state to another are accomplished with GOTO statements. The version of BASIC used here is CBASIC (Software Systems, Inc., Vallejo, CA), but the coding has been kept as much as possible to standard BASIC. CBASIC runs on 8080, 8085, or Z80 systems under the CP/M operating system.

The digital input/output port is accessed through the built-in functions IN and OUT, which take the port identification number as input, and either read or write the port. The bits on the input and output ports are masked by use of the operators AND and OR, which do bit by bit logical operations on their operands.

In the velocity-test program, Listing A2, the program must generate an output to clear the latch and then reset it. Since that is the only bit in use on the output port, it is not necessary to perform any masking operations to manipulate it. Although the conceptual diagrams show a high signal to clear the latch, in the actual system a low signal performs the clear operation. (This is a common occurrence in logic system design. In the system conceptualization *high* is associated with a positive action of some sort. When the system hardware is actually designed and built, however, the realities of hardware constraints, plus other considerations such as safety, often dictate the use of the opposite logic.)

The motor-test program, Listing A3, uses the output port to control the motor (on/off) and to clear the latch. The variable ISTAT is used to keep track of the current values of the output port's bits so that the appropriate masking operations can be performed to change only one bit at a time. To simplify use of this program, the user inputs have been expressed in engineering units rather than in the pulse count units used in the time and velocity-test programs.

Because BASIC programs are usually executed line-by-line by an *interpreter,* they generally run much slower than similarly complex compiled programs. These speed differences can be crucial to successful implementation of real-time programs and can limit the performance of the BASIC motor test programs compared to that of compiler-based languages.

A1   Time-Telling Program in BASIC

```
10 REM TIME TELLING PROGRAM
40 REM STATE INITIAL
50 INPUT "NUMBER OF TICKS TO ELAPSE BEFORE REPORT?";NTR
60 ICLOK1=NTR
70 GOTO 200
80 REM 200=STATE TICK DETECT
90 REM END STATE INITIAL
100 REM **********
110 REM STATE TICK DETECT
200 IF (INP(16) AND 2) NE 0 THEN GOTO 200
250 IF (INP(16) AND 2) EQ 0 THEN GOTO 250
260 REM TO HERE => RISING EDGE OF CLOCK DETECTED
270 GOTO 300
280 REM 300 = STATE CLOCK UPDATE
285 REM END STATE TICK DETECT
290 REM **********
```

```
295 REM STATE CLOCK UPDATE
300 ICLOK1=ICLOK1-1
310 IF ICLOK1 GT 0 THEN GOTO 200
320 REM 200 = STATE TICK DETECT
330 GOTO 400
340 REM 400 = STATE REPORT
350 REM END STATE CLOCK UPDATE
360 REM **********
370 REM STATE REPORT
400 PRINT "TIME IS UP"
410 GOTO 50
420 REM 50 = STATE INITIAL
430 REM END STATE REPORT
440 REM END OF PROGRAM
```

A2   Velocity Test Program in BASIC

```
10 REM PROGRAM VELTES
11 REM THIS PROGRAM IS THE VELOCITY TEST PROGRAM
12 REM (SECOND EXAMPLE PROGRAM OF CHAPTER 3).
13 REM THE USER IS ASKED FOR TWO VALUES: FIRST, THE
14 REM LENGTH OF THE TEST, CLOCK1 (IN TICKS OF THE CLOCK)
15 REM AND SECOND, THE SAMPLING INTERVAL TO RESET VARIABLE
16 REM CLOCKV (ALSO IN TICKS).
17 REM AT EXPIRATION OF CLOCK1, LAST COMPLETE TACHOMETER
18 REM PULSE COUNT IS PRINTED.
19 REM
40 MASKTK=1
45 MASKCK=2
46 REM MASKS FOR TACHOMETER AND CLOCKS
47 REM **********
48 REM STATE INITIAL
50 INPUT "LENGTH OF THE TEST (IN TICKS)?";ICLOK1
60 INPUT "LENGTH OF SAMPLING INTERVAL (TICKS)?";LENSAM
70 ICLOCKV=LENSAM
80 NUMPLS=0
90 LSTPLS=0
100 OUT 17,2
105 REM RESET TACHOMETER LATCH (TRUE LOW).
110 GOTO 200
120 REM 200 = STATE TICK DETECT
130 REM END STATE INITIAL
140 REM **********
150 REM STATE TICK DETECT
200 IF (INP(16) AND MASKCK) NE 0 THEN GOTO 200
250 IF (INP(16) AND MASKCK) EQ 0 THEN GOTO 250
260 REM TO HERE => RISING EDGE OF CLOCK DETECTED
270 GOTO 300
280 REM 300 = STATE CLOCK UPDATE
290 REM END STATE TICK DETECT
295 REM **********
296 REM STATE CLOCK UPDATE
300 ICLOK1=ICLOK1-1
310 ICLOKV=ICLOKV-1
320 IF ICLOKV GT 0 THEN GOTO 325
321 ICLOKV=LENSAM
322 GOTO 400
323 REM 400 = STATE SAMPLE
325 IF ICLOK1 GT 0 THEN GOTO 500
330 REM 500 = STATE VELOCITY
340 GOTO 600
350 REM 600 = STATE TIMEOUT
360 REM END STATE CLOCK UPDATE
370 **********
380 REM STATE SAMPLE
```

```
400 LSTPLS=NUMPLS
410 NUMPLS=0
420 GOTO 500
430 REM 500 = STATE VELOCITY
440 REM END STATE SAMPLE
450 REM *********
460 REM STATE VELOCITY
500 IF (INP(16) AND MASKTK) EQ 0 THEN GOTO 200
510 REM 200 = STATE TICK DETECT
520 NUMPLS=NUMPLS+1
530 OUT 17,0
540 OUT 17,2
550 REM BIT 1 (BINARY 10) IS TACHOMETER LATCH CLEAR (0 => TRUE)
560 GOTO 200
570 REM 200 = STATE TICK DETECT
580 REM END STATE VELOCITY
590 REM *********
595 REM STATE TIMEOUT
600 PRINT "LAST VELOCITY= ";LSTPLS
610 GOTO 50
620 REM 50 = STATE INITIAL
630 REM END STATE TIMEOUT
640 REM END OF PROGRAM
```

A3   Motor Test Program in BASIC

```
10 REM PROGRAM MOTEST
11 REM THIS PROGRAM IS THE MOTOR TEST PROGRAM
12 REM (THIRD EXAMPLE PROGRAM OF CHAPTER 3).
13 REM THE USER IS ASKED FOR FIVE VALUES:
14 REM 1) CLOCK RATE IN HZ, 2) LENGTH OF TEST IN SECONDS,
15 REM 3) VELOCITY SAMPLE INTERVAL (SECONDS), 4) MOTOR
16 REM ACTUATION PULSE FREQUENCY, 5) MOTOR ACTUATION PULSE
17 REM DUTY CYCLE (IN PERCENT).
18 REM THE MOTOR STARTS AND RUNS AT SPEED DETERMINED
19 REM BY ACTUATION PULSE TRAIN.  VELOCITY IS SAMPLED.
20 REM AT END OF TEST, LAST VELOCITY IS PRINTED (IN RPM
21 REM ASSUMING TWO TACHOMETER PULSES PER REVOLUTION).
22 REM MOTOR THEN STOPS.
23 REM
38 TRUE=-1
39 FALSE=0
40 MASKCK=2
41 MASKTK=1
42 MSKCL1=1
43 MSKCL2=2
44 REM PROGRAM STATE INITIALIZATION
45 START=TRUE
46 REM START <-- TRUE
47 REM END PROGRAM STATE INITIALIZATION
48 REM *********
49 REM STATE MOTOR OFF
50 OUT 17,3
60 ISTAT=1
65 REM STORED VALUE ISTAT IS CURRENT STATE OF MOTOR (1=> OFF)
70 REM MOTOR OFF, TACHOMETER PULSE LATCH CLEAR <-- FALSE
75 REM LATCH CLEAR IS TRUE LOW
76 IF START EQ TRUE THEN GOTO 100
77 REM 100 = STATE INITIAL
80 IF ICLOKV GT 0 THEN GOTO 500
85 REM 500 = STATE VELOCITY
90 GOTO 400
91 REM 400 = STATE SAMPLE
92 REM END STATE MOTOR OFF
93 REM *********
```

```
94 REM STATE INITIAL
100 INPUT "CLOCK FREQUENCY (HZ)?";ICLKRT
110 INPUT "LENGTH OF TEST (SEC)?";LENTST
120 INPUT "VELOCITY SAMPLE INTERVAL (SEC)?";INTVEL
130 INPUT "MOTOR ACTUATION PULSE FREQUENCY (HZ)?";IFREQ
140 INPUT "MOTOR ACTUATION PULSE DUTY CYCLE (%)?";IDUTY
150 REM NOW, COMPUTE CLOCK VALUES.
155 ICLOK1=LENTST*ICLKRT
160 ICLKV1=INTVEL*ICLKRT
165 IPLST1=ICLKRT/IFREQ
170 ITMON1=(IPLST1*IDUTY)/100
171 REM
175 ICLOKV=ICLKV1
180 ITIMON=ITMON1
185 IPLSTM=IPLST1
190 START=FALSE
195 GOTO 200
196 REM 200 = STATE TICK DETECT
197 REM END STATE INITIAL
198 **********
199 REM STATE TICK DETECT
200 IF(INP(16) AND MASKCK) NE 0 THEN GOTO 200
250 IF(INP(16) AND MASKCK) EQ 0 THEN GOTO 250
260 REM TO HERE => RISING EDGE OF CLOCK DETECTED
270 GOTO 300
275 REM 300 = STATE CLOCK UPDATE
280 REM END STATE TICK DETECT
285 REM **********
290 REM STATE CLOCK UPDATE
300 ICLOK1=ICLOK1-1
310 ICLOKV=ICLOKV-1
320 ITIMON=ITIMON-1
330 IPLSTM=IPLSTM-1
340 IF ICLOK1 LE 0 THEN GOTO 600
350 REM 600 = STATE TIME-OUT
360 IF ITIMON GT 0 THEN GOTO 700
370 REM 700 = STATE MOTOR ON
375 IF IPLSTM GT 0 THEN GOTO 50
380 REM 50 = STATE MOTOR OFF
385 IPLSTM=IPLST1
386 ITIMON=ITMON1
390 GOTO 700
391 REM 700 = STATE MOTOR ON
395 REM END STATE CLOCK UPDATE
396 REM **********
397 REM STATE SAMPLE
400 LSTPLS=NUMPLS
410 NUMPLS=0
420 ICLOKV=ICLKV1
430 GOTO 500
440 REM 500 = STATE VELOCITY
450 REM END STATE SAMPLE
460 REM **********
470 REM STATE VELOCITY
500 IF (INP(16) AND MASKTK) EQ 0 THEN GOTO 200
510 REM 200 = STATE TICK DETECT
520 NUMPLS=NUMPLS+1
530 OUT 17,(ISTAT AND MSKCL1)
540 OUT 17,(ISTAT OR MSKCL2)
550 REM ABOVE CLEARS TACHOMETER LATCH
560 GOTO 200
570 REM 200 = STATE TICK DETECT
580 REM END STATE VELOCITY
590 REM **********
595 REM STATE TIME-OUT
600 PRINT "LAST VELOCITY (RPM)= ";((LSTPLS*30)/INTVEL)
```

```
610 START=TRUE
620 GOTO 50
630 REM 50 = STATE MOTOR OFF
640 REM END STATE TIME-OUT
650 REM **********
660 REM STATE MOTOR ON
700 OUT 17,2
710 REM TURN MOTOR ON
720 ISTAT=0
730 REM STORED VARIABLE IS CURRENT STATE OF MOTOR (1 => OFF).
740 IF ICLOKV LE 0 THEN GOTO 400
750 REM 400 = STATE SAMPLE
760 GOTO 500
770 REM 500 = STATE VELOCITY
780 REM END STATE MOTOR ON
790 REM END OF PROGRAM
```

DC MOTOR CONTROL PROGRAMS IN PASCAL

The Pascal version of the time-telling program appears in Listing A4. The four states in Figure 3.7 are defined by numbered statement labels and set off by comments. The correspondance of state names and numbers is given at the beginning of the program. Transitions are implemented in the Pascal program by GOTO's. All internal program variables are of type integer, and all are global to the entire program.

The transition diagram logic can also be structured by using the "case" structure of Pascal; instead of actually performing a transition to the next state with a GOTO, a variable can be set to indicate the next state and control, then returned to the beginning of the case from which the transfer to the next state module is made. This construct could be used with Pascals that do not support statement labels or GOTO's. It is also a convenient construct for debugging, as it is easy to print the previous state and next state each time a transition occurs. It does require more overhead than the direct transition, however.

The digital input/output port must be accessed through a library function. In the programs given here, that function is named *ptin* (for port-in). It takes the port identification number as an argument, and returns the value read from that port as an integer. The digital input port must be wired so that all unused inputs appear as zeros when read by the Pascal program. In this way, the value returned can be tested for zero/non-zero to detect the clock pulse.

The program shown was run on a Z80 system and compiled using the Pascal/Z compiler of Ithaca Intersystems, Inc. The function ptin (and ptout, which is used later) was added.

The velocity test program appears in Listing A5. In this program, it is necessary to distinguish individual bits on the input port to separate the clock pulse signal from the tachometer signal. Masking operations were described in the text to accomplish this, but standard Pascal does not include any masking operators or functions.

Although special functions could have been added to the library in assembly language, our goal is to write these programs in standard Pascal. Therefore, we wrote a Pascal function named btest (for bit-test), which takes a different approach. Its arguments are the input word to be tested and an integer that specifies the number of the bit to be tested (using the convention that the bits are numbered from right to left, starting with 0).

The function returns a Boolean value which is true if the bit were 1 and false if it were a 0. It works by using the property of binary arithmetic that division by 2 is equivalent to moving all of the bits one position to the right (this is actually true in any base — division by the radix moves the entire number one position to the right). The division is carried out n times, where n is the number of the bit to be tested (if n is zero, no divisions are done). This has the effect of moving the bit in question to position zero. The standard Pascal function *odd* can then be used to test that bit.

In the velocity test, an output must be generated to clear the latch. Since only one bit of the output port is being used, it is not necessary to mask the other bits. The tachometer latch was assigned to bit number 1 of the digital output port, so sending out a 2 sets that bit, and sending out a 0 clears it.

Although the conceptual diagrams show a high signal to clear the latch, in the actual system a low signal performs the clear operation. (This is a common occurrence in logic system design. In the system conceptualization, high is associated with a positive action of some sort. When the system hardware is actually built, however, the realities of hardware constraints, plus other considerations such as safety, sometimes dictate the use of the opposite logic.) The latch is cleared and rearmed by sending a 0 followed by a 2. The actual output is done with the function ptout, which takes the port identification number and value to be sent out as arguments.

The third program is the motor control and test program corresponding to the transition diagram of Figure 3.20. Two new functions, bset (bit-set) and bclear (bit-

clear), are introduced to allow setting or clearing of individual bits on the output port. Also, the program's inputs and outputs have been expressed in engineering units to make the program easier to use. For convenience in the unit conversions, some floating point (real) calculations have been used. Since these are very much slower than integer calculations, their use is restricted to portions of the program where computing speed is not critical.

To control the digital output port, we have defined a Pascal integer variable named mostate. Its value is always the same as the current output of the port. To set a particular bit on the output port, that bit is first set in mostate, using the bset function, and then sent out using the ptout function. An output bit is cleared in a similar manner.

The functions bset and bclear are just dummies that call another function, bsc, which does all the work. Bsc has three main parts. First, it uses btest to find out if the bit in question already has the desired value. If it does, bsc returns. If the bit must be changed, bsc tests to see whether the bit to be changed is the leftmost bit of the word (the constant intsize can be changed if the function is to be used on a different computing system). This is a special case because most computer systems use a convention called *two's complement* for signed integers. Attempting to manipulate the left bit in such systems will cause overflows, which may get flagged as computational errors. Finally, for any other bits, bsc constructs a number that has a 1 bit in the desired position by repeated multiplications of 1 times 2. That number is either added (to set) or subtracted (to clear) from the original number.

A4   Time-Telling Program in Pascal

```
(* Time-Telling program. Counts ticks from an external clock.
Implements the transition diagram of Fig. 3.7.  *)
PROGRAM TIME;
LABEL 100,200,300,400;   (* Statement labels *)

CONST
        inport = 120;    (* identifier for digital input port,
                            120D = 78H  *)
        incntrl = 121;          (* control port to configure input *)
        incnword = 79;          (* control word for input port set-up,4FH *)

TYPE BYTE = 0..255;

VAR
        clockl : INTEGER;       (* tick counter *)

(* State Definitions:
        100 Initial
        200 Tick Detect
        300 Clock Update
        400 Report
*)

PROCEDURE out(outp,val : INTEGER); EXTERNAL;

PROCEDURE digset;
(* This procedure does whatever set-up is necessary to use the digital
I/O port.  *)
BEGIN
        out(incntrl,incnword);
END;

PROCEDURE inp(port : BYTE; VAR value : BYTE); EXTERNAL;

FUNCTION ptin (inpt : BYTE) : INTEGER;
VAR
        x :INTEGER;
BEGIN
        inp(inpt,x);
        ptin := x;
END;
BEGIN
(* Initial *)
100:    writeln(' Number of ticks?');
        readln(clockl);
        GOTO 200;               (* transition to Tick Detect *)

(* Tick Detect *)
200:    WHILE   ptin(inport) <> 0 DO ;  (* The semi-colon delimits
                                        a null statement, so this statement
                                        will do nothing until a zero
                                        input is detected. *)
        WHILE ptin(inport) = 0 DO ;     (* Now wait for a nonzero *)
        GOTO 300;                       (* to Clock Update *)

(* Clock Update *)
300:    clockl := clockl - 1;           (* decrement the tick counter *)
        IF clockl > 0
                THEN GOTO 200           (* to Tick Detect *)
```

```
            ELSE GOTO 400;              (* to Report *)

(* Report *)
400:    writeln(' Time is up.');
        GOTO 100                        (* to Initial *)
END.
```

A5   Velocity Test Program in Pascal

```
PROGRAM VELTES;
(* VELTES measures the velocity of a motor by counting clock
pulses. The user is asked to supply two input values: 1) the
length of the test, (in units of clock ticks) and 2) the sampling
interval for measuring velocity (also in units of clock ticks).
  The program prints the last complete sample value on termination.
*)
(*$c-,m-,r-,s-      disable run-time error checking  *)
(* State Definitions:
        100   Initial
        200   Tick Detect
        300   Clock Update
        400 Sample
        500 Velocity
        600 Time-out
*)
LABEL 100,200,300,400,500,600;  (* statement labels *)
CONST
        inport = 120;    (* digital input port, 78H *)
        incnpt = 121;    (* input port control, 79H *)
        incnwd = 79;     (* control word for input port, 4FH*)
        outport = 122;   (* digital ouput port, 7AH *)
        outcnpt = 123;   (* output port control, 7BH *)
        outcnwd = 15;    (* control word for output port, 0FH *)
        clkbit = 0;      (* bit number for clock *)
        tkbit = 1;       (* bit number for tachometer *)
        lhigh =2;        (* latch output values for high and low *)
        llow = 0;
VAR
        clockl,clockv : INTEGER;        (* tick counters *)
        lensam : INTEGER;       (* sample time in ticks *)
        numpls : INTEGER;       (* tachometer pulse count *)
        lstpls : INTEGER;       (* most recent complete count *)

(* ptout is the routine to write to a Z-80 output port. *)
PROCEDURE ptout(outp, value :INTEGER )   ; EXTERNAL;

(* ptin reads a Z-80 input port *)
FUNCTION ptin(inp : INTEGER) : INTEGER; EXTERNAL;

FUNCTION btest(x,n : INTEGER) : BOOLEAN;
(* Tests bit n of word x. Returns TRUE for 1, FALSE for 0.
This version is written in standard Pascal and uses divisions by
two to move the bit in question to the rightmost position where the
function ODD can be used to test it.
 The bits are numbered from right-to-left, starting with zero.
 Much more efficient implementations can be written in either assembly
language, or by taking advantage of compiler-dependent features such
as using the SET structure's internal storage format.
*)
CONST
```

```
          bigneg = -32768;               (* largest negative number for this system --
                                         2's complement notation is assumed for signed
                                         numbers. *)
          intsiz = 16;                   (* number of bits used for integers *)
VAR
          i,y : INTEGER;
          neg : BOOLEAN;                 (* flag for negative numbers *)
BEGIN
          y := x;            (* copy input value so it won't be modified *)
          IF y = bigneg
                    THEN BEGIN
                              IF n = intsiz - 1 THEN btest := TRUE
                                                ELSE btest := FALSE;
                    END
          ELSE
          BEGIN
                    IF y < 0
                    THEN BEGIN
                              neg := TRUE;
                              y := -y - 1;
                          END
                    ELSE neg := FALSE;
          i := 0;           (* counter *)
          WHILE i < n DO
                    BEGIN
                              y := y DIV 2;
                              i := i + 1;
                          END;
          IF neg
                    THEN btest := NOT ODD(y)
                    ELSE btest := ODD(y);
          END
END;
BEGIN

(* Initial *)
100:      writeln(' length of test (in ticks)?');
          readln(clockl);
          writeln(' length of sampling interval (in ticks)?');
          readln(lensam);
          clockv := lensam;         (* initialize counters *)
          numpls := 0;
          lstpls := 0;
          ptout(incnpt,incnwd);     (* set up parallel ports for reading
                                       and writing *)
          ptout(outcnpt,outcnwd);
          ptout(outport,lhigh);             (* reset latch *)
          GOTO 200;                 (* to Tick Detect *)

(* Tick Detect *)
200:      WHILE btest(ptin(inport),clkbit) DO ;
                                          (* wait for zero *)
          WHILE NOT btest(ptin(inport),clkbit) DO ;       (* wait for nonzero*)
          GOTO 300;                 (* to Clock Update *)

(* Clock Update *)
300:      clockl := clockl - 1;     (* decrement tick counters *)
          clockv := clockv - 1;
          IF clockv <= 0
                    THEN BEGIN
                              clockv := lensam;         (* reset clock *)
```

```
                        GOTO 400                      (* to Sample *)
                    END;
            IF clock1 > 0 THEN GOTO 500;      (* to Velocity *)
            GOTO 600;                         (* to Time-Out *)
(* Sample *)
400:     lstpls := numpls;         (* update most recent value *)
         numpls := 0;
         GOTO 500;                 (* to Velocity *)


(* Velocity *)
500:     IF NOT btest(ptin(inport),tkbit) THEN GOTO 200;
                    (* to Tick Detect if no tach. signal is present *)
         numpls := numpls + 1;    (* incrment pulse counter *)
         ptout(outport,llow);     (* clear then re-arm latch *)
         ptout(outport,lhigh);
         GOTO 200;                 (* to Tick Detect *)

(* TIme-Out *)
600:     writeln(' last velocity = ',lstpls);
         GOTO 100;                 (* to Initial *)
END.
```

A6   Motor Test Program in Pascal

```
PROGRAM MOTEST;
(*$c-,m-,r-,s-      disable run-time error checking   *)
(* Motor test program - implements the transition diagram of
Fig.  3.20. The user is asked for six values:
         clock rate, Hz            (clkrate)
         length of test, sec       (lentest)
         velocity sample interval, sec    (samintvl)
         motor actuation pulse frequency, Hz      (pfreq)
         motor actuation duty cycle, %            (dcycle)
         number of tachometer pulses per revolution      (ntach)
The most recent motor velocity is printed at the end of the test.
*)
(* State Definitions:
         100 Initial
         200 Tick Detect
         300 Clock Update
         400 Sample
         500 Velocity
         600 Time-out
         700 Motor-On
         800 Motor-Off
*)
LABEL 100,200,300,400,500,600,700,800;  (* statement labels *)

CONST
         inport = 120;    (* digital input port, 78H *)
         incnpt = 121;    (* input port control, 79H *)
         incnwd = 79;     (* control word for input port, 4FH*)
         outport = 122;   (* digital ouput port, 7AH *)
         outcnpt = 123;   (* output port control, 7BH *)
         outcnwd = 15;    (* control word for output port, 0FH *)
         clkbit = 0;      (* bit number for clock *)
         tkbit = 1;       (* bit number for tachometer *)
         onoffbit = 0;    (* motor on/off control bit *)
         latchbit = 1;
VAR
         start : BOOLEAN;          (* indicates first time program is run *)
```

```
        mostate: INTEGER;           (* stored value indicating current values
                                       of motor control output bits *)
        clockv,clockl : INTEGER;        (* tick counters *)
        clockvl : INTEGER;          (* reset value for clockv *)
        ch : CHAR;
        clkrate,lentest,samintvl,pfreq,dcycle,ntach : INTEGER; (* Inputs *)
        cltimeon,timeon : INTEGER;      (* tick counter for pulse width
                                           modullation and its reset value *)
        clpulse,pulstime : INTEGER;     (* tick counter for motor pulse and
                                           its reset value *)
        lstpls,numpls : INTEGER;        (* most recent complete count and
                                           tach. pulse counter *)
        rpm : REAL;

(* ptout is the routine to write to a Z-80 output port. *)
PROCEDURE ptout(outp, value :INTEGER )  ; EXTERNAL;

(* ptin reads a Z-80 input port *)
FUNCTION ptin(inp : INTEGER) : INTEGER; EXTERNAL;

FUNCTION btest(x,n : INTEGER) : BOOLEAN;
(* Tests bit n of word x. Returns TRUE for 1, FALSE for 0.
This version is written in standard Pascal and uses divisions by
two to move the bit in question to the rightmost position where the
function ODD can be used to test it.
 The bits are numbered from right-to-left, starting with zero.
 Much more efficient implementations can be written in either assembly
language, or by taking advantage of compiler-dependent features such
as using the SET structure's internal storage format.
*)
CONST
        bigneg = -32768;            (* largest negative number for this system --
                                       2's complement notation is assumed for signed
                                       numbers. *)
        intsiz = 16;                (* number of bits used for integers *)
VAR
        i,y : INTEGER;
        neg : BOOLEAN;              (* flag for negative numbers *)
BEGIN
        y := x;             (* copy input value so it won't be modified *)
        IF y = bigneg
                THEN BEGIN
                        IF n = intsiz - 1 THEN btest := TRUE
                                          ELSE btest := FALSE;
                END
        ELSE
        BEGIN
                IF y < 0
                THEN BEGIN
                        neg := TRUE;
                        y := -y - 1;
                    END
                ELSE neg := FALSE;
        i := 0;             (* counter *)
        WHILE i < n DO
                BEGIN
                        y := y DIV 2;
                        i := i + 1;
                END;
        IF neg
                THEN btest := NOT ODD(y)
```

```
                        ELSE btest := ODD(y);
              END
END;
FUNCTION bsc(x,n : INTEGER; sc : BOOLEAN) : INTEGER;
(* bsc sets of clears bit n in x. Sets the bit if sc = TRUE.
It uses btest to find out if the bit in question already
has the desired value. If it doesn't, bsc sets up a data word with
a "1" in the correct position and adds (or subtracts) it from the original
word to set (clear) the bit.  This routine could be coded in assembly
language or use known internal formats such as SET'S to do this task
much more efficiently.  This version, however, should work with any
Pascal implementation for which signed arithmetic is done
using two's complement notation.
*)
CONST
        intsize = 16;    (* number of bits in type INTEGER *)
        bigpos = 32767; (* largest positive and negative numbers *)
        bigneg = -32768;

VAR
        f,i : INTEGER;
        bt : BOOLEAN;

BEGIN
        bt := btest(x,n);         (* is bit already at proper value? *)
        IF (bt AND sc) OR (NOT bt AND NOT sc)
                THEN bsc := x          (* bit is correct already *)
                ELSE BEGIN
                        IF n = intsize - 1     (* operating on the
                                        leftmost bit is a special case  *)
                        THEN BEGIN
                                IF x < 0
                                        THEN bsc := (x + bigpos) + 1
                                        ELSE bsc := x - bigpos - 1
                        END
                        ELSE BEGIN
                                f := 1;  (* f will have bit moved *)
                                i := 0;
                                WHILE i < n DO
                                        BEGIN
                                                f := f * 2;
                                                i := i + 1
                                        END;
                                IF sc
                                        THEN bsc := x + f
                                        ELSE bsc := x - f
                        END
                END;
END;

FUNCTION bset(x,n : INTEGER) : INTEGER;
(* Sets bit #n in x without disturbing other bits.  Bits are numbered
from right-to-left starting with zero.  Two's complement notation
is assumed for signed integers.
*)
BEGIN
        bset := bsc(x,n,TRUE)
END;

FUNCTION bclear(x,n : INTEGER) : INTEGER;
(* Clears bit #n ... otherwise the same as bset.  *)
```

```
BEGIN
        bclear := bsc(x,n,FALSE);
END;
BEGIN
        ptout(incnpt,incnwd);    (* set up parallel ports for reading
                                    and writing *)
        ptout(outcnpt,outcnwd);
        start := TRUE;  (* initialize state variables *)
        mostate := 0;
        GOTO 800;         (* to Motor-Off *)
(* Initial *)
100:    writeln('Use current data values (Y/N)?');
        readln(ch);
        IF (ch <> 'y') AND (ch <> 'Y') THEN
                BEGIN
                        writeln(' Clock Freq. (Hz)?');
                        readln(clkrate);
                        writeln(' Length of test (sec)?');
                        readln(lentest);
                        writeln(' Velocity sample interval (sec)?');
                        readln(samintvl);
                        writeln(' Motor actuation pulse frequency (Hz)?');
                        readln(pfreq);
                        writeln(' Motor actuation pulse duty cycle (%)?');
                        readln(dcycle);
                        writeln(' Number of tach. pulses per rev.?');
                        readln(ntach)
                END;
(* Compute clock reset values and initialize clocks *)
        clockl := lentest * clkrate;
        clockvl := samintvl * clkrate;
        pulstime := round(clkrate/pfreq);
        timeon := round((pulstime * dcycle)/100);

        clockv := clockvl;
        clpulse := pulstime;
        cltimeon := timeon;
        lstpls := 0;
        numpls := 0;
        start := FALSE;
        GOTO 200;         (* to Tick Detect *)

(* Tick Detect *)
200:    WHILE btest(ptin(inport),clkbit) DO ;   (* wait for zero *)
        WHILE NOT btest(ptin(inport),clkbit) DO ;      (* wait for nonzero*)
        GOTO 300;                (* to Clock Update *)
(* Clock Update *)
300:    clockl := clockl - 1;   (* decrement tick counters *)
        clockv := clockv - 1;
        cltimeon := cltimeon - 1;
        clpulse := clpulse - 1;

        IF clockl <= 0 THEN GOTO 600;   (* to Time-Out *)
        IF cltimeon >= 0 THEN GOTO 700; (* to Motor-On *)
        IF clpulse > 0 THEN GOTO 800;   (* to Motor-Off *)
        clpulse := pulstime;            (* reset pulse timer *)
        cltimeon := timeon;             (* reset time-on timer *)
        IF cltimeon = 0 THEN GOTO 800;  (* to Motor-Off *)
        GOTO 700;                       (* to Motor-On *)

(* Sample *)
```

```
400:     lstpls := numpls;        (* update most recent value *)
         numpls := 0;
         clockv := clockv1;       (* reset sample clock *)
         GOTO 500;                (* to Velocity *)

(* Velocity *)
500:     IF NOT btest(ptin(inport),tkbit) THEN GOTO 200;
                  (* to Tick Detect if no tach. signal is present *)
         numpls := numpls + 1;    (* incrment pulse counter *)
         mostate := bclear(mostate,latchbit);    (* clear and re-arm latch*)
         ptout(outport,mostate);
         mostate := bset(mostate,latchbit);
         ptout(outport,mostate);
         GOTO 200;                (* to Tick Detect *)

(* TIme-Out *)
600:     rpm := lstpls * 60.0 / (samintvl * ntach);
         writeln(' Motor speed = ',rpm,' rpm');
         start := TRUE;
         GOTO 800;                (* to Motor-Off *)
(* Motor-On *)
700:     mostate := bclear(mostate,onoffbit);
         ptout(outport,mostate);
         IF clockv <= 0 THEN GOTO 400;   (* to Sample *)
         GOTO 500;                       (* to Velocity *)

(* Motor-Off *)
800:     mostate := bset(mostate,onoffbit);       (* Motor off *)
         mostate := bset(mostate,latchbit);       (* clear latch *)
         ptout(outport,mostate);
         IF start THEN GOTO 100;          (* to Initial *)
         IF clockv > 0 THEN GOTO 500;     (* to Velocity *)
         GOTO 400;                        (* to Sample *)
END.
```

DC MOTOR CONTROL PROGRAMS IN C

The time-telling program written in C is shown in Listing A7. The four states in Figure 3.7 are defined by statement labels with names resembling the state names as closely as possible. Transitions are implemented by use of GOTO's. All internal program variables are of type integer to achieve maximum computing speed.

The programs have been compiled using a C compiler (written by Whitesmiths, Inc., New York, N.Y.). The library functions *in* and *out* are used to gain access to the digital input/output ports. These functions take the port identification number as input and either read or write to that port. In the time-telling program, all unused inputs on the input port must be set to zero, since the program tests the input value for zero/non-zero to detect the clock pulse.

The velocity test program, Listing A8, uses the bitwise AND operator (&) to perform the masking operation on the input values from the digital input port to separate the clock input from the tachometer latch signal. Although the conceptual diagrams show a high signal to clear the latch, in the actual system a low signal performs the clear operation. (This is a common occurrence in logic system design. In the system conceptualization, high is associated with a positive action of some sort. When the system hardware is actually built, however, the realities of hardware constraints, plus other considerations such as safety, sometimes dictate the use of the opposite logic.)

The third program, the motor test and control program corresponding to the transition diagram of Figure 3.20, is shown in Listing A9. In this program the C operators for bitwise AND (&) and OR (|) are used to set or clear individual bits in the output port corresponding to the latch clear signal and the motor on/off signal. A variable, mostate, with a value that corresponds to the current value of the output port is defined. To change individual bits in the output port, the corresponding bits in mostate are set (or cleared) with masking operations. The value of mostate is then sent to the output port with the out function.

A7   Time-Telling Program In C

```
#include <std.h>
/* Time-telling program.  Counts Ticks from an external
clock.  Implements the transition diagram of Fig. 3.7.  */

extern int inport=0,incnpt=0,incnwd=0;  /* parallel port variables */
extern int outport=0,outcnpt=0,outcnwd=0;

COUNT _main()
{
int clockl;             /* tick counter */

setup();        /* input/output port setup*/

/* Initial   */
INITIAL:        putfmt(" Number of ticks\n");
                getfmt("%i",&clockl);
                goto TKDETECT;

/* Tick Detect */
TKDETECT:       while((in(inport) & 1) != 0) ;  /* wait for zero ..
                                  The semicolon represents a
                            null statement following the 'while'
                            so it does nothing until the condition
                            is satisfied.  */
                while((in(inport) & 1) == 0) ;  /* wait for nonzero  */
                goto CLKUPDT;

/* Clock  Update   */
CLKUPDT:        if( --clockl > 0)goto TKDETECT;
                        goto REPORT;

/* Report */
REPORT:         putfmt(" Time is up!\n");
                goto INITIAL;
}
/* Setup queries the user for the port addresses and set-up data
for the input and output parallel ports. */

setup()
{
extern int inport,incnpt,incnwd,outport,outcnpt,outcnwd;

putfmt("type input port data (in HEX):\n");
putfmt(" address, control address, control word\n");
```

```
getfmt("%hi%hi%hi",&inport,&incnpt,&incnwd);

if((inport >= 0) && (incnpt >= 0))out(incnpt,incnwd);

putfmt("type output port data (in HEX):\n");
putfmt(" address, control address, control word\n");
getfmt("%hi%hi%hi",&outport,&outcnpt,&outcnwd);

if((outport >= 0) && (outcnpt >= 0))out(outcnpt,outcnwd);

}
```

A8   Velocity Test Program in C

```
#include <std.h>

/* VELTES measures the velocity of a motor by counting clock
   pulses. The user is asked to supply two input values: 1) the
   length of test, (in units of clock ticks) and 2) the sampling
   interval for measuring velocity (also in units of clock ticks).
     The program prints the last complete sample value on termination. */

#define maskbit0 0x01    /* mask for bit 0 */
#define maskbit1 0x02    /* mask for bit 1 */
#define lhigh    2       /* latch output values for high and low */
#define llow     0

extern int inport=0,incnpt=0,incnwd=0;  /* parallel port varaibles */
extern int outport=0,outcnpt=0,outcnwd=0;

COUNT _main()
{
int clockl,clockv ;     /* tick counters */
int lensam ;            /* sample time in ticks */
int numpls ;            /* tachometer pulse count */
int lstpls ;            /* most recent complete count */

setup();        /* setup parallel input and output */

/* Initial */
INITIAL:        putfmt(" Length of test (in ticks)?\n");
                getfmt("%i",&clockl);
                putfmt(" Length of sampling interval (in ticks)?\n");
                getfmt("%i",&lensam);
                clockv = lensam;  /* initialize counters */
                numpls = 0;
                lstpls = 0;


                out(outport,lhigh);  /* reset latch */
                goto TKDETECT;  /* to Tick Detect */
/* Tick Detect */
TKDETECT: while((in(inport) & maskbit0) != 0) ; /* wait for zero */
       while((in(inport) & maskbit0) == 0) ;  /* wiat for nonzero */
       goto CLKUPDT;   /* to Clock Update */

/* Clock Update */
CLKUPDT: --clockl;      /* decrement tick counters */
       if ( --clockv <= 0) {
                        clockv = lensam ; /* reset clock */
                        goto SAMPLE; /* to Sample */                }
```

```
          if (clock1 > 0) goto VELOC;  /* to Velocity */
          goto TIMEOT;    /* to Time-Out */

/* Sample */
SAMPLE: lstpls = numpls;         /* update most recent value */
        numpls = 0;
        goto VELOC;     /* to Velocity */

/* Velocity */
VELOC: if((in(inport) & maskbit1) == 0 )  goto TKDETECT;
               /* to Tick Detect if no tach. signal is present */
        ++numpls;       /* increment pulse counter */
        out(outport,llow);       /* clear then re-arm latch */
        out(outport,lhigh);
        goto TKDETECT;  /* to Tick Detect */

/* Time-Out */
TIMEOT: putfmt(" Last velocity = %i\n",lstpls);
        goto INITIAL;   /* to Initial */
}
/* Setup queries the user for the port addresses and set-up data
for the input and output parallel ports. */

setup()
{
extern int inport,incnpt,incnwd,outport,outcnpt,outcnwd;

putfmt("type input port data (in HEX):\n");
putfmt(" address, control address, control word\n");
getfmt("%hi%hi%hi",&inport,&incnpt,&incnwd);

if((inport >= 0) && (incnpt >= 0))out(incnpt,incnwd);

putfmt("type output port data (in HEX):\n");
putfmt(" address, control address, control word\n");
getfmt("%hi%hi%hi",&outport,&outcnpt,&outcnwd);

if((outport >= 0) && (outcnpt >= 0))out(outcnpt,outcnwd);

}
```

A9   Motor Test Program In C

```
#include <std.h>

/* Motor test program - implements the transition diagram of
   Fig.   3.20. The user is asked for six values:
        clock rate, Hz  (clkrate)
        length of test, sec      (lentest)
        velocity sample interval, sec   (samintvl)
        motor actuation pulse frequency, Hz     (pfreq)
        motor actuation duty cycle, %   (dcycle)
        number of tachometer pulses per revolution     (ntach)
   The most recent motor velocity is printed at the end of the test.
*/
#define maskbit0 0x01   /* mask for bit 0 */
#define maskbit1 0x02   /* mask for bit 1 */

extern int inport=0,incnpt=0,incnwd=0;  /* parallel port variables */
extern int outport=0;outcnpt=0,outcnwd=0;
```

```
COUNT _main()
{
int start;        /* indicates first time program is run */
int mostate;      /* stored value indicating current values of
                     motor control output bits */
int clockv,clockl;    /* tick counters */
int clockvl;      /* reset value for clockv */
int ch;           /* used for Y/N answer */
int clkrate,lentest,samintvl,pfreq,dcycle,ntach;        /* Inputs */
int cltimeon,timeon;   /* tick counter for pulse width modullation and
                          its reset value */
int clpulse,pulstime;   /* tick counter for motor pulse and its reset value */
int lstpls,numpls;      /* most recent complete count and tach. pulse counter */
float rpm;

setup();          /* Set up parallel input and output ports */

start = YES;      /* initialize state variables */
mostate = 0;
goto MOTOFF;      /* to Motor-Off */
/* Initial */
INITIAL: putfmt("Use current data values (Y/N)?\n");
        getfmt("%a",&ch);
        if ((ch != 'y') & (ch != 'Y'))    {
                putfmt(" Clock Freq. (Hz)?\n");
                getfmt("%i",&clkrate);
                putfmt(" Length of test (sec)?\n");
                getfmt("%i",&lentest);
                putfmt(" Velocity sample interval (sec)?\n");
                getfmt("%i",&samintvl);
                putfmt(" Motor actuation pulse frequency (Hz)?\n");
                getfmt("%i",&pfreq);
                putfmt(" Motor actuation pulse duty cycle (%%)?\n");
                getfmt("%i",&dcycle);
                putfmt(" Number of tach. pulses per rev.?\n");
                getfmt("%i",&ntach);            }
/* Compute clock reset values and initialize clocks */
        clockl = lentest * clkrate;
        clockvl = samintvl * clkrate;
        pulstime = clkrate * 1.0 / pfreq + 0.5;
        timeon = (pulstime * dcycle) / 100.0 + 0.5;

        clockv = clockvl;
        clpulse = pulstime;
        cltimeon = timeon;
        lstpls = 0;
        numpls = 0;
        start = NO;
        goto TKDETECT;   /* to Tick Detect */

/* Tick Detect */
TKDETECT: while((in(inport) & maskbit0) != 0) ; /* wait for zero */
        while((in(inport) & maskbit0) == 0) ; /* wait for nonzero */
        goto CLKUPDT;   /* to Clock Update */
/* Clock Update */
CLKUPDT: clockl--;   /* decrement tick counters */
        clockv--;
        cltimeon--;
        clpulse--;

        if ( clockl <= 0 ) goto TIMEOUT; /* to Time-Out */
```

```
              if ( cltimeon > 0 ) goto MOTON; /* to Motor-On */
              if ( clpulse > 0 ) goto MOTOFF; /* to Motor-Off */
              clpulse = pulstime; /* reset pulse timer */
              cltimeon = timeon;  /* reset time-on timer */
              if ( cltimeon > 0 ) goto MOTON; /* to Motor-On */
              goto MOTOFF;  /* to Motor-Off */

/* Sample */
SAMPLE: lstpls = numpls ;  /* update most recent value */
        numpls = 0;
        clockv = clockvl;  /* reset sample clock */
        goto VELOC;  /* to Velocity */

/* Velocity */
VELOC:  if((in(inport) & maskbitl) == 0) goto TKDETECT;
                    /* to Tick Detect if no tach. signal is present */
        numpls++ ;  /* increment pulse counter */
        mostate &= (~maskbitl);  /* clear and re-arm latch */
        out(outport,mostate);
        mostate |= maskbitl;
        out(outport,mostate);
        goto TKDETECT;  /* to Tick Detect */

/* Time-Out */
TIMEOUT: rpm = lstpls * 60.0 / (samintvl * ntach);
        putfmt(" Motor speed = %f rpm\n",rpm);
        start = YES;
        goto MOTOFF;  /* to Motor-Off */
/* Motor-On */
MOTON:  mostate &= (~maskbit0);
        out(outport,mostate);
        if (clockv <= 0) goto SAMPLE;  /* to Sample */
        goto VELOC;  /* to Velocity */

/* Motor-Off */
MOTOFF: mostate |= maskbit0;  /* Motor off */
        mostate |= maskbitl;  /* clear latch */
        out(outport,mostate);
        if (start == YES)  goto INITIAL;  /* to Initial */
        if (clockv > 0)  goto VELOC; /* to Velocity */
        goto SAMPLE;  /* to Sample */
}

/* Setup queries the user for the port addresses and set-up data
for the input and output parallel ports. */

setup()
{
extern int inport,incnpt,incnwd,outport,outcnpt,outcnwd;

putfmt("type input port data (in HEX):\n");
putfmt(" address, control address, control word\n");
getfmt("%hi%hi%hi",&inport,&incnpt,&incnwd);

if((inport >= 0) && (incnpt >= 0))out(incnpt,incnwd);

putfmt("type output port data (in HEX):\n");
putfmt(" address, control address, control word\n");
getfmt("%hi%hi%hi",&outport,&outcnpt,&outcnwd);

if((outport >= 0) && (outcnpt >= 0))out(outcnpt,outcnwd);
```

STEPPING MOTOR PROGRAMS

The 8080 microprocessor was designed by the Intel Corporation. Although a generation of microprocessors has come forth since the 8080's introduction, the 8080 is still widely used, primarily because great investments have been made in software and dedicated hardware.

Zilog's Z80 represents an enhancement of the 8080. The Z80 is faster, has a larger instruction set, more sophisticated interrupt structure, and an extra set of CPU registers to facilitate rapid interrupt response.

Intel's enhancement of the 8080 is the 8085, which is faster than the 8080, requires fewer support chips, has a more sophisticated interrupt structure, and has several extra instructions. But the 8080 instruction set is a subset of the Z80 and 8085 instruction sets. For this reason, we will describe only the 8080 instructions and treat the Z80 and 8085 as fast 8080s.

The 8080 is an *8-bit processor,* which means that data is transferred 8 bits at a time and memory is organized in terms of 8-bit words (or bytes). In order not to be limited to $2^8 = 256$ memory locations, however, the 8080's addressing mechanism is 16 bits wide allowing direct addressing of $2^{16} = 65,536$ memory locations. Addresses are stored in memory as two consecutive bytes, usually with the least significant byte stored first, that is, at the lower address.

The 8-bit/16-bit duality is reflected in the internal CPU registers. Instead of general purpose registers, the 8080 contains an 8-bit main register called the *accumulator* (the A register). Many operations may only be performed on data in the accumulator. For example, rotates, most immediate instructions, and many arithmetic instructions are either partially or totally performed in the accumulator. All data transmitted and received by the microprocessor (via IN and OUT instructions) must pass through the accumulator.

Six 8-bit registers, B,C,D,E,H, and L, which can also be viewed as three 16-bit *register pairs* (BC,DE,HL), are also contained within the CPU. Some instructions (e.g., decrement register, DCR) may operate on one 8-bit register while other instructions (e.g., decrement register pair, DCX) operate on the combined 16-bit register.

The 16-bit instructions are particularly useful for manipulating addresses. A dedicated 16-bit stack pointer (called SP) and a 16-bit program counter (PC) are also within the CPU.

Finally, five condition bits which reflect the outcome of the last condition-code-changing instruction are contained within the CPU. (Many instructions do not affect the condition codes, however.) The bits are carry, auxiliary carry, sign, zero, and parity.

Copy-type operations using the immediate mode come in 8- and 16-bit versions. The 8-bit instruction, which has the assembly mnemonic of move-immediate, MVI, specifies one of the seven CPU registers or a memory location whose address is in the HL register pair. The 8080 assembly format convention for move instructions is usually from right to left, thus MVI A,15 would cause the value 15 to be copied into the accumulator. (Decimal is the default convention in many 8080 assemblers.) Copying the accumulator's contents to an output port is achieved by executing the OUT instruction. The instruction OUT 55 would copy the accumulator to port number fifty-five. Listing A10 is a three instruction sequence which will turn on bit zero of output port number 55.

The instruction code for the 8080 MVI instruction follows the pattern shown in Figure 4.2. Bits 7,6,2,1, and 0 are the operation code for the MVI instruction, while bits 5,4, and 3 specify the register into which the copy is to take place. The immediate data (15 in our example) is stored in the memory location immediately following the first byte of the instruction. The full operation code is commonly represented in hexadecimal notation. For our example MVI A,15, the instruction code would be 3EH for the operation followed by the immediate data 0FH. Our program of Listing A10 is shown with hex instruction codes in Listing A11.

Monitors abound for 8080 systems. Unlike some processors which contain built-in monitors, all 8080 monitors are actually programs stored somewhere in memory. Some monitors are ROM resident while others are provided through the operating systems. The capabilities and operating procedures vary widely, but the functions are similar. Most monitors are operated via keyboard and display.

Listed roughly in order of complexity, monitor functions are: examine and change any memory location or any register; display large blocks of data in hexadecimal and its ASCII (character) equivalent; insert and remove breakpoints (instructions which, when executed, cause the monitor to regain control of the processor); single step through code in memory; assemble instructions at an arbitrary address; disassemble memory (or display, when possible, the assembly mnemonics which represent memory locations); edit or insert sequences of instructions without re-entering subsequent code. Listing A12 shows the use of a program called DDT written by Digital Research and distributed in their CP/M operating system.

The timed-loop programs, Listings A13 and A14, use several additional instructions, the copy-direct (where direct is a synonym for absolute) from accumulator to memory called STA (for store), the copy direct from memory to accumulator called LDA (for load), the decrement instruction DCR, the load immediate 16-bit register pair LXI, the decrement register pair DCX, the move from register to register MOV, the logical operator ORA, and the conditional branch JNZ. The logical OR is used, in this case, to test if two 8-bit registers are both zero. If any bits of either are set, the resulting bit or bits will appear in the accumulator.

The 8080 CPU condition codes described earlier are set or cleared by some instructions. The logical OR (ORA) affects the Z bit, so we can find out whether or not the result of the OR operation was zero. The conditional branch JNZ will cause a jump if the zero bit is not set. The jump address is given in the two bytes following the jump instruction byte. If the logical operation produces a zero result, the program *drops out* of the loop by not branching. The DCR instruction also affects the zero bit.

Two versions of the timed-loop program are shown with hexadecimal instruction codes. Listing A13 uses a memory location to save the outer-loop count, while Listing A14 uses a 16-bit register pair to store the inner loop count and an 8-bit register to store the outer loop count. Using the numbers shown in Listing A13, the total time to run the program was 0.02 seconds for A13 and 10 seconds for A14.

All of the components needed to output a pulse train are now available. The program is shown in Listing A15 with hexadecimal instruction codes.

Since the 8080 instruction set and most 8080 I/O ports do not allow individual bits of an output port to be manipulated, it is necessary to perform a logical OR operation on a value which represents the current state of the output in order to leave the direction bit unchanged while we toggle the output. This value will be stored in a memory location and called CUROUT. If we wish to set bit one (second least significant bit), we would use an OR-immediate instruction with the immediate value 10B

(two base ten). To clear bit one, we would AND immediate the current state with the immediate value 11111101B (FDH). This AND immediate operation leaves all bits except bit one unaffected. These masking instructions are used in the move-wait-return program (Listing A16) and the final program (Listing A18) which uses as its delay device the external clock algorithm described in Listing A17.

A10   Instructions to Turn On Output Bit

```
MVI A,1        ;COPY A ONE TO THE ACCUMULATOR
OUT 55         ;COPY THE ACCUMULATOR TO
               ;OUTPUT PORT FIFTY-FIVE.
HLT            ;END OF SEQUENCE
```

A11   Program with Hexadecimal Codes

```
0000 3E01      MVI A,1      ;COPY A ONE TO THE ACCUMULATOR
0002 D337      OUT 55       ;COPY THE ACCUMULATOR TO
                            ;OUTPUT PORT FIFTY-FIVE.
0004 76        HLT
```

A12   Using a Debugging Aid to Enter and Run a Program

```
B>DDT
DDT VER 1.4
-A100
0100  MVI A,1
0102  OUT 55
0104  RST 7
0105
-G100
*104
-
```

A13   Timed Loop Program Using a Memory Location and a Register

```
0000 3E0C              MVI A,12     ;INITIALIZE ACCUMULATOR WITH OUTER
                                    ;LOOP COUNT USING COPY IMMEDIATE
0002 321300    W1:     STA COUNT    ;SAVE THE OUTER LOOP COUNT IN MEMORY
0005 3EFF              MVI A,0FFH   ;COPY INNER LOOP VALUE TO ACCUMULATOR
0007 3D        W2:     DCR A        ;DECREMENT INNER LOOP COUNTER
0008 C20700            JNZ W2       ;IF NOT ZERO, CONTINUE LOOP
000B 3A1300            LDA COUNT    ;COPY TO THE ACCUMULATOR THE
                                    ;VALUE AT THE ADDRESS "COUNT".
000E 3D                DCR A        ;DECREMENT OUTER LOOP COUNT
000F C20200            JNZ W1       ;IF NOT ZERO, LOOP
0012 FF                RST 7        ;TRAP TO DEBUGGING TOOL
                  ;
0013 00        COUNT:  DB 0         ;RESERVE SPACE FOR VALUE CALLED "COUNT"
```

A14   Timed Loop Program Using Two Registers

```
0000 3E0C              MVI A,12       ;REGISTER B IS INITIALIZED WITH
                                      ;OUTER LOOP COUNT
0002 21FFFF    W1:     LXI H,0FFFFH   ;REGISTER PAIR HL IS INITIALIZED
                                      ;WITH INNER LOOP COUNT USING
                                      ;COPY IMMEDIATE
0005 2B        W2:     DCX H          ;DECREMENT REGISTER PAIR.
                                      ;NOTE: THE DCX INSTRUCTION DOES
                                      ;NOT SET ANY CONDITION CODES, THUS
                                      ;WE MUST TEST IF HL IS ZERO.
0006 7D                MOV A,L        ;COPY REGISTER L TO THE ACCUMULATOR
0007 B4                ORA H          ;(ACCUMULATOR OR REGISTER H).  THE
                                      ;RESULT IS ZERO IF AND ONLY IF
                                      ;H AND A (ACTUALLY L) ARE BOTH ZERO.
0008 C20500            JNZ W2         ;IF NOT ZERO, CONTINUE LOOP
000B 05                DCR B          ;DECREMENT OUTER LOOP COUNT
000C C20200            JNZ W1         ;IF NOT ZERO, CONTINUE LOOP
000F FF                RST 7          ;AS FOR FIGURE B.4-4.
```

A15   Pulse Train Program

```
               ;REGISTER USAGE:    B CONTAINS NUMBER OF PULSES
               ;                   HL CONTAINS WAIT LOOP COUNTER
               ;
0000 060C              MVI B,12       ;INITIALIZE REGISTER B FOR TWELVE PULSES
0002 3E01      P1:     MVI A,1        ;PREPARE TO TURN ON OUTPUT
0004 D311              OUT 11H        ;OUTPUT CONTENTS OF ACCUMULATOR
                                      ;TO OUTPUT PORT SEVENTEEN BASE TEN
0006 212301            LXI H,123H     ;INITIALIZE ON-TIME WAIT
0009 2B        P2:     DCX H          ;DECREMENT COUNTER
000A 7D                MOV A,L
000B B4                ORA H
000C C20900            JNZ P2         ;IF NOT ZERO, LOOP
               ;
000F 3E00              MVI A,0        ;PREPARE TO TURN OUTPUT OFF
                                      ;NOTE: THE INSTRUCTIONS "SUB A" OR
                                      ;"XRA A" WILL ZERO THE ACCUMULATOR
                                      ;WITH A SINGLE BYTE INSTRUCTION.
                                      ;THE MVI TAKES TWO.
0011 D311              OUT 11H        ;TURN OFF THE OUTPUT
0013 215604            LXI H,456H     ;INITIALIZE OFF-TIME WAIT
0016 2B        P3:     DCX H
0017 7D                MOV A,L
0018 B4                ORA H          ;AS ABOVE
0019 C21600            JNZ P3         ;IS OFF-TIME COUNTER
001C 05                DCR B          ;HAVE ALL PULSES BEEN SENT?
001D C20200            JNZ P1         ;IF NOT, SEND ANOTHER
0020 FF                RST 7          ;TRAP TO THE DEBUGGING AID
```

A16   Move-Wait-Return Program Using Delay Loop

```
               ;REGISTER USAGE:    REGISTER PAIR BC = PULSE COUNT
               ;                   REGISTER PAIR DE = WAIT LOOP COUNT
               ;                   REGISTER PAIR HL = INNER WAIT LOOP COUNT
               ;MEMORY USAGE:      VARIABLE SEQUEN = SEQUENCE COUNT
               ;                   VARIABLE CUROUT = CURRENT STATE OF
                                                    PARALLEL OUTPUT
               ;
               ;INITIALIZE MODULE
```

```
                    ;
0000 3E02   INIT:    MVI A,2          ;COPY IMMEDIATE 2 TO ACCUMULATOR
0002 326B00          STA SEQUEN       ;STORE ACCUMULATOR IN SEQUENCE COUNT
0005 010002          LXI B,512        ;PULSE COUNT INITIALIZED TO 512
                    ;
0008 3A6C00          LDA CUROUT       ;COPY CURRENT STATE OF PARALLEL
                                      ;OUTPUT TO ACCUMULATOR
000B F602            ORI 2            ;SET DIRECTION BIT
000D 326C00          STA CUROUT       ;SAVE NEW STATE
0010 D311            OUT 11H          ;WRITE VALUE TO PARALLEL OUTPUT PORT
                    ;
0012 3A6C00  PG1:    LDA CUROUT       ;ACCUMULATOR <-- CURRENT PARALLEL
                                      ;OUTPUT STATE
0015 F601            ORI 1            ;SET STEP PULSE BIT
0017 326C00          STA CUROUT       ;SAVE NEW STATE
001A D311            OUT 11H          ;WRITE VALUE TO PARALLEL OUTPUT PORT
                    ;
001C 110800          LXI D,8          ;PULSE ON-TIME COUNT
                    ;
                    ; WAIT LOOP. THESE INSTRUCTIONS WILL
                    ; BE REPEATED SEVERAL TIMES.
                    ;
001F 1B      W1:     DCX D            ;DECREMENT REGISTER PAIR
0020 7B              MOV A,E
0021 B2              ORA D            ;TEST IF DE IS YET ZERO
0022 C21F00          JNZ W1
                    ;
0025 3A6C00          LDA CUROUT       ;ACCUMULATOR <-- CURRENT PARALLEL OUTPUT
0028 E6FE            ANI 0FEH         ;MASK SUCH THAT BIT ZERO IS TURNED OFF
                                      ;BUT ALL OTHER BITS ARE UNAFFECTED
002A 326C00          STA CUROUT       ;SAVE CURRENT STATE
002D D311            OUT 11H          ;WRITE VALUE TO PARALLEL OUTPUT PORT
                    ;
002F 111027          LXI D,10000      ;OFF TIME DELAY LOOP COUNT
                    ;
                    ; WAIT LOOP, AGAIN.
                    ;
0032 1B      W2:     DCX D
0033 7B              MOV A,E
0034 B2              ORA D
0035 C23200          JNZ W2           ;AS ABOVE FOR W1
                    ;
0038 0B              DCX B            ;DECREMENT PULSE COUNT
0039 79              MOV A,C
003A B0              ORA B
003B C21200          JNZ PG1          ;IF PULSE COUNT NOT ZERO,
                                      ;DO ANOTHER PULSE
                    ; END OF PULSE GENERATION MODULE
                    ;
                    ; DECREMENT SEQUENCE COUNT MODULE
                    ;
003E 3A6B00          LDA SEQUEN       ;ACCUMULATOR <-- SEQUENCE COUNT
0041 3D              DCR A            ;DECREMENT SEQUENCE COUNT
0042 326B00          STA SEQUEN       ;SAVE SEQUENCE COUNT
0045 C24900          JNZ RESET        ;IF NOT ZERO, SET UP FOR RETURN MOTION
                    ;
                    ; END DECREMENT SEQUENCE COUNT MODULE
                    ;
                    ; STOP MODULE.  TO HERE => SEQUENCE COUNT = 0
                    ;
```

```
 0048 FF                   RST 7               ;TRAP TO DEBUGGING AID
1LT                                            ;OR JMP 0, BRANCH TO OPERATING SYSTEM
                   ; END STOP MODULE
                   ;
                   ; RESET MODULE
                   ;
 0049 3A6C00      RESET:  LDA CUROUT           ;ACCUMULATOR <-- CURRENT OUTPUT STATE
 004C E6FD                ANI 0FDH             ;MASK SUCH THAT BIT 1, THE
                                               ;DIRECTION BIT, IS RESET TO ZERO.
 004E 326C00              STA CUROUT           ;SAVE CURRENT STATE
 0051 D311                OUT 11H              ;WRITE VALUE TO PARALLEL OUTPUT PORT
 0053 010002              LXI B,512            ;INITIALIZE PULSE COUNT FOR
                                               ;REVERSE DIRECTION
                   ; A LONGER WAIT WILL NOW BE GENERATED
                   ;
 0056 110800              LXI D,8              ;EIGHT PASSES THROUGH OUTER LOOP
 0059 21FFFF      W3:     LXI H,0FFFFH         ;MAXIMUM INNER LOOP COUNT

 005C 2B          W4:     DCX H                ;DECREMENT INNER LOOP
 005D 7D                  MOV A,L
 005E B4                  ORA H                ;IS HL ZERO?
 005F C25C00              JNZ W4
                   ; END OF INNER LOOP
 0062 1B                  DCX D                ;DECREMENT OUTER LOOP
 0063 7B                  MOV A,E
 0064 B2                  ORA D
 0065 C25900              JNZ W3               ;LOOP TO START OF INNER LOOP
                   ; END OF OUTER LOOP
 0068 C31200              JMP PG1              ;RETURN TO PULSE TRAIN
                                               ;GENERATION ROUTINE
                   ; END RESET MODULE
                   ;
 006B 00          SEQUEN: DB 0                 ;DEFINE STORAGE LOCATION FOR
                                               ;SEQUENCE COUNT
 006C 00          CUROUT: DB 0                 ;DEFINE STORAGE LOCATION FOR
                                               ;CURRENT OUTPUT STATE
                   ;
                   ; END OF PROGRAM
```

A17   Test Program for External Clock Timing

```
                   ; TEST PROGRAM FOR TIMING WITH EXTERNAL CLOCK
                   ; REGISTER PAIR DE IS USED TO HOLD THE CLOCK TICK COUNT
                   ;
 0000 110002              LXI D,512            ;INITIALIZE CLOCK TICK COUNT REGISTER
                   ;
                   ; BEGINNING OF WAIT-LOOP MACRO
                   ;
 0003 DB10        CLK1:   IN 10H               ;EXAMINE PARALLEL INPUT PORT
 0005 E601                ANI 1                ;MASK SUCH THAT ALL INPUTS EXCEPT
                                               ;BIT ZERO (CLOCK)ARE IGNORED.
 0007 C20300              JNZ CLK1             ;IF NOT ZERO, WAIT
                   ;
 000A DB10        CLK2:   IN 10H               ;LOOK AT CLOCK AGAIN
 000C E601                ANI 1
 000E CA0A00              JZ CLK2              ;IF CLOCK IS ZERO (I.E. NOT 1), WAIT
                   ;
 0011 1B                  DCX D                ;DECREMENT TICK COUNT
 0012 7B                  MOV A,E
 0013 B2                  ORA D
 0014 C20300              JNZ CLK1             ;IF CLOCK TICK COUNT NOT ZERO, LOOP
                                               ;AND WAIT FOR NEXT CLOCK TICK
 0017 FF                  RST 7                ;TRAP TO DEBUGGING AID.
```

A18   **Move-Wait-Return Program Using an External Clock**

```
                     ;REGISTER USAGE:          REGISTER PAIR BC = PULSE COUNT
                     ;                         REGISTER PAIR DE = EXTERNAL
                     ;                         CLOCK WAIT LOOP COUNT
                     ;                         REGISTER PAIR HL = OUTER WAIT LOOP COUNT
                     ;MEMORY USAGE:            VARIABLE SEQUEN = SEQUENCE COUNT
                     ;                         VARIABLE CUROUT = CURRENT STATE OF
                     ;                                             PARALLEL OUTPUT
                     ;
                     ;INITIALIZE MODULE
                     ;
0000 3E02    INIT:    MVI A,2            ;COPY IMMEDIATE 2 TO ACCUMULATOR
0002 329300           STA SEQUEN         ;STORE ACCUMULATOR IN SEQUENCE COUNT
0005 010002           LXI B,512          ;PULSE COUNT INITIALIZED TO 512
                     ;
0008 3A9400           LDA CUROUT         ;COPY CURRENT STATE OF PARALLEL
                                         ;OUTPUT TO ACCUMULATOR
000B F602             ORI 2              ;SET DIRECTION BIT
000D 329400           STA CUROUT         ;SAVE NEW STATE
0010 D311             OUT 11H            ;WRITE VALUE TO PARALLEL OUTPUT PORT
                     ;
0012 3A9400    PG1:   LDA CUROUT         ;ACCUMULATOR <-- CURRENT PARALLEL
                                         ;OUTPUT STATE
0015 F601             ORI 1              ;SET STEP PULSE BIT
0017 329400           STA CUROUT         ;SAVE NEW STATE
001A D311             OUT 11H            ;WRITE VALUE TO PARALLEL OUTPUT PORT
                     ;
001C 110100           LXI D,1            ;PULSE ON-TIME COUNT
                     ;
                     ; EXTERNAL CLOCK WAIT LOOP. THESE INSTRUCTIONS WILL
                     ; BE REPEATED SEVERAL TIMES.
001F DB10    CLK11:   IN 10H             ;LOOK AT INPUT PORT
0021 E601             ANI 1
0023 C21F00           JNZ CLK11          ;BRANCH IF CLOCK HIGH
                     ;
0026 DB10    CLK12:   IN 10H             ;LOOK AT INPUT PORT AGAIN
0028 E601             ANI 1
002A CA2600           JZ CLK12           ;BRANCH IF CLOCK LOW
                     ;
002D 1B               DCX D              ;DECREMENT COUNTER
002E 7B               MOV A,E
002F B2               ORA D
0030 C21F00           JNZ CLK11          ;BRANCH IF COUNTER NOT ZERO
                     ;
                     ;
0033 3A9400           LDA CUROUT         ;ACCUMULATOR <-- CURRENT PARALLEL OUTPUT
0036 E6FE             ANI 0FEH           ;MASK SUCH THAT BIT ZERO IS TURNED OFF
                                         ;BUT ALL OTHER BITS ARE UNAFFECTED
0038 329400           STA CUROUT         ;SAVE CURRENT STATE
                      OUT  4             ;SEND DATA TO PORT
                                         ;NOTE: THIS IS A CORRECTION LINE
                                         ;AND WILL CAUSE SUBSEQUENT HEX
                                         ;ADDRESSES TO BE INCORRECT
                     ;
003B 114000           LXI D,64           ;OFF TIME DELAY LOOP COUNT
                     ;
                     ; EXTERNAL CLOCK WAIT LOOP, AGAIN.
003E DB10    CLK21:   IN 10H             ;AS ABOVE
0040 E601             ANI 1
0042 C23E00           JNZ CLK21
                     ;
0045 DB10    CLK22:   IN 10H
0047 E601             ANI 1
0049 CA4500           JZ CLK22
```

```
                          ;
004C 1B                   DCX D
004D 7B                   MOV A,E
004E B2                   ORA D
004F C23E00               JNZ CLK21
                          ;
0052 0B                   DCX B              ;DECREMENT PULSE COUNT
0053 79                   MOV A,C
0054 B0                   ORA B
0055 C21200               JNZ PG1            ;IF PULSE COUNT NOT ZERO,
                                             ;DO ANOTHER PULSE
                 ; END OF PULSE GENERATION MODULE
                          ;
                 ; DECREMENT SEQUENCE COUNT MODULE
0058 3A9300               LDA SEQUEN         ;ACCUMULATOR <-- SEQUENCE COUNT
005B 3D                   DCR A              ;DECREMENT SEQUENCE COUNT
005C 329300               STA SEQUEN         ;SAVE SEQUENCE COUNT
005F C26300               JNZ RESET          ;IF NOT ZERO, SET UP FOR RETURN MOTION
                          ;
                 ; END DECREMENT SEQUENCE COUNT MODULE
                          ;
                 ; STOP MODULE.  TO HERE => SEQUENCE COUNT = 0
                          ;
0062 FF                   RST 7              ;TRAP TO DEBUGGING AID
                                             ;OR JMP 0, BRANCH TO OPERATING SYSTEM
                 ; END STOP MODULE
                          ;
                 ; RESET MODULE
0063 3A9400       RESET:   LDA CUROUT        ;ACCUMULATOR <-- CURRENT OUTPUT STATE
0066 E6FD                  ANI 0FDH          ;MASK SUCH THAT BIT 1, THE
                                             ;DIRECTION BIT, IS RESET TO ZERO.
0068 329400                STA CUROUT        ;SAVE CURRENT STATE
006B D311                  OUT 11H           ;WRITE VALUE TO PARALLEL OUTPUT PORT
006D 010002                LXI B,512         ;INITIALIZE PULSE COUNT FOR
                                             ;REVERSE DIRECTION
                 ; A LONGER WAIT WILL NOW BE GENERATED
                          ;
0070 210800                LXI H,8           ;EIGHT PASSES THROUGH OUTER LOOP
0073 11FFFF       W3:      LXI D,0FFFFH      ;MAXIMUM INNER LOOP COUNT
                                             ;(0FFFFH = (2**16)-1 = 65535
0076 DB10         CLK31:   IN 10H
0078 E601                  ANI 1
007A C27600                JNZ CLK31
                          ;
007D DB10         CLK32:   IN 10H
007F E601                  ANI 1
0081 CA7D00                JZ CLK32
                          ;
0084 1B                    DCX D
0085 7B                    MOV A,E
0086 B2                    ORA D
0087 C27600                JNZ CLK31
                          ;
                 ; END OF INNER LOOP
                          ;
008A 2B                    DCX H             ;DECREMENT OUTER LOOP
008B 7D                    MOV A,L
008C B4                    ORA H
008D C27300                JNZ W3            ;LOOP TO START OF INNER LOOP
                          ;
                 ; END OF OUTER LOOP
```

```
                    ;
0090 C31200                  JMP PG1              ;RETURN TO PULSE TRAIN
                                                  ;GENERATION ROUTINE
                    ; END RESET MODULE
                    ;
0093 00             SEQUEN: DB 0                  ;DEFINE STORAGE LOCATION FOR
                                                  ;SEQUENCE COUNT
0094 00             CUROUT: DB 0                  ;DEFINE STORAGE LOCATION FOR
                                                  ;CURRENT OUTPUT STATE
                    ; END OF PROGRAM
```

TEMPERATURE CONTROL PROGRAMS

There is a wide variety of serial input/output circuits available which interface with Z80 and 8080 processors. Usually, an 8-bit data port is available for input of received serial characters and output of characters to be sent. Circuit manufacturers have attempted to produce flexible serial interfaces by allowing software programming of such attributes as transmission mode (synchronous or asynchronous), packet length, parity, baud rate, and so forth. These attributes are typically selected by writing a series of bytes to one or more *control registers* of the serial input/output circuits.

Some serial circuits have twenty or more registers which may be read or written in order to perform efficient serial communication. All serial circuits allow the program to determine if a character has been received or if the transmitter has finished sending the previous character. A manufacturer's data sheet must be consulted for the status register format of the circuit being used. Figure A.1 shows two typical status register formats. Only the status bits which relate to this chapter are labeled.

Programs which read the keyboard and exercise the display are shown in Listing A19. The programs are written in a format which closely follows the Intel standard. The directive .=2000H tells the assembler to set its address counter to the value 2000H. (The Intel format is ORG 2000H where ORG stands for origin.) Listings in this appendix were assembled with an absolute assembler to be run in a machine whose RAM begins at 2000H. Note that the leftmost column of the listing indicates that the first instruction is located at 2000H. Symbols are defined with an equivalence statement. KBCSR=0 defines a symbol with a fixed value. (Many 8080 assemblers use the symbol EQU instead of =.) In this case, a symbol which represents the address of the keyboard control and

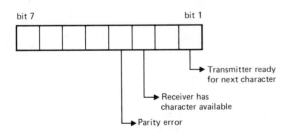

bit 7   bit 1

→ Transmitter ready for next character

→ Receiver has character available

→ Parity error

a. Intel 8251 status register partial format

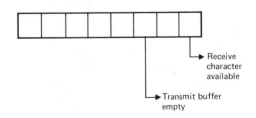

→ Receive character available

→ Transmit buffer empty

b. Zilog Z80-SIO status register partial format

Figure A.1: Typical Serial Circuit Status Registers

status register is defined to have the value zero.

The instruction IN KBCSR is exactly equivalent to IN 0. These equivalence statements are used for two reasons. Mnemonics make the assembly listing more readable, and the value of the symbol may be changed by changing only the definition. The two equivalence statements CHARED = 40H and TXMPTY = 80H are masks which allow us to test the status bits representing the state of the serial interface. The instructions used in Listings A19 and A20 were introduced in the previous section, Stepping Motor Programs. The form of the instruction MVI A, 'A' is new, however. The operand 'A' represents the ASCII character A. Note that the assembler has inserted the code 41H following the code for MVI in Listing A20.

Listing A21, the shifted echo program, contains the subroutines CHIN and CHOUT. These subroutines are executed with the CALL instruction. The CPU pushes onto the stack the address of the instruction immediately following the call. The return from subroutine instruction, RET, causes the top of stack to be popped into the program counter. The character which CHIN receives is passed to the calling program in the accumulator. Similarly, the character to be sent to the display is placed in the accumulator before CHOUT is called.

The instruction CPI or compare immediate is introduced here to help us determine if a carriage return was typed. The compare instruction subtracts the immediate value (0DH in this case) from the contents of the accumulator. Although the result of the subtraction is thrown away, the condition codes are updated in order that a conditional branch (JZ or jump on zero in this case) may be performed.

The multiply subroutine, with a short test program, is shown in Listing A22. An 8-bit multiplicand is passed in register L, and an 8-bit multiplier is passed in register E. A 16-bit product is returned in register pair HL. We designed this routine to preserve all registers not used to pass arguments. For this reason, the first two instructions preserve the registers and the two instructions immediately preceding the return from subroutine instruction restore the register pairs.

Since the 8080 instruction set does not include arithmetic shifts, we must combine two to make one. Clearing the carry bit (using an exclusive or XRA A) and then rotating the accumulator left through the carry bit performs an arithmetic left shift. In an arithmetic left shift, a zero must be shifted into the lowest order bit. Clearing the carry and then rotating it into the low-order bit position performs the arithmetic shift. The multiply algorithm requires that we add an 8-bit multiplier to a 16-bit product. The double add instruction DAD is used.

Listing A23 shows the D/A test program. The subroutines CHIN and CHOUT are used to accept and echo entered characters. ASCII to decimal-binary conversion is accomplished by subtracting the value of an ASCII zero from the entered character. The instruction SUI '0' subtracts 30H (the ASCII code for the character zero) from the entered value. Decimal-binary to binary conversion is accomplished by multiplying the first-entered character by ten and adding it to the binary value of the second-entered character.

A listing of the analog to digital converter (A/D) test program and subroutine is shown in listing A24. Because the control program uses two's complement representation, we have written a 7-bit conversion routine. The counting loop takes roughly twenty-five microseconds; thus a full-scale conversion takes about three milliseconds. The program contains only two new instructions. The set carry instruction (STC) and the complement carry (CMC) are used to signal the calling routine if an overflow has occurred. An overflow is any value greater than 127.

The divide subroutine, Listing A25, expects a 16-bit dividend in register-pair HL and an 8-bit divisor in Register E. An 8-bit quotient is returned in register L with the 8-bit remainder in H. As with the multiply subroutine, the divide subroutine preserves all other registers except the accumulator. No new instructions are introduced here. The divide subroutine is needed to convert from binary to decimal in order for our A/D

calibration program to function (Listing A26). The calibration program uses the character subroutines to accept and echo characters and print the converted value.

The final program, Listing A27, incorporates all the modules described in this appendix. Although the code is written to make the listing readable rather than efficient, we have added a few instructions which simplify the process of writing the programs. For example, the two instructions:

```
LXI H, RSET
ADD M
```

cause the accumulator to be updated with the sum of the old accumulator contents and the byte at location RSET. This is a form of indirect addressing which will be introduced in Chapter 6.

A19   Read Keyboard and Echo

```
2000                        .= 2000H
                      ;
0000 =          KBCSR   = 0          ;ADDRESS OF KEYBOARD STATUS REGISTER
0001 =          KBBUF   = 1          ;ADDRESS OF KEYBOARD DATA REGISTER
0000 =          DISCSR  = 0          ;ADDRESS OF DISPLAY STATUS REGISTER
0001 =          DISBUF  = 1          ;ADDRESS OF DISPLAY STATUS REGISTER
                      ;
0040 =          CHARED  = 40H        ;MASK FOR CHARACTER READY FROM SERIAL INTERFACE
0080 =          TXMPTY  = 80H        ;MASK FOR SERIAL TRANSMITTER EMPTY
                      ;
                      ;
2000 DB00       START:  IN KBCSR     ;READ KEYBOARD STATUS
2002 E640               ANI CHARED   ;CHECK FOR CHARACTER READY
2004 CA0020             JZ START     ;IF NOT READY, CHECK AGAIN
                      ;
2007 DB01               IN KBBUF     ;GET CHARACTER
2009 D301               OUT DISBUF   ;ECHO CHARACTER
                      ;
200B DB00       K2:     IN DISCSR    ;READ DISPLAY STATUS REGISTER
200D E680               ANI TXMPTY   ;SEE IF TRANSMITTER IS FINISHED
                                     ;WITH CHARACTER
200F CA0B20             JZ K2        ;IF NOT DONE, WAIT
                      ;
2012 F7                 RST 6        ;RETURN TO MONITOR
                      ;
                      ; END OF PROGRAM
```

A20   Print a Character

```
                ;FIGURE B.5-2B PRINT A CHARACTER
                ;
2000                    .= 2000H
```

```
                  ;
0000 =            DISCSR  = 0        ;ADDRESS OF DISPLAY STATUS REGISTER
0001 =            DISBUF  = 1        ;ADDRESS OF DISPLAY DATA BUFFER
                  ;
0080 =            TXMPTY  = 80H      ;MASK FOR TRANSMITTER EMPTY
                  ;
2000 AF           START:  XRA A         ;CLEAR ACCUMULATOR
2001 D301                 OUT DISBUF    ;SEND NULL TO START TRANSMITTER
                  ;
2003 DB00         D1:     IN DISCSR     ;READ DISPLAY STATUS REGISTER
2005 E680                 ANI TXMPTY    ;SEE IF TRANSMITTER IS FINISHED
                                        ;WITH CHARACTER
2007 CA0320               JZ D1         ;IF NOT DONE, WAIT
                  ;
200A 3E41                 MVI A,'A'     ;ACCUMULATOR <-- ASCII "A"
200C D301                 OUT DISBUF    ;SEND TO DISPLAY
                  ;
200E DB00         D2:     IN DISCSR     ;READ DISPLAY STATUS REGISTER
2010 E680                 ANI TXMPTY    ;SEE IF TRANSMITTER IS FINISHED
                                        ;WITH CHARACTER
2012 CA0E20               JZ D2         ;IF NOT DONE, WAIT
                  ;
2015 F7                   RST 6         ;RETURN TO MONITOR
                  ;
                  ; END OF PROGRAM
```

A21   Shifted Echo Program

```
2000                      .= 2000H
                  ;
000D =            CR      = 13       ;ASCII CODE FOR CARRIAGE RETURN
000A =            LF      = 10       ;ASCII CODE FOR LINE FEED
                  ;
2000 CD1720       START:  CALL CHIN     ;CHARACTER-IN SUBROUTINE WILL
                                        ;RETURN KEYBOARD ENTRY IN
                                        ;ACCUMULATOR
2003 FE0D                 CPI CR        ;IS CHARACTER A RETURN?
2005 CA0C20               JZ S1
2008 3C                   INR A         ;TO HERE       => NOT A RETURN, THUS
                                        ;INCREMENT CHARACTER CODE
2009 C31120               JMP S2
200C CD2320       S1:     CALL CHOUT    ;ECHO RETURN
200F 3E0A                 MVI A,LF      ;SET UP TO ECHO LINE FEED
2011 CD2320       S2:     CALL CHOUT    ;ECHO
2014 C30020               JMP START     ;DO IT AGAIN
                  ;
                  ; CHARACTER IN AND CHARACTER OUT SUBROUTINES
                  ;
0000 =            KBCSR   = 0        ;ADDRESS OF KEYBOARD STATUS REGISTER
0001 =            KBBUF   = 1        ;ADDRESS OF KEYBOARD DATA REGISTER
0000 =            DISCSR  = 0        ;ADDRESS OF DISPLAY STATUS REGISTER
0001 =            DISBUF  = 1        ;ADDRESS OF DISPLAY DATA BUFFER
                  ;
0040 =            CHARED  = 40H      ;MASK FOR CHARACTER READY FROM SERIAL INTERFACE
0080 =            TXMPTY  = 80H      ;MASK FOR SERIAL TRANSMITTER EMPTY
                  ;
2017 DB00         CHIN:   IN KBCSR      ;READ KEYBOARD STATUS REGISTER
2019 E640                 ANI CHARED    ;SEE IF CHARACTER IS READY
201B CA1720               JZ CHIN       ;IF NOT, WAIT
                  ;
```

```
201E DB01                 IN KBBUF        ;ACCUMULATOR <-- CHARACTER
2020 E67F                 ANI 7FH         ;CLEAR PARITY BIT
2022 C9                   RET             ;RETURN FROM SUBROUTINE
                    ;
                    ;
2023 F5       CHOUT:      PUSH PSW        ;SAVE CHARACTER PASSED ON SYSTEM STACK
2024 DB00     C1:         IN DISCSR       ;READ DISPLAY STATUS REGISTER
2026 E680                 ANI TXMPTY      ;SEE IF TRANSMITTER IS READY FOR CHARACTER
2028 CA2420               JZ C1           ;IF NOT READY, WAIT
                    ;
202B F1                   POP PSW         ;RESTORE ACCUMULATOR WITH CHARACTER TO SEND
202C D301                 OUT DISBUF      ;SEND CHARACTER
202E C9                   RET             ;RETURN FROM SUBROUTINE
                    ;
                    ; END OF SUBROUTINES
                    ;
                    ; END OF PROGRAM
```

A22   Multiply Subroutine and Test Program

```
2000                          .=2000H
                    ;
                    ; CALL THIS SUBROUTINE WITH 8-BIT MULTIPLICAND IN "L" AND
                    ; 8-BIT MULTIPLIER IN "E".  16-BIT PRODUCT IS RETURNED
                    ; IN "HL".  MULTIPLIER IS RETURNED UNCHANGED.
                    ; THIS ROUTINE USES THE STACK, THUS IT MUST HAVE BEEN
                    ; INITIALIZED.
                    ; THIS SUBROUTINE IS REENTRANT.
                    ;
2000 C5       MULT:       PUSH B          ;SAVE REGISTER B ON STACK
2001 D5                   PUSH D          ;WE'LL USE REGISTER D FOR COUNT,
                                          ;THUS WE'LL SAVE OLD VALUE OF D.
2002 4D                   MOV C,L         ;REGISTER C <-- MULTIPLICAND
2003 0600                 MVI B,0         ;NOW REGISTER PAIR BC CONTAINS
                                          ;MULTIPLICAND
2005 210000               LXI H,0         ;ZERO PRODUCT REGISTER PAIR
2008 1608                 MVI D,8         ;D <-- STEP COUNT
                    ;
200A AF       M1:         XRA A           ;CLEAR CARRY
200B 7D                   MOV A,L         ;ACCUMULATOR <-- LOWER ORDER BYTE
                                          ;OF PRODUCT
200C 17                   RAL             ;CLEAR CARRY AND RAL IS EQUIVALENT
                                          ;TO ARITHMETIC LEFT SHIFT.
200D 6F                   MOV L,A         ;PLACE BACK (CARRY IS NOW SHIFTED
                                          ;VALUE OF LOWER ORDER).
200E 7C                   MOV A,H         ;ACCUMULATOR <-- HIGH ORDER OR
                                          ;PRODUCT
200F 17                   RAL             ;SHIFT HIGH ORDER OF PRODUCT AND
                                          ;SHIFT IN CARRY WHICH IS SHIFT OF
                                          ;BIT 7 OF LOWER ORDER BYTE OF PRODUCT
2010 67                   MOV H,A         ;PLACE HIGH-ORDER PRODUCT BACK
2011 7B                   MOV A,E         ;ACCUMULATOR <-- MULTIPLICAND
2012 07                   RLC             ;ROTATE MULTIPLIER LEFT
2013 5F                   MOV E,A         ;PLACE REGISTER E BACK
2014 D21820               JNC M3          ;BRANCH IF NO BIT ROTATED OUT
2017 09                   DAD B           ;PRODUCT <-- PRODUCT + MULTIPLICAND
                    ;
2018 15       M3:         DCR D           ;DECREMENT STEP COUNT
2019 C20A20               JNZ M1          ;LOOP FOR EIGHT BITS
                    ;
201C D1                   POP D           ;RESTORE DE
201D C1                   POP B           ;RESTORE BC
201E C9                   RET
                    ;
```

```
                    ; END OF MULTIPLY SUBROUTINE
                    ;
                    ; MULTIPLY TEST PROGRAM
                    ;
201F 1E0A    TEST:    MVI E,10        ;MULTIPLIER <-- TEN
2021 2E10             MVI L,16        ;MULTIPLICAND <-- SIXTEEN
2023 1605             MVI D,5         ;CHECK THAT REGISTER D IS
                                      ;NOT AFFECTED
2025 0606             MVI B,6         ;REGISTER B SHOULD ALSO BE
                                      ;UNAFFECTED
2027 CD0020           CALL MULT       ;CALL MULTIPLY SUBROUTINE
202A F7               RST 6           ;RETURN TO MONITOR
                    ;
                    ; END OF PROGRAM
```

A23   D/A Test Program

```
2000                     .= 2000H
                    ;
                    ;
0024 =          DIGOUT = 24H     ;ADDRESS OF PARALLEL DIGITAL OUTPUT PORT
                    ;
2000 CD3D20    START:   CALL CHIN       ;GET FIRST CHARACTER
2003 CD4920             CALL CHOUT      ;ECHO IT
2006 323B20             STA CHAR1       ;STORE CHARACTER
                    ;
2009 CD3D20             CALL CHIN       ;GET SECOND CHARCTER
200C CD4920             CALL CHOUT      ;ECHO SECOND CHARACTER
200F 323C20             STA CHAR2       ;STORE SECOND CHARACTER
                    ;
2012 CD3D20    D1:      CALL CHIN       ;GET NEXT CHARACTER
2015 FE0D               CPI CR          ;WAIT FOR "RETURN"
2017 C21220             JNZ D1          ;DON'T ECHO UNLESS A RETURN
                    ;
201A CD4920             CALL CHOUT      ;ECHO RETURN
201D 3E0A               MVI A,LF        ;ACCUMULATOR <-- LINE FEED
201F CD4920             CALL CHOUT      ;SEND LINEFEED
                    ;
                    ; NOW WE WILL CONVERT FROM DECIMAL-ASCII TO BINARY
                    ;
2022 210A00             LXI H,10        ;WE'LL MULTIPLY CHARACTER #1 BY 10
2025 3A3B20             LDA CHAR1       ;ACCUMULATOR <-- CHARACTER#1
2028 D630               SUI '0'         ;SUBTRACT  CODE FOR ASCII ZERO
                                        ;TO YIELD BINARY
202A 5F                 MOV E,A
202B 1600               MVI D,0         ;DE NOW CONTAINS BINARY
202D CD5520             CALL MULT       ;HL <-- 10*<CHAR1>
                    ;
2030 3A3C20             LDA CHAR2       ;ACCUMULATOR <-- CHARACTER #2
2033 D630               SUI '0'         ;MAKE CHARACTER #2 BINARY
                    ;
2035 85                 ADD L           ;ACCUMULATOR <-- (CHAR2)+ 10*(CHAR1)
                    ;
2036 D324               OUT DIGOUT      ;WRITE VALUE TO D/A
                    ;
2038 C30020             JMP START       ;DO IT AGAIN
                    ;
203B 00        CHAR1:   DB 0            ;STORAGE FOR CHARACTER #1
203C 00        CHAR2:   DB 0            ;STORAGE FOR CHARACTER #2
                    ;
                    ; END OF D/A TEST PROGRAM
                    ;
```

```
0000 =          KBCSR   = 0               ;ADDRESS OF KEYBOARD STATUS REGISTER
0001 =          KBBUF   = 1               ;ADDRESS OF KEYBOARD DATA REGISTER
0000 =          DISCSR  = 0              ;ADDRESS OF DISPLAY STATUS REGISTER
0001 =          DISBUF  = 1              ;ADDRESS OF DISPLAY DATA BUFFER
                ;
000D =          CR      = 13              ;ASCII CODE FOR CARRIAGE RETURN
000A =          LF      = 10              ;ASCII CODE FOR LINE FEED
                ;
0040 =          CHARED  = 40H    ;MASK FOR CHARACTER READY FROM SERIAL INTERFACE
0080 =          TXMPTY  = 80H    ;MASK FOR SERIAL TRANSMITTER EMPTY
                ;
203D DB00       CHIN:   IN KBCSR         ;READ KEYBOARD STATUS REGISTER
203F E640               ANI CHARED       ;SEE IF CHARACTER IS READY
2041 CA3D20             JZ CHIN          ;IF NOT, WAIT
                ;
2044 DB01               IN KBBUF         ;ACCUMULATOR <-- CHARACTER
2046 E67F               ANI 7FH          ;CLEAR PARITY BIT
2048 C9                 RET              ;RETURN FROM SUBROUTINE
                ;
                ;
2049 F5         CHOUT:  PUSH PSW         ;SAVE CHARACTER PASSED ON SYSTEM STACK
204A DB00       C1:     IN DISCSR        ;READ DISPLAY STATUS REGISTER
204C E680               ANI TXMPTY       ;SEE IF TRANSMITTER IS READY FOR CHARACTER
204E CA4A20             JZ C1            ;IF NOT READY, WAIT
                ;
2051 F1                 POP PSW          ;RESTORE ACCUMULATOR WITH CHARACTER TO SEND
2052 D301               OUT DISBUF       ;SEND CHARACTER
2054 C9                 RET              ;RETURN FROM SUBROUTINE
                ;
                ; END OF CHARACTER IN/OUT SUBROUTINES
                ; MULTIPLY SUBROUTINE FOLLOWS
                ;
                ;
                ; CALL THIS SUBROUTINE WITH 8-BIT MULTIPLICAND IN "L" AND
                ; 8-BIT MULTIPLIER IN "E".  16-BIT PRODUCT IS RETURNED
                ; IN "HL".  MULTIPLIER IS RETURNED UNCHANGED.
                ; THIS ROUTINE USES THE STACK, THUS IT MUST HAVE BEEN
                ; INITIALIZED.
                ; THIS SUBROUTINE IS REENTRANT.
                ;
2055 C5         MULT:   PUSH B           ;SAVE REGISTER B ON STACK
2056 D5                 PUSH D           ;WE'LL USE REGISTER D FOR COUNT,
                                         ;THUS WE'LL SAVE OLD VALUE OF D.
2057 4D                 MOV C,L          ;REGISTER C <-- MULTIPLICAND
2058 0600               MVI B,0          ;NOW REGISTER PAIR BC CONTAINS
                                         ;MULTIPLICAND
205A 210000             LXI H,0          ;ZERO PRODUCT REGISTER PAIR
205D 1608               MVI D,8          ;D <-- STEP COUNT
                ;
205F AF         M1:     XRA A            ;CLEAR CARRY
2060 7D                 MOV A,L          ;ACCUMULATOR <-- LOWER ORDER BYTE
                                         ;OF PRODUCT
2061 17                 RAL              ;CLEAR CARRY AND RAL IS EQUIVALENT
                                         ;TO ARITHMETIC LEFT SHIFT.
2062 6F                 MOV L,A          ;PLACE BACK (CARRY IS NOW SHIFTED
                                         ;VALUE OF LOWER ORDER).
2063 7C                 MOV A,H          ;ACCUMULATOR <-- HIGH ORDER OR
                                         ;PRODUCT
2064 17                 RAL              ;SHIFT HIGH ORDER OF PRODUCT AND
                                         ;SHIFT IN CARRY WHICH IS SHIFT OF
                                         ;BIT 7 OF LOWER ORDER BYTE OF PRODUCT
```

```
2065 67                   MOV  H,A         ;PLACE HIGH-ORDER PRODUCT BACK
2066 7B                   MOV  A,E         ;ACCUMULATOR <-- MULTIPLICAND
2067 07                   RLC              ;ROTATE MULTIPLIER LEFT
2068 5F                   MOV  E,A         ;PLACE REGISTER E BACK
2069 D26D20               JNC  M3          ;BRANCH IF NO BIT ROTATED OUT
206C 09                   DAD  B           ;PRODUCT <-- PRODUCT + MULTIPLICAND
               ;
206D 15          M3:      DCR  D           ;DECREMENT STEP COUNT
206E C25F20               JNZ  M1          ;LOOP FOR EIGHT BITS
               ;
2071 D1                   POP  D           ;RESTORE DE
2072 C1                   POP  B           ;RESTORE BC
2073 C9                   RET
               ;
               ; END OF MULTIPLY SUBROUTINE
               ;
               ; END OF PROGRAM
```

A24   A/D Test Program

```
2000                      .= 2000H
               ;
               ; CONVERTED VALUE IS RETURNED IN ACCUMULATOR.
               ; SETS CARRY ON OVERFLOW, CLEARS CARRY OTHERWISE.
               ;
0024 =           DIGIN   = 24H            ;ADDRESS OF DIGITAL PARALLEL INPUT PORT
0024 =           DIGOUT  = 24H            ;ADDRESS OF DIGITAL PARALLEL OUTPUT PORT
               ;
               ;
2000 0E00        AD:      MVI  C,0         ;REGISTER "C" CONTAINS A/D COUNT
2002 3A3220               LDA  CURDIG      ;ACCUMULATOR <-- CURRENT PARALLEL
                                          ;DIGITAL OUTPUT PORT STATE
2005 F680                 ORI  80H         ;OPEN RESET SWITCH
2007 323220               STA  CURDIG      ;STORE VALUE
               ;
200A D324                 OUT  DIGOUT      ;OPEN INTEGRATOR RESET SWITCH
               ;
200C DB24        A1:      IN   DIGIN       ;LOOK AT COMPARATOR
200E E601                 ANI  1           ;MASK FOR COMPARATOR
2010 C22420               JNZ  A2          ;BRANCH IF COMPARATOR HAS SWITCHED
               ;
2013 0C                   INR  C           ;INCREMENT COUNT
2014 C20C20               JNZ  A1          ;NO CARRY => NO OVERFLOW
               ;
               ; TO HERE => COUNTER HAS OVERFLOWED
2017 3A3220               LDA  CURDIG      ;ACCUMULATOR <-- CURRENT PARALLEL OUTPUT
201A E67F                 ANI  7FH         ;CLOSE RESET SWITCH
201C 323220               STA  CURDIG      ;STORE CURRENT OUTPUT STATE
201F D324                 OUT  DIGOUT      ;CLOSE RESET SWITCH
               ;
2021 79                   MOV  A,C         ;ACCUMULATOR <-- VALUE OF COUNTER
2022 37                   STC              ;SET CARRY INDICATING OVERFLOW
2023 C9                   RET
               ;
               ; TO HERE => COMPARATOR HAS SWITCHED WITHOUT OVERFLOW
               ;
2024 3A3220      A2:      LDA  CURDIG      ;ACCUMULATOR <-- CURRENT PARALLEL OUTPUT
2027 E67F                 ANI  7FH         ;CLEAR INTEGRATOR RESET BIT
2029 323220               STA  CURDIG
202C D324                 OUT  DIGOUT      ;CLOSE INTEGRATOR RESET SWITCH
```

```
202E 79              MOV A,C           ;ACCUMULATOR <-- VALUE OF COUNTER
202F 37              STC
2030 3F              CMC               ;CLEAR CARRY
2031 C9              RET
                 ;
2032 00     CURDIG: DB 0               ;CURRENT STATE OF PARALLEL DIGITAL
                                       ;OUTPUT PORT
                 ;
                 ; END OF A/D PROGRAM
                 ;
                 ; A/D TEST PROGRAM
                 ;
2033 CD0020 ADTEST: CALL AD            ;PERFORM CONVERSION
2036 F7              RST 6             ;RETURN TO MONITOR IN ORDER TO ALLOW
                                       ;EXAMINATION OF VALUE RETURNED IN
                                       ;ACCUMULATOR.
                 ;
                 ; END OF PROGRAM
```

A25   Divide Subroutine and Test Program

```
2000                     .= 2000H
                 ;
                 ; CALL WITH 16-BIT DIVIDEND IN REGISTER-PAIR HL, 8-BIT
                 ; DIVISOR IN REGISTER E.  THE 8-BIT QUOTIENT IS RETURNED
                 ; IN REGISTER L AND AN 8-BIT REMAINDER IS RETURNED IN
                 ; REGISTER H.  REGISTER-PAIR BC IS UNAFFECTED AS IS
                 ; REGISTER D.  THE ACCUMULATOR IS DESTROYED.  THIS
                 ; SUBROUTINE USES THE SYSTEM STACK.  IT IS REENTRANT.
                 ;
                 ;
2000 C5     DIVIDE: PUSH B             ;SAVE REGISTER-PAIR BC
2001 D5             PUSH D             ;SAVE REGISTER D
2002 0E00           MVI C,0            ;ZERO QUOTIENT
2004 0608           MVI B,8            ;STEP COUNT
                 ;
2006 AF     DV0:    XRA A              ;CLEAR CARRY
2007 7D             MOV A,L            ;SHIFT LEFT REGISTER-PAIR HL
2008 17             RAL                ;ARITHMETIC LEFT SHIFT
2009 6F             MOV L,A
200A 7C             MOV A,H
200B 17             RAL
200C 67             MOV H,A            ;SHIFT COMPLETE
                 ;
200D 79             MOV A,C            ;LEFT SHIFT QUOTIENT
200E 07             RLC                ;ARITHMETIC LEFT SHIFT
200F 4F             MOV C,A
                 ;
2010 7C             MOV A,H            ;COMPARE E AND H
2011 93             SUB E              ;PERFORM H-E
2012 FA1720         JM DV1             ;BRANCH => (H>E)
2015 67             MOV H,A            ;H <-- H-E
2016 0C             INR C              ;INCREMENT QUOTIENT
                 ;
2017 05     DV1:    DCR B
2018 C20620         JNZ DV0
                 ;
201B 69             MOV L,C            ;LEAVE QUOTIENT IN L
                 ;
201C D1             POP D              ;RESTORE DE
```

```
201D  C1                    POP  B             ;RESTORE BC
201E  C9                    RET
                     ;
                     ; END OF DIVIDE SUBROUTINE
                     ;
                     ; DIVIDE TEST PROGRAM
                     ;
201F  1E0A          DEVTST: MVI  E,10          ;DIVISOR <-- TEN
2021  214000                LXI  H,64          ;DIVIDEND <-- SIXTY-FOUR
                     ;
2024  CD0020                CALL DIVIDE        ;DO DIVISION
2027  F7                    RST  6             ;RETURN TO MONITOR IN ORDER
                                               ;TO EXAMINE REGISTER RESULT.
                     ;
                     ; END OF PROGRAM
```

A26   A/D Calibration Program

```
2000                        .= 2000H
                     ;
                     ;
2000  CD9E20        START:  CALL AD            ;DO ONE CONVERSION TO MAKE SURE
                                               ;THAT THE RESET SWITCH IS SET
                                               ;CORRECTLY (I.E. CLOSED TO DIS-
                                               ;CHARGE THE INTEGRATOR).
2003  CD6720        AD0:    CALL CHIN          ;GET A CHARACTER
2006  CD7320                CALL CHOUT         ;ECHO IT
                     ;
2009  326420                STA  CHAR          ;STORE CHARACTER
                     ;
200C  CD6720        AD1:    CALL CHIN          ;NOW WAIT FOR "RETURN"
200F  FE0D                  CPI  CR            ;IS IT A CARRIAGE RETURN?
2011  C20C20                JNZ  AD1           ;IF NOT, TRY AGAIN
                     ;
2014  CD7320                CALL CHOUT         ;ECHO RETURN
2017  3E0A                  MVI  A,LF
2019  CD7320                CALL CHOUT         ;SEND LINE FEED
                     ;
201C  3A6420                LDA  CHAR          ;EXAMINE CHARACTER
201F  FE47                  CPI  'G'           ;IS IT A "G"?
2021  C20320                JNZ  AD0           ;IF NOT, GET A NEW MESSAGE
                     ;
2024  CD9E20                CALL AD            ;PERFORM CONVERSION
                     ;
                     ; NOW PREPARE TO DIVIDE
                     ;
2027  6F                    MOV  L,A           ;PLACE A/D VALUE IN DIVIDEND
2028  2600                  MVI  H,0           ;CLEAR HIGH ORDER BYTE OF DIVIDEND
202A  1E0A                  MVI  E,10          ;DIVISOR <-- TEN
                     ;
202C  CD7F20                CALL DIVIDE        ;L CONTAINS QUOTIENT, H THE REMAINDER
                     ;
202F  7C                    MOV  A,H           ;ACCUMULATOR <-- REMAINDER
2030  C630                  ADI  '0'           ;MAKE ASCII
2032  326520                STA  CHAR1         ;STORE LEAST SIGNIFICANT CHARACTER
                                               ;FOR LATER OUTPUT
2035  2600                  MVI  H,0           ;ZERO HIGH ORDER BYTE OF DIVIDEND
                                               ;NOTE: PREVIOUS QUOTIENT IS IN DIVIDEND
                                               ;AND DIVISOR IS STILL VALID.
2037  CD7F20                CALL DIVIDE
```

```
203A 7C                 MOV A,H           ;AS ABOVE FOR NEXT CHARACTER
203B C630               ADI '0'
203D 326620             STA CHAR2
              ;
2040 2600               MVI H,0           ;THIRD DIVIDE
2042 CD7F20             CALL DIVIDE
2045 7C                 MOV A,H
2046 C630               ADI '0'           ;CHARACTER #3 IS IN ACCUMULATOR
              ;
2048 CD7320             CALL CHOUT        ;PRINT MOST SIGNIFICANT
204B 3A6620             LDA CHAR2
204E CD7320             CALL CHOUT        ;AND NEXT LEAST SIGNIFICANT
2051 3A6520             LDA CHAR1
2054 CD7320             CALL CHOUT        ;AND LEAST SIGNIFICANT
              ;
2057 3E0D               MVI A,CR
2059 CD7320             CALL CHOUT        ;SEND RETURN
205C 3E0A               MVI A,LF
205E CD7320             CALL CHOUT        ;SEND LINE FEED
              ;
2061 C30320             JMP AD0           ;GO BACK AND DO AGAIN
              ;
2064 00      CHAR:      DB 0              ;CHARACTER STORAGE AREA
2065 00      CHAR1:     DB 0
2066 00      CHAR2:     DB 0
              ;
             ; END OF A/D CALIBRATION PROGRAM
             ; CHARACTER INPUT AND OUTPUT SUBROUTINES FOLLOW
              ;
0000 =       KBCSR     = 0       ;ADDRESS OF KEYBOARD STATUS REGISTER
0001 =       KBBUF     = 1       ;ADDRESS OF KEYBOARD DATA REGISTER
0000 =       DISCSR    = 0       ;ADDRESS OF DISPLAY STATUS REGISTER
0001 =       DISBUF    = 1       ;ADDRESS OF DISPLAY DATA BUFFER
              ;
0040 =       CHARED    = 40H     ;MASK FOR CHARACTER READY FROM SERIAL INTERFACE
0080 =       TXMPTY    = 80H     ;MASK FOR SERIAL TRANSMITTER EMPTY
              ;
000D =       CR        = 13      ;ASCII CODE FOR CARRIAGE RETURN
000A =       LF        = 10      ;ASCII CODE FOR LINE FEED
              ;
2067 DB00    CHIN:      IN KBCSR          ;READ KEYBOARD STATUS REGISTER
2069 E640               ANI CHARED        ;SEE IF CHARACTER IS READY
206B CA6720             JZ CHIN           ;IF NOT, WAIT
              ;
206E DB01               IN KBBUF          ;ACCUMULATOR <-- CHARACTER
2070 E67F               ANI 7FH           ;CLEAR PARITY BIT
2072 C9                 RET               ;RETURN FROM SUBROUTINE
              ;
              ;
2073 F5      CHOUT:     PUSH PSW          ;SAVE CHARACTER PASSED ON SYSTEM STACK
2074 DB00    C1:        IN DISCSR         ;READ DISPLAY STATUS REGISTER
2076 E680               ANI TXMPTY        ;SEE IF TRANSMITTER IS READY FOR CHARACTER
2078 CA7420             JZ C1             ;IF NOT READY, WAIT
              ;
207B F1                 POP PSW           ;RESTORE ACCUMULATOR WITH CHARACTER TO SEND
207C D301               OUT DISBUF        ;SEND CHARACTER
207E C9                 RET               ;RETURN FROM SUBROUTINE
              ;
             ; END OF CHARACTER INPUT AND OUTPUT SUBROUTNES
             ; DIVIDE SUBROUTINE FOLLOWS
```

```
                    ;
                    ;
                    ; CALL WITH 16-BIT DIVIDEND IN REGISTER-PAIR HL, 8-BIT
                    ; DIVISOR IN REGISTER E.  THE 8-BIT QUOTIENT IS RETURNED
                    ; IN REGISTER L AND AN 8-BIT REMAINDER IS RETURNED IN
                    ; REGISTER H.  REGISTER-PAIR BC IS UNAFFECTED AS IS
                    ; REGISTER D.  THE ACCUMULATOR IS DESTROYED.  THIS
                    ; SUBROUTINE USES THE SYSTEM STACK.  IT IS REENTRANT.
                    ;
                    ;
207F C5        DIVIDE: PUSH B              ;SAVE REGISTER-PAIR BC
2080 D5                PUSH D              ;SAVE REGISTER D
2081 0E00              MVI C,0             ;ZERO QUOTIENT
2083 0608              MVI B,8             ;STEP COUNT IS ONE EXTRA
                    ;
2085 AF        DV0:    XRA A               ;CLEAR CARRY
2086 7D                MOV A,L             ;SHIFT LEFT REGISTER-PAIR HL
2087 17                RAL                 ;ARITHMETIC LEFT SHIFT
2088 6F                MOV L,A
2089 7C                MOV A,H
208A 17                RAL
208B 67                MOV H,A             ;SHIFT COMPLETE
                    ;
208C 79                MOV A,C             ;LEFT SHIFT QUOTIENT
208D 07                RLC                 ;ARITHMETIC LEFT SHIFT
208E 4F                MOV C,A
                    ;
208F 7C                MOV A,H             ;COMPARE E AND H
2090 93                SUB E               ;PERFORM H-E
2091 FA9620            JM DV1              ;BRANCH => (H>E)
2094 67                MOV H,A             ;H <-- H-E
2095 0C                INR C               ;INCREMENT QUOTIENT
                    ;
2096 05        DV1:    DCR B
2097 C28520            JNZ DV0
                    ;
209A 69                MOV L,C             ;LEAVE QUOTIENT IN L
                    ;
209B D1                POP D               ;RESTORE DE
209C C1                POP B               ;RESTORE BC
209D C9                RET
                    ;
                    ; END OF DIVIDE SUBROUTINE
                    ; A/D SUBROUTINE FOLLOWS
                    ;
                    ;
                    ; CONVERTED VALUE IS RETURNED IN ACCUMULATOR.
                    ; SETS CARRY ON OVERFLOW, CLEARS CARRY OTHERWISE.
                    ;
0024 =         DIGIN  = 24H                ;ADDRESS OF DIGITAL PARALLEL INPUT PORT
0024 =         DIGOUT = 24H                ;ADDRESS OF DIGITAL PARALLEL OUTPUT PORT
                    ;
                    ;
209E 0E00      AD:     MVI C,0             ;REGISTER "C" CONTAINS A/D COUNT
20A0 3AD020            LDA CURDIG          ;ACCUMULATOR <-- CURRENT PARALLEL
                                           ;DIGITAL OUTPUT PORT STATE
20A3 F680              ORI 80H             ;OPEN RESET SWITCH
20A5 32D020            STA CURDIG          ;STORE VALUE
                    ;
20A8 D324              OUT DIGOUT          ;OPEN INTEGRATOR RESET SWITCH
                    ;
20AA DB24      A1:     IN DIGIN            ;LOOK AT COMPARATOR
```

```
20AC E601                 ANI 1               ;MASK FOR COMPARATOR
20AE C2C220               JNZ A2              ;BRANCH IF COMPARATOR HAS SWITCHED
                      ;
20B1 0C                   INR C               ;INCREMENT COUNT
20B2 C2AA20               JNZ A1              ;NO CARRY => NO OVERFLOW
                      ;
                      ; TO HERE => COUNTER HAS OVERFLOWED
20B5 3AD020               LDA CURDIG          ;ACCUMULATOR <-- CURRENT PARALLEL OUTPUT
20B8 E67F                 ANI 7FH             ;CLOSE RESET SWITCH
20BA 32D020               STA CURDIG          ;STORE CURRENT OUTPUT STATE
20BD D324                 OUT DIGOUT          ;CLOSE RESET SWITCH
                      ;
20BF 79                   MOV A,C             ;ACCUMULATOR <-- VALUE OF COUNTER
20C0 37                   STC                 ;SET CARRY INDICATING OVERFLOW
20C1 C9                   RET
                      ;
                      ; TO HERE => COMPARATOR HAS SWITCHED WITHOUT OVERFLOW
                      ;
20C2 3AD020   A2:         LDA CURDIG          ;ACCUMULATOR <-- CURRENT PARALLEL OUTPUT
20C5 E67F                 ANI 7FH             ;CLEAR INTEGRATOR RESET BIT
20C7 32D020               STA CURDIG
20CA D324                 OUT DIGOUT          ;CLOSE INTEGRATOR RESET SWITCH
20CC 79                   MOV A,C             ;ACCUMULATOR <-- VALUE OF COUNTER
20CD 37                   STC
20CE 3F                   CMC                 ;CLEAR CARRY
20CF C9                   RET
                      ;
20D0 00       CURDIG: DB 0                    ;CURRENT STATE OF PARALLEL DIGITAL
                                              ;OUTPUT PORT
                      ;
                      ; END OF A/D PROGRAM
                      ; END OF PROGRAM
```

A27   Temperature Control Program

```
3000                      .= 3000H
                      ;
                      ; DIGITAL INPUT BIT 0 IS A/D COMPARATOR
                      ; DIGITAL OUTBIT 7 IS INTEGRATOR RESET
                      ;
0002 =        CLKMSK  = 2         ;MASK FOR CLOCK INPUT
0001 =        COMASK  = 1         ;MASK FOR COMPARATOR
                      ;
003F =        DAMAX   = 3FH       ;MAXIMUM D/A OUTPUT ALLOWED
0000 =        DAMIN   = 0         ;MINIMUM D/A OUTPUT ALLOWED
                      ;
                      ; REGISTER USAGE:  REGISTER C USED BY CLOCK UPDATE AND SHOULD
                      ; BE PRESERVED.  REGISTER B IS SCRATCH REGISTER FOR FEEDBACK
                      ; CONTROL PROGRAM.
                      ;
                      ;
                      ; INITIALIZATION MODULE
                      ;
3000 31CF32   INIT:   LXI SP,STACK    ;INITIALIZE STACK POINTER
3003 3A2330           LDA TSAMP
3006 4F               MOV C,A         ;SAMPLE TIME COUNT
                                      ;IN REGISTER C
3007 AF               XRA A           ;CLEAR CARRY
3008 32D531           STA CHAR1       ;INITIALIZE CHARACTER STORAGE AREA
300B 32D631           STA CHAR2
300E 32D731           STA CHAR3
3011 32D831           STA CHAR4
3014 32D931           STA CHAR5
3017 32DA31           STA CHAR6
```

```
301A 32DB31          STA CHAR7
301D 32DC31          STA CHAR8
                ;
3020 C32830          JMP TICDT        ;TO TICK-DETECT
                ;
3023 80     TSAMP:   DB 80H  ;SAMPLE-TIME CLOCK
3024 01     KNUM:    DB 1    ;INITIAL VALUES FOR GAINS
3025 01     KDEN:    DB 1
3026 00     CCX:     DB 0    ;OFFSET
3027 00     RSET:    DB 0    ;SETPOINT
                ;
                ; END INITIALIZE MODULE
                ;
                ; TICK-DETECT MODULE
                ;
3028 DB24   TICDT:   IN DIGIN
302A E602            ANI CLKMSK       ;LOOK AT CLODK
302C C22830          JNZ TICDT        ;WAIT FOR ZERO
                ;
302F DB24   TIC1:    IN DIGIN
3031 E602            ANI CLKMSK       ;LOOK AT CLOCK AGAIN
3033 CA2F30          JZ TIC1          ;WAIT FOR ONE
                ;
                ; END OF TICK-DETECT MODULE
                ;
                ; CLOCK-UPDATE MODULE
                ;
3036 0D     CLKUP:   DCR C            ;DECREMENT SAMPLE-TIME CLOCK
3037 C2A430          JNZ TERMIN       ;IF NOT ZERO, GO TO TERMINAL-IN
303A 3A2330          LDA TSAMP
303D 4F             MOV C,A          ;RESET SAMPLE-TIME CLOCK
                ;
                ; NOW PERFORM A/D AND CONTROL
                ;
                ; END CLOCK-UPDATE MODULE
                ;
                ; A/D MODULE
                ;
303E CD1432          CALL AD          ;ACCUMULATOR <-- VALUE
3041 D24630          JNC AD11         ;TEST FOR OVERFLOW
3044 3E7F            MVI A,7FH        ;MAXIMUM VALUE PERMITTED
3046 00     AD11:    NOP
                ;
                ; END A/D MODULE
                ;
                ; CONTROL MODULE
                ;
3047 F5             PUSH PSW         ;SAVE TEMPERATURE A/D VALUE
3048 AF             XRA A
3049 329330         STA NFLAG        ;NFLAG <-- ZERO => ERROR IS POSITIVE
304C F1             POP PSW          ;RESTORE TEMPERATURE A/D VALUE
                ;
304D 2F             CMA              ;MAKE TEMPERATURE NEGATIVE
304E 3C             INR A            ;TWO'S COMPLEMENT
                ;
304F 212730         LXI H,RSET       ;POINT TO RSET
3052 86             ADD M            ;ACCUMULATOR <-- SETPONT - TEMPERATURE
                                     ;WHICH IS ERROR
                ;
                ; NOW SEE IF RESULT IS POSITIVE OR NEGATIVE
                ;
3053 F25F30         JP CC1
3056 F5             PUSH PSW         ;SAVE ERROR
3057 3E01           MVI A,1
3059 329330         STA NFLAG        ;SET NFLAG TRUE IF ERROR IF NEGATIVE
```

```
305C F1              POP PSW          ;RESTORE ERROR
         ;
305D 2F              CMA
305E 3C              INR A            ;NEGATE ERROR TO MAKE POSITIVE
         ;
         ; NOW PREPARE FOR (KNUM*ERROR)/KDEN
         ;
305F 5F     CC1:     MOV E,A          ;E <-- MULTIPLIER WHICH IS ERROR
3060 3A2430          LDA KNUM
3063 6F              MOV L,A          ;MULTIPLICAND <-- KNUM
3064 CDF531          CALL MULT        ;KNUM*ERROR
         ;
3067 3A2530          LDA KDEN
306A 5F              MOV E,A          ;DIVISOR <-- KDEN
306B CD4C32          CALL DIVIDE      ; (KNUM*ERROR)/KDEN
         ;
306E 3A9330          LDA NFLAG        ;SEE IF WE'RE TO NEGATE RESULT
3071 FE00            CPI 0            ;FALSE?
3073 CA7A30          JZ C2
         ;
         ; TO HERE, WE MUST NEGATE OUTPUT SINCE ERROR WAS NEGATIVE
         ;
3076 7D              MOV A,L          ;ACCUMULATOR <-- QUOTIENT
3077 2F              CMA
3078 3C              INR A            ;TWO'S COMPLEMENT
3079 6F              MOV L,A          ;PLACE BACK
         ;
307A 7D     C2:      MOV A,L
307B 212630          LXI H,CCX        ;POINT TO OFFSET
307E 86              ADD M            ;ACCUMULATOR <-- (KNUM*ERROR)/KDEN+OFFSET
307F FA8E30          JM C5            ;LESS THAN ZERO => OUTPUT ZERO
3082 FE3F            CPI DAMAX        ;LIMIT OUTPUT TO BETWEEN MIN AND MAX
3084 FA8930          JM C3            ;BRANCH IF LESS THAN MAXIMUM
3087 3E3F            MVI A,DAMAX      ;LIMIT
         ;
3089 FE00   C3:      CPI DAMIN        ;COMPARE TO MINIMUM
308B F29030          JP C4            ;BRANCH IF GREATER THAN MINIMUM
308E 3E00   C5:      MVI A,DAMIN      ;LIMIT
         ;
3090 C39430 C4:      JMP DA1          ;TO D/A MODULE
         ;
3093 00     NFLAG:   DB 0             ;NEGATE FLAG
         ;
         ; END OF COMPUTE MODULE
         ;
         ; D/A MODULE
         ;
3094 47     DA1:     MOV B,A          ;SAVE OUTPUT
3095 3AA330          LDA CURDIG       ;LOOK AT CURRENT DIGITAL OUTPUT STATE
3098 E6C0            ANI 0C0H         ;CLEAR LOWER SIX BITS OF D/A
309A B0              ORA B            ;SET OUTPUT OF D/A
309B D324            OUT DIGOUT       ;NEW D/A OUTPUT
309D 32A330          STA CURDIG       ;STORE VALUE WHICH IS CURRENT STATE
         ;
30A0 C3A430          JMP TERMIN       ;TO TERMINAL-IN MODULE
         ;
30A3 00     CURDIG:  DB 0             ;CURRENT PARALLEL DIGITAL OUTPUT STATE
         ;
         ; END D/A MODULE
         ;
         ; TERMINAL-IN MODULE
         ;
30A4 DB00   TERMIN:  IN KBCSR
30A6 E640            ANI CHARED       ;CHECK FOR CHARACTER READY
30A8 CA2830          JZ TICDT         ;IF NOT READY, TO TICK-DETECT
```

```
                         ;
30AB CDDD31              CALL CHIN        ;GET CHARACTER
30AE CDE931              CALL CHOUT       ;ECHO CHARACTER
                         ;
30B1 FE0D                CPI CR           ;A "RETURN"?
30B3 C2BE30              JNZ TER1         ;IF NOT, BRANCH
                         ;
30B6 3E0A                MVI A,LF         ;IF YES, ECHO A LINE FEED
30B8 CDE931              CALL CHOUT
                         ;
30BB C33B31              JMP MSGDCD       ;TO MESSAGE-DECODER
                         ;
                         ; THE FOLLOWING SEQUENCE TESTS CHARACTERS FROM CHAR1 TO
                         ; CHAR8 TO FIND THE FIRST NULL.  IT PUTS THE CURRENT
                         ; CHARACTER INTO THAT POSITION.
                         ;
30BE F5        TER1:     PUSH PSW         ;SAVE CHARACTER TO PLACE IN MEMORY
30BF 3AD531              LDA CHAR1
30C2 FE00                CPI 0            ;NULL?
30C4 C2CE30              JNZ TER2
30C7 F1                  POP PSW
30C8 32D531              STA CHAR1
30CB C32830              JMP TICDT        ;TO TICK-DETECT
                         ;
30CE 3AD631    TER2:     LDA CHAR2
30D1 FE00                CPI 0
30D3 C2DD30              JNZ TER3
30D6 F1                  POP PSW
30D7 32D631              STA CHAR2
30DA C32830              JMP TICDT        ;AS ABOVE
                         ;
30DD 3AD731    TER3:     LDA CHAR3
30E0 FE00                CPI 0
30E2 C2EC30              JNZ TER4
30E5 F1                  POP PSW
30E6 32D731              STA CHAR3
30E9 C32830              JMP TICDT
                         ;
30EC 3AD831    TER4:     LDA CHAR4
30EF FE00                CPI 0
30F1 C2FB30              JNZ TER5
30F4 F1                  POP PSW
30F5 32D831              STA CHAR4
30F8 C32830              JMP TICDT
                         ;
30FB 3AD931    TER5:     LDA CHAR5
30FE FE00                CPI 0
3100 C20A31              JNZ TER6
3103 F1                  POP PSW
3104 32D931              STA CHAR5
3107 C32830              JMP TICDT
                         ;
310A 3ADA31    TER6:     LDA CHAR6
310D FE00                CPI 0
310F C21931              JNZ TER7
3112 F1                  POP PSW
3113 32DA31              STA CHAR6
3116 C32830              JMP TICDT
                         ;
3119 3ADB31    TER7:     LDA CHAR7
311C FE00                CPI 0
311E C22831              JNZ TER8
3121 F1                  POP PSW
3122 32DB31              STA CHAR7
3125 C32830              JMP TICDT
```

```
                ;
3128 3ADC31     TER8:   LDA CHAR8
312B FE00               CPI 0
312D C23731             JNZ TER9
3130 F1                 POP PSW
3131 32DC31             STA CHAR8
3134 C32830             JMP TICDT
                ;
3137 F1         TER9:   POP PSW             ;NO PLACE FOR CHARACTER, IGNORE IT.
                ;
3138 C32830             JMP TICDT           ;TO TICK-DETECT
                ;
                ; END OF TERMNAL-IN MODULE
                ;
                ; MESSAGE DECODE MODULE
                ;
313B 3AD531     MSGDCD: LDA CHAR1           ;EXAMINE FIRST CHARACTER OF COMMAND
313E FE52               CPI 'R'             ;IS COMMAND AN R?
3140 C24C31             JNZ MSG1
3143 CD9831             CALL VALUE          ;YES, GET VALUE, RETURN IN ACCUMULATOR
3146 322730             STA RSET            ;UPDATE SETPOINT
3149 C3B931             JMP CHCLR           ;CLEAR CHARACTERS
                ;
314C FE4B       MSG1:   CPI 'K'             ;IS IT UPDATE GAIN COMMAND?
314E C27231             JNZ MSG2
3151 CD9831             CALL VALUE
3154 322430             STA KNUM
3157 3ADA31             LDA CHAR6
315A 32D631             STA CHAR2
315D 3ADB31             LDA CHAR7
3160 32D731             STA CHAR3
3163 3ADC31             LDA CHAR8
3166 32D831             STA CHAR4           ;WE HAVE MOVED KDEN TO "NORMAL"
                                            ;POSITION FOR VALUE
3169 CD9831             CALL VALUE
316C 322530             STA KDEN
316F C3B931             JMP CHCLR           ;AS ABOVE
                ;
3172 FE43       MSG2:   CPI 'C'             ;UPDATE OFFSET?
3174 C28031             JNZ MSG3
3177 CD9831             CALL VALUE
317A 320100             STA CCX
317D C3B931             JMP CHCLR
                ;
3180 FE53       MSG3:   CPI 'S'             ;STOP COMMAND?
3182 C28631             JNZ MSG4            ;LAST VALID CHARACTER
3185 F7                 RST 6               ;STOP COMMAND.  RETURN TO MONITOR
                ;
3186 3E3F       MSG4:   MVI A,'?'           ;UNRECOGNIZABLE COMMAND
3188 CDE931             CALL CHOUT          ;SEND CHARACTER
318B 3E0D               MVI A,CR            ;RETURN
318D CDE931             CALL CHOUT
3190 3E0A               MVI A,LF            ;LINEFEED
3192 CDE931             CALL CHOUT
3195 C3B931             JMP CHCLR           ;CLEAR CHARACTERS
                ;
                ; VALUE SUBROUTINE CONVERTS 3 ASCII CHARACTERS TO
                ; BINARY BY REPEATED MULTIPLICATION.
                ;
3198 1E64       VALUE:  MVI E,100           ;MULTIPLIER
319A 3AD631             LDA CHAR2           ;MOST SIGNIFICANT CHARACTER
319D D630               SUI '0'             ;MAKE BINARY
319F 6F                 MOV L,A             ;BECOMES MULTIPLICAND
31A0 CDF531             CALL MULT           ;PERFORM (CHAR1)*100
31A3 45                 MOV B,L             ;FIRST PRODUCT
```

```
                      ;
31A4 1E0A             MVI E,10          ;MULTIPLIER
31A6 3AD731           LDA CHAR3
31A9 D630             SUI '0'           ;AS ABOVE
31AB 6F               MOV L,A           ;MULTIPLICAND
31AC CDF531           CALL MULT
31AF 7D               MOV A,L           ;ACCUMULATOR <-- SECOND PRODUCT
31B0 80               ADD B             ;ACCUMULATOR <-- FIRST + SECOND PRODUCT
31B1 47               MOV B,A
                      ;
31B2 3AD831           LDA CHAR4         ;FINAL CHARACTER (LEAST SIGNIFICANT)
31B5 D630             SUI '0'           ;MAKE BINARY
31B7 80               ADD B             ;ACCUMULATOR <-- FINAL VALUE
31B8 C9               RET
                   ;
                   ; END VALUE SUBROUTINE
                   ;
                   ; CHARACTER CLEAR MODULE
                   ;
31B9 AF            CHCLR:  XRA A         ;CLEAR ACCUMULATOR
31BA 32D531                STA CHAR1
31BD 32D631                STA CHAR2
31C0 32D731                STA CHAR3
31C3 32D831                STA CHAR4
31C6 32D931                STA CHAR5
31C9 32DA31                STA CHAR6
31CC 32DB31                STA CHAR7
31CF 32DC31                STA CHAR8
                   ;
31D2 C32830               JMP TICDT      ;TO TICK-DETECT
                   ;
                   ;
31D5 00            CHAR1:  DB 0          ;CHARACTER STORAGE AREA
31D6 00            CHAR2:  DB 0
31D7 00            CHAR3:  DB 0
31D8 00            CHAR4:  DB 0
31D9 00            CHAR5:  DB 0
31DA 00            CHAR6:  DB 0
31DB 00            CHAR7:  DB 0
31DC 00            CHAR8:  DB 0
                   ;
                   ; END OF FEED BACK CONTROL PROGRAM
                   ; SUBROUTINES FOLLOW
                   ;
0000 =             KBCSR   = 0           ;ADDRESS OF KEYBOARD STATUS REGISTER
0001 =             KBBUF   = 1           ;ADDRESS OF KEYBOARD DATA REGISTER
0000 =             DISCSR  = 0           ;ADDRESS OF DISPLAY STATUS REGISTER
0001 =             DISBUF  = 1           ;ADDRESS OF DISPLAY DATA BUFFER
                   ;
0040 =             CHARED  = 40H         ;MASK FOR CHARACTER READY FROM SERIAL INTERFACE
0080 =             TXMPTY  = 80H         ;MASK FOR SERIAL TRANSMITTER EMPTY
                   ;
000D =             CR      = 13          ;ASCII CODE FOR CARRIAGE RETURN
000A =             LF      = 10          ;ASCII CODE FOR LINE FEED
                   ;
31DD DB00          CHIN:   IN KBCSR      ;READ KEYBOARD STATUS REGISTER
31DF E640                  ANI CHARED    ;SEE IF CHARACTER IS READY
31E1 CADD31                JZ CHIN       ;IF NOT, WAIT
                   ;
31E4 DB01                  IN KBBUF      ;ACCUMULATOR <-- CHARACTER
31E6 E67F                  ANI 7FH       ;CLEAR PARITY BIT
31E8 C9                    RET           ;RETURN FROM SUBROUTINE
                   ;
                   ;
31E9 F5            CHOUT:  PUSH PSW      ;SAVE CHARACTER PASSED ON SYSTEM STACK
```

```
31EA DB00      Cl:     IN DISCSR       ;READ DISPLAY STATUS REGISTER
31EC E680              ANI TXMPTY      ;SEE IF TRANSMITTER IS READY FOR CHARACTER
31EE CAEA31            JZ Cl           ;IF NOT READY, WAIT
               ;
31F1 F1                POP PSW         ;RESTORE ACCUMULATOR WITH CHARACTER TO SEND
31F2 D301              OUT DISBUF      ;SEND CHARACTER
31F4 C9                RET             ;RETURN FROM SUBROUTINE
               ;
               ;
               ;
               ; CALL THIS SUBROUTINE WITH 8-BIT MULTIPLICAND IN "L" AND
               ; 8-BIT MULTIPLIER IN "E".  16-BIT PRODUCT IS RETURNED
               ; IN "HL".  MULTIPLIER IS RETURNED UNCHANGED.
               ; THIS ROUTINE USES THE STACK, THUS IT MUST HAVE BEEN
               ; INITIALIZED.
               ; THIS SUBROUTINE IS REENTRANT.
               ;
31F5 C5        MULT:   PUSH B          ;SAVE REGISTER B ON STACK
31F6 D5                PUSH D          ;WE'LL USE REGISTER D FOR COUNT,
                                       ;THUS WE'LL SAVE OLD VALUE OF D.
31F7 4D                MOV C,L         ;REGISTER C <-- MULTIPLICAND
31F8 0600              MVI B,0         ;NOW REGISTER PAIR BC CONTAINS
                                       ;MULTIPLICAND
31FA 210000            LXI H,0         ;ZERO PRODUCT REGISTER PAIR
31FD 1608              MVI D,8         ;D <-- STEP COUNT
               ;
31FF AF        M1:     XRA A           ;CLEAR CARRY
3200 7D                MOV A,L         ;ACCUMULATOR <-- LOWER ORDER BYTE
                                       ;OF PRODUCT
3201 17                RAL             ;CLEAR CARRY AND RAL IS EQUIVALENT
                                       ;TO ARITHMETIC LEFT SHIFT.
3202 6F                MOV L,A         ;PLACE BACK (CARRY IS NOW SHIFTED
                                       ;BIT OF LOWER ORDER).
3203 7C                MOV A,H         ;ACCUMULATOR <-- HIGH ORDER OR
                                       ;PRODUCT
3204 17                RAL             ;SHIFT HIGH ORDER OF PRODUCT AND
                                       ;SHIFT IN CARRY WHICH IS SHIFT OF
                                       ;BIT 7 OF LOWER ORDER BYTE OF PRODUCT
3205 67                MOV H,A         ;PLACE HIGH-ORDER PRODUCT BACK
3206 7B                MOV A,E         ;ACCUMULATOR <-- MULTIPLICAND
3207 07                RLC             ;ROTATE MULTIPLIER LEFT
3208 5F                MOV E,A         ;PLACE REGISTER E BACK
3209 D20D32            JNC M3          ;BRANCH IF NO BIT ROTATED OUT
320C 09                DAD B           ;PRODUCT <-- PRODUCT + MULTIPLICAND
               ;
320D 15        M3:     DCR D           ;DECREMENT STEP COUNT
320E C2FF31            JNZ M1          ;LOOP FOR EIGHT BITS
               ;
3211 D1                POP D           ;RESTORE DE
3212 C1                POP B           ;RESTORE BC
3213 C9                RET
               ;
               ; END OF MULTIPLY SUBROUTINE
               ;
               ;
               ;
               ; CONVERTED VALUE IS RETURNED IN ACCUMULATOR.
               ; SETS CARRY ON OVERFLOW, CLEARS CARRY OTHERWISE.
               ;
0024 =         DIGIN   = 24H           ;ADDRESS OF DIGITAL PARALLEL INPUT PORT
0024 =         DIGOUT  = 24H           ;ADDRESS OF DIGITAL PARALLEL OUTPUT PORT
               ;
               ;
3214 C5        AD:     PUSH B          ;SAVE B,C ACCROSS CALL
3215 0E00              MVI C,0         ;REGISTER "C" CONTAINS A/D COUNT
```

```
3217 3AA330            LDA CURDIG     ;ACCUMULATOR <-- CURRENT PARALLEL
                                      ;DIGITAL OUTPUT PORT STATE
321A F680              ORI 80H        ;OPEN RESET SWITCH
321C 32A330            STA CURDIG     ;STORE VALUE
              ;
321F D324              OUT DIGOUT     ;OPEN INTEGRATOR RESET SWITCH
              ;
3221 DB24     A1:      IN DIGIN       ;LOOK AT COMPARATOR
3223 E601              ANI COMASK     ;MASK FOR COMPARATOR
3225 C23D32            JNZ A2         ;BRANCH IF COMPARATOR HAS SWITCHED
              ;
3228 0C                INR C          ;INCREMENT COUNT
              ;
3229 79                MOV A,C
322A E680              ANI 80H        ;TEST FOR OVERFLOW INTO BIT 7
322C CA2132            JZ A1          ;BIT 7 CLEAR => NO OVERFLOW
              ; TO HERE => COUNTER HAS OVERFLOWED
322F 3AA330            LDA CURDIG     ;ACCUMULATOR <-- CURRENT PARALLEL OUTPUT
3232 E67F              ANI 7FH        ;CLOSE RESET SWITCH
3234 32A330            STA CURDIG     ;STORE CURRENT OUTPUT STATE
3237 D324              OUT DIGOUT     ;CLOSE RESET SWITCH
              ;
3239 79                MOV A,C        ;ACCUMULATOR <-- VALUE OF COUNTER
323A C1                POP B          ;RESTORE BC
323B 37                STC            ;SET CARRY INDICATING OVERFLOW
323C C9                RET
              ;
              ; TO HERE => COMPARATOR HAS SWITCHED WITHOUT OVERFLOW
              ;
323D 3AA330   A2:      LDA CURDIG     ;ACCUMULATOR <-- CURRENT PARALLEL OUTPUT
3240 E67F              ANI 7FH        ;CLEAR INTEGRATOR RESET BIT
3242 32A330            STA CURDIG
3245 D324              OUT DIGOUT     ;CLOSE INTEGRATOR RESET SWITCH
3247 79                MOV A,C        ;ACCUMULATOR <-- VALUE OF COUNTER
3248 C1                POP B          ;RESTORE BC
3249 37                STC
324A 3F                CMC            ;CLEAR CARRY
324B C9                RET
              ;
              ; END OF A/D PROGRAM
              ;
              ;
              ;
              ;
              ; CALL WITH 16-BIT DIVIDEND IN REGISTER-PAIR HL, 8-BIT
              ; DIVISOR IN REGISTER E.  THE 8-BIT QUOTIENT IS RETURNED
              ; IN REGISTER L AND AN 8-BIT REMAINDER IS RETURNED IN
              ; REGISTER H.  REGISTER-PAIR BC IS UNAFFECTED AS IS
              ; REGISTER D.  THE ACCUMULATOR IS DESTROYED.  THIS
              ; SUBROUTINE USES THE SYSTEM STACK.  IT IS REENTRANT.
              ;
              ;
324C C5       DIVIDE:  PUSH B         ;SAVE REGISTER-PAIR BC
324D D5                PUSH D         ;SAVE REGISTER D
324E 0E00              MVI C,0        ;ZERO QUOTIENT
3250 0608              MVI B,8        ;STEP COUNT
              ;
3252 AF       DV0:     XRA A          ;CLEAR CARRY
3253 7D                MOV A,L        ;SHIFT LEFT REGISTER-PAIR HL
3254 17                RAL            ;ARITHMETIC LEFT SHIFT
3255 6F                MOV L,A
3256 7C                MOV A,H
3257 17                RAL
3258 67                MOV H,A        ;SHIFT COMPLETE
```

```
                    ;
3259 79             MOV A,C          ;LEFT SHIFT QUOTIENT
325A 07             RLC              ;ARITHMETIC LEFT SHIFT
325B 4F             MOV C,A
                    ;
325C 7C             MOV A,H          ;COMPARE E AND H
325D 93             SUB E            ;PERFORM H-E
325E FA6332         JM DV1           ;BRANCH => (H>E)
3261 67             MOV H,A          ;H <-- H-E
3262 0C             INR C            ;INCREMENT QUOTIENT
                    ;
3263 05      DV1:   DCR B
3264 C25232         JNZ DV0
                    ;
3267 69             MOV L,C          ;LEAVE QUOTIENT IN L
                    ;
3268 D1             POP D            ;RESTORE DE
3269 C1             POP B            ;RESTORE BC
326A C9             RET
                    ;
                    ; END OF DIVIDE SUBROUTINE
                    ;
326B                DS   100    ;RESERVE SPACE FOR STACK
32CF 00      STACK: DB 0
                    ;
                    ; END OF PROGRAM
```

BLENDING CONTROL PROGRAMS

These programs demonstrate the use of interrupts in a control problem. By using interrupts, the interaction with the operator via a terminal can be separated into a high priority part, the actual transfer of characters back and forth from the terminal, and a lower priority part, the decoding of messages from the operator and generation of output for the operator. The sampling and control continues to run at high priority. Since the actual amount of CPU time required for the terminal interaction is very low, there is virtually no conflict between the terminal service routines and the control portion of the program. Since message decoding takes longer than reading a character from the terminal, the message decoding task is put in the background at a lower priority than other tasks in order that it not interfere with the control activity.

The 8080/8085/Z80 processors have several interrupt modes. The 8080 itself has only a single interrupt mode. When a device requests an interrupt, if the processor has its interrupt enabled, the device will follow the interrupt request with a three bit code. The CPU will then execute the instruction RST N, where N is the three bit number sent by the interrupting device. This amounts to a vectored interrupt having a total of eight possible vectors.

If more than eight devices can interrupt, some polling must be done to find out which device actually caused the interrupt. In the 8085, priority interrupts have been added so that lower priority interrupts tasks can be interrupted by higher priority tasks. Each of the four priority levels has an associated RST instruction that is executed when an interrupt is requested; thus there is no vectoring within the priority levels. In addition, the 8085 has the full 8080 interrupt system.

The Z80 has three interrupt modes, numbered 0, 1, and 2. Mode 0 is the same as the 8080 interrupt. Mode 1 is a simpler mode in which the CPU will always do a RST 7. This mode is very useful for systems with only one or two interrupts sources because the interface hardware is considerably simplified and the CPU can process the interrupt quickly.

Mode 2 is a fully vectored interrupt. When a mode 2 interrupt occurs, a 16-bit vector address is constructed by taking the high-order 8 bits from the I register (a Z80 CPU register that can be loaded with the instruction STAI) and getting the low-order 8 bits from the interrupting device. The CPU uses that vector address as a pointer to memory and loads the program counter from the address pointed to by the vector. The vector is thus the address of the address of the beginning of the interrupt service routine. With this system, a maximum of 128 unique interrupt vectors can be defined, since the contents of the I register should not be changed once it has been initialized.

The programs we give here all use Z80 mode 2 interrupts. The first program, Listing A28, uses just a clock interrupt. The clock in this case is a programmable clock, which means that the amount of time that will elapse between interrupts can be set from the user program. Non-programmable clocks also exist, in which the time between interrupts is fixed. Programmable clocks are more expensive but use less CPU overhead, because, in many applications, a software counter to determine when an event (such as sampling) should occur is not needed; even if one is required, there are usually fewer interrupts between samples.

Programmable clocks are usually designed for maximum flexibility. Like serial interfaces, they often have many set-up parameters that must be initialized to determine their operating modes and the time between samples. In addition, when

using mode 2 interrupts, the value of the low-order 8 bits of the interrupt vector must be sent to the device interface as part of the initialization procedure.

The background part of Listing A28 is a dummy that keeps testing to see that the accumulator has not been changed. The foreground part of the program runs a counter that is decremented each time the clock interrupts and is reset to its initial value every time it reaches zero. At every interrupt, the value of the counter is sent to the D/A converter. A sawtooth pattern can be observed at the D/A output.

Listings A29 and A30 are programs that demonstrate the use of the terminal's interrupts. In both cases, the clock interrupt is also present and functions the same as in Listing A28. In the terminal input test program, user typed characters are placed in a buffer as they are received. Each time a character is typed, an interrupt is generated. The characters are not echoed at the time they are typed. Instead, when the program detects that the user has typed a RETURN, the entire buffer is echoed in reverse order.

The terminal output test program illustrates a common way to send messages to a terminal under interrupt control. A buffer is set up for the message, and a pointer is established to the buffer. Every time the terminal interrupts to indicate that it is ready to receive a character, the character pointed at is sent, and the pointer is incremented.

The blending control program, Listing A31, uses all three interrupts. The clock interrupt controls the sampling and control calculation process, while the two terminal interrupts control the interaction with the operator. Other than the instructions associated with the interrupts, the calculation procedures use most of the same instruction sequences and subroutines as the temperature control program. Some enhancements have been made in the form of overflow and limit checking.

Because all of the major control variables are defined as 8 bit quantities, the precision is extremely limited. For that reason, the limit check routine used in the temperature control program is of little value, because any number that goes past the maximum (or minimum) value will actually cause an overflow and *wraparound*. For example, if two numbers were added together to give a result of 129, that result would be interpreted as -127, since 129 represents a negative two's complement number. If -127 went through a limit check with limits of 0 and 127, the output would be set to zero, certainly not the desired result!

To avoid this error, a subroutine that performs additions with overflow check, ADDCHK, has been added. It checks for overflow by comparing the sign of the result with the sign of the inputs. In any addition process for which the operands both have the same sign, the result must have that sign. If the operands have different signs, overflow cannot occur.

An additional problem in checking for limits occurs when the check is done by subtracting the quantity being tested from the limits. The result of such a subtraction can be larger than the largest allowable two's complement number. If that condition were to occur, an erroneous limit indication would result. For that reason, a subroutine MAX has been added to determine which of two numbers is larger. If the numbers have opposite signs, the determination is made on the basis of sign. If they have the same sign, it is made by subtraction. (Some computers include hardware to make this test; the Z80 has such hardware, but the 8080 does not.)

A28   Clock Interrupt Test Program

```
                          1 ; INTERRUPT TEST PROGRAM
                          2 ;
                          3 ; THIS CLOCK INTERRUPT ROUTINE SENDS A SAWTOOTH WAVEFORM
                          4 ; TO A D/A CONVERTER.  THIS PROGRAM ALSO DEMONSTRATES THE
                          5 ; IMPORTANCE OF PRESERVING THE MACHINE STATE IN THE
                          6 ; INTERRUPT ENVIRONMENT.
                          7 ; THIS PROGRAM ASSUMES THE USE OF A PROGRAMABLE TIMER (8253).
                          8 ; Z-80 MODE TWO INTERRUPT RESPONSE AND
                          9 ; A PROGRAMABLE INTERRUPT CONTROLLER (8214) ARE USED.
                         10 ; ALTHOUGH THE CODE FOR THIS PROGRAM IS DEPENDENT UPON THE
                         11 ; TIMER AND INTERRUPT CONTROLLER HARDWARE, THE STRUCTURE OF
                         12 ; A PROGRAM USING ARBITRARY HARDWARE IS SIMILAR.
                         13 ;
00df                     14 TIMCON  = 0DFH          ;TIMER CONTROL PORT ADDRESS
00dc                     15 TIMDAT  = 0DCH          ;TIMER DATA PORT ADDRESS
00d7                     16 CONTRL  = 0D7H          ;INTERRUPT CONTROLLER ADDRESS
fff0                     17 INADR   = 0FFF0H        ;INTERRUPT VECTOR ADDRESS
00ad                     18 DA0     = 0ADH          ;LOWER ORDER D/A
00ac                     19 DA1     = 0ACH          ;HIGHER ORDER D/A
00ed                     20 KBCSR   = 0EDH          ;KEYBOARD STATUS REGISTER
00ec                     21 KBBUF   = 0ECH          ;KEYBOARD DATA BUFFER
0002                     22 CHARED  = 2             ;MASK FOR CHARACTER-READY FLAG
00ec                     23 DISBUF  = 0ECH          ;DISPLAY DATA BUFFER
000d                     24 CR      = 13            ;ASCII CARRIAGE RETURN
                         25 ;
e000                     26         .=0E000H        ;STARTING ADDRESS OF PROGRAM
                         27 ;
e000 db ed               28 GO:     IN KBCSR        ;GET CHARACTER
e002 e6 02               29         ANI CHARED
```

```
e004 ca 00 e0   30              JZ GO           ;WAIT IF NO CHAR READY
e007 db ec      31              IN KBBUF        ;GET CHARACTER
e009 fe 47      32              CPI 'G'         ;G?
e00b c2 00 e0   33              JNZ GO          ;IF NOT WAIT FOR NEXT CHAR.
e00e d3 ec      34              OUT DISBUF      ;ECHO G (NOTHING ELSE WILL BE ECHOED)
                35 ;
e010 31 f0 ff   36              LXI SP,0FFF0H   ;INITIALIZE STACK POINTER
                37 ;
e013 21 43 e0   38              LXI H,TIMER     ;HL <-- ADDRESS OF INTERRUPT ROUTINE
e016 22 f0 ff   39              SHLD INADR      ;STORE ADDRESS OF INTERRUPT ROUTINE AT VECTOR
                40                              ;LOCATION
e019 3e ff      41              MVI A,0FFH      ;ACCUMULATOR <-- MOST SIGNIFICANT BYTE OF
                42                              ;INTERRUPT VECTOR
e01b ed 47      43              DB 0EDH,47H     ;THIS IS THE OPERATION CODE FOR THE Z-80
                44                              ;INSTRUCTION STAI OR REGISTER I <-- ACCUMULATOR
e01d ed 5e      45              DB 0EDH,5EH     ;Z-80 CODE FOR IM2, SELECT INTERRUPT MODE 2
e01f 3e 30      46              MVI A,30H       ;INITIALIZE (8253) COUNTER:
                47                              ;MODE ZERO, LOAD LSB FIRST
e021 d3 df      48              OUT TIMCON      ;TIMER CONTROL PORT
e023 21 d0 07   49              LXI H,2000      ;2MHZ/2000 = 1KHZ COUNTER INTERRUPT RATE
e026 7d         50              MOV A,L
e027 d3 dc      51              OUT TIMDAT      ;WRITE TO TIMER DATA PORT
e029 7c         52              MOV A,H
e02a d3 dc      53              OUT TIMDAT      ;WRITE MOST SIGNIFICANT BYTE
                54 ;
e02c 3e 81      55              MVI A,81H       ;INITIALIZE 8214 INTERRUPT CONTROLLER
e02e d3 d7      56              OUT CONTRL
                57 ;
e030 21 ff 00   58              LXI H,0FFH      ;NUMBER OF CLOCK COUNTS
e033 22 6e e0   59              SHLD COUNT
e036 3e 02      60              MVI A,2         ;VALUE IN A TO CHECK FOR REGISTER PRESERVATION
e038 fb         61              EI              ;ENABLE INTERRUPTS -- TIMER IS NOW RUNNING
                62 ;
                63 ;BACK IS THE START OF THE BACKGROUND ROUTINE... IT RUNS WHENEVER THE
                64 ;INTERRUPT ROUTINE IS NOT RUNNING.
                65 ;
e039 fe 02      66 BACK:        CPI 2           ;DOES A HAVE A 2?
e03b c2 41 e0   67              JNZ B2          ;IF NOT, GO BACK TO DDT TO INDICATE AN ERROR
e03e c3 39 e0   68              JMP BACK        ;KEEP LOOKING
                69 ;
e041 f3         70 B2:          DI              ;DISABLE INTERRUPTS
e042 c9         71              RET             ;RETURN TO MONITOR
                72 ;
                73 ; INTERRUPT SERVICE ROUTINE
                74 ;
e043 f5         75 TIMER:       PUSH PSW        ;PRESERVE MACHINE STATE
e044 e5         76              PUSH H
                77 ;
e045 21 d0 07   78              LXI H,2000      ;RESET TIMER
e048 7d         79              MOV A,L
e049 d3 dc      80              OUT TIMDAT      ;WRITE LEAST SIGNIFICANT BYTE
e04b 7c         81              MOV A,H
e04c d3 dc      82              OUT TIMDAT      ;WRITE MOST SIGNIFICANT BYTE
                83 ;
e04e 2a 6e e0   84              LHLD COUNT      ;HL <-- COUNT
e051 7c         85              MOV A,H         ;AC <-- HIGH ORDER BYTE OF COUNT
e052 f6 80      86              ORI 80H         ;SELECT D/A CHANNEL
e054 d3 ac      87              OUT DA1         ;WRITE TO D/A
e056 7d         88              MOV A,L         ;AC <-- LOWER ORDER BYTE OF COUNT
e057 d3 ad      89              OUT DA0
e059 2b         90              DCX H           ;DECREMENT COUNT
e05a 7c         91              MOV A,H
e05b b5         92              ORA L           ;TEST COUNT FOR ZERO
e05c c2 62 e0   93              JNZ TIM1
e05f 21 ff 0f   94              LXI H,0FFFH     ;HL <-- NEW COUNT
e062 22 6e e0   95 TIM1:        SHLD COUNT      ;STORE COUNT
```

```
                     96 ;
e065 3e 81           97          MVI A,81H    ;RESET INTERRUPT CONTROLLER (8214)
e067 d3 d7           98          OUT CONTRL
                     99 ;
e069 e1             100          POP H
e06a f1             101          POP PSW      ;RESTORE ACCUMULATOR AND FLAGS
e06b fb             102          EI           ;RE-ENABLE INTERRUPTS
e06c ed 4d          103          DB 0EDH,4DH  ;Z-80 CODE FOR RETURN FROM MASKABLE INTERRUPT
                    104 ;
e06e 00 00          105 COUNT:   DW 0         ;MEMORY LOCATION FOR COUNT VARIABLE.
                    106 ;
                    107 ; END OF PROGRAM
```

A29   Terminal Input Interrupt Test Program

```
                      1 ; TERMINAL INPUT INTERRUPT TEST PROGRAM
                      2 ;
                      3 ; THIS PROGRAM RECEIVES CHARACTERS FROM THE KEYBOARD AND
                      4 ; STORES THEM WITHOUT ECHO.  WHEN A RETURN IS TYPED, THE
                      5 ; ENTIRE STRING IS ECHOED BACKWARDS (THIS IS EQUIVALENT
                      6 ; TO A LAST-IN, FIRST-OUT (LIFO) STACK).
                      7 ;
                      8 ; THIS PROGRAM USES THE SAME MAIN ROUTINE AND CLOCK INTERRUPT
                      9 ; ROUTINE AS THE CLOCK INTERRUPT PROGRAM.
                     10 ;
00df                 11 TIMCON  = 0DFH        ;TIMER CONTROL PORT ADDRESS
00dc                 12 TIMDAT  = 0DCH        ;TIMER DATA PORT ADDRESS
00d7                 13 CONTRL  = 0D7H        ;INTERRUPT CONTROLLER ADDRESS
fff0                 14 INADR   = 0FFF0H      ;INTERRUPT VECTOR ADDRESS, CLOCK
fffc                 15 KEYADR  = 0FFFCH      ;INTERRUPT VECTOR ADDRESS, KEYBOARD
00ad                 16 DA0     = 0ADH        ;LOWER ORDER D/A
00ac                 17 DA1     = 0ACH        ;HIGHER ORDER D/A
00ed                 18 KBCSR   = 0EDH        ;KEYBOARD COMMAND STATUS REGISTER
00ec                 19 KBBUF   = 0ECH        ;KEYBOARD DATA BUFFER
00ed                 20 DISCSR  = 0EDH        ;CONSOLE DISPLAY COMMAND STATUS REGISTER
00ec                 21 DISBUF  = 0ECH        ;CONSOLE DISPLAY DATA BUFFER
0002                 22 CHARED  = 2           ;MASK FOR CHARACTER READY FLAG
0001                 23 TXMPTY  = 1           ;MASK FOR SERIAL TRANSMITTER READY
000d                 24 CR      = 13          ;ASCII CARRIAGE RETURN
                     25 ;
e000                 26          .=0E000H     ;STARTING ADDRESS OF PROGRAM
                     27 ;
e000 db ed           28 GO:      IN KBCSR     ;GET CHAR.
e002 e6 02           29          ANI CHARED
e004 ca 00 e0        30          JZ GO        ;WAIT IF NO CHAR READY
e007 db ec           31          IN KBBUF     ;GET CHARACTER
e009 fe 47           32          CPI 'G'      ;G?
e00b c2 00 e0        33          JNZ GO       ;IF NOT WAIT FOR NEXT CHAR.
e00e d3 ec           34          OUT DISBUF   ;ECHO G (NOTHING ELSE WILL BE ECHOED)
                     35 ;
e010 31 f0 ff        36          LXI SP,0FFF0H ;INITIALIZE STACK POINTER
                     37 ;
e013 21 49 e0        38          LXI H,TIMER  ;HL <-- ADDRESS OF INTERRUPT ROUTINE
e016 22 f0 ff        39          SHLD INADR   ;STORE ADDRESS OF INTERRUPT ROUTINE AT VECTOR
                     40                       ;LOCATION
e019 21 76 e0        41          LXI H,KINT   ;HL <-- KEYBOARD INTERRUPT ROUTINE ADDRESS
e01c 22 fc ff        42          SHLD KEYADR  ;STORE ADDRESS AT VECTOR LOCATION
e01f 3e ff           43          MVI A,0FFH   ;ACCUMULATOR <-- MOST SIGNIFICANT BYTE OF
                     44                       ;INTERRUPT VECTOR
e021 ed 47           45          DB 0EDH,47H  ;THIS IS THE OPERATION CODE FOR THE Z-80
                     46                       ;INSTRUCTION STAI OR REGISTER I <-- ACCUMULATOR
e023 ed 5e           47          DB 0EDH,5EH  ;Z-80 CODE FOR IM2, SELECT INTERRUPT MODE 2
e025 3e 30           48          MVI A,30H    ;INITIALIZE (8253) COUNTER
                     49                       ;MODE ZERO, LOAD LSB FIRST
e027 d3 df           50          OUT TIMCON   ;TIMER CONTROL PORT
e029 21 d0 07        51          LXI H,2000   ;2MHZ/2000 = 1KHZ COUNTER INTERRUPT RATE
```

```
e02c 7d        52              MOV A,L
e02d d3 dc     53              OUT TIMDAT      ;WRITE TO TIMER DATA PORT
e02f 7c        54              MOV A,H
e030 d3 dc     55              OUT TIMDAT      ;WRITE MOST SIGNIFICANT BYTE
               56 ;
e032 3e 87     57              MVI A,87H       ;INITIALIZE 8214 INTERRUPT CONTROLLER
e034 d3 d7     58              OUT CONTRL
               59 ;
e036 21 ff 00  60              LXI H,0FFH      ;NUMBER OF CLOCK COUNTS
e039 22 74 e0  61              SHLD COUNT
e03c 3e 02     62              MVI A,2         ;VALUE IN ACCUMULATOR TO CHECK FOR REGISTER
               63                              ;PRESERVATION
e03e fb        64              EI              ;ENABLE INTERRUPTS -- TIMER IS NOW RUNNING
               65 ;
               66 ; BACK IS THE START OF THE BACKGROUND ROUTINE ... IT RUNS WHENEVER
               67 ; THE INTERRUPT ROUTINE IS NOT RUNNING.
               68 ;
e03f fe 02     69 BACK:        CPI 2           ;DOES A HAVE A 2?
e041 c2 47 e0  70              JNZ B2          ;IF NOT, GO BACK TO DDT TO INDICATE AN ERROR
e044 c3 3f e0  71              JMP BACK        ;KEEP LOOKING
               72 ;
e047 f3        73 B2:          DI              ;DISABLE INTERRUPTS
e048 c9        74              RET             ;RETURN TO MONITOR
               75 ;
               76 ;
               77 ;CLOCK INTERRUPT SERVICE ROUTINE
               78 ;
e049 f5        79 TIMER:       PUSH PSW        ;PRESERVE MACHINE STATE
e04a e5        80              PUSH H
               81 ;
e04b 21 d0 07  82              LXI H,2000      ;RESET TIMER
e04e 7d        83              MOV A,L
e04f d3 dc     84              OUT TIMDAT      ;WRITE LEAST SIGNIFICANT BYTE
e051 7c        85              MOV A,H
e052 d3 dc     86              OUT TIMDAT      ;WRITE MOST SIGNIFICANT BYTE
               87 ;
e054 2a 74 e0  88              LHLD COUNT      ;HL <-- COUNT
e057 7c        89              MOV A,H         ;AC <-- HIGH ORDER BYTE OF COUNT
e058 f6 80     90              ORI 80H         ;SELECT D/A CHANNEL
e05a d3 ac     91              OUT DA1         ;WRITE TO D/A
e05c 7d        92              MOV A,L         ;AC <-- LOWER ORDER BYTE OF COUNT
e05d d3 ad     93              OUT DA0
e05f 2b        94              DCX H           ;DECREMENT COUNT
e060 7c        95              MOV A,H
e061 b5        96              ORA L           ;TEST FOR ZERO
e062 c2 68 e0  97              JNZ TIM1
e065 21 ff 0f  98              LXI H,0FFFH     ;HL <-- NEW COUNT
e068 22 74 e0  99 TIM1:        SHLD COUNT      ;STORE COUNT
               100 ;
e06b 3e 87     101             MVI A,87H       ;RESET INTERRUPT CONTROLLER (8214)
e06d d3 d7     102             OUT CONTRL
               103 ;
e06f e1        104             POP H
e070 f1        105             POP PSW         ;RESTORE ACCUMULATOR AND FLAGS
e071 fb        106             EI              ;RE-ENABLE INTERRUPTS
e072 ed 4d     107             DB 0EDH,4DH     ;Z-80 CODE FOR RETURN FROM MASKABLE INTERRUPT
               108 ;
e074 00 00     109 COUNT:      DW 0            ;MEMORY LOCATION FOR COUNT VARIABLE
               110 ;
               111 ; END OF CLOCK INTERRUPT SERVICE RETURN
               112 ;
               113 ; KEYBOARD INTERRUPT SERVICE RETURN
               114 ;
e076 f5        115 KINT:       PUSH PSW        ;PRESERVE MACHINE STATE
e077 c5        116             PUSH B
e078 d5        117             PUSH D
```

```
e079 e5          118          PUSH H
                 119 ;
e07a 2a bd e0    120          LHLD BPOINT    ;HL <-- POINTER TO BUFFER
e07d db ec       121          IN KBBUF       ;AC <-- CHARACTER
e07f e6 7f       122          ANI 7FH        ;REMOVE ANY PARITY
e081 77          123          MOV M,A        ;PLACE CHARACTER IN BUFFER
e082 23          124          INX H          ;INCREMENT POINTER TO NEXT FREE LOCATION
e083 22 bd e0    125          SHLD BPOINT    ;STORE POINTER
e086 47          126          MOV B,A        ;SAVE CHARACTER IN REGISTER B
e087 3a bc e0    127          LDA NCH        ;AC <-- CHARACTER COUNT
e08a 3c          128          INR A
e08b 32 bc e0    129          STA NCH        ;CHARACTER COUNT += 1
e08e 78          130          MOV A,B        ;LOOK AGAIN AT CHARACTER
e08f fe 0d       131          CPI CR         ;IS CHARACTER A CARRIAGE RETURN?
e091 ca 9f e0    132          JZ KECHO       ;IF YES, ECHO BUFFER
                 133 ;
e094 3e 87       134 KXIT:    MVI A,87H      ;RESET INTERRUPT CONTROLLER
e096 d3 d7       135          OUT CONTRL
                 136 ;
e098 e1          137          POP H          ;RESTORE MACHINE STATE
e099 d1          138          POP D
e09a c1          139          POP B
e09b f1          140          POP PSW
e09c fb          141          EI
e09d ed 4d       142          DB 0EDH,4DH    ;Z-80 CODE FOR RETURN FROM MASKABLE INTERRUPT
                 143 ;
e09f 2b          144 KECHO:   DCX H          ;DECREMENT POINTER
e0a0 22 bd e0    145          SHLD BPOINT    ;STORE IT
e0a3 7e          146          MOV A,M        ;AC <-- BUFFER CHARACTER
e0a4 d3 ec       147          OUT DISBUF     ;SEND CHARACTER
e0a6 3a bc e0    148          LDA NCH        ;CHECK CHARACTER COUNT
e0a9 3d          149          DCR A          ;DECREMENT COUNT
e0aa 32 bc e0    150          STA NCH
e0ad fe 00       151          CPI 0          ;IS COUNT ZERO?
e0af ca 94 e0    152          JZ KXIT        ;RETURN IS DONE
                 153 ;
e0b2 db ed       154 KE2:     IN DISCSR      ;IS DISPLAY READY?
e0b4 e6 01       155          ANI TXMPTY
e0b6 ca b2 e0    156          JZ KE2         ;WAIT IF NOT READY
e0b9 c3 9f e0    157          JMP KECHO
                 158 ;
                 159 ; DATA STORAGE AREA
                 160 ;
e0bc 00          161 NCH:     DB 0           ;CHARACTER COUNT
e0bd bf e0       162 BPOINT:  DW BUFFER      ;POINTER TO BUFFER -- 16 BIT ADDRESS
e0bf             163 BUFFER:  DS 100         ;SET ASIDE SPACE FOR BUFFER
                 164 ;
                 165 ; END OF KEYBOARD INTERRUPT ROUTINE
                 166 ;
                 167 ; END OF PROGRAM
```

A30   Terminal Output Interrupt Test Program

```
                 1 ; TERMINAL OUTPUT INTERRUPT TEST PROGRAM
                 2 ;
                 3 ; THIS PROGRAM SENDS OUT A MESSAGE WHOSE BEGINNING IS
                 4 ; SPECIFIED BY A POINTER AND WHOSE END IS MARKED BY A
                 5 ; NULL CHARACTER.
                 6 ;
                 7 ; THIS PROGRAM USES THE SAME MAIN ROUTINE AND CLOCK INTERRUPT
                 8 ; ROUTINE AS THE CLOCK INTERRUPT PROGRAM.
                 9 ;
00df             10 TIMCON  = 0DFH          ;TIMER CONTROL PORT ADDRESS
00dc             11 TIMDAT  = 0DCH          ;TIMER DATA PORT ADDRESS
00d7             12 CONTRL  = 0D7H          ;INTERRUPT CONTROLLER ADDRESS
```

```
fff0              13 INADR   = 0FFF0H    ;INTERRUPT VECTOR ADDRESS, CLOCK
fffc              14 KEYADR  = 0FFFCH    ;INTERRUPT VECTOR ADDRESS, KEYBOARD
fffe              15 DISADR  = 0FFFEH    ;INTERRUPT VECTOR ADDRESS, DISPLAY
00ad              16 DA0     = 0ADH      ;LOWER ORDER D/A
00ac              17 DA1     = 0ACH      ;HIGHER ORDER D/A
00ed              18 KBCSR   = 0EDH      ;KEYBOARD COMMAND STATUS REGISTER
00ec              19 KBBUF   = 0ECH      ;KEYBOARD DATA BUFFER
00ed              20 DISCSR  = 0EDH      ;CONSOLE DISPLAY COMMAND STATUS REGISTER
00ec              21 DISBUF  = 0ECH      ;CONSOLE DISPLAY DATA BUFFER
0002              22 CHARED  = 2         ;MASK FOR CHARACTER READY FLAG
0001              23 TXMPTY  = 1         ;MASK FOR SERIAL TRANSMITTER READY
000d              24 CR      = 13        ;ASCII CARRIAGE RETURN
000a              25 LF      = 10        ;ASCII LINEFEED
0000              26 NULL    = 0         ;ASCII NULL CHARACTER
                  27 ;
e000              28         .=0E000H    ;STARTING ADDRESS OF PROGRAM
                  29 ;
e000 db ed        30 GO:     IN KBCSR    ;GET CHAR.
e002 e6 02        31         ANI CHARED
e004 ca 00 e0     32         JZ GO       ;WAIT IF NO CHAR READY
e007 db ec        33         IN KBBUF    ;GET CHARACTER
e009 fe 47        34         CPI 'G'     ;G?
e00b c2 00 e0     35         JNZ GO      ;IF NOT WAIT FOR NEXT CHAR.
e00e d3 ec        36         OUT DISBUF  ;ECHO G (NOTHING ELSE WILL BE ECHOED)
                  37 ;
e010 31 f0 ff     38         LXI SP,0FFF0H;INITIALIZE STACK POINTER
                  39 ;
e013 21 4c e0     40         LXI H,TIMER  ;HL <-- ADDRESS OF INTERRUPT ROUTINE
e016 22 f0 ff     41         SHLD INADR   ;STORE ADDRESS OF INTERRUPT ROUTINE AT VECTOR
                  42                      ;LOCATION
e019 21 7b e0     43         LXI H,DINT   ;HL <-- DISPLAY INTERRUPT ROUTINE ADDRESS
e01c 22 fe ff     44         SHLD DISADR  ;STORE ADDRESS AT VECTOR LOCATION
e01f 3e ff        45         MVI A,0FFH   ;ACCUMULATOR <-- MOST SIGNIFICANT BYTE OF
                  46                      ;INTERRUPT VECTOR
e021 ed 47        47         DB 0EDH,47H  ;THIS IS THE OPERATION CODE FOR THE Z-80
                  48                      ;INSTRUCTION STAI OR REGISTER I <-- ACCUMULATOR
e023 ed 5e        49         DB 0EDH,5EH  ;Z-80 CODE FOR IM2, SELECT INTERRUPT MODE 2
e025 3e 30        50         MVI A,30H    ;INITIALIZE (8253) COUNTER:
                  51                      ;MODE ZERO, LOAD LSB FIRST
e027 d3 df        52         OUT TIMCON   ;TIMER CONTROL PORT
e029 21 d0 07     53         LXI H,2000   ;2MHZ/2000 = 1KHZ COUNTER INTERRUPT RATE
e02c 7d           54         MOV A,L
e02d d3 dc        55         OUT TIMDAT   ;WRITE TO TIMER DATA PORT
e02f 7c           56         MOV A,H
e030 d3 dc        57         OUT TIMDAT   ;WRITE MOST SIGNIFICANT BYTE
                  58 ;
e032 3e 88        59         MVI A,88H    ;INITIALIZE 8214 INTERRUPT CONTROLLER
e034 32 7a e0     60         STA MASK     ;INITIALIZE MASK WORD
e037 d3 d7        61         OUT CONTRL
                  62 ;
e039 21 ff 00     63         LXI H,0FFH   ;NUMBER OF CLOCK COUNTS
e03c 22 78 e0     64         SHLD COUNT
e03f 3e 02        65         MVI A,2      ;VALUE IN ACCUMULATOR TO CHECK FOR REGISTER
                  66                      ;PRESERVATION
e041 fb           67         EI           ;ENABLE INTERRUPTS -- TIMER IS NOW RUNNING
                  68 ;
                  69 ; BACK IS THE START OF THE BACKGROUND ROUTINE ... IT RUNS WHENEVER
                  70 ; THE INTERRUPT ROUTINE IS NOT RUNNING.
                  71 ;
e042 fe 02        72 BACK:   CPI 2        ;DOES A HAVE A 2?
e044 c2 4a e0     73         JNZ B2       ;IF NOT, GO BACK TO DDT TO INDICATE AN ERROR
e047 c3 42 e0     74         JMP BACK     ;KEEP LOOKING
                  75 ;
e04a f3           76 B2:     DI           ;DISABLE INTERRUPTS
e04b c9           77         RET          ;RETURN TO MONITOR
                  78 ;
```

```
                    79 ;
                    80 ;CLOCK INTERRUPT SERVICE ROUTINE
                    81 ;
e04c  f5            82 TIMER:    PUSH PSW        ;PRESERVE MACHINE STATE
e04d  e5            83           PUSH H
                    84 ;
e04e  21 d0 07      85           LXI H,2000      ;RESET TIMER
e051  7d            86           MOV A,L
e052  d3 dc         87           OUT TIMDAT      ;WRITE LEAST SIGNIFICANT BYTE
e054  7c            88           MOV A,H
e055  d3 dc         89           OUT TIMDAT      ;WRITE MOST SIGNIFICANT BYTE
                    90 ;
e057  2a 78 e0      91           LHLD COUNT      ;HL <-- COUNT
e05a  7c            92           MOV A,H         ;AC <-- HIGH ORDER BYTE OF COUNT
e05b  f6 80         93           ORI 80H         ;SELECT D/A CHANNEL
e05d  d3 ac         94           OUT DA1         ;WRITE TO D/A
e05f  7d            95           MOV A,L         ;AC <-- LOWER ORDER BYTE OF COUNT
e060  d3 ad         96           OUT DA0
e062  2b            97           DCX H           ;DECREMENT COUNT
e063  7c            98           MOV A,H
e064  b5            99           ORA L           ;TEST FOR ZERO
e065  c2 6b e0     100           JNZ TIM1
e068  21 ff 0f     101           LXI H,0FFFH     ;HL <-- NEW COUNT
e06b  22 78 e0     102 TIM1:     SHLD COUNT      ;STORE COUNT
                   103 ;
e06e  3a 7a e0     104           LDA MASK        ;RESET INTERRUPT CONTROLLER (8214)
e071  d3 d7        105           OUT CONTRL
                   106 ;
e073  e1           107           POP H
e074  f1           108           POP PSW         ;RESTORE ACCUMULATOR AND FLAGS
e075  fb           109           EI              ;RE-ENABLE INTERRUPTS
e076  ed 4d        110           DB 0EDH,4DH     ;Z-80 CODE FOR RETURN FROM MASKABLE INTERRUPT
                   111 ;
e078  00 00        112 COUNT:    DW 0            ;MEMORY LOCATION FOR COUNT VARIABLE
                   113 ;
e07a  00           114 MASK:     DB 0            ;INTERRUPT CONTROLLER MASK
                   115 ;
                   116 ; END OF CLOCK INTERRUPT SERVICE RETURN
                   117 ;
                   118 ; DISPLAY INTERRUPT ROUTINE
                   119 ;
e07b  f5           120 DINT:     PUSH PSW        ;PRESERVE MACHINE STATE
e07c  c5           121           PUSH B
e07d  d5           122           PUSH D
e07e  e5           123           PUSH H
                   124 ;
e07f  2a a0 e0     125           LHLD MPOINT     ;HL <-- BUFFER POINTER
e082  7e           126           MOV A,M         ;AC <-- CHARACTER FROM BUFFER
e083  d3 ec        127           OUT DISBUF      ;SEND CHARACTER
e085  23           128           INX H           ;INCREMENT POINTER
e086  22 a0 e0     129           SHLD MPOINT     ;STORE POINTER
e089  7e           130           MOV A,M         ;CHECK FOR END OF MESSAGE
e08a  fe 00        131           CPI NULL
e08c  c2 94 e0     132           JNZ DXIT        ;NOT END YES, THUS RETURN
                   133 ;
e08f  3e 87        134           MVI A,87H       ;NEW INTERRUPT CONTROLLER MASK
e091  32 7a e0     135           STA MASK
                   136 ;
e094  3a 7a e0     137 DXIT:     LDA MASK
e097  d3 d7        138           OUT CONTRL      ;RESET INTERRUPT CONTROLLER
e099  e1           139           POP H
e09a  d1           140           POP D
e09b  c1           141           POP B
e09c  f1           142           POP PSW         ;RESTORE MACHINE STATE
e09d  fb           143           EI
e09e  ed 4d        144           DB 0EDH,4DH     ;Z-80 CODE FOR RETURN FROM MASKABLE INTERRUPT
```

```
              145 ;
              146 ; DATA STORAGE AREA
              147 ;
e0a0 a2 e0    148 MPOINT: DW MBUF         ;POINTER TO MESSAGE BUFFER (16-BIT ADDRESS)
              149 ;
e0a2 54 45 53 150 MBUF:    .ASCII 'TESTING, TESTING, 1, 2, 3, ...'
     54 49 4e
     47 2c 20
     54 45 53
     54 49 4e
     47 2c 20
     31 2c 20
     32 2c 20
     33 2c 20
     2e 2e 2e
e0c0 0d 0a 00 151          DB CR,LF,NULL
              152 ;
              153 ; END OF DISPLAY INTERRUPT ROUTINE
              154 ;
              155 ; END OF PROGRAM
```

A31   Blending Program

```
                1 ; BLENDING CONTROL PROGRAM
                2 ;
                3 ; THIS IS THE FINAL PROGRAM OF CHAPTER 6.
                4 ; IT USES TERMINAL INPUT AND OUTPUT INTERRUPT ROUTINES AND A CLOCK
                5 ; INTERRUPT ROUTINE.
                6 ;
                7 ; SYMBOL DEFINITIONS:
                8 ;
00a8            9 ADMUX   = 0A8H          ;ADDRESS OF A/D MULTIPLEXER
00a9           10 ADCSR   = 0A9H          ;ADDRESS OF A/D STATUS REGISTER
00ab           11 ADDATL  = 0ABH          ;ADDRESS OF LOWER ORDER 8 BITS OF A/D DATA
00aa           12 ADDATH  = 0AAH          ;ADDRESS OF HIGHER ORDER 2 BITS AND BUSY FLAG
00ad           13 DA0     = 0ADH          ;LOWER ORDER D/A
00ac           14 DA1     = 0ACH          ;HIGHER ORDER D/A
00df           15 TIMCON  = 0DFH          ;TIMER CONTROL PORT ADDRESS
00dc           16 TIMDAT  = 0DCH          ;TIMER DATA PORT ADDRESS
07d0           17 CLTIME  = 2000          ;TIMER INTERRUPT RATE
00d7           18 CONTRL  = 0D7H          ;INTERRUPT CONTROLLER ADDRESS
fff0           19 INADR   = 0FFF0H        ;INTERRUPT VECTOR ADDRESS, CLOCK
fffc           20 KEYADR  = 0FFFCH        ;INTERRUPT VECTOR ADDRESS, KEYBOARD
fffe           21 DISADR  = 0FFFEH        ;INTERRUPT VECTOR ADDRESS, DISPLAY
00ff           22 CLTIME  = 0FFH          ;TIME COUNT FOR CLOCK
0003           23 NTICK   = 3             ;NUMBER OF CLOCK TICKS PER SAMPLE
               24 ;
0000           25 VACANT  = 0             ;BUFFER STATUS CODES, 0 = VACANT
0001           26 BUSY    = 1
0002           27 READY   = 2
0001           28 TRUE    = 1
0000           29 FALSE   = 0
000d           30 CR      = 13            ;ASCII FOR RETURN
000a           31 LF      = 10            ;ASCII FOR LINEFEED
               32 ;
 )00           33          .=0E000H       ;STARTING ADDRESS
               34 ;
 )00 21 e4 e1  35 MAIN:    LXI H,INBF1    ;INITIALIZE INPUT BUFFER POINTER
 )03 22 84 e2  36          SHLD INPOIN
 )06 3e 01     37          MVI A,BUSY     ;SET INPUT BUFFER STATUS TO BUSY
 )08 32 e2 e1  38          STA BF1STT
 )0b 3e 00     39          MVI A,VACANT   ;SET BUFFER#2 STATUS TO VACANT
 )0d 32 e3 e1  40          STA BF2STT
               41 ;
 )10 97        42          SUB A          ;TURN OFF PUMPS
```

```
)11 d3 ac      43         OUT DA1        ;HIGHER ORDER HOT PUMP
)13 d3 ad      44         OUT DA0        ;LOWER ORDER HOT PUMP
)15 f6 80      45         ORI 80H        ;SELECT COLD PUMP D/A
)17 d3 ac      46         OUT DA1        ;HIGHER ORDER COLD PUMP
)19 af         47         XRA A
)1a d3 ad      48         OUT DA0        ;LOWER ORDER COLD PUMP
               49 ;
               50 ; SET UP INTERRUPTS
               51 ; OUR TIMER IS AN 8253 WITH AN 8214 INTERRUPT CONTROLLER
               52 ;
01c 31 f0 ff   53         LXI SP,0FFF0H  ;INITIALIZE STACK POINTER
               54 ;
01f 21 a1 e4   55         LXI H,CLKINT   ;HL <-- ADDRESS OF CLOCK INTERRUPT ROUTINE
022 22 f0 ff   56         SHLD INADR     ;STORE ADDRESS OF INTERRUPT ROUTINE AT
               57                        ;VECTOR LOCATION
025 21 b4 e6   58         LXI H,KINT     ;HL <-- ADDRESS OF KEYBOARD INTERRUPT ROUTINE
028 22 fc ff   59         SHLD KEYADR    ;STORE AT KEYBOARD VECTOR LOCATION
               60 ;
02b 21 fb e7   61         LXI H,DINT     ;HL <-- ADDRESS OF DISPLAY INTERRUPT ROUTINE
02e 22 fe ff   62         SHLD DISADR    ;STORE AT DISPLAY VECTOR LOCATION
               63 ;
031 3e ff      64         MVI A,0FFH     ;ACCUMULATOR <-- MOST SIGNIFICANT BYTE
               65                        ;OF INTERRUPT VECTOR
033 ed 47      66         DB 0EDH,47H    ;THIS IS THE OPERATION CODE FOR THE Z-80
               67                        ;INSTRUCTION STAI OR REGISTER I <-- ACCUMULATOR
035 ed 5e      68         DB 0EDH,5EH    ;Z-80 CODE FOR IM2, SELECT INTERRUPT MODE 2
               69 ;
037 3e 30      70         MVI A,30H      ;INITIALIZE (8253) TIMER:
               71                        ;MODE ZERO, LOAD LSB FIRST
e039 d3 df     72         OUT TIMCON     ;TIMER CONTROL PORT
e03b 3e 87     73         MVI A,87H      ;INITIALIZE 8214 INTERRUPT CONTROLLER
e03d 32 e1 e1  74         STA MASK       ;INITIALIZE MASK WORD
e040 d3 d7     75         OUT CONTRL
e042 fb        76         EI
               77 ;
               78 ;
               79 ; AWAIT A TYPED "G" FROM USER
               80 ;
               81 ;
e043 3a e2 e1  82 M1:     LDA BF1STT     ;IS BUFFER#1 READY?
e046 fe 02     83         CPI READY
e048 c2 54 e0  84         JNZ M2
e04b 21 e4 e1  85         LXI H,INBF1    ;INITIALIZE MESSAGE POINTER
e04e 22 1f e3  86         SHLD MPOINT
e051 c3 62 e0  87         JMP M3
               88 ;
e054 3a e3 e1  89 M2:     LDA BF2STT     ;IS BUFFER#2 READY?
e057 fe 02     90         CPI READY
e059 c2 43 e0  91         JNZ M1         ;BRANCH IF NOT READY
e05c 21 34 e2  92         LXI H,INBF2    ;INITIALIZE MESSAGE POINTER
e05f 22 1f e3  93         SHLD MPOINT
               94 ;
               95 ; TO HERE, A MESSAGE EXISTS.
               96 ; POSSIBLE MESSAGES ARE: E EXIT TO MONITOR;S STOP PUMPS
               97 ; G BEGIN CONTROL (GO);L LIST VARIABLES;R NEW SETPOINT
               98 ; K GAINS (FOUR POSSIBLE GAINS)
               99 ;
e062 2a 1f e3  100 M3:    LHLD MPOINT    ;ADDRESS OF BEGINNING OF MESSAGE TO HL
e065 3e 45     101        MVI A,'E'      ;COMMAND = E?
e067 be        102        CMP M          ;COMPARE A TO MEMORY POINTED AT BY HL
e068 c2 92 e0  103        JNZ M4
               104 ;
               105 ; EXIT => STOP PUMPS, DISARM INTERRUPTS, RETURN TO MONITOR
               106 ;
e06b f3        107        DI             ;DISABLE CPU INTERRUPTS
e06c 3e 30     108        MVI A,30H      ;RESET AND THEREFORE STOP CLOCK
```

```
e06e d3 df    109            OUT TIMCON
              110 ;
e070 97       111            SUB A         ;ZERO A
e071 d3 ac    112            OUT DA1       ;HIGHER ORDER COLD PUMP D/A
e073 d3 ad    113            OUT DA0       ;STOP COLD PUMP
e075 f6 80    114            ORI 80H       ;SELECT HOT PUMP
e077 d3 ac    115            OUT DA1       ;HIGHER ORDER HOT PUMP
e079 af       116            XRA A
e07a d3 ad    117            OUT DA0       ;STOP HOT PUMP
              118 ;
e07c 3a e2 e1 119            LDA BF1STT    ;NOW VACATE BUFFER WHICH CONTAINED EXIT COMMAND
e07f fe 02    120            CPI READY
e081 c2 8c e0 121            JNZ B1
e084 3e 00    122            MVI A,VACANT
e086 32 e2 e1 123            STA BF1STT
e089 c3 91 e0 124            JMP B2
e08c 3e 00    125 B1:        MVI A,VACANT
e08e 32 e3 e1 126            STA BF2STT
e091 c9       127 B2:        RET           ;RETURN TO MONITOR
              128 ;
e092 3e 53    129 M4:        MVI A,'S'     ;COMMAND = STOP?
e094 be       130            CMP M
e095 c2 b4 e0 131            JNZ M5
              132 ;
              133 ; STOP => DISARM INTERRUPT, STOP PUMPS, PRINT "STOPPED"
              134 ;
e098 3e 30    135            MVI A,30H     ;RESET TIMER, DISABLE
e09a d3 df    136            OUT TIMCON    ;TIMER CONTROL PORT
              137 ;
e09c 97       138            SUB A         ;STOP PUMPS
e09d d3 ac    139            OUT DA1       ;HIGHER ORDER HOT PUMP
e09f d3 ad    140            OUT DA0       ;STOP HOT PUMP
e0a1 f6 80    141            ORI 80H       ;SELECT COLD PUMP
e0a3 d3 ac    142            OUT DA1
e0a5 af       143            XRA A
e0a6 d3 ad    144            OUT DA0       ;STOP COLD PUMP
              145 ;
e0a8 21 21 e3 146            LXI H,SBUF    ;INITIALIZE OUTPUT BUFFER POINTER
e0ab 22 86 e2 147            SHLD OUTPNT
e0ae cd 51 e8 148            CALL DISPON   ;ENABLE DISPLAY FOR FIRST CHARACTER
e0b1 c3 bd e1 149            JMP VACAT
              150 ;
e0b4 3e 47    151 M5:        MVI A,'G'     ;COMMAND = GO?
e0b6 be       152            CMP M
e0b7 c2 cf e0 153            JNZ M6
              154 ;
              155 ; GO => ARM INTERRUPT, PRINT "RUNNING"
              156 ;
e0ba 21 ff 00 157 M5GO:      LXI H,CLTIME  ;START CLOCK
e0bd 7d       158            MOV A,L
e0be d3 dc    159            OUT TIMDAT    ;RESET TIMER
e0c0 7c       160            MOV A,H
e0c1 d3 dc    161            OUT TIMDAT
              162 ;
e0c3 21 26 e3 163            LXI H,GOBUF   ;INITIALIZE OUTPUT BUFFER
e0c6 22 86 e2 164            SHLD OUTPNT
e0c9 cd 51 e8 165            CALL DISPON   ;WAKE UP DISPLAY
e0cc c3 bd e1 166            JMP VACAT
              167 ;
e0cf 3e 54    168 M6:        MVI A,'T'     ;COMMAND = TEMPERATURE SETPOINT?
e0d1 be       169            CMP M
e0d2 c2 e5 e0 170            JNZ M7
              171 ;
              172 ; SETPOINT => UPDATE RTN WITH VALUE OF THREE DECIMAL DIGITS
              173 ;
e0d5 2a 1f e3 174            LHLD MPOINT   ;MOVE POINTER TO FIRST NUMBER
```

```
e0d8 23          175        INX  H
e0d9 cd 0b e4    176        CALL VALUE        ;VALUE EXPECTS ADDRESS OF FIRST NUMBER IN HL,
                 177                          ;RETURNS VALUE IN A
e0dc da d5 e1    178        JC   ERR          ;VALUE SETS CARRY ON ERROR
e0df 32 a8 e3    179        STA  RTN          ;UPDATE VALUE
e0e2 c3 bd e1    180        JMP  VACAT
                 181 ;
e0e5 3e 46       182 M7:    MVI  A,'F'        ;COMMAND = FLOW SETPOINT?
e0e7 be          183        CMP  M
e0e8 c2 fb e0    184        JNZ  M8
                 185 ;
                 186 ; FLOW SETPOINT => UPDATE RFN
                 187 ;
e0eb 2a 1f e3    188        LHLD MPOINT       ;POINTER TO NUMBER
e0ee 23          189        INX  H
e0ef cd 0b e4    190        CALL VALUE        ;CONVERT FROM ASCII TO BINARY
e0f2 da d5 e1    191        JC   ERR          ;ERROR CHECK
e0f5 32 a9 e3    192        STA  RFN          ;STORE RESULT
e0f8 c3 bd e1    193        JMP  VACAT
                 194 ;
e0fb 3e 4b       195 M8:    MVI  A,'K'        ;COMMAND = NEW GAIN?
e0fd be          196        CMP  M
e0fe c2 73 e1    197        JNZ  M12
                 198 ;
                 199 ; GAIN UPDATE CAN BE KPF,KPT,KIF,KIT
                 200 ;
e101 2a 1f e3    201        LHLD MPOINT       ;CONVERT FIRST VALUE
e104 11 03 00    202        LXI  D,3          ;GET FIRST DIGIT
e107 19          203        DAD  D
e108 cd 0b e4    204        CALL VALUE        ;CONVERT
e10b da d5 e1    205        JC   ERR
e10e 47          206        MOV  B,A          ;LEAVE RESULT IN B FOR LATER USE
e10f 2a 1f e3    207        LHLD MPOINT       ;GET NEXT VALUE
e112 11 07 00    208        LXI  D,7
e115 19          209        DAD  D            ;ADDRESS OF FIRST DIGIT OF SECOND NUMBER
e116 cd 0b e4    210        CALL VALUE        ;CONVERT
e119 da d5 e1    211        JC   ERR
e11c 4f          212        MOV  C,A          ;LEAVE RESULT IN C
e11d 2a 1f e3    213        LHLD MPOINT       ;NOW FIND WHERE TO STORE IT
e120 23          214        INX  H
e121 3e 50       215        MVI  A,'P'        ;PROPORTIONAL GAIN?
e123 be          216        CMP  M
e124 c2 4a e1    217        JNZ  M9
e127 23          218        INX  H            ;NOW LOOK AT NEXT CHARACTER
e128 3e 46       219        MVI  A,'F'        ;FLOW?
e12a be          220        CMP  M
e12b c2 39 e1    221        JNZ  M10
e12e 78          222        MOV  A,B          ;YES, GET VALUES FOR STORING
e12f 32 ae e3    223        STA  KPFNUM       ;STORE NUMERATOR
e132 79          224        MOV  A,C
e133 32 af e3    225        STA  KPFDEN       ;STORE DENOMINATOR
e136 c3 bd e1    226        JMP  VACAT
                 227 ;
e139 3e 54       228 M10:   MVI  A,'T'        ;TEMPERATURE?
e13b be          229        CMP  M
e13c c2 d5 e1    230        JNZ  ERR          ;ERROR IF NOT F OR T
e13f 78          231        MOV  A,B
e140 32 b0 e3    232        STA  KPTNUM
e143 79          233        MOV  A,C
e144 32 b1 e3    234        STA  KPTDEN
e147 c3 bd e1    235        JMP  VACAT
                 236 ;
e14a 3e 49       237 M9:    MVI  A,'I'        ;IF NOT P IT SHOULD BE I
e14c be          238        CMP  M
e14d c2 d5 e1    239        JNZ  ERR
e150 23          240        INX  H
```

```
e151 3e 46      241         MVI A,'F'       ;FLOW?
e153 be         242         CMP M
e154 c2 62 el   243         JNZ M11
e157 78         244         MOV A,B
e158 32 aa e3   245         STA KIFNUM
e15b 79         246         MOV A,C
e15c 32 ab e3   247         STA KIFDEN
e15f c3 bd el   248         JMP VACAT
                249 ;
e162 3e 54      250 M11:    MVI A,'T'       ;TEMPERATURE?
e164 be         251         CMP M
e165 c2 d5 el   252         JNZ ERR
e168 78         253         MOV A,B
e169 32 ac e3   254         STA KITNUM
e16c 79         255         MOV A,C
e16d 32 ad e3   256         STA KITDEN
e170 c3 bd el   257         JMP VACAT
                258 ;
                259 ;
e173 3e 4c      260 M12:    MVI A,'L'       ;COMMAND = LIST?
e175 be         261         CMP M
e176 c2 d5 el   262         JNZ ERR
                263 ;
                264 ; LIST VALUES OF SYSTEM VARIABLES AS SPECIFIED IN "LIST"
                265 ;
e179 3a a7 e3   266         LDA HEDCNT      ;CHECK TO SEE IF IT IS TIME FOR THE HEADER
e17c 3d         267         DCR A           ;DECREMENT COUNT
e17d 32 a7 e3   268         STA HEDCNT
e180 b7         269         ORA A           ;IF NOT ZERO, NO HEADING
e181 c2 95 el   270         JNZ MM11
e184 3e 0a      271         MVI A,10        ;RESET COUNT
e186 32 a7 e3   272         STA HEDCNT
e189 21 56 e3   273         LXI H,HEAD
e18c 22 86 e2   274         SHLD OUTPNT     ;SET UP POINTER TO HEADING
e18f cd 51 e8   275         CALL DISPON     ;WAKE UP DISPLAY
e192 c3 bd el   276         JMP VACAT
                277 ;
e195 21 88 e2   278 MM11:   LXI H,OUTBUF    ;SET UP POINTER TO OUTPUT BUFFER
e198 22 86 e2   279         SHLD OUTPNT
e19b 21 34 e3   280         LXI H,LIST      ;POINTER TO LIST IN HL
e19e 46         281 MM12:   MOV B,M         ;CHECK FOR NULL ADDRESS
e19f 23         282         INX H
e1a0 7e         283         MOV A,M
e1a1 2b         284         DCX H           ;RESET HL
e1a2 b0         285         ORA B           ;CHECK FOR ZERO
e1a3 ca ae el   286         JZ MM13
                287 ;
e1a6 cd b2 e3   288         CALL FORMAT     ;CONVERT BINARY TO ASCII
e1a9 23         289         INX H           ;POINT TO NEXT ITEM
e1aa 23         290         INX H
e1ab c3 9e el   291         JMP MM12
                292 ;
e1ae 2a 86 e2   293 MM13:   LHLD OUTPNT     ;TERMINATE MESSAGE WITH RETURN
e1b1 3e 0d      294         MVI A,CR
e1b3 77         295         MOV M,A
e1b4 21 88 e2   296         LXI H,OUTBUF    ;RESET DISPLAY POINTER
e1b7 22 86 e2   297         SHLD OUTPNT
e1ba cd 51 e8   298         CALL DISPON     ;WAKE UP DISPLAY
                299 ;
e1bd 3a e2 el   300 VACAT:  LDA BF1STT      ;IS BUFFER#1 READY?
e1c0 fe 02      301         CPI READY
e1c2 c2 cd el   302         JNZ V1
e1c5 3e 00      303         MVI A,VACANT    ;VACATE BUFFER#1
e1c7 32 e2 el   304         STA BF1STT
e1ca c3 d2 el   305         JMP V2
e1cd 3e 00      306 V1:     MVI A,VACANT
```

```
e1cf 32 e3 e1   307           STA BF2STT        ;VACATE BUFFER#2
e1d2 c3 43 e0   308 V2:       JMP M1            ;BACK TO LOOK FOR MORE MESSAGES
                309 ;
e1d5 21 2e e3   310 ERR:      LXI H,ERRBUF      ;PRINT ERROR MESSAGE
e1d8 22 86 e2   311           SHLD OUTPNT
e1db cd 51 e8   312           CALL DISPON
e1de c3 bd e1   313           JMP VACAT
                314 ;
                315 ;DATA STORAGE AREA
                316 ;
e1e1 00         317 MASK:     DB 0      ;INTERRUPT CONTROLLER MASK
                318 ;
e1e2 00         319 BF1STT:   DB 0        ;STATUS OF BUFFER#1
e1e3 00         320 BF2STT:   DB 0        ;STATUS OF BUFFER#2
e1e4            321 INBF1:    DS 80       ;INPUT BUFFER#1
e234            322 INBF2:    DS 80       ;INPUT BUFFER #2
                323 ;
e284 00 00      324 INPOIN:   DW 0        ;POINTER TO INPUT BUFFER
                325 ;
e286 00 00      326 OUTPNT:   DW 0        ;POINTER TO OUTPUT BUFFER
e288            327 OUTBUF:   DS 80       ;OUTPUT BUFFER
e2d8            328           DS 70
e31e 00         329 BUF:      DB 0        ;DISPLAY MESSAGE READY FLAG
                330 ;
e31f 00 00      331 MPOINT:   DW 0        ;POINTER TO CURRENT MESSAGE BUFFER
                332 ;
e321 53 54 4f   333 SBUF:     .ASCII 'STOP'
     50
e325 0d         334           DB CR
e326 52 55 4e   335 GOBUF:    .ASCII 'RUNNING'
     4e 49 4e
     47
e32d 0d         336           DB CR
e32e 45 52 52   337 ERRBUF:   .ASCII 'ERROR'
     4f 52
e333 0d         338           DB CR
                339 ;
e334 a8 e3 a9   340 LIST:     DW RTN,RFN,KIFNUM,KIFDEN,KITNUM,KITDEN,KPFNUM,KPFDEN
     e3 aa e3
     ab e3 ac
     e3 ad e3
     ae e3 af
     e3
e344 b0 e3 b1   341           DW KPTNUM,KPTDEN,CTN,CFN,MCN,MHN,DELMT,DELMF,0
     e3 a8 e6
     aa e6 ae
     e6 ac e6
     b0 e6 b1
     e6 00 00
e356 20 52 54   342 HEAD:     .ASCII ' RTN RFN KIFN KIFD KITN KITD KPFN KPFD'
     4e 20 52
     46 4e 20
     4b 49 46
     4e 20 4b
     49 46 44
     20 4b 49
     54 4e 20
     4b 49 54
     44 20 4b
     50 46 4e
     20 4b 50
     46 44
e37c 20 4b 50   343           .ASCII ' KPTN KPTD CTN  CFN  MCN  MHN  DELMT DELMF'
     54 4e 20
     4b 50 54
     44 20 43
```

```
          54 4e 20
          20 43 46
          4e 20 20
          4d 43 4e
          20 20 4d
          48 4e 20
          20 44 45
          4c 4d 54
          20 44 45
          4c 4d 46
e3a6 0d        344          DB CR
e3a7 01        345 HEDCNT: DB 1      ;COUNT FOR HEADING (ALWAYS PRINTED FIRST TIME)
e3a8 00        346 RTN:    DB 0      ;TEMPERATURE SETPOINT
e3a9 00        347 RFN:    DB 0      ;FLOW SETPOINT
e3aa 00        348 KIFNUM: DB 0      ;GAINS
e3ab 01        349 KIFDEN: DB 1
e3ac 00        350 KITNUM: DB 0
e3ad 01        351 KITDEN: DB 1
e3ae 00        352 KPFNUM: DB 0
e3af 01        353 KPFDEN: DB 1
e3b0 00        354 KPTNUM: DB 0
e3b1 01        355 KPTDEN: DB 1
               356 ;
               357 ; END OF MAIN ROUTINE...START OF SUBROUTINES
               358 ;
               359 ;FORMAT...
               360 ;TAKES AN 8-BIT BINARY VALUE (2'S COMPLEMENT) WHOSE ADDRESS'S
               361 ;ADDRESS IS IN HL AND CONVERTS IT   INTO 3 ASCII CHARACTERS
               362 ;PRECEDED BY A SIGN AND FOLLOWED BY 1 ASCII SPACE. THE RESULTING
               363 ;STRING IS PLACED IN THE BUFFER POINTED TO BY OUTPNT. OUTPNT IS
               364 ;INCREMENTED TO POINT TO THE NEXT FREE LOCATION IN THE OUTPUT
               365 ;BUFFER.
               366 ;
e3b2 f5        367 FORMAT: PUSH PSW      ;SAVE REGISTERS
e3b3 c5        368          PUSH B
e3b4 d5        369          PUSH D
e3b5 e5        370          PUSH H
e3b6 5e        371          MOV E,M      ;GET ADDRESS OF DATA
e3b7 23        372          INX H
e3b8 56        373          MOV D,M
e3b9 2a 86 e2  374          LHLD OUTPNT  ;GET ADDRESS OF OUTPUT BUFFER
e3bc eb        375          XCHG         ;HL <-- ADDRESS OF DATA
e3bd 7e        376          MOV A,M      ;A <-- DATA TO BE CONVERTED
e3be b7        377          ORA A        ;TEST SIGN
e3bf f2 ce e3  378          JP F1
e3c2 eb        379          XCHG         ;EXCHANGE HL AND DE
e3c3 2f        380          CMA          ;MAKE VALUE POSITIVE FOR CORRECT CONVERSION
e3c4 3c        381          INR A
e3c5 32 0a e4  382          STA TEMP     ;PUT IT IN TEMPORARY STORAGE
e3c8 3e 2d     383          MVI A,'-'    ;PRINT MINUS SIGN
e3ca 77        384          MOV M,A
e3cb c3 d5 e3  385          JMP F2
e3ce eb        386 F1:      XCHG         ;EXCHANGE HL AND DE
e3cf 32 0a e4  387          STA TEMP     ;STORE VALUE IN TEMPORARY STORAGE
e3d2 3e 2b     388          MVI A,'+'    ;PRINT PLUS SIGN
e3d4 77        389          MOV M,A
               390 ;
e3d5 0e 04     391 F2:      MVI C,4      ;SET UP TO INCREMENT HL ...
e3d7 06 00     392          MVI B,0
e3d9 09        393          DAD B        ;INCREMENT HL SO THAT BUFFER CAN BE FILLED
               394                       ;BACKWARDS
e3da 3e 20     395          MVI A,' '    ;PUT IN SPACES
e3dc 77        396          MOV M,A
e3dd 2b        397          DCX H        ;DECREMENT POINTER
e3de eb        398          XCHG         ;DE <-- OUTPUT BUFFER POINTER
               399                       ;HL <-- DATA ADDRESS
```

```
e3df 0e 03       400          MVI C,3        ;ITERATION COUNT
e3el 3a 0a e4    401          LDA TEMP       ;GET DATA -- USE B FOR SUCCESSIVE DIVIDES.
e3e4 47          402          MOV B,A
                 403 ;
e3e5 d5          404 FLOP:    PUSH D         ;SAVE DE
e3e6 68          405          MOV L,B        ;SET UP FOR DIVIDE
e3e7 26 00       406          MVI H,0        ;HIGH-ORDER PART OF DIVIDEND
e3e9 le 0a       407          MVI E,10       ;DIVISOR
e3eb cd 82 e4    408          CALL DIVIDE
e3ee 45          409          MOV B,L
e3ef 3e 30       410          MVI A,'0'      ;ASCII-ZERO
e3f1 84          411          ADD H          ;A <-- CHARACTER
e3f2 d1          412          POP D          ;GET BACK OUTPUT BUFFER ADDRESS
e3f3 eb          413          XCHG           ;HL <-- OUTPUT BUFFER ADDRESS
e3f4 77          414          MOV M,A        ;CHAR. TO BUFFER
e3f5 2b          415          DCX H          ;DECREMENT POINTER
e3f6 eb          416          XCHG           ;EXCHANGE DE AND HL
e3f7 0d          417          DCR C          ;DECREMENT ITERATION COUNT
e3f8 c2 e5 e3    418          JNZ FLOP
                 419 ;
e3fb 2a 86 e2    420          LHLD OUTPNT    ;MOVE OUTPUT POINTER FORWARD
e3fe 11 05 00    421          LXI D,5
e401 19          422          DAD D
e402 22 86 e2    423          SHLD OUTPNT
                 424 ;
e405 el          425          POP H          ;RESTORE REGISTERS
e406 dl          426          POP D
e407 cl          427          POP B
e408 fl          428          POP PSW
e409 c9          429          RET            ;RETURN
e40a 00          430 TEMP:    DB 0           ;TEMPORARY STORAGE
                 431 ;
                 432 ;END OF FORMAT SUBROUTINE
                 433 ;
                 434 ;
                 435 ; VALUE SUBROUTINE CONVERTS 3 ASCII CHARACTERS TO
                 436 ; BINARY BY REPEATED MULTIPLICATION.
                 437 ; ENTER WITH HL POINTING TO THE FIRST CHARACTER
                 438 ;
e40b c5          439 VALUE:   PUSH B
e40c d5          440          PUSH D
e40d e5          441          PUSH H
e40e 97          442          SUB A          ;A <-- 0
e40f 32 62 e4    443          STA ERRFLG     ;INITIALIZE ERROR FLAG
e412 le 64       444          MVI E,100      ;MULTIPLIER
e414 7e          445          MOV A,M        ;A <-- MOST SIGNIFICANT CHARACTER
e415 23          446          INX H          ;POINT TO NEXT CHAR.
e416 e5          447          PUSH H         ;SAVE HL
e417 d6 30       448          SUI '0'        ;MAKE BINARY
e419 cd 51 e4    449          CALL VCHAR     ;CHECK CHAR. FOR VALIDITY
e41c 6f          450          MOV L,A        ;BECOMES MULTIPLICAND
e41d cd 63 e4    451          CALL MULT      ;PERFORM (CHAR1)*100
e420 45          452          MOV B,L        ;FIRST PRODUCT
                 453 ;
e421 le 0a       454          MVI E,10       ;MULTIPLIER
e423 el          455          POP H          ;RESTORE POINTER
e424 7e          456          MOV A,M
e425 23          457          INX H
e426 e5          458          PUSH H
e427 d6 30       459          SUI '0'        ;AS ABOVE
e429 cd 51 e4    460          CALL VCHAR     ;CHECK VALIDITY
e42c 6f          461          MOV L,A        ;MULTIPLICAND
e42d cd 63 e4    462          CALL MULT
e430 7d          463          MOV A,L        ;ACCUMULATOR <-- SECOND PRODUCT
e431 80          464          ADD B          ;ACCUMULATOR <-- FIRST + SECOND PRODUCT
e432 47          465          MOV B,A
```

```
                    466 ;
e433 e1             467          POP  H
e434 7e             468          MOV  A,M
e435 23             469          INX  H            ;GET NEXT CHAR
e436 d6 30          470          SUI  '0'          ;MAKE BINARY
e438 cd 51 e4       471          CALL VCHAR        ;VALIDITY CHECK
e43b 80             472          ADD  B            ;ACCUMULATOR <-- FINAL VALUE
                    473 ;
e43c 47             474          MOV  B,A          ;SAVE RESULT
e43d 3a 62 e4       475          LDA  ERRFLG       ;CHECK FOR GOOD RESULT
e440 b7             476          ORA  A
e441 ca 4a e4       477          JZ   VAL1         ;ZERO => OK
e444 37             478          STC               ;CARRY SET => ERROR
e445 97             479          SUB  A            ;RETURN ZERO
e446 e1             480          POP  H            ;RESTORE REGISTERS
e447 d1             481          POP  D
e448 c1             482          POP  B
e449 c9             483          RET               ;ERROR RETURN
                    484 ;
e44a 37             485 VAL1:    STC
e44b 3f             486          CMC               ;CLEAR CARRY
e44c 78             487          MOV  A,B          ;RESTORE RESULT
e44d e1             488          POP  H
e44e d1             489          POP  D
e44f c1             490          POP  B
e450 c9             491          RET               ;VALID RETURN
                    492 ;
                    493 ; END VALUE SUBROUTINE
                    494 ;
                    495 ;SUBROUTINE TO CHECK FOR VALID CHARACTERS, I.E., THAT THE VALUE
                    496 ;ASSOCIATED WITH THE CHARACTER IS IN THE RANGE 0 - 9.
                    497 ;SETS ERROR FLAG IF NOT VALID.  DOES NOTHING IF VALID.
                    498 ;
e451 fe 00          499 VCHAR:   CPI  0            ;VALUE IN A ON ENTRY AND EXIT
e453 f2 5c e4       500          JP   VC1
e456 3e 01          501 VC0:     MVI  A,1          ;SET ERROR INDICATOR
e458 32 62 e4       502          STA  ERRFLG
e45b c9             503          RET               ;ERROR RETURN
e45c fe 0a          504 VC1:     CPI  10           ;LARGER THAN 9?
e45e f2 56 e4       505          JP   VC0
e461 c9             506          RET               ;VALID RETURN
                    507 ;
e462 00             508 ERRFLG:  DB   0            ;ERROR FLAG
                    509 ;
                    510 ;END OF VALID-CHARACTER ROUTINE
                    511 ;
                    512 ;
                    513 ;MULTIPLY SUBROUTINE
                    514 ;
                    515 ; CALL THIS SUBROUTINE WITH 8-BIT MULTIPLICAND IN "L" AND
                    516 ; 8-BIT MULTIPLIER IN "E".  16-BIT PRODUCT IS RETURNED
                    517 ; IN "HL".  MULTIPLIER IS RETURNED UNCHANGED.
                    518 ; THIS ROUTINE USES THE STACK, THUS IT MUST HAVE BEEN
                    519 ; INITIALIZED.
                    520 ; THIS SUBROUTINE IS REENTRANT.
                    521 ;
e463 c5             522 MULT:    PUSH B            ;SAVE REGISTER B ON STACK
e464 d5             523          PUSH D            ;WE'LL USE REGISTER D FOR COUNT,
                    524                            ;THUS WE'LL SAVE OLD VALUE OF D.
e465 4d             525          MOV  C,L          ;REGISTER C <-- MULTIPLICAND
e466 06 00          526          MVI  B,0          ;NOW REGISTER PAIR BC CONTAINS
                    527                            ;MULTIPLICAND
e468 21 00 00       528          LXI  H,0          ;ZERO PRODUCT REGISTER PAIR
e46b 16 08          529          MVI  D,8          ;D <-- STEP COUNT
                    530 ;
e46d af             531 MLT1:    XRA  A            ;CLEAR CARRY
```

```
e46e 7d        532         MOV A,L        ;ACCUMULATOR <-- LOWER ORDER BYTE
               533                         ;OF PRODUCT
e46f 17        534         RAL            ;CLEAR CARRY AND RAL IS EQUIVALENT
               535                         ;TO ARITHMETIC LEFT SHIFT.
e470 6f        536         MOV L,A        ;PLACE BACK (CARRY IS NOW SHIFTED
               537                         ;VALUE OF LOWER ORDER).
e471 7c        538         MOV A,H        ;ACCUMULATOR <-- HIGH ORDER OR
               539                         ;PRODUCT
e472 17        540         RAL            ;SHIFT HIGH ORDER OF PRODUCT AND
               541                         ;SHIFT IN CARRY WHICH IS SHIFT OF
               542                         ;BIT 7 OF LOWER ORDER BYTE OF PRODUCT
e473 67        543         MOV H,A        ;PLACE HIGH-ORDER PRODUCT BACK
e474 7b        544         MOV A,E        ;ACCUMULATOR <-- MULTIPLICAND
e475 07        545         RLC            ;ROTATE MULTIPLIER LEFT
e476 5f        546         MOV E,A        ;PLACE REGISTER E BACK
e477 d2 7b e4  547         JNC MLT3       ;BRANCH IF NO BIT ROTATED OUT
e47a 09        548         DAD B          ;PRODUCT <-- PRODUCT + MULTIPLICAND
               549 ;
e47b 15        550 MLT3:   DCR D          ;DECREMENT STEP COUNT
e47c c2 6d e4  551         JNZ MLT1       ;LOOP FOR EIGHT BITS
               552 ;
e47f d1        553         POP D          ;RESTORE DE
e480 c1        554         POP B          ;RESTORE BC
e481 c9        555         RET
               556 ;
               557 ; END OF MULTIPLY SUBROUTINE
               558 ;
               559 ;DIVIDE SUBROUTINE
               560 ;
               561 ; CALL WITH 16-BIT DIVIDEND IN REGISTER-PAIR HL, 8-BIT
               562 ; DIVISOR IN REGISTER E.  THE 8-BIT QUOTIENT IS RETURNED
               563 ; IN REGISTER L AND AN 8-BIT REMAINDER IS RETURNED IN
               564 ; REGISTER H.  REGISTER-PAIR BC IS UNAFFECTED AS IS
               565 ; REGISTER D.  THE ACCUMULATOR IS DESTROYED.  THIS
               566 ; SUBROUTINE USES THE SYSTEM STACK.  IT IS REENTRANT.
               567 ;
               568 ;
e482 c5        569 DIVIDE: PUSH B         ;SAVE REGISTER-PAIR BC
e483 d5        570         PUSH D         ;SAVE REGISTER D
e484 0e 00     571         MVI C,0        ;ZERO QUOTIENT
e486 06 08     572         MVI B,8        ;STEP COUNT IS ONE EXTRA
               573 ;
e488 af        574 DV0:    XRA A          ;CLEAR CARRY
e489 7d        575         MOV A,L        ;SHIFT LEFT REGISTER-PAIR HL
e48a 17        576         RAL            ;ARITHMETIC LEFT SHIFT
e48b 6f        577         MOV L,A
e48c 7c        578         MOV A,H
e48d 17        579         RAL
e48e 67        580         MOV H,A        ;SHIFT COMPLETE
               581 ;
e48f 79        582         MOV A,C        ;LEFT SHIFT QUOTIENT
e490 07        583         RLC            ;ARITHMETIC LEFT SHIFT
e491 4f        584         MOV C,A
               585 ;
e492 7c        586         MOV A,H        ;COMPARE E AND H
e493 93        587         SUB E          ;PERFORM H-E
e494 fa 99 e4  588         JM DV1         ;BRANCH => (H>E)
e497 67        589         MOV H,A        ;H <-- H-E
e498 0c        590         INR C          ;INCREMENT QUOTIENT
               591 ;
e499 05        592 DV1:    DCR B
e49a c2 88 e4  593         JNZ DV0
               594 ;
e49d 69        595         MOV L,C        ;LEAVE QUOTIENT IN L
               596 ;
e49e d1        597         POP D          ;RESTORE DE
```

```
e49f c1            598            POP B          ;RESTORE BC
e4a0 c9            599            RET
                   600 ;
                   601 ; END OF DIVIDE SUBROUTINE
                   602 ;
                   603 ;INTERRUPT SERVICE ROUTINES
                   604 ;
                   605 ;CLOCK INTERRUPT ROUTINE
                   606 ;SAMPLES THE A/D CONVERTER THEN COMPUTES VALUES OF MANIPULATED
                   607 ;VARIABLES AND SENDS THEM OUT TO THE D/A.
                   608 ;
                   609 ;PROGRAM RUNS EVERY TIME THE CLOCK RUNS OUT.
                   610 ;
                   611 ;
e4al f5            612 CLKINT: PUSH PSW          ;SAVE REGISTERS
e4a2 c5            613            PUSH B
e4a3 d5            614            PUSH D
e4a4 e5            615            PUSH H
                   616 ;
e4a5 21 ff 00      617            LXI H,CLTIME    ;RESET TIMER
e4a8 7d            618            MOV A,L
e4a9 d3 dc         619            OUT TIMDAT
e4ab 7c            620            MOV A,H
e4ac d3 dc         621            OUT TIMDAT
                   622 ;
e4ae 3a b3 e6      623            LDA TCOUNT      ;CHECK TO SEE IF THIS IS TIME FOR A SAMPLE
e4bl 3d            624            DCR A
e4b2 32 b3 e6      625            STA TCOUNT
e4b5 c2 la e6      626            JNZ CLKXIT      ;IF NOT, RETURN
e4b8 3e 03         627            MVI A,NTICK     ;IF IT IS, RESET TCOUNT, THEN PROCEED
e4ba 32 b3 e6      628            STA TCOUNT
                   629 ;
                   630 ;A/D CONVERSIONS -       CH#0 : TEMP   (CTN)
                   631 ;                        CH#1 : FLOW   (CFN)
e4bd 3e 00         632            MVI A,0         ;DO CH #0
e4bf cd 8a e6      633            CALL AD
e4c2 32 a8 e6      634            STA CTN
e4c5 3e 01         635            MVI A,1         ;DO CH #1
e4c7 cd 8a e6      636            CALL AD
e4ca 32 aa e6      637            STA CFN
                   638 ;
                   639 ;CALCULATE DELTA MT:
                   640 ;DELMT=[KPTNUM*(CTNM1-CTN)/KPTDEN]+[KITNUM*(RTN-CTN)/KITDEN]
                   641 ;
e4cd 3e 00         642            MVI A,FALSE     ;FLAG TO ACCOUNT FOR NEGATIVE VALUES
e4cf 32 b2 e6      643            STA NEGFLG
e4d2 3a a8 e6      644            LDA CTN
e4d5 5f            645            MOV E,A
e4d6 3a a9 e6      646            LDA CTNM1
e4d9 93            647            SUB E           ;A <-- (CTNM1-CTN)
e4da 5f            648            MOV E,A         ;SET UP FOR MULTIPLICATION
e4db f2 e6 e4      649            JP CC1          ;SET FLAG IF VALUE IS NEGATIVE.
e4de 2f            650            CMA             ;MAKE VALUE POSITIVE SO MULT WILL WORK
e4df 3c            651            INR A
e4e0 5f            652            MOV E,A
e4el 3e 01         653            MVI A,TRUE
e4e3 32 b2 e6      654            STA NEGFLG      ;SET SIGN FLAG
                   655 ;
e4e6 3a b0 e3      656 CC1:       LDA KPTNUM
e4e9 6f            657            MOV L,A
e4ea cd 63 e4      658            CALL MULT       ;HL <-- PRODUCT
e4ed 3a bl e3      659            LDA KPTDEN      ;NOW GET READY FOR DIVIDE
e4f0 5f            660            MOV E,A         ;DIVISOR IN E, DIVIDEND IN HL
e4f1 cd 82 e4      661            CALL DIVIDE
e4f4 45            662            MOV B,L         ;SAVE RESULT IN B
e4f5 3a b2 e6      663            LDA NEGFLG      ;CHECK SIGN FLAG
```

```
e4f8 b7          664          ORA  A
e4f9 f2 05 e5    665          JP   CC2        ;NOTHING TO DO IF POSITIVE
e4fc 78          666          MOV  A,B        ;NEGATE RESULT
e4fd 2f          667          CMA
e4fe 3c          668          INR  A
e4ff 47          669          MOV  B,A        ;BACK TO B
e500 3e 00       670          MVI  A,FALSE
e502 32 b2 e6    671          STA  NEGFLG     ;RESET FLAG
                 672  ;
e505 3a a8 e6    673 CC2:     LDA  CTN        ;SECOND TERM
e508 5f          674          MOV  E,A
e509 3a a8 e3    675          LDA  RTN
e50c 93          676          SUB  E          ;A <-- (RTN-CTN)
e50d 5f          677          MOV  E,A        ;SET UP FOR MULTIPLICATION
e50e f2 19 e5    678          JP   CC3
e511 2f          679          CMA
e512 3c          680          INR  A          ;MAKE RESULT POSITIVE
e513 5f          681          MOV  E,A
e514 3e 01       682          MVI  A,TRUE
e516 32 b2 e6    683          STA  NEGFLG     ;SET FLAG TO NEGATIVE.
                 684  ;
e519 3a ac e3    685 CC3:     LDA  KITNUM     ;REST OF MULT.
e51c 6f          686          MOV  L,A
e51d cd 63 e4    687          CALL MULT
e520 3a ad e3    688          LDA  KITDEN     ;DIVISOR
e523 5f          689          MOV  E,A
e524 cd 82 e4    690          CALL DIVIDE
e527 3a b2 e6    691          LDA  NEGFLG
e52a b7          692          ORA  A
e52b ca 37 e5    693          JZ   CC4        ;NO CHANGE IF POSITIVE
e52e 7d          694          MOV  A,L        ;NEGATE RESULT
e52f 2f          695          CMA
e530 3c          696          INR  A
e531 6f          697          MOV  L,A
e532 3e 00       698          MVI  A,FALSE
e534 32 b2 e6    699          STA  NEGFLG     ;RESET FLAG
                 700  ;
e537 7d          701 CC4:     MOV  A,L        ;COMPUTE DELMT
e538 80          702          ADD  B
e539 32 b0 e6    703          STA  DELMT
                 704  ;
                 705  ;NOW CALCULATE DELTA MF AS:
                 706  ;DELMF=[KPFNUM*(CFNM1-CFN)/KPFDEN]+[KIFNUM*(RFN-CFN)/KIFDEN]
                 707  ;
                 708  ;THE PATTERN OF THE CALCULATION IS THE SAME AS THE DELMT
                           CALCULATION
                 709  ;
e53c 3a aa e6    710          LDA  CFN
e53f 5f          711          MOV  E,A
e540 3a ab e6    712          LDA  CFNM1
e543 93          713          SUB  E
e544 5f          714          MOV  E,A
e545 f2 50 e5    715          JP   CC5
e548 2f          716          CMA
e549 3c          717          INR  A
e54a 5f          718          MOV  E,A
e54b 3e 01       719          MVI  A,TRUE
e54d 32 b2 e6    720          STA  NEGFLG
                 721  ;
e550 3a ae e3    722 CC5:     LDA  KPFNUM
e553 6f          723          MOV  L,A
e554 cd 63 e4    724          CALL MULT
e557 3a af e3    725          LDA  KPFDEN
e55a 5f          726          MOV  E,A
e55b cd 82 e4    727          CALL DIVIDE
e55e 45          728          MOV  B,L
```

```
e55f 3a b2 e6    729           LDA NEGFLG
e562 b7          730           ORA A
e563 f2 6f e5    731           JP CC6
e566 78          732           MOV A,B
e567 2f          733           CMA
e568 3c          734           INR A
e569 47          735           MOV B,A
e56a 3e 00       736           MVI A,FALSE
e56c 32 b2 e6    737           STA NEGFLG
                 738 ;
e56f 3a aa e6    739 CC6:      LDA CFN
e572 5f          740           MOV E,A
e573 3a a9 e3    741           LDA RFN
e576 93          742           SUB E
e577 5f          743           MOV E,A
e578 f2 83 e5    744           JP CC7
e57b 2f          745           CMA
e57c 3c          746           INR A
e57d 5f          747           MOV E,A
e57e 3e 01       748           MVI A,TRUE
e580 32 b2 e6    749           STA NEGFLG
                 750 ;
e583 3a aa e3    751 CC7:      LDA KIFNUM
e586 6f          752           MOV L,A
e587 cd 63 e4    753           CALL MULT
e58a 3a ab e3    754           LDA KIFDEN
e58d 5f          755           MOV E,A
e58e cd 82 e4    756           CALL DIVIDE
e591 3a b2 e6    757           LDA NEGFLG
e594 b7          758           ORA A
e595 ca a1 e5    759           JZ CC8
e598 7d          760           MOV A,L
e599 2f          761           CMA
e59a 3c          762           INR A
e59b 6f          763           MOV L,A
e59c 3e 00       764           MVI A,FALSE
e59e 32 b2 e6    765           STA NEGFLG
e5a1 7d          766 CC8:      MOV A,L
e5a2 80          767           ADD B
e5a3 32 b1 e6    768           STA DELMF
                 769 ;
                 770 ;NOW UPDATE THE MANIPULATED AND CONTROL VARIABLES
                 771 ;
e5a6 3a ac e6    772           LDA MHN        ;MH(N-1) <-- MH(N), ETC.
e5a9 32 ad e6    773           STA MHNM1
e5ac 3a ae e6    774           LDA MCN
e5af 32 af e6    775           STA MCNM1
                 776 ;
                 777 ;OUTPUTS:
                 778 ;MHN <-- MHN(N-1) + (DELTA MF) + (DELTA MT)
                 779 ;MCN <-- MCN(N-1) + (DELTA MF) - (DELTA MT)
                 780 ;
e5b2 3a ac e6    781           LDA MHN
e5b5 47          782           MOV B,A
e5b6 3a b1 e6    783           LDA DELMF
e5b9 cd 26 e6    784           CALL ADDCHK    ;ADD WITH CHECK FOR OVERFLOW
e5bc 47          785           MOV B,A
e5bd 3a b0 e6    786           LDA DELMT
e5c0 cd 26 e6    787           CALL ADDCHK    ;THIS LEAVES MHN IN A
e5c3 cd 54 e6    788           CALL CHLIM     ;CHECK FOR MAX., MIN. LIMITS
e5c6 32 ac e6    789           STA MHN        ;STORE RESULT
                 790 ;
e5c9 3a b0 e6    791           LDA DELMT
e5cc 2f          792           CMA            ;NEGATE VALUE FOR SUBTRACT
e5cd 3c          793           INR A
e5ce 47          794           MOV B,A
```

```
e5cf 3a bl e6   795              LDA DELMF
e5d2 cd 26 e6   796              CALL ADDCHK    ;A <--- (DELMF - DELMT)
e5d5 47         797              MOV B,A
e5d6 3a ae e6   798              LDA MCN
e5d9 cd 26 e6   799              CALL ADDCHK    ;NEW MCN IN A
e5dc cd 54 e6   800              CALL CHLIM     ;CHECK LIMITS
e5df 32 ae e6   801              STA MCN        ;STORE RESULT
                802 ;
                803 ; UPDATE CONTROL MEMORY VARIABLES
                804 ;
e5e2 3a a8 e6   805              LDA CTN
e5e5 32 a9 e6   806              STA CTNM1
e5e8 3a aa e6   807              LDA CFN
e5eb 32 ab e6   808              STA CFNM1
                809 ;
                810 ; OUTPUT TO D/A
                811 ;
e5ee 3a ac e6   812              LDA MHN        ;SEND CONTROL OUTPUTS OUT TO D/A'S
e5f1 f5         813              PUSH PSW       ;STORE FOR LATER USE
e5f2 lf         814              RAR            ;WE USE A 12-BIT D/A HERE, BUT BECAUSE
e5f3 lf         815              RAR            ;8-BIT D/A'S ARE MORE COMMON, WE MIMIC
e5f4 lf         816              RAR            ;THE USE OF AN 8-BIT D/A AND MERELY THROW
e5f5 lf         817              RAR            ;AWAY FOUR BITS
e5f6 e6 0f      818              ANI 0FH        ;MASK FOR SAMPLE
e5f8 d3 ac      819              OUT DA1        ;WRITE HIGHER ORDER TO D/A
e5fa fl         820              POP PSW
e5fb 17         821              RAL            ;PREPARE TO WRITE LOWER FOUR BITS
e5fc 17         822              RAL
e5fd 17         823              RAL
e5fe 17         824              RAL
e5ff e6 f0      825              ANI 0F0H       ;MASK FOR UPPER FOUR BITS
e601 d3 ad      826              OUT DA0        ;WRITE LOWER FOUR BITS
                827 ;
e603 3a ae e6   828              LDA MCN
e606 f5         829              PUSH PSW
e607 lf         830              RAR
e608 lf         831              RAR
e609 lf         832              RAR
e60a lf         833              RAR
e60b e6 0f      834              ANI 0FH
e60d f6 80      835              ORI 80H        ;SELECT D/A, COLD PUMP
e60f d3 ac      836              OUT DA1        ;WRITE UPPER FOUR BITS, COLD PUMP
e611 fl         837              POP PSW
e612 17         838              RAL
e613 17         839              RAL
e614 17         840              RAL
e615 17         841              RAL
e616 e6 f0      842              ANI 0F0H       ;MASK FOR LOWER FOUR BITS, COLD
e618 d3 ad      843              OUT DA0        ;WRITE TO D/A
                844 ;
e61a 3a el el   845 CLKXIT:      LDA MASK
e61d d3 d7      846              OUT CONTRL     ;RESET INTERRUPT CONTROLLER
e61f el         847              POP H          ;RESTORE REGISTERS
e620 dl         848              POP D
e621 cl         849              POP B
e622 fl         850              POP PSW
e623 fb         851              EI             ;ENABLE INTERRUPT
e624 ed 4d      852              DB 0EDH,4DH    ;Z-80 CODE FOR RETURN FROM MASKABLE INTERRUPT
                853 ;
                854 ;ADD WITH CHECK FOR OVERFLOW
                855 ;THIS ROUTINE ADDS B TO A AND LEAVES THE RESULT IN A.
                856 ;B IS DESTROYED.
                857 ;OVERFLOW IS CHECKED.  IF FOUND, THE LARGEST POSSIBLE
                858 ;VALUE WITH APPROPRIATE SIGN IS RETURNED.
                859 ;
e626 32 53 e6   860 ADDCHK:      STA ADDTMP     ;TEMPORARY STORAGE
```

```
e629 a8        861        XRA B           ;CHECK WHETHER A AND B HAVE THE SAME SIGNS
e62a f2 34 e6  862        JP ADD1         ;+ => SIGNS ARE THE SAME
e62d 3a 53 e6  863        LDA ADDTMP      ;SIGNS ARE OPPOSITE .. NO OVERFLOW IS POSSIBLE
e630 80        864        ADD B
e631 c3 52 e6  865        JMP ADDXIT
               866 ;
e634 3a 53 e6  867 ADD1:  LDA ADDTMP      ;SIGNS ARE THE SAME, SO OVERFLOW MIGHT OCCUR
e637 80        868        ADD B
e638 47        869        MOV B,A         ;RESULT TO B
e639 3a 53 e6  870        LDA ADDTMP      ;RESULT SHOULD BE SAME SIGN AS ORIGINAL VALUE
               871                        ;IF NOT, OVERFLOW HAS OCCURRED
e63c a8        872        XRA B
e63d f2 51 e6  873        JP ADD3         ;+ => SAME SIGNS, THEREFORE OK.
e640 3a 53 e6  874        LDA ADDTMP      ;- => OPPOSITE SIGNS, THEREFORE OVERFLOW
e643 b7        875        ORA A           ;CHECK THE SIGN SO APPROPRIATE OVERFLOW
e644 f2 4c e6  876        JP ADD2         ;VALUE CAN BE USED
e647 3e 80     877        MVI A,80H       ;LARGEST NEGATIVE VALUE
e649 c3 52 e6  878        JMP ADDXIT
e64c 3e 7f     879 ADD2:  MVI A,7FH       ;LARGEST POSITIVE
e64e c3 52 e6  880        JMP ADDXIT
e651 78        881 ADD3:  MOV A,B         ;NO OVERFLOW.. RESULT IN A
e652 c9        882 ADDXIT: RET            ;RETURN
e653 00        883 ADDTMP: DB 0           ;TEMPORARY STORAGE
               884 ;
               885 ;LIMIT CHECK ROUTINE
               886 ;ENTER AND EXIT WITH VALUE IN A
               887 ;
0000           888 DAMIN  = 0
007f           889 DAMAX  = 127
e654 c5        890 CHLIM:  PUSH B          ;SAVE BC
e655 47        891        MOV B,A         ;SAVE NUMBER ENTERED IN B
e656 3e 00     892        MVI A,DAMIN     ;CHECK AGAINST MINIMUM
e658 cd 6c e6  893        CALL MAX        ;MAX RETURNS INDICATOR (IN CARRY) OF WHETHER
               894                        ;THE NUMBER IN A IS LARGER THAN THE ONE IN B.
e65b d2 61 e6  895        JNC CHL1
e65e c3 6a e6  896        JMP CHXIT       ;CARRY SET IMPLIES VALUE <= DAMIN, SO DAMIN
               897                        ;SHOULD BE RETURNED
e661 3e 7f     898 CHL1:  MVI A,DAMAX     ;NOW CHECK AGAINST UPPER LIMIT
e663 cd 6c e6  899        CALL MAX
e666 d2 6a e6  900        JNC CHXIT       ;CARRY CLEAR IMPLIES DAMAX < VALUE, SO DAMAX
               901                        ;SHOULD BE RETURNED
e669 78        902        MOV A,B         ;VALUE WITHIN LIMITS SO RETURN ORIGINAL VALUE
e66a c1        903 CHXIT:  POP B
e66b c9        904        RET             ;RESTORE BC THEN RETURN
               905 ;
               906 ;END OF CHLIM
               907 ;
               908 ;SUBROUTINE MAX -- GIVEN TWO 2'S COMPLEMENT NUMBERS, ONE IN A THE
               909 ;OTHER IN B, RETURNS WITH CARRY SET IF NUMBER IN A IS EQUAL TO OR
               910 ;GREATER THAN THE NUMBER IN B.
               911 ;ORDINARY SUBTRACT WILL NOT WORK RELIABLY IN THIS APPLICATION
                                                                       BECAUSE
               912 ;THE DIFFERENCE OF TWO ARBITRARY 2'S COMPLEMENT NUMBERS CAN BE
               913 ;LARGER THAN THE LARGEST ALLOWABLE 2'S COMPLEMENT NUMBER.  THE
                                                                       RELATIVE
               914 ;SIGNS OF A AND B ARE CHECKED FORST TO AVOID THIS PROBLEM.
               915 ;
               916 ;MAX RETURNS WITH A AND B UNCHANGED.
               917 ;
e66c c5        918 MAX:   PUSH B          ;SAVE BC
e66d 4f        919        MOV C,A         ;SAVE A VALUE
e66e a8        920        XRA B           ;EXCLUSIVE-OR TO FIND IF THE SIGNS ARE THE
               921                        ;SAME OR DIFFERENT.
e66f fa 7f e6  922        JM MAX2         ;NEG. RESULT => OPPOSITE SIGN
e672 79        923        MOV A,C         ;ORIGINAL VALUE BACK TO A
e673 90        924        SUB B           ;A <-- (A - B) .. SUBTRACTION IS OK
```

```
                  925                      ;IF BOTH NUMBERS HAVE SAME SIGN.
e674 f2 7b e6     926          JP MAX1
e677 af           927 MAX0:    XRA A       ;CLEARS CARRY .. AFFECT ON A INCONSEQUENTIAL HERE
e678 c3 87 e6     928          JMP MXIT    ;CARRY CLEAR MEANS A < B
e67b 37           929 MAX1:    STC         ;SET CARRY MEANS A => B
e67c c3 87 e6     930          JMP MXIT
                  931 ;
e67f 79           932 MAX2:    MOV A,C     ;SIGN IS OPPOSITE -- CHECK SIGN OF A
e680 b7           933          ORA A
e681 f2 7b e6     934          JP MAX1     ;A IS POSITIVE SO A > B
e684 c3 77 e6     935          JMP MAX0    ;A NEGATIVE, SO A < B
e687 79           936 MXIT:    MOV A,C     ;RESTORE VALUE TO A
e688 c1           937          POP B       ;RESTORE BC
e689 c9           938          RET
                  939 ;
                  940 ;END OF MAX
                  941 ;
                  942 ;A/D SUBROUTINE
                  943 ;THIS SYSTEM USES 10 BIT A/D'S, BUT THIS PROGRAM ONLY USES THE
                  944 ;HIGHER ORDER 8 BITS.  CALL AD WITH THE MULTIPLEXER CHANNEL
                  945 ;NUMBER IN A...IT RETURNS WITH THE CONVERTED VALUE IN A
                  946 ;
e68a c5           947 AD:      PUSH B      ;SAVE B REGISTER AS IT WILL BE USED HERE
e68b d3 a8        948          OUT ADMUX   ;SELECTING THE MUX CHANNEL ALSO STARTS THE
                  949                      ;CONVERSION
e68d db a9        950 ADWAIT:  IN ADCSR    ;THIS PORT CONTAINS THE A/D DONE FLAG
e68f e6 80        951          ANI 80H     ;MASK FOR DONE FLAG
e691 ca 8d e6     952          JZ ADWAIT   ;WAIT FOR CONVERSION
e694 db aa        953          IN ADDATH   ;AC <-- HIGHER ORDER OF CHANNEL
e696 17           954          RAL         ;NOW START PROCEDURE TO TRUNCATE 4 LOWER BITS
e697 17           955          RAL
e698 17           956          RAL
e699 17           957          RAL
e69a e6 f0        958          ANI 0F0H    ;MASK FOR UPPER FOUR BITS
e69c 47           959          MOV B,A     ;SAVE INTERMEDIATE RESULT
e69d db ab        960          IN ADDATL   ;GET LOWER-ORDER PART
e69f 1f           961          RAR
e6a0 1f           962          RAR
e6a1 1f           963          RAR
e6a2 1f           964          RAR         ;SAVE LOW ORDER
e6a3 e6 0f        965          ANI 0FH     ;MASK FOR LOWER-ORDER
e6a5 b0           966          ORA B       ;AC <-- FULL SAMPLE
e6a6 c1           967          POP B       ;RESTORE BC
e6a7 c9           968          RET
                  969 ;
                  970 ;END OF AD
                  971 ;
                  972 ;
                  973 ;DATA STORAGE AREA FOR CLKINT:
                  974 ;
e6a8 00           975 CTN:     DB 0        ;SAMPLED TEMPERATURE
e6a9 00           976 CTNM1:   DB 0        ;CT(N-1)
e6aa 00           977 CFN:     DB 0        ;SAMPLED FLOW
e6ab 00           978 CFNM1:   DB 0
e6ac 00           979 MHN:     DB 0        ;MANIPULATED VAR., HOT WATER PUMP
e6ad 00           980 MHNM1:   DB 0
e6ae 00           981 MCN:     DB 0        ;MANIPULATED VARIABLE, COLD WATER PUMP
e6af 00           982 MCNM1:   DB 0
e6b0 00           983 DELMT:   DB 0        ;CHANGE IN MANIPULATED VARIABLE, TEMPERATURE
e6b1 00           984 DELMF:   DB 0        ;CHANGE IN MANIPULATED VARIABLE, FLOW
e6b2 00           985 NEGFLG:  DB 0        ;FLAG FOR NEGATIVE VALUES.
e6b3 03           986 TCOUNT:  DB NTICK         ;CLOCK TICK COUNTER
                  987 ;
                  988 ;END OF CLOCK INTERRUPT ROUTINE
                  989 ;
                  990 ;
```

```
                    991 ;KEYBOARD INTERRUPT ROUTINE
                    992 ;
                    993 ;
00ed                994 KBCSR    = 0EDH   ;KEYBOARD STATUS REGISTER
00ec                995 KBBUF    = 0ECH   ;KEYBOARD DATA BUFFER
0002                996 CHARED   = 2            ;MASK FOR CHARACTER READY.
0015                997 CNTRLU   = 21           ;ASCII FOR CONTROL-U
007f                998 DELETE   = 127          ;ASCII FOR DELETE
                    999 ;
e6b4 f5            1000 KINT:    PUSH PSW       ;SAVE REGISTERS
e6b5 c5            1001          PUSH B
e6b6 d5            1002          PUSH D
e6b7 e5            1003          PUSH H
                   1004 ;
e6b8 3a ca e7      1005          LDA NCB        ;INCREMENT CHARACTER-IN-BUFFER COUNT
e6bb 3c            1006          INR A
e6bc 32 ca e7      1007          STA NCB
e6bf db ec         1008          IN KBBUF       ;AC <-- CHAR.
e6c1 e6 7f         1009          ANI 7FH        ;STRIP PARITY BIT
e6c3 2a 84 e2      1010          LHLD INPOIN    ;SET UP POINTER
e6c6 77            1011          MOV M,A        ;STORE CHARACTER
e6c7 23            1012          INX H          ;INCREMENT POINTER
e6c8 22 84 e2      1013          SHLD INPOIN
e6cb fe 0d         1014          CPI CR         ;IS CHAR A RETURN?
e6cd c2 29 e7      1015          JNZ K2
                   1016 ;
e6d0 21 cb e7      1017          LXI H,CRBUF    ;ECHO RETURN, LINEFEED
e6d3 22 86 e2      1018          SHLD OUTPNT    ;THIS WILL GET LFED SET AUTOMATICALLY!
e6d6 cd 51 e8      1019          CALL DISPON    ;WAKE UP DISPLAY
                   1020 ;
e6d9 3a e2 e1      1021          LDA BF1STT     ;SET BUFFER STATUS FLAGS
e6dc fe 02         1022          CPI READY      ;STILL READY MEANS DATA NOT PROCESSED
e6de ca b2 e7      1023          JZ KBERR
e6e1 fe 00         1024          CPI VACANT
e6e3 c2 05 e7      1025          JNZ K1
e6e6 3e 01         1026          MVI A,BUSY     ;IF NOW VACANT, SET TO BUSY FOR NEXT INPUTS
e6e8 32 e2 e1      1027          STA BF1STT
e6eb 97            1028          SUB A          ;INITIALIZE COUNTER
e6ec 32 ca e7      1029          STA NCB
e6ef 21 e4 e1      1030          LXI H,INBF1    ;SET UP POINTER
e6f2 22 84 e2      1031          SHLD INPOIN
e6f5 3a e3 e1      1032          LDA BF2STT     ;BUF2 STATE SHOULD BE BUSY
e6f8 fe 01         1033          CPI BUSY
e6fa c2 be e7      1034          JNZ KBER2      ;IF NOT, BUFFERS ARE IN AN ILLEGAL STATE
e6fd 3e 02         1035          MVI A,READY
e6ff 32 e3 e1      1036          STA BF2STT
e702 c3 a6 e7      1037          JMP KXIT
                   1038 ;
e705 fe 01         1039 K1:      CPI BUSY
e707 c2 be e7      1040          JNZ KBER2      ;INVALID STATUS
e70a 3e 02         1041          MVI A,READY    ;SET STATUS TO READY
e70c 32 e2 e1      1042          STA BF1STT
e70f 3a e3 e1      1043          LDA BF2STT     ;IF BUF1 WAS BUSY, BUF2 SHOULD BE VACANT
e712 fe 00         1044          CPI VACANT
e714 c2 b2 e7      1045          JNZ KBERR      ;IF NOT, ERROR
e717 3e 01         1046          MVI A,BUSY     ;MAKE IT BUSY, AND SET POINTER
e719 32 e3 e1      1047          STA BF2STT
e71c 97            1048          SUB A
e71d 32 ca e7      1049          STA NCB        ;INITIALIZE CHAR. COUNTER
e720 21 34 e2      1050          LXI H,INBF2
e723 22 84 e2      1051          SHLD INPOIN    ;INITIALIZE POINTER
e726 c3 a6 e7      1052          JMP KXIT
                   1053 ;
e729 fe 7f         1054 K2:      CPI DELETE     ;IS CHAR. DELETE?
e72b c2 61 e7      1055          JNZ K4
e72e 3a ca e7      1056          LDA NCB
```

```
e731 3d          1057           DCR  A
e732 32 ca e7    1058           STA  NCB           ;DECREMENT COUNT
e735 c2 47 e7    1059           JNZ  K3
                 1060 ;
e738 3e 87       1061           MVI  A,87H         ;DISABLE OUTPUT INTERRUPTS
e73a 32 e1 e1    1062           STA  MASK
                 1063 ;
e73d 2a 84 e2    1064           LHLD INPOIN        ;DECREMENT POINTER
e740 2b          1065           DCX  H
e741 22 84 e2    1066           SHLD INPOIN
e744 c3 a6 e7    1067           JMP  KXIT
                 1068 ;
e747 2a 84 e2    1069 K3:       LHLD INPOIN        ;ECHO ERASED CHARACTER
e74a 2b          1070           DCX  H             ;DECREMENT BACK TO ERASED CHARACTER
e74b 2b          1071           DCX  H
e74c 7e          1072           MOV  A,M
e74d d3 ec       1073           OUT  DISBUF        ;SEND OUT CHAR FOR ECHOING
e74f 22 84 e2    1074           SHLD INPOIN
e752 3a ca e7    1075           LDA  NCB           ;DECREMENT COUNT BY ONE MORE
e755 3d          1076           DCR  A
e756 32 ca e7    1077           STA  NCB
                 1078 ;
e759 3e 87       1079           MVI  A,87H         ;DISABLE OUTPUT INTERRUPTS
e75b 32 e1 e1    1080           STA  MASK
                 1081 ;
e75e c3 a6 e7    1082           JMP  KXIT
                 1083 ;
e761 fe 15       1084 K4:       CPI  CNTRLU        ;IS CHAR CONTROL-U?
e763 c2 9f e7    1085           JNZ  K6
e766 21 cb e7    1086           LXI  H,CRBUF       ;SET UP TO ECHO RETURN, LINEFEED
e769 22 86 e2    1087           SHLD OUTPNT
e76c cd 51 e8    1088           CALL DISPON        ;WAKE UP DISPLAY
e76f 97          1089           SUB  A             ;RESET COUNT
e770 32 ca e7    1090           STA  NCB
e773 3a e2 e1    1091           LDA  BF1STT        ;FIND OUT WHICH BUFFER IS ACTIVE
e776 fe 01       1092           CPI  BUSY
e778 c2 89 e7    1093           JNZ  K5
e77b 21 e4 e1    1094           LXI  H,INBF1       ;RESET POINTER
e77e 22 84 e2    1095           SHLD INPOIN
                 1096 ;
e781 3e 88       1097           MVI  A,88H         ;ENABLE OUTPUT INTERRUPTS
e783 32 e1 e1    1098           STA  MASK
e786 c3 a6 e7    1099           JMP  KXIT
                 1100 ;
e789 3a e3 e1    1101 K5:       LDA  BF2STT
e78c fe 01       1102           CPI  BUSY
e78e c2 be e7    1103           JNZ  KBER2         ;IF NEITHER IS BUSY, STATUS IS INVALID
e791 21 34 e2    1104           LXI  H,INBF2
e794 22 84 e2    1105           SHLD INPOIN        ;SET UP POINTER TO BEGINNING OF BUFFER
                 1106 ;
e797 3e 88       1107           MVI  A,88H         ;ENABLE OUTPUT INTERRUPTS
e799 32 e1 e1    1108           STA  MASK
                 1109 ;
e79c c3 a6 e7    1110           JMP  KXIT
                 1111 ;
e79f d3 ec       1112 K6:       OUT  DISBUF        ;NOT A SPECIAL CHARACTER -- ECHO IT
                 1113 ;
e7a1 3e 87       1114           MVI  A,87H         ;DISABLE OUTPUT INTERRUPTS
e7a3 32 e1 e1    1115           STA  MASK
                 1116 ;
e7a6 3a e1 e1    1117 KXIT:     LDA  MASK          ;RESET INTERRUPT CONTROLLER
e7a9 d3 d7       1118           OUT  CONTRL
                 1119 ;
e7ab e1          1120           POP  H             ;RESTORE REGISTERS
e7ac d1          1121           POP  D
e7ad c1          1122           POP  B
```

```
e7ae f1          1123          POP PSW
e7af fb          1124          EI
e7b0 ed 4d       1125          DB 0EDH,4DH ;Z-80 CODE FOR RETURN FROM MASKABLE INTERRUPT
                 1126 ;
e7b2 21 cc e7    1127 KBERR:   LXI H,KBR1  ;PRINT ERROR MESSAGE
e7b5 22 86 e2    1128          SHLD OUTPNT
e7b8 cd 51 e8    1129          CALL DISPON
e7bb c3 a6 e7    1130          JMP KXIT
                 1131 ;
e7be 21 e5 e7    1132 KBER2:   LXI H,KBR2
e7c1 22 86 e2    1133          SHLD OUTPNT
e7c4 cd 51 e8    1134          CALL DISPON
e7c7 c3 a6 e7    1135          JMP KXIT
                 1136 ;
e7ca 00          1137 NCB:     DB 0     ;NUMBER OF CHAR IN BUFFER
e7cb 0d          1138 CRBUF:   DB CR    ;OUTPUT BUFFER TO PRINT RETURN, LINEFEED
e7cc 49 4e 50    1139 KBR1:    .ASCII 'INPUT BUFFER NOT VACATED'
     55 54 20
     42 55 46
     46 45 52
     20 4e 4f
     54 20 56
     41 43 41
     54 45 44
e7e4 0d          1140          DB CR
e7e5 49 4e 56    1141 KBR2:    .ASCII 'INVALID BUFFER STATUS'
     41 4c 49
     44 20 42
     55 46 46
     45 52 20
     53 54 41
     54 55 53
e7fa 0d          1142          DB CR
                 1143 ;
                 1144 ; END OF KEYBOARD INTERRUPT ROUTINE
                 1145 ;
                 1146 ; TERMINAL OUTPUT INTERRUPT PROGRAM
                 1147 ;
00ed             1148 DISCSR = 0EDH   ;DISPLAY REGISTERS
00ec             1149 DISBUF = 0ECH
0001             1150 TXMPTY = 1           ;MASK FOR DISPLAY READY (TRANSMITTER EMPTY)
                 1151 ;
e7fb f5          1152 DINT:    PUSH PSW    ;SAVE REGISTERS
e7fc c5          1153          PUSH B
e7fd d5          1154          PUSH D
e7fe e5          1155          PUSH H
                 1156 ;
e7ff 3a 5e e8    1157          LDA LFED    ;CHECK LINEFEED FLAG
e802 fe 01       1158          CPI TRUE
e804 c2 13 e8    1159          JNZ D1
e807 3e 0a       1160          MVI A,LF    ;SEND LINEFEED
e809 d3 ec       1161          OUT DISBUF
e80b 3e 00       1162          MVI A,FALSE
e80d 32 5e e8    1163          STA LFED    ;RESET FLAG
e810 c3 45 e8    1164          JMP DXIT    ;RETURN
                 1165 ;
e813 3a 1e e3    1166 D1:      LDA BUF     ;IS A MESSAGE READY TO SEND?
e816 fe 01       1167          CPI TRUE
e818 ca 23 e8    1168          JZ D4       ;JUMP IF YES.
                 1169 ;
e81b 3e 87       1170          MVI A,87H   ;DISABLE OUTPUT INTERRUPTS
e81d 32 e1 e1    1171          STA MASK
                 1172 ;
e820 c3 45 e8    1173          JMP DXIT
                 1174 ;
e823 2a 86 e2    1175 D4:      LHLD OUTPNT ;SEND CHAR.
```

```
e826 7e        1176         MOV A,M      ;A <-- CHAR. POINTED TO BY HL
e827 d3 ec     1177         OUT DISBUF
e829 fe 0d     1178         CPI CR       ;IS IT A RETURN?
e82b c2 3b e8  1179         JNZ D2
e82e 3e 00     1180         MVI A,FALSE ;YES, BUF <-- FALSE
e830 32 1e e3  1181         STA BUF
e833 3e 01     1182         MVI A,TRUE   ;LFED <-- TRUE
e835 32 5e e8  1183         STA LFED
e838 c3 3f e8  1184         JMP D3
               1185 ;
e83b 23        1186 D2:     INX H        ;POINT TO NEXT CHAR.
e83c 22 86 e2  1187         SHLD OUTPNT
e83f 00        1188 D3:     NOP
               1189 ;
e840 3e 88     1190         MVI A,88H    ;ENABLE OUTPUT INTERRUPTS
e842 32 e1 e1  1191         STA MASK
               1192 ;
e845 3a e1 e1  1193 DXIT:   LDA MASK     ;RESET INTERRUPT CONTROLLER
e848 d3 d7     1194         OUT CONTRL
               1195 ;
e84a e1        1196         POP H        ;RESTORE REGISTERS
e84b d1        1197         POP D
e84c c1        1198         POP B
e84d f1        1199         POP PSW
e84e fb        1200         EI
e84f ed 4d     1201         DB 0EDH,4DH ;Z-80 CODE FOR RETURN FROM MASKABLE INTERRUPT
               1202 ;
e851 3e 01     1203 DISPON: MVI A,TRUE   ;THIS ROUTINE WAKES UP THE DISPLAY
e853 32 1e e3  1204         STA BUF
               1205 ;
e856 3e 88     1206         MVI A,88H    ;ENABLE OUTPUT INTERRUPTS
e858 32 e1 e1  1207         STA MASK
e85b d3 d7     1208         OUT CONTRL
               1209 ;
e85d c9        1210 DISXIT: RET
e85e 00        1211 LFED:   DB 0         ;LINEFEED FLAG
               1212 ;
               1213 ;END OF DISPLAY INTERRUPT ROUTINE
               1214 ;
               1215 ; END OF PROGRAM
```

APPENDIX B—PDP-11/LSI-11

AUTOMATED WEIGHING PROGRAMS IN FORTRAN
- B29   Background Program in FORTRAN
- B30   Assembly Language Interrupt Routine

AUTOMATED WEIGHING PROGRAMS IN C
- B31   C Programs
- B32   Assembly Language Routine

POLAR PLOTTER PROGRAMS IN FORTRAN
- B33   Vector Generation Subroutine
- B34   Assembly Language Subroutine to Initialize Interrupts
- B35   Assembly Language Subroutines for Sequencing Stepping Motors

DC MOTOR CONTROL PROGRAMS IN FORTRAN

A listing of the FORTRAN time-telling program appears in Listing B1. The four program states defined in Figure 3.7 are labeled and separated by asterisks to improve readability. Each GOTO branch is followed by a comment line which indicates to which state the branch is aimed. FORTRAN allows the user to specify integer or real variables. Real variables (often called floating point variables) contain a mantissa and exponent in order to provide a greater range than integer variables.

The penalties paid for increased range include greater storage requirements and substantially greater computation times. The time-telling program is written using only integer arithmetic in order to avoid the time penalty. The IPEEK function is used to interrogate the parallel input interface. All unused inputs are connected so that they appear as zeros to the FORTRAN program. The function IPEEK, therefore, returns a one if the clock is high and a zero if it is low. The program was run on a Digital Equipment Corporation LSI-11 (PDP-11/03) using an external clock operating at 1000Hz.

The velocity test program listing is presented in Listing B2. Masking was introduced in Chapter 3 to allow us to ignore all bits of a parallel input word except those desired. Two mask words are defined at the beginning of the velocity test program. The tachometer mask, MASKTK, has a value of 1 to allow examination of bit zero, the tachometer pulse input bit. The second mask word, MASKCK, enables test-ing bit one, the clock input bit.

Although Figure 3.18c shows the ideal tachometer clear signal as active high, the actual circuit built requires an active low clear signal. Had this fact not been realized when signals were verified, the program would not have functioned properly when first tried. The tachometer latch is cleared by calling subroutine IPOKE, which writes one 16-bit word to a parallel output interface. POKE-ing a zero and then a two causes bit one of the parallel output to pulse low, thereby clearing the tachometer latch.

The third and final program is the motor control and test program. Listing B3 is a listing of precisely the algorithm described in the test (Figure 3.20). Two additional mask words have been introduced to allow the tachometer latch to be cleared without affecting the state of the motor. The logical variable called START (Figure 3.20) is initialized to ensure that the program advances to the initial state after program loading. This program is made more convenient for the operator to use than the two previous programs by having the program calculate the proper number of ticks for the length of the test, the sampling interval, and the motor on and off times. As in earlier programs, integer variables are used.

The system as shown in Figure 3.4 was assembled and run. The structured design approach recommended in Chapter 3 provided us with a program whose logical structure was correct the first time. The completed system functions precisely as described in the test.

B1   Time-Telling Program in FORTRAN

```
      PROGRAM TIMTEL
C
C THIS PROGRAM IS THE TIME  TELLING PROGRAM
C (FIRST EXAMPLE OF CHAPTER  3 .)
```

```
C THE USER IS ASKED FOR THE NUMBER OF TICKS WHICH
C ARE TO ELAPSE BEFORE A "REPORT" IS TO BE MADE.
C THE REPORT SAYS "TIME IS UP"
C
C
C STATE INITIAL
50        CONTINUE
          TYPE 100
100       FORMAT(1X'NUMBER OF TICKS TO ELAPSE BEFORE REPORT?')
C
          ACCEPT 110,NTR
110       FORMAT(I6)
C
          ICLOK1=NTR
          GO TO 200
C 200 = STATE TICK DETECT
C END STATE INITIAL
C
C ******************
C
C STATE TICK DETECT
200       CONTINUE
C
          IF(IPEEK("167774").NE.0)GO TO 200
250       CONTINUE
          IF(IPEEK("167774").EQ.0)GO TO 250
C
C TO HERE => RISING EDGE OF CLOCK DETECTED
C
          GO TO 300
C 300 = STATE CLOCK UPDATE
C END STATE TICK DETECT
C
C ******************
C
C STATE CLOCK UPDATE
300       CONTINUE
C
          ICLOK1=ICLOK1-1
          IF(ICLOK1.GT.0)GO TO 200
C 200 = STATE TICK DETECT
          GO TO 400
C 400 = STATE REPORT
C END STATE CLOCK UPDATE
C
C ******************
C
C STATE REPORT
400       CONTINUE
          TYPE 425
425       FORMAT(1X'TIME IS UP')
C
          GO TO 50
C 50 = STATE INITIAL
C
          END
```

B2   Velocity Test Program in FORTRAN

```
          PROGRAM VELTES
C
C THIS PROGRAM IS THE VELOCITY TEST PROGRAM
C
C THE USER IS ASKED FOR TWO VALUES: FIRST, THE
C LENGTH OF THE TEST, CLOCK1 (IN TICKS OF THE CLOCK)
```

```
C AND SECOND, THE SAMPLING INTERVAL TO RESET VARIABLE
C CLOCKV (ALSO IN TICKS).
C AT EXPIRATION OF CLOCK1, LAST COMPLETE TACHOMETER
C PULSE COUNT IS PRINTED.
C
C
        DATA MASKTK,MASKCK/1,2/
C MASKS FOR TACHOMETER AND CLOCK
C
C STATE INITIAL
50      CONTINUE
        TYPE 100
100     FORMAT(1X'LENGTH OF THE TEST (IN TICKS)?')
        ACCEPT 110,ICLOK1
110     FORMAT(I6)
C
        TYPE 120
120     FORMAT(1X'LENGTH OF SAMPLING INTERVAL (TICKS)?')
        ACCEPT 130,LENSAM
130     FORMAT(I6)
C
        ICLOKV=LENSAM
        NUMPLS=0
        LSTPLS=0
C
        CALL IPOKE("167772,2)
C RESET TACHOMETER LATCH LINE (TRUE LOW)
C
        GO TO 200
C 200 = STATE TICK DETECT
C END STATE INITIAL
C
C ********************
C
C STATE TICK DETECT
200     CONTINUE
C
        IF((IPEEK("167774).AND.MASKCK).NE.0)GO TO 200
250     CONTINUE
        IF((IPEEK("167774).AND.MASKCK).EQ.0)GO TO 250
C
C TO HERE => RISING EDGE OF CLOCK DETECTED
C
        GO TO 300
C 300 = STATE CLOCK UPDATE
C END OF STATE TICK DETECT
C
C ********************
C
C STATE CLOCK UPDATE
300     CONTINUE
C
        ICLOK1=ICLOK1-1
        ICLOKV=ICLOKV-1
C
        IF(ICLOKV.GT.0)GO TO 325
        ICLOKV=LENSAM
        GO TO 400
C 400 = STATE SAMPLE
C
325     CONTINUE
        IF(ICLOK1.GT.0)GO TO 500
C 500 = STATE VELOCITY
C
        GO TO 600
```

```
C 600 = TIMEOUT
C END OF STATE CLOCK UPDATE
C
C *********************
C
C STATE SAMPLE
400       CONTINUE
C
          LSTPLS=NUMPLS
          NUMPLS=0
          GO TO 500
C 500 = STATE VELOCITY
C END OF STATE SAMPLE
C
C **********************
C
C STATE VELOCITY
500       CONTINUE
C
          IF((IPEEK("167774).AND.MASKTK).EQ.0)GO TO 200
C 200 = STATE TICK DETECT
C
          NUMPLS=NUMPLS+1
C
          CALL IPOKE("167772,0)
          CALL IPOKE("167772,2)
C BIT 1 (BINARY 10) IS TACHOMETER CLEAR PULSE (0 => TRUE)
C
          GO TO 200
C 200 = STATE TICK DETECT
C END STATE VELOCITY
C
C *******************
C
C STATE TIME-OUT
600       CONTINUE
C
          TYPE 625,LSTPLS
625       FORMAT(1X'LAST VELOCITY= ',I6)
C
          GO TO 50
C 50 = STATE INITIAL
C END OF STATE TIME-OUT
C
          END
```

B3   Motor Test Program In FORTRAN

```
          PROGRAM MOTEST
C
C THIS PROGRAM IS THE MOTOR TEST PROGRAM
C
C THE USER IS ASKED FOR FIVE VALUES:
C 1)CLOCK RATE IN HZ, 2)LENGTH OF TEST IN SECONDS,
C 3)VELOCITY SAMPLE INTERVAL (SECONDS), 4)MOTOR
C ACTUATION PULSE FREQUENCY, 5)MOTOR ACTUATION PULSE
C DUTY CYCLE (IN PERCENT).
C THE MOTOR STARTS AND RUNS AT SPEED DETERMINED
C BY ACTUATION PULSE TRAIN.   VELOCITY IS SAMPLED.
C AT END OF TEST, LAST VELOCITY IS PRINTED (IN RPM
C ASSUMING TWO TACHOMETER PULSES PER REVOLUTION).
C MOTOR THEN STOPS.
C
C
          LOGICAL START
```

```
        DATA MASKTK,MASKCK,MSKCL1,MSKCL2/1,2,1,2/
C
C PROGRAM STATE INITIALIZATION
C
        START=.TRUE.
C
C END PROGRAM STATE INITIALIZATION
C
C * * * * * * * * * *
C
C STATE MOTOR-OFF
800     CONTINUE
C
        CALL IPOKE("167772,3)
        ISTAT=1
C STORED VALUE IS CURRENT STATE OF MOTOR (1 => OFF)
C MOTOR OFF, TACHOMETER PULSE LATCH CLEAR <-- FALSE
C LATCH CLEAR IS TRUE LOW
C
        IF(START)GO TO 50
C 50 = STATE INITIAL
C
        IF(ICLOKV.GT.0)GO TO 500
C 500 = STATE VELOCITY
C
        GO TO 400
C 400 = STATE SAMPLE
C
C END STATE MOTOR OFF
C
C *******************
C
C STATE INITIAL
50      CONTINUE
C
        TYPE 60
60      FORMAT(1X'CLOCK FREQUENCY (HZ)?')
        ACCEPT 65,ICLKRT
65      FORMAT(I6)
C
        TYPE 70
70      FORMAT(1X'LENGTH OF TEST (SEC)?')
        ACCEPT 75,LENTST
75      FORMAT(I6)
C
        TYPE 80
80      FORMAT(1X'VELOCITY SAMPLE INTERVAL (SEC)?')
        ACCEPT 85,INTVEL
85      FORMAT(I6)
C
        TYPE 90
90      FORMAT(1X'MOTOR ACTUATION PULSE FREQUENCY (HZ)?')
        ACCEPT 95,IFREQ
95      FORMAT(I6)
C
        TYPE 100
100     FORMAT(1X'MOTOR ACTUATION PULSE DUTY CYCLE (%)?')
        ACCEPT 105,IDUTY
105     FORMAT(I6)
C
C NOW, COMPUTE CLOCK VALUES
C
        ICLOK1=LENTST*ICLKRT
        ICLKV1=INTVEL*ICLKRT
        IPLST1=ICLKRT/IFREQ
```

```
            ITMON1=(IPLST1*IDUTY)/100
C
            ICLOKV=ICLKV1
            ITIMON=ITMON1
            IPLSTM=IPLST1
C
            START=.FALSE.
C
            GO TO 200
C 200 = STATE TICK DETECT
C END STATE INITIAL
C
C ********************
C
C STATE TICK DETECT
200       CONTINUE
C
            IF((IPEEK("167774).AND.MASKCK).NE.0)GO TO 200
250       CONTINUE
            IF((IPEEK("167774).AND.MASKCK).EQ.0)GO TO 250
C
C TO HERE => RISING EDGE OF CLOCK DETECTED
C
            GO TO 300
C 300 = STATE CLOCK UPDATE
C END STATE TICK DETECT
C
C **********************
C
C STATE CLOCK UPDATE
300       CONTINUE
C
            ICLOK1=ICLOK1-1
            ICLOKV=ICLOKV-1
            ITIMON=ITIMON-1
            IPLSTM=IPLSTM-1
C
            IF(ICLOK1.LE.0)GO TO 600
C 600 = STATE TIME-OUT
C
            IF(ITIMON.GT.0)GO TO 700
C 700 = STATE MOTOR ON
C
            IF(IPLSTM.GT.0)GO TO 800
C 800 = STATE MOTOR OFF
C
            IPLSTM=IPLST1
            ITIMON=ITMON1
C
            GO TO 700
C 700 = STATE MOTOR ON
C END STATE CLOCK UPDATE
C
C ********************
C
C STATE SAMPLE
400       CONTINUE
C
            LSTPLS=NUMPLS
            NUMPLS=0
            ICLOKV=ICLKV1
C
            GO TO 500
C 500 = STATE VELOCITY
C END STATE SAMPLE
```

```
C
C ********************
C
C STATE VELOCITY
500       CONTINUE
C
          IF((IPEEK("167774).AND.MASKTK).EQ.0)GO TO 200
C 200 = STATE TICK DETECT
C
          NUMPLS=NUMPLS+1
C
          CALL IPOKE("167772,(ISTAT.AND.MSKCL1))
          CALL IPOKE("167772,(ISTAT.OR.MSKCL2))
C
C CLEAR TACHOMETER LATCH
C
          GO TO 200
C 200 = STATE TICK DETECT
C END STATE VELOCITY
C
C ********************
C
C STATE TIME-OUT
600       CONTINUE
C
          ANTVEL=INTVEL
          TYPE 625,(LSTPLS/ANTVEL)*0.5*60
C
C (PULSE/INTERVAL)*(INTERVAL/SEC)*(REV/PULSE)*(SEC/MIN)=RPM
C
625       FORMAT(1X'LAST VELOCITY (RPM)= ',F8.2)
C
          START=.TRUE.
C
          GO TO 800
C 800 = STATE MOTOR OFF
C END STATE TIME-OUT
C
C ********************
C
C STATE MOTOR ON
700       CONTINUE
C
          CALL IPOKE("167772,2)
C
C TURN MOTOR ON
C
          ISTAT=0
C
C STORED VARIABLE IS CURRENT STATE OF MOTOR (1 => OFF)
C
          IF(ICLOKV.LE.0)GO TO 400
C 400 = STATE SAMPLE
C
          GO TO 500
C 500 = STATE VELOCITY
C END STATE MOTOR ON
C
          END
```

STEPPING MOTOR PROGRAMS

The PDP-11, LSI-11 series of computers is manufactured by the Digital Equipment Corporation (DEC). The PDP-11 series is a set of upward compatible minicomputer processors; the LSI-11 series fits into the area between minicomputers and microcomputers. PDP-11s and LSI-11s will run more or less the same programs because their CPUs will respond to almost the same command (instruction) set. They differ in that peripheral devices can only be used with one series or the other, but cannot be interchanged. For brevity, we will use the term PDP-11 to refer to both PDP-11 and LSI-11 unless specified otherwise. We should also note that the computer systems that Digital Equipment calls the PDP-11/03 and PDP-11/23 are actually part of the LSI-11 series rather than the PDP-11 series.

PDP-11s use 16-bit words and do 16-bit arithmetic. The memory, however, can be accessed either by 16-bit words or by 8-bit bytes. The address structure of the memory uses one address for each byte; words take up two bytes. Full 16-bit words must always start on *even* addresses. Instruction codes always take one or more full 16-bit words, and thus must always start on even addresses. In programs that deal mostly with words, only even addresses are used. However, it is important to remember the factor of two when computing the number of memory addresses occupied by data or instructions.

The CPU contains six, 16-bit general purpose registers named R0, R1,...,R5. The program counter is also 16 bits which provides a nominal address space having 65,536 (2^{16}) addresses. These are byte addresses, however, so the nominal address space in words is only half that, 32,768. All manuals written by DEC concerning PDP-11s use octal to represent instruction codes.

Copy-type operations on PDP-11s are implemented with an instruction called *move,* which has an assembly-format mnemonic of MOV. Immediate data is indicated in assembly format by use of the symbol # and registers are indicated either by R0, R1, etc., or by %0, %1, etc. Thus, in assembly format, a copy-immediate to register 0 would be MOV #101,R0. The direction of the copy is from left to right. In this case, the data 101Q would be copied to register 0. Octal is the default number base in PDP-11 assembly format. Copying from the register to the output port is also done with the move instruction. The output port is identified by a number preceded by the combined symbol @#. The program to turn bit zero of the output port on is shown in Listing B4.

PDP-11s do not require that data destined for output ports be passed through a CPU register, as was done in Listing B4, although it is sometimes convenient if some intermediate processing is to be done. The program in Listing B5 shows the use of a move instruction to copy data directly to the output port.

The MOV instruction code follows the pattern shown in Figure 4.2. Bits 15-12 are used for the 4-bit operation code, bits 11-6 for the source operand, and bits 5-0 for the destination operand. If either the source or destination operand (or both) is a register, the number of the register in binary is used in that operand portion of the instruction. Immediate data is specified by using the code 27Q in the 6-bit operand portion of the instruction. The immediate data itself follows the instruction in memory. The operation code for MOV is 01Q, =0001B.

To construct the instruction MOV #1,R1, we combine the op-code,

01Q, the code for immediate data, 27Q, for the source operand, and the register number, 01Q for the destination (second) operand to get 012701Q (=0001010111000001B). The immediate data, 1Q, follows in the word immediately after the instruction code. The operand code for copying data to an output port is 37Q, so the instruction MOV R1,@#167772 becomes 010137Q. The complete program, with octal instruction codes and memory addresses, is shown in Listing B6.

The instruction to copy data directly to the output port, MOV #1,@#167772, requires three memory words. The first for the instruction code, which is 012737Q (01Q for the op-code, 27Q to indicate that the first [source] operand is immediate data, and 37Q to indicate that the second [destination] operand is the output port), the second for the immediate data, 1Q, the third for the output port identifier, 167772Q. This program, with octal instruction codes, is shown in Listing B7.

The PDP-11 monitor is called ODT, for octal debugging technique. For LSI-11s, a version of ODT is built into the CPU and can be entered by pressing the CPU halt switch on the console. For other PDP-11s, an ODT is available through the operating system, which is RT-11 V4 for these examples. References here will be both to the LSI-11 built-in ODT (*console* ODT) and RT-11 V4 ODT. All interaction with ODT is via the console terminal. There are only two ODT commands that we need know to load and run this program: one for both examining and changing memory locations, and the other to start the CPU running.

To examine a memory location, the user types the memory location desired (in octal) followed by a slash (/). ODT then types the contents of the memory location, leaving the print head (or cursor on a CRT terminal) positioned one space beyond where it stopped. The user can now do one of three things: 1) type a RETURN so that another memory location can be entered for examination, 2) type a LINEFEED (LF), which will cause ODT to automatically open the next sequential memory location (the next word is accessed, i.e., current location plus 2 for examination and possible modification, or 3) type an octal number to replace the contents of the memory location with the number typed.

After typing the replacement information, either RETURN or LINEFEED can be used. To start the program running, the user types the address in memory at which the CPU is to start followed by the command ;G (the semicolon is not needed for LSI-11 console ODT). The instruction breakpoint trap (BPT), with an operation code of 3, causes control to be returned to ODT. Listing B8 shows the user-ODT interaction to run this program.

The timed-loop program uses several additional instructions, copy-absolute to memory, decrement, and conditional branch. The MOV instruction is used for the copy-absolute. It uses exactly the same form as the copy to output port MOV used earlier because PDP-11s use the same set of addresses for both memory and input and output ports (this is called memory-mapped I/O). Thus the operand code 37Q is used to specify that a memory address will be accessed, and the address to be accessed is specified in the word following the instruction. Although decrementing immediate data is technically possible, it rarely makes any sense to do it. Thus, the instruction DEC R0 has the instruction code 053300Q.

Conditional branch instructions are implemented in PDP-11s by testing condition codes that are set by instructions operating on data. In this instance we are concerned with testing for a zero or non-zero result, so we will use instructions that test the Z bit. Both MOV and DEC (as well as most other instructions that manipulate data) set the Z bit to 1 if the result of the operations was zero and set it to 0 (clear it) if the result was not zero. The BNE (branch on not equal to zero) instruction tests the Z bit and performs the indicated change of sequence if Z is 0. If Z is 1, it just goes on to the next sequential instruction. Its instruction code format uses bits 15-8 for its op-code (which is 0010Q) and bits 7-0 to indicate where in memory the next instruction to be executed is if its test is true.

Since there are too few bits to indicate an actual memory address, the branch location is given by an offset from the instruction that would normally be executed next. The offset is expressed in *words,* not bytes. For example, an offset of zero turns the branch instruction into a no-operation since, regardless of the result of its test, the instruction immediately following the branch will be executed. An offset of 1 will skip one word and execute the instruction one word beyond the instruction that would be executed if the test failed.

In programming branch instructions, the offset used must take account of the variable number of words occupied by instructions so as not to land in the middle of an instruction. To branch backwards as in implementing a loop, the 8-bit branch offset must be written as a negative number in two's complement form. Two's complement is formed by counting backwards from zero in binary. One less than 00000000B is 11111111B. One less than that is 11111110B, etc. A quick trick for getting two's complement numbers is to first write the number as a positive binary number, for example, 00001101B ($=15Q = 13$). Getting the two's complement is a two-step

process. First, change all the zeros to ones and all the ones to zero. This gives 11110010B. Then add 1 to that number to get 11110011B ($=363Q$). This is the two's complement negative of 15Q.

Two versions of the timed loop program are shown in Listings B9 and B10 with octal instruction codes. Listing B9 uses a memory location to save the outer-loop counter, and B10 uses several registers to avoid the necessity of saving registers. Using the numbers shown in the figure, the total time to run the program on an LSI-11 was 5.8 seconds.

All of the components needed to output a pulse train are now available. The program is shown in Listing B11, with octal instruction codes.

The PDP-11 instruction set provides specifically for manipulating bits within a word, so it is not necessary to perform the OR operations to do that. The two instructions that accomplish what is needed to provide the pulse generation program with direction control are bit-set (BIS) and bit-clear (BIC). Their instruction codes are constructed using the same bit pattern as is used for the MOV instruction. The op-codes are 05Q for BIS and 04Q for BIC. The first operand specifies a mask to indicate which bit is to be operated on. The mask word should have a 1 in any bit position that is to be operated on and zero in bit positions that are not to be operated on. The same mask rules are used for both BIS and BIC.

In our case, it is most convenient to specify the mask with immediate data, which is specified by a 27Q in the first operand position. Using 37Q in the second operand position specifies absolute mode for either memory or I/O addresses. For example, the instruction BIS #2,@#167772 will take three words—052737Q, 000002Q, and 167772Q—and will turn bit 1 of the output port on because the number 2 has a 1 in bit position 1 and zeros elsewhere. With this, the move-wait-return program can be completed and is shown in Listing B12.

The bit-test instruction (BIT) can be used to test individual bits on an input port to implement the external clock-timed wait loop. It is constructed in the same manner as BIT and BIC and the mask word follows the same rules. A program to test external clock timing is shown in Listing B13 and the complete move-wait-return program using the external clock is shown in Listing B14.

B4   Instructions to Turn On Output Bit Using a Register

```
MOV #1,R1              ;COPY-IMMEDIATE 1 TO REGISTER 1

MOV R1,@#167772       ;COPY REGISTER 1 TO OUTPUT
                      ;PORT SPECIFIED BY 167772Q.
BPT                   ;THIS INSTRUCTION RETURNS TO MONITOR
```

B5   Instructions to Turn On Output Bit with Direct Copy to Output Port

```
MOV #1,@#167772       ;COPY-IMMEDIATE DATA DIRECTLY
                      ;TO OUTPUT PORT.
BPT
```

B6   Program with Octal Codes Using a Register

```
address    instruction

010000     012701          MOV #1,R1              ;COPY-IMMEDIATE 1 TO REGISTER 1
           000001

010004     010137          MOV R1,@#167772        ;COPY REGISTER 1 TO OUTPUT
           167772
                                                  ;PORT SPECIFIED BY 167772Q.
010010     000003          BPT              ;THIS INSTRUCTION RETURNS TO MONITOR
```

B7   Program with Octal Codes with Direct Copy to Output Port

```
address    instruction

010000     012737          MOV #1,@#167772        ;COPY-IMMEDIATE DATA DIRECTLY
           000001
           167772
                                                  ;TO OUTPUT PORT.
010006     000003          BPT
```

B8   Using a Debugging Aid to Enter and Run a Program

```
.R ODT

ODT V01.06
*10000/000000 12701
010002 /000000 1              Enter the program
010004 /000000 10137
010006 /000000 167772
010010 /000000 3
*10000/012701                 Verify the program entry
010002 /000001
010004 /010137
010006 /167772
```

```
010010 /000003
*10000;G                        Run it

BE010010
*10002/000001 0                 Change the output to turn bit off
*10000;G                        Run it again

BE010010
*
```

B9   Timed Loop Program Using a Memory Location and a Register

```
010000   012700         MOV #12,R0      ;INITIALIZE OUTER LOOP COUNT
         000012
010004   010037   W1:    MOV R0,@#COUNT  ;SAVE OUTER LOOP COUNTER IN MEMORY
         010032
010010   012700         MOV #177777,R0  ;INNER LOOP COUNT
         177777
010014   005300   W2:    DEC R0          ;DECREMENT LOOP COUNT
010016   001376         BNE W2          ;IF NOT ZERO GO BACK TO W2
010020   013700         MOV @#COUNT,R0   ;RESTORE OUTER LOOP COUNT
         010032
010024   005300         DEC R0          ;DECREMENT OUTER LOOP COUNT
010026   001366         BNE W1          ;IF NOT ZERO GO BACK TO W1
010030   000003         BPT             ;THIS GETS BACK TO THE MONITOR
                                        ;HALT WOULD GET BACK FOR CONSOLE ODT.
010032   000000   COUNT:   .WORD 0       ;DEFINE A MEMORY LOCATION FOR COUNT
```

B10   Timed Loop Program Using Two Registers

```
010000   012700         MOV #12,R0      ;USE REGISTER 0 FOR OUTER LOOP
         000012
010004   012701   W1:    MOV #177777,R1  ;USE REGISTER 1 FOR INNER LOOP
         177777
010010   005301   W2:    DEC R1          ;DECREMENT INNER LOOP
010012   001376         BNE W2
010014   005300         DEC R0          ;DECREMENT OUTER LOOP
010016   001372         BNE W1
010020   000003         BPT             ;RETURN TO MONITOR
```

B11   Pulse Train Program

```
                 ;REGISTER USAGE:      R0   COUNTS NUMBER OF PULSES
                 ;                     R1   WAIT LOOP COUNTER
                 ;
010000   012700         MOV #12,R0      ;INITIALIZE REGISTER 0 FOR 12B =10
         000012
                                        ;PULSES
010004   012737   P1:    MOV #1,@#167772 ;COPY-IMMEDIATE TO OUTPUT PORT TO
         000001
         167772
                                        ;TURN OUTPUT ON
010012   012701         MOV #100,R1     ;INITIALIZE ON-TIME WAIT
         000100
010016   005301   P2:    DEC R1          ;DECREMENT COUNTER
010020   001376         BNE P2          ;IF NOT ZERO, DECREMENT AGAIN
010022   012737         MOV #0,@#167772 ;TURN OUTPUT BIT OFF. CLR (CLEAR)
         000000
         167772
                                        ;INSTRUCTION WOULD ALSO DO THIS.
010030   012701         MOV #1000,R1    ;OFF-TIME WAIT LOOP
         001000
010034   005301   P3:    DEC R1
010036   001376         BNE P3
```

```
010040   005300        DEC R0          ;HAVE ALL PULSES BEEN SENT?
010042   001360        BNE P1          ;IF NOT, SEND ANOTHER
010044   000137        JMP @#1232      ;DONE...RETURN TO MONITOR
         001232
```

B12   Move-Wait-Return Program Using Delay Loop

```
              ;REGISTER USAGE        ;R0   SEQUENCE COUNT
                                     ;R1   PULSE COUNT
                                     ;R2   WAIT LOOP COUNT
                                     ;R3   WAIT LOOP, INNER LOOP COUNT

              ;
              ;INITIALIZE MODULE
010000   012700   INIT:   MOV #2,R0       ;INITIALIZE SEQUENCE COUNT
         000002
010004   012701           MOV #1000,R1    ;PULSE COUNT, 1000B=512 PULSES
         001000
010010   052737           BIS #2,@#167772 ;SET INITIAL DIRECTION
         000002
         167772
              ;
              ;PULSE GENERATION MODULE
010016   052737   PG1:    BIS #1,@#167772 ;TURN BIT ON
         000001
         167772
010024   012702           MOV #10,R2      ;ON-TIME
         000010
              ;
              ;WAIT LOOP.   THESE INSTRUCTIONS WILL BE REPEATED
              ;SEVERAL TIMES.
010030   005302   W1:     DEC R2          ;DECREMENT, THEN TEST
010032   001376           BNE W1
010034   042737           BIC #1,@#167772 ;TURN BIT OFF.
         000001
         167772
010042   012702           MOV #1000,R2    ;OFF-TIME
         001000
              ;
              ;WAIT LOOP AGAIN
010046   005302   W2:     DEC R2
010050   001376           BNE W2
010052   005301           DEC R1          ;DECREMENT PULSE COUNT
010054   001360           BNE PG1         ;IF NOT ZERO, DO ANOTHER PULSE
              ;END OF PULSE GENERATION MODULE.
              ;DECREMENT SEQUENCE COUNT..
010056   005300           DEC R0
010060   001002           BNE RESET       ;IF NOT ZERO, SET UP FOR RETURN MOTION
              ;
              ;STOP MODULE.  GET HERE IF SEQUENCE COUNT=0
010062   000137           JMP @#1232      ;RETURN TO MONITOR
         001232
              ;
              ;RESET MODULE
010066   042737   RESET:  BIC #2,@#167772 ;SET DIRECTION TO RETURN
         000002
         167772
010074   012701           MOV #1000,R1    ;SET PULSE COUNT FOR RETURN
         001000
              ;
              ;ANOTHER WAIT.  USE DOUBLE LOOP HERE TO MAXIMIZE WAIT TIME.
              ;USE REGISTER 3 FOR INNER LOOP COUNT
010100   012702           MOV #100,R2
         000100
010104   012703   W3:     MOV #177777,R3  ;MAXIMUM INNER LOOP COUNT
         177777
```

```
010110   005303   W4:     DEC R3
010112   001376           BNE W4
010114   005302           DEC R2
010116   001372           BNE W3
010120   000137           JMP @#PG1          ;WAIT IS OVER.  GENERATE PULSE TRAIN AGAIN.
         010016
```

B13   Test Program for External Clock Timing

```
                  ;REGISTER USAGE        R2  CLOCK TICK COUNT
                  ;
010000   012702           MOV #100,R2      ;WAIT FOR 100B=64 CLOCK TICKS
         000100
                  ;BEGINNING OF WAIT-LOOP MACRO
010004   032737   CLK1:   BIT #1,@#167774 ;TEST BIT-0
         000001
         167774
010012   001374           BNE CLK1        ;IF NOT ZERO, WAIT
010014   032737   CLK2:   BIT #1,@#167774 ;TEST AGAIN
         000001
         167774
010022   001774           BEQ CLK2        ;IF ZERO (I.E., NOT 1), WAIT
010024   005302           DEC R2
010026   001366           BNE CLK1        ;IF NOT ZERO, GO BACK AND WAIT FOR
                                          ;NEXT CLOCK PULSE.
010030   000137           JMP @#1232      ;RETURN TO MONITOR
         001232
```

B14   Move-Wait-Return Program Using an External Clock

```
                  ;REGISTER USAGE        ;R0   SEQUENCE COUNT
                                         ;R1   PULSE COUNT
                                         ;R2   WAIT LOOP COUNT
                  ;
                  ;INITIALIZE MODULE
010000   012700   INIT:   MOV #2,R0       ;INITIALIZE SEQUENCE COUNT
         000002
010004   012701           MOV #1000,R1    ;PULSE COUNT, 1000Q=512 PULSES
         001000
010010   052737           BIS #2,@#167772 ;SET INITIAL DIRECTION
         000002
         167772
                  ;
                  ;PULSE GENERATION MODULE
010016   052737   PG1:    BIS #1,@#167772 ;TURN BIT ON
         000001
         167772
010024   012702           MOV #10,R2      ;ON-TIME
         000010
                  ;
                  ;THE ON-TIME IS USUALLY VERY SHORT SO THE CLOCK
                  ;WON'T BE USED FOR TIMING HERE.
010030   005302   W1:     DEC R2          ;DECREMENT, THEN TEST
010032   001376           BNE W1
010034   042737           BIC #1,@#167772 ;TURN BIT OFF.
         000001
         167772
010042   012702           MOV #5,R2       ;OFF-TIME
         000005
                  ;
                  ;PUT CLOCK TIMER MACRO HERE FOR OFF-TIME WAIT
010046   032737   CLK1:   BIT #1,@#167774 ;TEST BIT-0
         000001
         167774
```

```
010054  001374         BNE CLK1          ;IF NOT ZERO, WAIT
010056  032737  CLK2:  BIT #1,@#167774   ;TEST AGAIN
        000001
        167774
010064  001774         BEQ CLK2          ;IF ZERO, WAIT
010066  005302         DEC R2            ;DECREMENT TICK COUNT
010070  001366         BNE CLK1          ;IF NOT ZERO, WAIT FOR ANOTHER TICK.
010072  005301         DEC R1            ;DECREMENT PULSE COUNT
010074  001350         BNE PG1           ;IF NOT ZERO, DO ANOTHER PULSE
                ;END OF PULSE GENERATION MODULE.
                ;DECREMENT SEQUENCE COUNT..
010076  005300         DEC R0
010100  001001         BNE RESET         ;IF NOT ZERO, SET UP FOR RETURN MOTION
                ;
                ;STOP MODULE.  GET HERE IF SEQUENCE COUNT=0
010102  000003         BPT               ;RETURN TO MONITOR
                ;
                ;RESET MODULE
010104  042737  RESET: BIC #2,@#167772   ;SET DIRECTION TO RETURN
        000002
        167772
010112  012701         MOV #1000,R1      ;SET PULSE COUNT FOR RETURN
        001000
                ;
                ;PUT CLOCK TIMER MACRO HERE ALSO.
010116  012702         MOV #1000,R2
        001000
010122  032737  CLK3:  BIT #1,@#167774   ;TEST BIT-0
        000001
        167774
010130  001374         BNE CLK3
010132  032737  CLK4:  BIT #1,@#167774   ;TEST AGAIN
        000001
        167774
010140  001774         BEQ CLK4
010142  005302         DEC R2            ;DECREMENT TICK COUNTER
010144  001366         BNE CLK3          ;IF NOT ZERO, WAIT FOR ANOTHER TICK.
010146  000137         JMP @#PG1         ;WAIT IS OVER.  GENERATE PULSE TRAIN AGAIN.
        010016
```

TEMPERATURE CONTROL PROGRAMS

Control of terminals on PDP-11s is done with registers known as control and status registers (CSR). Each PDP-11 I/O device has such a register. The register is physically located on the device interface. A second interface register, the data buffer, is used for transferring data to or from the device. The keyboard and display CSRs are shown in Figure B.1. The two bits that are of concern to us are the ready/done flag (bit 7)

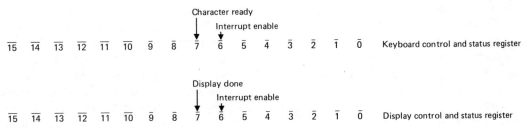

Figure B.1: Terminal Status Registers (CSR's)

and the interrupt enable. These bits are normally tested with the bit-test (BIT) instruction and set or cleared using bit-set (BIS) or bit-clear (BIC). The RT-11 operating system makes use of interrupts to operate the terminal while the programs in this case study do not. Thus, the interrupts must be disabled (bit 6 cleared) before attempting to access the terminal.

Programs to read a character from the keyboard and print a character on the display are shown in Listings B15 and B16. The programs are written in PDP-11 assembly format for use with the RT-11 assembler called Macro. Names beginning with a period, such as .CSECT, are assembler directives. They do not cause generation of any machine language instructions but give instructions to the assembler on how to proceed. The .CSECT directive tells the assembler that a section of relocatable code as named follows.

Macro is a relocatable assembler, meaning that it can generate machine language modules which are then combined using a linking loader to produce a complete program. Because .CSECTs are program modules, the assembler listing shown in these programs always has an origin address of zero. The linker assigns actual starting addresses to each of the modules as it links them and produces a memory map showing the starting address of each module.

Following the .CSECT, the lines with equal signs indicate symbol definitions. Again, these are a form of assembler directive indicating how to define a symbol. Later use of that symbol in an assembly format instruction has the same effect as using the number directly, but makes for more readable and more easily modified programs. For example, using KBCSR=177560 and then writing BIT #200,@#KBCSR is the same as writing BIT #200,@#177560.

The .END directive indicates the last line of a program. The symbol following the .END indicates the starting address for the program and is optional.

The console terminal interaction for assembling, linking, and running the keyboard program is shown in Listing B17. The original source file is called C32A.MAC.

The terminal input and output functions have been put in subroutine form in the shifted echo program of Listing B18a. The PDP-11 subroutine call statement is JSR PC, CHIN (for jump to subroutine), to call the character-in subroutine, CHIN, for example. The PC in the instruction indicates that the program counter is to be pushed onto the stack as part of the calling sequence. The return is RTS PC. The character read by CHIN is passed in register zero and the character to be printed is passed to CHOUT in register zero also. Subroutines CHIN and CHOUT are shown in Listing B18b.

The compare (CMP) instruction used in the program is a standard double-operand instruction like MOV or ADD in which the destination operand is subtracted from the source. No result is produced, however. The function of the instruction is just to set condition codes for use by a subsequent conditional branch. The load map for the complete program Listing B18c shows the actual memory locations for each of the program sections.

The multiply subroutine, with a short test program, is shown in Listing B19. The arguments to the multiply routine, the multiplicand and the multiplier are passed in registers zero and two. The 32-bit result is returned in registers zero and one with the high-order part in register zero. Registers three and four are used for scratch workspace. The instructions MOV R3,-(SP) and MOV R4,-(SP) push the contents of these registers on the system stack to save them. They are restored by popping them off the stack with MOV (SP)+,R4 and MOV (SP)+,R3 (notice the reversed order).

The shifts required for the multiply are done with the arithmetic shift left (ASL) instruction. The operand is left-shifted one bit, with the leftmost bit (bit 15) going to the carry (C) bit of the condition codes and the rightmost bit getting filled with a zero. The add-carry (ADC) instruction is used to keep the carry-overs correct when shifting or adding double-precision (32-bit) quantities.

The D/A program is given in Listing B20a. It makes use of the CHIN and CHOUT suboutines (B20b) which are supplied in a separate file and linked with the D/A test program.

The A/D subroutine, Listing B21, is set up to do 8-bit conversions. The counting loop has five instructions so, at about 10 microseconds per instruction, a full-scale

voltage should take 10 to 15 milliseconds for conversion. Using the divide routine of Listing B22, the full A/D calibration program of Listing B23a is built. It uses the terminal to receive start commands from the operator and prints the converted value, in decimal, on the terminal in order that the A/D can be set up and calibrated.

All of the pieces are put together in the temperature control program, Listing B24. It makes use of one additional feature of the Macro assembler, its ability to handle macros. Macros were introduced in Chapter 4 as a means of showing text substitution for a repeated instruction sequence. Defining a macro with the .MACRO directive automates this procedure. By using the macro, only one line need be written instead of the entire instruction sequence. The assembler then *expands* the macros to produce the actual assembly code. The single quote character concatenates the items on each side of it to produce a new symbol. Thus, TER'N will produce the symbol TER1 if expanded with N=1.

B15　　Read Keyboard and Echo

```
 1                     ;              READ KEYBOARD AND ECHO
 2                     ;
 3 000000             .CSECT KEYBD
 4                     ;
 5        177560       KBCSR=177560
 6        177562       KBBUF=177562
 7        177564       DISCSR=177564
 8        177566       DISBUF=177566
 9                     ;
10                     ; THESE ARE THE ADDRESSES FOR THE KEYBOARD AND DISPLAY
11                     ; STATUS REGISTERS AND DATA BUFFERS.
12                     ;
13 000000 042737 START: BIC #100,@#KBCSR       ;DISABLE RT-11'S INTERRUPTS
          000100
          177560
14 000006 042737      BIC #100,@#DISCSR        ; SO THEY DON'T INTERFERE.
          000100
          177564
15 000014 032737 K1:  BIT #200,@#KBCSR         ;CHECK FOR CHAR. READY
          000200
          177560
16 000022 001774      BEQ K1                   ;IF NOT READY, CHECK AGAIN
17 000024 013700      MOV @#KBBUF,R0           ;GET CHARACTER
```

```
                      177562
          18 000030   010037         MOV R0,@#DISBUF        ;ECHO IT.
                      177566
          19 000034   032737  K2:    BIT #200,@#DISCSR      ;WAIT TO FINISH PRINTING
                      000200
                      177564
          20 000042   001774         BEQ K2                 ;BEFORE RETURNING TO
          21 000044   000003         BPT                    ;MONITOR.
          22                   ;
          23           000000'       .END START             ;"START" IS THE ENTRY ADDRESS.
ERRORS DETECTED:  0

VIRTUAL MEMORY USED:  8192 WORDS  ( 32 PAGES)
DYNAMIC MEMORY AVAILABLE FOR  66 PAGES
C32A,C32A.L/N:SYM/L:TTM=C32A
```

B16   Print a Character

```
           1                    ;                 PRINT A CHARACTER
           2                    ;
           3 000000                    .CSECT DISPLY
           4                    ;
           5           177564   DISCSR=177564
           6           177566   DISBUF=177566
           7                    ;
           8 000000    042737   START: BIC #100,@#DISCSR     ;DISABLE RT-11'S
                       000100
                       177564
           9                                                 ;INTERRUPTS.
          10 000006    005037          CLR @#DISBUF          ;SEND OUT NULL TO
                       177566
          11                                                 ;START PRINTER.
          12 000012    012700          MOV #'A,R0            ;PUT CHAR. TO PRINT INTO R0
                       000101
          13 000016    032737   D1:    BIT #200,@#DISCSR     ;CHECK FOR DONE FLAG
                       000200
                       177564
          14 000024    001774          BEQ D1
          15 000026    010037          MOV R0,@#DISBUF       ;SEND OUT CHAR.
                       177566
          16 000032    032737   D2:    BIT #200,@#DISCSR     ;WAIT FOR DISPLAY TO
                       000200
                       177564
          17 000040    001774          BEQ D2                ;FINISH BEFORE RETURNING
          18 000042    000003          BPT                   ;TO ODT.
          19                    ;
          20            000000'        .END START
ERRORS DETECTED:   0

VIRTUAL MEMORY USED:  8192 WORDS  ( 32 PAGES)
DYNAMIC MEMORY AVAILABLE FOR  66 PAGES
C32B,C32B.L/N:SYM/L:TTM=C32B
```

B17   Assembling, Linking, and Running the Terminal Program

```
.R MACRO
*C32A,LS:/N:SYM=C32A
*^C

.R LINK
*C32A,TT:=ODT,C32A
RT-11 LINK  V05.04A    Load Map
C12A .SAV       Title: ODT     Ident:
```

```
Section  Addr    Size    Global  Value   Global  Value   Global  Value

. ABS.   000000  001000     (RW,I,GBL,ABS,OVR)
         001000  006100     (RW,I,LCL,REL,CON)
                         O.ODT    001232
KEYBD    007100  000046     (RW,I,GBL,REL,OVR)

Transfer address = 001232, High limit = 007146 =  1843. words
*^C

.R C32A

 ODT  V01.06
*7100;0R
*0,0/042737
*0,0;G
f
BE0,000044
*0,0;G
G
BE0,000044
*^C

.
```

B18a   Shifted Echo Program

```
 1                    ;            SHIFTED ECHO PROGRAM
 2                    ;
 3 000000                    .CSECT SHIFT
 4                    ;
 5        177560   KBCSR=177560
 6        177564   DISCSR=177564
 7        000015   CR=15
 8        000012   LF=12
 9                    ;
10                         .GLOBL CHIN,CHOUT
11                    ;
12 000000  042737   START:  BIC #100,@#KBCSR       ;CLEAT RT-11 INTERRUPT
           000100
           177560
13 000006  042737           BIC #100,@#DISCSR
           000100
           177564
14 000014  004767   S0:     JSR PC,CHIN            ;CALL CHAR.-IN SUBROUTINE
           000000G
15                                                 ;CHAR. RETURNED IN R0
16 000020  022700           CMP #CR,R0             ;IS IT A RETURN?
           000015
17 000024  001402           BEQ S1
18 000026  005200           INC R0                 ;GET HERE IF NOT A RET.
19                                                 ;INCREMENT CHAR. CODE
20 000030  000404           BR S2
21 000032  004767   S1:     JSR PC,CHOUT           ;ECHO RETURN
           000000G
22 000036  012700           MOV #LF,R0             ;SET UP TO ECHO LINE FEED
           000012
23 000042  004767   S2:     JSR PC,CHOUT           ;ECHO
           000000G
24 000046  000167           JMP S0                 ;DO IT AGAIN
           177742
25                    ;
26 000000'                  .END START
ERRORS DETECTED:  0
```

```
VIRTUAL MEMORY USED:  8192 WORDS  ( 32 PAGES)
DYNAMIC MEMORY AVAILABLE FOR  66 PAGES
C34A,C34A.L/N:SYM/L:TTM=C34A
```

B18b   Character I/O Subroutines

```
  1                          ; CHARACTER-IN (CHIN) AND CHARACTER-OUT (CHOUT) SUBROUTINES
  2                          ;
  3 000000                          .CSECT CHAR
  4                          ;
  5         177560   KBCSR=177560
  6         177562   KBBUF=177562
  7         177564   DISCSR=177564
  8         177566   DISBUF=177566
  9                          ;
 10                                  .GLOBL CHIN,CHOUT
 11                          ;
 12 000000  032737   CHIN:   BIT #200,@#KBCSR        ;WAIT FOR CHAR.
            000200
            177560
 13                          ;
 14 000006  001774           BEQ CHIN
 15 000010  013700           MOV  @#KBBUF,R0         ;GET CHARACTER.
            177562
 16 000014  042700           BIC #200,R0             ;CLEAR PARITY BIT
            000200
 17 000020  000207           RTS PC                  ;RETURN
 18 000022  032737   CHOUT:  BIT #200,@#DISCSR       ;IS DISPLAY READY?
            000200
            177564
 19 000030  001774           BEQ CHOUT
 20 000032  010037           MOV R0,@#DISBUF         ;YES, SEND OUT CHAR.
            177566
 21 000036  000207           RTS PC                  ;RETURN
 22                          ;
 23         000001           .END
ERRORS DETECTED:  0
```

```
VIRTUAL MEMORY USED:  8192 WORDS  ( 32 PAGES)
DYNAMIC MEMORY AVAILABLE FOR  66 PAGES
C34B,C34B.L/N:SYM/L:TTM=C34B
```

B18c   Load Map for Shifted Echo Program

```
RT-11 LINK  V05.04A     Load Map
C34A   .SAV     Title: ODT      Ident:

Section  Addr   Size    Global  Value    Global  Value    Global  Value

. ABS.   000000 001000  (RW,I,GBL,ABS,OVR)
         001000 006100  (RW,I,LCL,REL,CON)
                        O.ODT    001232
SHIFT    007100 000052  (RW,I,GBL,REL,OVR)
CHAR     007152 000040  (RW,I,GBL,REL,OVR)
                        CHIN     007152   CHOUT   007174

Transfer address = 001232, High limit = 007212 =  1861. words
```

B19   Multiply Subroutine and Test Program

```
  1                      ;                MULTIPLY SUBROUTINE AND TEST PROGRAM
  2                      ;
  3                      ; CALL WITH MULTIPLICAND IN R0, MULTIPLIER IN R2
  4                      ; 32-BIT RESULT IN R0 & R1; R0 IS HIGH-ORDER PART.
```

```
 5                               ; USES R3 AS SCRATCH SPACE, R4 FOR COUNT
 6                               ; FORMAT IS COMPATIBLE WITH EIS MUL INSTRUCTION.
 7                               ;
 8 000000                               .CSECT MLTPLY
 9                                       .GLOBL MULT
10                               ;
11 000000   010346    MULT:      MOV R3,-(SP)      ;SAVE R3 & R4 ON SYSTEM
12 000002   010446               MOV R4,-(SP)      ;STACK.
13 000004   010003               MOV R0,R3         ;COPY MULTIPLICAND TO R3
14 000006   005000               CLR R0
15 000010   005001               CLR R1
16 000012   012704               MOV #20,R4        ;20Q=16, THE STEP COUNT.
           000020
17 000016   006300    M1:        ASL R0            ;SHIFT H.O. PART OF PRODUCT LEFT
18 000020   006301               ASL R1            ;SHIFT L.O. PART
19 000022   005500               ADC R0            ;ADD CARRY TO H.O. PART.
20 000024   006302    M2:        ASL R2            ;SHIFT MULTIPLIER
21 000026   103002               BCC M3            ;CHECK FOR 1 FROM MULTIPLIER
22 000030   060301               ADD R3,R1         ;PRODUCT=PRODUCT+MULTIPLICAND
23 000032   005500               ADC R0            ;ADD CARRY INTO H.O. PART.
24 000034   005304    M3:        DEC R4            ;DECREMENT STEP COUNT
25 000036   001367               BNE M1
26 000040   012604               MOV (SP)+,R4      ;RESTORE R3 & R4.
27 000042   012603               MOV (SP)+,R3
28 000044   000207               RTS PC            ;RETURN
29                               ;
30                               ;TEST PROGRAM
31                               ;
32 000046   012702    TEST:      MOV #12,R2        ;MULTIPLIER=12Q=10
           000012
33 000052   012700               MOV #20,R0        ;MULTIPLICAND=20Q=16
           000020
34 000056   012703               MOV #5,R3         ;CHECK TO SEE IF REGISTERS
           000005
35 000062   012704               MOV #6,R4         ;ARE SAVED PROPERLY
           000006
36 000066   004767               JSR PC,MULT       ;CALL MULTIPLY
           177706
37 000072   000003               BPT               ;RETURN TO MONITOR TO CHECK RESULT
38                               ;
39 000046'                               .END TEST
ERRORS DETECTED:  0

VIRTUAL MEMORY USED:  8192 WORDS  ( 32 PAGES)
DYNAMIC MEMORY AVAILABLE FOR  66 PAGES
C35,C35.L/N:SYM/L:TTM=C35
```

B20a   D/A Test Program

```
 1                   ;              D/A TEST PROGRAM
 2                   ;
 3 000000                          .CSECT DATEST
 4                                 .GLOBL CHIN,CHOUT,MULT
 5                   ;
 6         177560    KBCSR=177560
 7         177564    DISCSR=177564
 8         000015    CR=15
 9         000012    LF=12
10         167772    DIGOUT=167772
11                   ;
12 000000   042737   START:  BIC #100,@@#KBCSR        ;CLEAR RT-11
           000100
           177560
13 000006   042737           BIC #100,@@#DISCSR       ;INTERRUPTS.
           000100
```

```
                   177564
      14 000014  004767  D0:     JSR PC,CHIN           ;GET FIRST CHARACTER
                   000000G
      15 000020  004767          JSR PC,CHOUT          ;ECHO IT
                   000000G
      16 000024  010037          MOV R0,@#CHAR1        ;STORE CHARACTER
                   000134'
      17 000030  004767          JSR PC,CHIN           ;GET SECOND CHAR.
                   000000G
      18 000034  010037          MOV R0,@#CHAR2        ;STORE IT.
                   000136'
      19 000040  004767          JSR PC,CHOUT          ;ECHO 2-ND CHAR.
                   000000G
      20 000044  004767  D1:     JSR PC,CHIN
                   000000G
      21 000050  022700          CMP #CR,R0            ;WAIT FOR RETURN. DON'T ECHO
                   000015
      22 000054  001373          BNE D1                ;OTHER CHARACTERS.
      23 000056  004767          JSR PC,CHOUT          ;ECHO RETURN
                   000000G
      24 000062  012700          MOV #LF,R0            ;ECHO LINEFEED.
                   000012
      25 000066  004767          JSR PC,CHOUT
                   000000G
      26 000072  012700          MOV #12,R0            ;NOW CONVERT FROM DECIMAL-ASCII
                   000012
      27 000076  013702          MOV @#CHAR1,R2        ;TO BINARY
                   000134'
      28 000102  162702          SUB #'0,R2            ;SUBTRACT CODE FOR ASCII-ZERO
                   000060
      29 000106  004767          JSR PC,MULT           ;10*<CHAR1> IN R1 ON RETURN
                   000000G
      30 000112  013700          MOV @#CHAR2,R0
                   000136'
      31 000116  162700          SUB #'0,R0            ;SECOND DIGIT
                   000060
      32 000122  060100          ADD R1,R0             ;RESULT IN R0
      33 000124  010037          MOV R0,@#DIGOUT       ;SEND VALUE OUT TO D/A
                   167772
      34 000130  000167          JMP D0                ;GO BACK FOR ANOTHER NUMBER.
                   177660
      35                  ;
      36 000134  000000  CHAR1:  .WORD 0               ;STORAGE FOR THE CHARACTERS
      37 000136  000000  CHAR2:  .WORD 0
      38                  ;
      39          000000'         .END START
ERRORS DETECTED:  0

VIRTUAL MEMORY USED:  8192 WORDS  ( 32 PAGES)
DYNAMIC MEMORY AVAILABLE FOR  66 PAGES
C36A,C36A.L/N:SYM/L:TTM=C36A
```

B2Ob   Load Map for D/A Test Program

```
RT-11 LINK  V05.04A      Load Map
C36A  .SAV     Title: ODT    Ident:

Section  Addr    Size    Global  Value   Global  Value   Global  Value

. ABS.   000000  001000  (RW,I,GBL,ABS,OVR)
         001000  006100  (RW,I,LCL,REL,CON)
                         O.ODT  001232
DATEST   007100  000140  (RW,I,GBL,REL,OVR)
CHAR     007240  000040  (RW,I,GBL,REL,OVR)
                         CHIN    007240  CHOUT   007262
```

```
MLTPLY  007300   000074    (RW,I,GBL,REL,OVR)
                     MULT    007300

Transfer address = 001232, High limit = 007374 =  1918. words
```

B21   A/D Test Program

```
 1                       ;               A/D SUBROUTINE AND TEST PROGRAM
 2                       ; RETURNS ANSWER IN R0. SETS CARRY (C) ON
 3                       ; OVERFLOW, CLEARS C OTHERWISE.
 4                       ;
 5  000000                      .CSECT ADCONV
 6                              .GLOBL AD
 7                       ;
 8        167774  DIGIN=167774    ;DIGITAL I/O PORTS.
 9        167772  DIGOUT=167772
10        000377  CMAX=377          ;SET MAXIMUM FOR 8-BIT CONVERSION.
11                       ;
12                       ; SUBROUTINE USES R0 FOR COUNT
13                       ;
14  000000  005000  AD:     CLR R0               ;CLEAR COUNT
15  000002  052737          BIS #100000,@#DIGOUT ;OPEN RESET SWITCH
            100000
            167772
16  000010  032767  A1:     BIT #1,DIGIN         ;TEST COMPARATOR SWITCH
            000001
            167774
17  000016  001006          BNE A2               ;DONE CONVERTING
18  000020  005200          INC R0               ;NOT DONE, INCREMENT AND TRY
19                                               ;AGAIN
20  000022  020027          CMP R0,#CMAX         ;CHECK FOR OVERFLOW
            000377
21  000026  002770          BLT A1               ;IF NO OVERFLOW, OK
22  000030  000261          SEC                  ;SET CARRY IF  OVERFLOW
23  000032  000401          BR A3
24  000034  000241  A2:     CLC                  ;CLEAR CARRY INDICATING
25                                               ;NO OVERFLOW
26  000036  042737  A3:     BIC #100000,@#DIGOUT ;CLOSE RESET SWITCH
            100000
            167772
27  000044  000207          RTS PC               ;RETURN
28                       ;
29                       ;TEST PROGRAM
30                       ;
31  000046  004767  ADTEST: JSR PC,AD
            177726
32  000052  000003          BPT
33                       ;
34        000046'          .END ADTEST
ERRORS DETECTED:  0
```

```
VIRTUAL MEMORY USED:  8192 WORDS   ( 32 PAGES)
DYNAMIC MEMORY AVAILABLE FOR  66 PAGES
C37,C37.L/N:SYM/L:TTM=C37
```

B22   Divide Subroutine and Test Program

```
 1                       ,              DIVIDE SUBROUTINE AND TEST PROGRAM
 2                       ;
 3                       ; DIVIDEND IN R0,R1 (HO PART IN R0)
 4                       ; DIVISOR IN R2
 5                       ; QUOTIENT RETURNED IN R0, REMAINDER IN R1
 6                       ; FOLLOWS FORMAT OF EIS DIV INSTRUCTION.
 7                       ; USES R3 AND R4 FOR SCRATCH (R3 FOR WORKING QUOT.)
```

```
   8                           ;
   9 000000                            .CSECT DIVD
  10                                    .GLOBL DIVIDE
  11                           ;
  12 000000   010346   DIVIDE: MOV R3,-(SP)        ;SAVE R3 AND R4 ON STACK.
  13 000002   010446           MOV R4,-(SP)
  14 000004   005003           CLR R3
  15 000006   012704           MOV #20,R4          ;STEP COUNT, 20Q=16
             000020
  16 000012   006300   DV0:    ASL R0              ;SHIFT DIVIDEND LEFT
  17 000014   006301           ASL R1
  18 000016   005500           ADC R0              ;ADD CARRY TO HO PART (R0) TO
  19                                                ;COMPLETE SHIFT.
  20 000020   006303           ASL R3              ;SHIFT QUOTIENT LEFT
  21 000022   020200           CMP R2,R0           ;COMPARE DIVISOR TO DIVIDEND.
  22 000024   003002           BGT DV1
  23 000026   160200           SUB R2,R0           ;NOT GREATER; SUBTRACT DIVISOR
  24                                                ;FROM HO PART OF DIVIDEND.
  25 000030   005203           INC R3              ;INCREMENT QUOTIENT
  26 000032   005304   DV1:    DEC R4              ;DECREMENT STEP COUNT
  27 000034   001366           BNE DV0             ;GO ROUND AGAIN IF NOT ZERO
  28 000036   010001           MOV R0,R1           ;REMAINDER IS HO DIVIDEND
  29 000040   010300           MOV R3,R0           ;QUOTIENT TO R0
  30 000042   012604           MOV (SP)+,R4        ;RESTORE R4
  31 000044   012603           MOV (SP)+,R3        ;RESTORE R3
  32 000046   000207           RTS PC              ;RETURN
  33                           ;
  34                           ;DIVIDE TEST PROGRAM
  35                           ;
  36 000050   012702   DIVTST: MOV #12,R2          ;DIVISOR=12Q=10
             000012
  37 000054   012701           MOV #100,R1         ;DIVIDEND=100Q=64
             000100
  38 000060   005000           CLR R0              ;HO PART OF DIVIDEND
  39 000062   004767           JSR PC,DIVIDE
             177712
  40 000066   000003           BPT                 ;RETURN TO ODT
  41                           ;
  42           000050'          .END DIVTST
ERRORS DETECTED:  0

VIRTUAL MEMORY USED:  8192 WORDS  ( 32 PAGES)
DYNAMIC MEMORY AVAILABLE FOR  66 PAGES
C38,C38.L/N:SYM/L:TTM=C38
```

B23a   A/D Calibration Program

```
   1                           ;           A/D TEST CALIBRATION PROGRAM
   2                           ;
   3 000000                            .CSECT ADCAL
   4                                    .GLOBL CHIN,CHOUT,AD,DIVIDE
   5                           ;
   6           177560   KBCSR=177560
   7           177564   DISCSR=177564
   8           000015   CR=15
   9           000012   LF=12
  10                           ;
  11 000000   042737   START:  BIC #100,@#KBCSR            ;DISABLE RT-11
             000100
             177560
  12 000006   042737           BIC #100,@#DISCSR           ;INTERRUPTS
             000100
             177564
  13 000014   004767           JSR PC,AD                   ;DO ONE A/D TO MAKE SURE
             000000G
```

```
14                                                  ;RESET SWITCH IS SET CORRECTLY.
15 000020  004767  AD0: JSR PC,CHIN                 ;GET CHAR.
           000000G
16 000024  004767       JSR PC,CHOUT                ;ECHO IT.
           000000G
17 000030  010037       MOV R0,@#CHAR
           000236'
18 000034  004767  AD1: JSR PC,CHIN                 ;NOW WAIT FOR RETURN
           000000G
19 000040  022700       CMP #CR,R0
           000015
20 000044  001373       BNE AD1
21 000046  004767       JSR PC,CHOUT                ;ECHO RETURN, LINEFEED
           000000G
22 000052  012700       MOV #LF,R0
           000012
23 000056  004767       JSR PC,CHOUT
           000000G
24 000062  022737       CMP #'G,@#CHAR              ;IS CHAR. A G?
           000107
           000236'
25 000070  001353       BNE AD0                     ;IF NOT, GET NEW MESSAGE
26 000072  004767       JSR PC,AD                   ;DO CONVERSION
           000000G
27 000076  010001       MOV R0,R1                   ;SET UP FOR DIVIDE. A/D RESULT IN R0
28 000100  005000       CLR R0
29 000102  012702       MOV #12,R2                  ;DIVIDE BY 10
           000012
30 000106  004767       JSR PC,DIVIDE
           000000G
31 000112  062701       ADD #'0,R1                  ;ADD ASCII-ZERO TO REMAINDER
           000060
32 000116  010137       MOV R1,@#CHAR1              ;OUTPUT CHARACTER.
           000240'
33 000122  010001       MOV R0,R1                   ;SET UP FOR NEXT DIVIDE
34 000124  005000       CLR R0                      ;12Q=10 IS STILL IN R2
35 000126  004767       JSR PC,DIVIDE
           000000G
36 000132  062701       ADD #'0,R1                  ;NEXT OUTPUT CHARACTER
           000060
37 000136  010137       MOV R1,@#CHAR2
           000242'
38 000142  010001       MOV R0,R1                   ;THIRD DIVIDE
39 000144  005000       CLR R0
40 000146  004767       JSR PC,DIVIDE
           000000G
41 000152  062701       ADD #'0,R1
           000060
42 000156  010137       MOV R1,@#CHAR3
           000244'
43 000162  013700       MOV @#CHAR3,R0              ;NOW PRINT ANSWER
           000244'
44 000166  004767       JSR PC,CHOUT
           000000G
45 000172  013700       MOV @#CHAR2,R0              ;CHARACTERS ARE OUTPUT IN
           000242'
46 000176  004767       JSR PC,CHOUT                ;REVERSE ORDER.
           000000G
47 000202  013700       MOV @#CHAR1,R0
           000240'
48 000206  004767       JSR PC,CHOUT
           000000G
49 000212  012700       MOV #CR,R0
           000015
50 000216  004767       JSR PC,CHOUT                ;SEND OUT RETURN,LINEFEED
```

```
                    000000G
      51 000222     012700            MOV #LF,R0
                    000012
      52 000226     004767            JSR PC,CHOUT
                    000000G
      53 000232     000167            JMP AD0              ;GO BACK TO BEGINNING.
                    177562
      54                        ;
      55 000236     000000   CHAR:    .WORD 0              ;STORAGE AREA
      56 000240     000000   CHAR1:   .WORD 0
      57 000242     000000   CHAR2:   .WORD 0
      58 000244     000000   CHAR3:   .WORD 0
      59                        ;
      60            000000'            .END START
ERRORS DETECTED:   0

VIRTUAL MEMORY USED:   8192 WORDS  ( 32 PAGES)
DYNAMIC MEMORY AVAILABLE FOR  66 PAGES
C39A,C39A.L/N:SYM/L:TTM=C39A
```

B23b   Load Map for A/D Calibration Program

```
RT-11 LINK  V05.04A      Load Map
C39A   .SAV    Title:    ODT    Ident:

Section  Addr    Size    Global  Value   Global  Value   Global  Value

. ABS.  000000  001000   (RW,I,GBL,ABS,OVR)
        001000  006100   (RW,I,LCL,REL,CON)
                         O.ODT   001232
ADCAL   007100  000246   (RW,I,GBL,REL,OVR)
CHAR    007346  000040   (RW,I,GBL,REL,OVR)
                         CHIN    007346  CHOUT   007370
DIVD    007406  000070   (RW,I,GBL,REL,OVR)
                         DIVIDE  007406
ADCONV  007476  000054   (RW,I,GBL,REL,OVR)
                         AD      007476

Transfer address = 001232, High limit = 007552 =  1973. words
```

B24   Temperature Control Program

```
       1                 ;              FEEDBACK CONTROL PROGRAM
       2                 ;
       3                 ;
       4                 ;              BIT      FUNCTION
       5                 ;              ---      --------
       6                 ; DIGITAL INPUT:
       7                 ;              0        A/D COMPARATOR
       8                 ;              1        CLOCK
       9                 ;
      10                 ; DIGITAL OUTPUT:
      11                 ;              5 TO 0   D/A OUTPUT
      12                 ;              15       A/D RESET SWITCH
      13                 ;
      14                 ;
      15 000000                 .CSECT TEMP
      16                         .GLOBL CHIN,CHOUT,AD,DIVIDE,MULT
      17                 ;
      18         177560  KBCSR=177560
      19         177562  KBBUF=177562
      20         177564  DISCSR=177564
      21         167774  DIGIN=167774
      22         167772  DIGOUT=167772
```

```
23          000015   CR=15
24          000012   LF=12
25          000077   DAMAX=77
26          000000   DAMIN=0
27                   ;
28                   ; INITIALIZE MODULE
29                   ;
30 000000   042737   INIT:    BIC #100,@#KBCSR        ;DISABLE RT-11'S
           000100
           177560
31 000006   042737            BIC #100,@#DISCSR       ;INTERRUPTS.
           000100
           177564
32 000014   013705            MOV @#TSAMP,R5          ;USE R5 AS COUNTER FOR
           000064'
33                                                    ;SAMPLE TIME.
34 000020   005037            CLR @#CHAR1             ;CLEAR INPUT CHARACTERS
           000774'
35 000024   005037            CLR @#CHAR2
           000776'
36 000030   005037            CLR @#CHAR3
           001000'
37 000034   005037            CLR @#CHAR4
           001002'
38 000040   005037            CLR @#CHAR5
           001004'
39 000044   005037            CLR @#CHAR6
           001006'
40 000050   005037            CLR @#CHAR7
           001010'
41 000054   005037            CLR @#CHAR8
           001012'
42 000060   000167            JMP TICDT               ;TO TICK-DETECT
           000012
43                   ;
44 000064   000200   TSAMP:   .WORD 200
45 000066   000001   KNUM:    .WORD 1                 ;INITIAL VALUES FOR GAINS
46 000070   000001   KDEN:    .WORD 1
47 000072   000000   C:       .WORD 0
48 000074   000100   RSET:    .WORD 100               ;SET POINT
49                   ;
50                   ;TICK-DETECT MODULE
51                   ;
52 000076   032737   TICDT:   BIT #2,@#DIGIN          ;GET CLOCK SIGNAL
           000002
           167774
53 000104   001374            BNE TICDT               ;WAIT FOR ZERO
54 000106   032737   TIC1:    BIT #2,@#DIGIN
           000002
           167774
55 000114   001774            BEQ TIC1                ;WAIT FOR ONE
56                   ;
57                   ;CLOCK UPDATE MODULE
58                   ;
59 000116   005305   CLKUP:   DEC R5                  ;DECREMENT SAMPLE-TIME CLOCK
60 000120   001057            BNE TERMIN              ;IF NOT ZERO, GO TO TERMINAL-IN
61 000122   013705            MOV @#TSAMP,R5          ;RESET CLOCK,   THEN A/D
           000064'
62                   ;
63                   ;A/D MODULE
64                   ;
65 000126   004767            JSR PC,AD               ;A/D SUBROUTINE LEAVES RESULT IN R0
           000000G
66                   ;
67                   ;COMPUTE CONTROLLER OUTPUT
```

```
 68                          ;
 69 000132    005067         CLR  NFLAG            ;NFLAG=0 MEANS ERROR=+
             000102
 70 000136    005400         NEG  R0               ;MAKE TEMP. NEGATIVE
 71 000140    063700         ADD  @#RSET,R0        ;ERROR -> R0
             000074'
 72 000144    002003         BGE  C1
 73 000146    005267         INC  NFLAG            ;SET NFLAG TRUE IF ERROR= -
             000066
 74 000152    005400         NEG  R0               ;MAKE ERROR POSITIVE FOR CALC.
 75 000154    013702   C1:   MOV  @#KNUM,R2        ;SET UP FOR MULTIPLY
             000066'
 76 000160    004767         JSR  PC,MULT          ;KNUM*ERROR
             000000G
 77 000164    013702         MOV  @#KDEN,R2        ;SET UP FOR DIVIDE
             000070'
 78 000170    004767         JSR  PC,DIVIDE
             000000G
 79 000174    005767         TST  NFLAG            ;CHECK FOR NEGATIVE ERROR
             000040
 80 000200    001401         BEQ  C2
 81 000202    005400         NEG  R0               ;NEGATE RESULT, IF NECESSARY
 82 000204    063700   C2:   ADD  @#C,R0           ;ADD OFFSET. CONTROLLER OUTPUT
             000072'
 83                                                ;NOW IN R0
 84 000210    020027         CMP  R0,#DAMAX        ;LIMIT OUTPUT TO DAMIN->DAMAX
             000077
 85 000214    003402         BLE  C3
 86 000216    012700         MOV  #DAMAX,R0        ;TO BIG, SET TO MAX.
             000077
 87 000222    020027   C3:   CMP  R0,#DAMIN
             000000
 88 000226    002002         BGE  C4
 89 000230    012700         MOV  #DAMIN,R0        ;TOO SMALL, SET TO MIN.
             000000
 90 000234    000167   C4:   JMP  DA1              ;TO D/A MODULE
             000002
 91                          ;
 92 000240    000000   NFLAG: .WORD 0
 93                          ;
 94                          ; D/A OUTPUT DO NOT DISTURB OTHER OUTPUT BITS
 95                          ;
 96 000242    042737   DA1:  BIC  #77,@#DIGOUT     ;CLEAR ALL D/A BITS
             000077
             167772
 97 000250    050037         BIS  R0,@#DIGOUT      ;SET NEW VALUE
             167772
 98 000254    000167         JMP  TERMIN           ;TO TERMINAL-IN MODULE
             000000
 99                          ;
100                          ; TERMINAL-IN MODULE
101                          ;
102 000260    032737   TERMIN: BIT #200,@#KBCSR    ;CHECK FOR CHARACTER
             000200
             177560
103 000266    001703         BEQ  TICDT            ;IF NOT, TO TICK-DETECT
104 000270    013700         MOV  @#KBBUF,R0       ;GET CHAR
             177562
105 000274    042700         BIC  #200,R0          ;CLEAR PARITY BIT.
             000200
106 000300    004767         JSR  PC,CHOUT         ;ECHO IT.
             000000G
107 000304    022700         CMP  #CR,R0           ;IS IT A RETURN?
             000015
108 000310    001006         BNE  TER1             ;IF NOT, BRANCH
```

```
109 000312  012700       MOV #LF,R0          ;YES, ECHO LINEFEED
            000012
110 000316  004767       JSR PC,CHOUT
            000000G
111 000322  000167       JMP MSGDCD          ;TO MESSAGE-DECODER
            000164
112                      ;
113                      ; THE FOLLOWING SEQUENCE TESTS CHARACTERS FROM CHAR1 TO
114                      ; CHAR8 TO FIND THE FIRST ZERO.  IT PUTS THE
115                      ; CURRENT CHARACTER INTO THAT POSITION.
116                      ; THE RT-11 MACRO FACILITY IS USED TO KEEP THE
117                      ; AMOUNT OF CODE WRITTEN TO A MINIMUM.
118                      ; MACRO WILL DO TEXT SUBSTITUTIONS AUTOMATICALLY.
119                      ;
120                          .MACRO TESTCH N,N1
121                      ;
122             TER'N:    TST @#CHAR'N        ;THE ' CHAR. CONCATENATES TO
123                                           ;FORM NEW NAMES.
124                       BNE TER'N1          ;IF NOT ZERO, TRY NEXT CHAR.
125                       MOV R0,@#CHAR'N     ;YES, PUT CHAR. IN PLACE
126                       JMP TICDT           ;TO TICK-DETECT.
127                          .ENDM
128                      ;
129                      ; THIS IS THE END OF THE MACRO DEFINITION. WE CAN NOW USE IT.
130                      ; ONLY THE TESTCH 1,2, ETC. IS IN THE SOURCE CODE.
131                      ; THE REST IS PUT IN BY THE ASSEMBLER WHEN IT EXPANDS THE
132                      ; MACRO NAMED TESTCH.
133                      ;
134 000326                  TESTCH 1,2
                         ;
    000326  005737   TER1:   TST @#CHAR1      ;THE ' CHAR. CONCATENATES TO
            000774'
                                              ;FORM NEW NAMES.
    000332  001004       BNE TER2             ;IF NOT ZERO, TRY NEXT CHAR.
    000334  010037       MOV R0,@#CHAR1       ;YES, PUT CHAR. IN PLACE
            000774'
    000340  000167       JMP TICDT            ;TO TICK-DETECT.
            177532
135 000344                  TESTCH 2,3
                         ;
    000344  005737   TER2:   TST @#CHAR2      ;THE ' CHAR. CONCATENATES TO
            000776'
                                              ;FORM NEW NAMES.
    000350  001004       BNE TER3             ;IF NOT ZERO, TRY NEXT CHAR.
    000352  010037       MOV R0,@#CHAR2       ;YES, PUT CHAR. IN PLACE
            000776'
    000356  000167       JMP TICDT            ;TO TICK-DETECT.
            177514
136 000362                  TESTCH 3,4
                         ;
    000362  005737   TER3:   TST @#CHAR3      ;THE ' CHAR. CONCATENATES TO
            001000'
                                              ;FORM NEW NAMES.
    000366  001004       BNE TER4             ;IF NOT ZERO, TRY NEXT CHAR.
    000370  010037       MOV R0,@#CHAR3       ;YES, PUT CHAR. IN PLACE
            001000'
    000374  000167       JMP TICDT            ;TO TICK-DETECT.
            177476
137 000400                  TESTCH 4,5
                         ;
    000400  005737   TER4:   TST @#CHAR4      ;THE ' CHAR. CONCATENATES TO
            001002'
                                              ;FORM NEW NAMES.
    000404  001004       BNE TER5             ;IF NOT ZERO, TRY NEXT CHAR.
    000406  010037       MOV R0,@#CHAR4       ;YES, PUT CHAR. IN PLACE
```

```
                001002'
      000412    000167              JMP TICDT              ;TO TICK-DETECT.
                177460
138   000416                        TESTCH 5,6
                                ;
      000416    005737   TER5:      TST @#CHAR5            ;THE ' CHAR. CONCATENATES TO
                001004'                                    ;FORM NEW NAMES.
      000422    001004              BNE TER6               ;IF NOT ZERO, TRY NEXT CHAR.
      000424    010037              MOV R0,@#CHAR5         ;YES, PUT CHAR. IN PLACE
                001004'
      000430    000167              JMP TICDT              ;TO TICK-DETECT.
                177442
139   000434                        TESTCH 6,7
                                ;
      000434    005737   TER6:      TST @#CHAR6            ;THE ' CHAR. CONCATENATES TO
                001006'                                    ;FORM NEW NAMES.
      000440    001004              BNE TER7               ;IF NOT ZERO, TRY NEXT CHAR.
      000442    010037              MOV R0,@#CHAR6         ;YES, PUT CHAR. IN PLACE
                001006'
      000446    000167              JMP TICDT              ;TO TICK-DETECT.
                177424
140   000452                        TESTCH 7,8
                                ;
      000452    005737   TER7:      TST @#CHAR7            ;THE ' CHAR. CONCATENATES TO
                001010'                                    ;FORM NEW NAMES.
      000456    001004              BNE TER8               ;IF NOT ZERO, TRY NEXT CHAR.
      000460    010037              MOV R0,@#CHAR7         ;YES, PUT CHAR. IN PLACE
                001010'
      000464    000167              JMP TICDT              ;TO TICK-DETECT.
                177406
141   000470                        TESTCH 8,9
                                ;
      000470    005737   TER8:      TST @#CHAR8            ;THE ' CHAR. CONCATENATES TO
                001012'                                    ;FORM NEW NAMES.
      000474    001004              BNE TER9               ;IF NOT ZERO, TRY NEXT CHAR.
      000476    010037              MOV R0,@#CHAR8         ;YES, PUT CHAR. IN PLACE
                001012'
      000502    000167              JMP TICDT              ;TO TICK-DETECT.
                177370
142                             ;
143   000506    000167   TER9:      JMP TICDT              ;THIS INSTRUCTION IS EXECUTED IF
                177364
144                                                        ;THERE IS NO P;ACE FOR THE CHAR.
145                             ;
146                             ; MESSAGE-DECODE MODULE
147                             ;
148   000512    023727   MSGDCD:    CMP @#CHAR1,#'R        ;IS COMMAND AN R?
                000774'
                000122
149   000520    001006              BNE MSG1
150   000522    004767              JSR PC,VALUE           ;YES GET VALUE, RESULT IN R0
                000120
151   000526    010037              MOV R0,@#RSET          ;SET NEW VALUE
                000074'
152   000532    000167              JMP CHCLR              ;CLEAR CHARACTERS
                000172
153   000536    023727   MSG1:      CMP @#CHAR1,#'K        ;IS IT K?
                000774'
                000113
154   000544    001023              BNE MSG2
155   000546    004767              JSR PC,VALUE           ;GET KNUM
```

```
               000074
156 000552     010037            MOV  R0,@#KNUM
               000066'
157 000556     013737            MOV  @#CHAR6,@#CHAR2    ;MOVE KDEN VALUES TO PROPER
               001006'
               000776'
158 000564     013737            MOV  @#CHAR7,@#CHAR3    ;PLACE FOR VALUE SUBROUTINE
               001010'
               001000'
159 000572     013737            MOV  @#CHAR8,@#CHAR4
               001012'
               001002'
160 000600     004767            JSR  PC,VALUE
               000042
161 000604     010037            MOV  R0,@#KDEN
               000070'
162 000610     000167            JMP  CHCLR
               000114
163 000614     023727  MSG2:     CMP  @#CHAR1,#'C        ;C?
               000774'
               000103
164 000622     001004            BNE  MSG3
165 000624     004767            JSR  PC,VALUE
               000016
166 000630     010037            MOV  R0,@#C
               000072'
167 000634     023727  MSG3:     CMP  @#CHAR1,#'S
               000774'
               000123
168 000642     001032            BNE  CHCLR
169 000644     000003            BPT                     ;STOP COMMAND. RETURN TO ODT
170                    ;
171                    ;VALUE SUBROUTINE
172                    ;
173 000646     005003  VALUE:    CLR  R3                 ;ACCUMULATE RESULT IN R3
174 000650     012702            MOV  #144,R2            ;144Q=100 FOR HO DIGIT
               000144
175 000654     013700            MOV  @#CHAR2,R0         ;SET UP FOR MULTIPLY
               000776'
176 000660     162700            SUB  #'0,R0             ;SUBTRACT ASCII-ZERO
               000060
177 000664     004767            JSR  PC,MULT
               000000G
178 000670     010103            MOV  R1,R3
179 000672     012702            MOV  #12,R2             ;12Q=10
               000012
180 000676     013700            MOV  @#CHAR3,R0
               001000'
181 000702     162700            SUB  #'0,R0
               000060
182 000706     004767            JSR  PC,MULT
               000000G
183 000712     060103            ADD  R1,R3
184 000714     013700            MOV  @#CHAR4,R0
               001002'
185 000720     162700            SUB  #'0,R0
               000060
186 000724     060300            ADD  R3,R0              ;RESULT IN R0
187 000726     000207            RTS  PC                 ;RETURN
188 000730     005037  CHCLR:    CLR  @#CHAR1            ;CLEAR CHARACTERS
               000774'
189 000734     005037            CLR  @#CHAR2
               000776'
190 000740     005037            CLR  @#CHAR3
               001000'
```

```
191 000744  005037          CLR @#CHAR4
            001002'
192 000750  005037          CLR @#CHAR5
            001004'
193 000754  005037          CLR @#CHAR6
            001006'
194 000760  005037          CLR @#CHAR7
            001010'
195 000764  005037          CLR @#CHAR8
            001012'
196 000770  000167          JMP TICDT                ;TO TICK-DETECT
            177102
197                 ;
198 000774  000000  CHAR1:  .WORD 0
199 000776  000000  CHAR2:  .WORD 0
200 001000  000000  CHAR3:  .WORD 0
201 001002  000000  CHAR4:  .WORD 0
202 001004  000000  CHAR5:  .WORD 0
203 001006  000000  CHAR6:  .WORD 0
204 001010  000000  CHAR7:  .WORD 0
205 001012  000000  CHAR8:  .WORD 0
206                 ;
207         000000'         .END INIT
ERRORS DETECTED:  0

VIRTUAL MEMORY USED:   8192 WORDS  ( 32 PAGES)
DYNAMIC MEMORY AVAILABLE FOR  66 PAGES
C310A,C310A.L[25]/N:SYM/L:TTM/L:ME=C310A
```

BLENDING CONTROL PROGRAMS

These programs demonstrate the use of interrupts in a control program. By using interrupts, the interaction with the operator via a terminal can be separated into a high priority part, the actual transfer of characters back and forth from the terminal, and a lower priority part, the decoding of messages from the operator and generation of output for the operator. The sampling and control continues to run at high priority. Since the actual amount of CPU time required for the terminal interaction is very low, there is virtually no conflict between the terminal service routines and the control portion of the program. Message decoding can take longer, however, so by putting it into the background at lower priority than other tasks, it will not interfere with the control activity.

The PDP-11 uses vectored interrupts. When an interrupt occurs, the CPU gets the interrupt vector, a 16-bit address, from the interrupting device. The CPU uses the vector as a pointer to a memory address. In processing the interrupt, the CPU loads the program counter from the memory location pointed to by the interrupt vector. The vector supplied by the interrupting device is thus the address of the address of the beginning of the interrupt service routine.

Before beginning execution of the interrupt service routine, the CPU uses the word in the address Vector + 2 (the word immediately following the memory location where the address of the interrupt service routine is stored) to load the processor status word (PSW). The old processor status word is pushed onto the system stack and will be restored upon returning from the interrupt. The new processor status word serves to set the priority at which the interrupt service will run. If the priority is set to the highest possible value, no other interrupts will be recognized. If the priority is set to the lowest possible value, all other interrupts will be recognized, so the service routine will itself be interruptable. Intermediate values allow some interrupts to be recognized and other not. PDP-11s (Unibus-based computers) have four priority levels and LSI-11s (Q-based computers) have two priority levels.

The first program, Listing B25, uses just a clock interrupt. The clock in this case is a non-programmable clock, which means that the amount of time that will elapse between interrupts is fixed. On PDP-11s and LSI-11s the clock used is called the Line Time Clock (LTC), although the connection to the utility line, where it interrupts at the 50 or 60 Hz line frequency, has been replaced with an external crystal clock.

Programmable clocks, in which the time between interrupts can be set from the user's program also exist. Such clocks are more expensive but use less CPU overhead, because, in many applications, a software counter to determine when an event (such as sampling) should occur will not be needed; even if one is required, there are usually fewer interrupts between samples.

Programmable clocks are usually designed for maximum flexibility and often have many set-up parameters that must be initialized to determine the mode in which they will operate and the time between samples.

Listings B26 and B27 are programs that demonstrate the use of the terminal's interrupts. In both cases, the clock interrupt is present also and functions the same as in the program B25. In the terminal input program, user-typed characters are placed in a buffer as they are received. Each time a character is typed, an interrupt is generated.

The terminal output program illustrates a common way to send messages to a terminal under interrupt control. A buffer is set up for the message, and a pointer is established to the buffer. Every time the terminal interrupts to indicate that it is ready to receive a character, the character pointed at is sent, and the pointer is incremented.

The blending control program, Listing B28, uses all three interrupts. The clock interrupt controls the sampling and control calculation process, while the terminal interrupts control the interaction with the operator. Other than the instructions associated with the interrupts, the calculation procedures use most of the same instruction sequences and subroutines as the temperature control program.

B25   Clock Interrupt Program

```
1              ;              CLOCK INTERRUPT PROGRAM
2              ;
3                       .TITLE C43
4                       .GLOBL  DIVIDE,KIFNUM,KIFDEN,KITNUM,KITDEN,KPFNUM,KPFDEN
5                       .GLOBL  KPTNUM,KPTDEN,MULT,RFN,RTN,CLKINT
6                       .GLOBL  CTN,CFN,MCN,MHN,DELMT,DELMF
7              ;
```

```
 8                      ; THIS INTERRUPT PROGRAM IS DRIVEN BY A CLOCK WHOSE FREQUENCY
 9                      ; MAY BE SWITCH SELECTED FOR 60,100, OR 1000 HZ.
10                      ; THE PROGRAM SAMPLES AN A/D, COMPUTES VALUES OF MANIPULATED
11                      ; VARIABLES, AND COPIES THE VALUES TO A D/A CONVERTER.
12                      ;
13          170440      DTOA1=170440
14          170442      DTOA2=170442
15                      ;
16          170400      ADCSR=170400              ;ADDRESS OF A/D STATUS REGISTER
17          170402      ADBUF=170402              ;ADDRESS OF A/D DATA BUFFER
18                      ;
19          003777      DAMAX=2047.               ;MAXIMUM ALLOWED D/A VALUE
20          174000      DAMIN=-2048.              ;MINIMUM ALLOWED D/A VALUE
21                      ;
22          000001      TRUE=1                    ;LOGICAL FLAG
23          000000      FALSE=0                   ;LOGICAL FLAG
24                      ;
25 000000   010046      CLKINT: MOV R0,-(SP)      ;PRESERVE STATE OF THE MACHINE
26 000002   010146              MOV R1,-(SP)
27 000004   010246              MOV R2,-(SP)
28 000006   010346              MOV R3,-(SP)
29 000010   010446              MOV R4,-(SP)
30                      ;
31 000012   012737              MOV #1,@#ADCSR    ;START CONVERSION FOR CHANNEL#0
            000001
            170400
32                      ;
33 000020   032737      C1:     BIT #200,@#ADCSR  ;TEST FOR END OF CONVERSION
            000200
            170400
34 000026   001774              BEQ C1            ;NOT DONE => BRANCH
35                      ;
36 000030   013767              MOV @#ADBUF,CTN   ;UPDATE SAMPLED CONTROL VARIABLE (TEMP)
            170402
            000610
37 000036   162767              SUB #2047.,CTN    ;ADJUST FOR ZERO LEVEL
            003777
            000602
38                      ;
39 000044   012737              MOV #401,@#ADCSR  ;START CONVERSION FOR CHANNEL#1
            000401
            170400
40                      ;
41 000052   032737      C2:     BIT #200,@#ADCSR  ;TEST FOR END OF CONVERSION
            000200
            170400
42 000060   001774              BEQ C2            ;NOT DONE => BRANCH
43                      ;
44 000062   013767              MOV @#ADBUF,CFN   ;UPDATE SAMPLED CONTROL VARIABLE (FLOW)
            170402
            000562
45 000070   162767              SUB #2047.,CFN    ;ADJUST FOR ZERO LEVEL
            003777
            000554
46                      ;
47                      ; NOW CALCULATE DELTA MT AS:
48                      ;
49                      ; DELMT=[KPTNUM*(CTNM1-CTN)/KPTDEN] + [KITNUM*(RTN-CTN)/KITDEN]
50                      ;
51 000076   012767              MOV #FALSE,NEGFLG ;NEGATE FLAG <-- FALSE
            000000
            000566
52                      ;
53 000104   016700              MOV CTNM1,R0
            000540
```

```
54 000110   166700          SUB CTN,R0           ;R0 <-- (CTNM1-CTN) WHICH IS MULTIPLICAND
           000532
55                   ;
56 000114   005700          TST R0               ;WE WILL TEST EACH SUBTRACTION FOR NEGATIVE
57 000116   002004          BGE CC1              ;BRANCH => NO NEED TO NEGATE
58 000120   012767          MOV #TRUE,NEGFLG     ;NEGATE AFTER MULT AND DIVISION
           000001
           000544
59 000126   005400          NEG R0               ;MAKE POSITIVE
60                   ;
61 000130   016702   CC1: MOV KPTNUM,R2          ;R2 <-- MULTIPLIER
           000000G
62 000134   004767          JSR PC,MULT          ;R0 AND R1 <-- PRODUCT
           000000G
63                   ;
64 000140   016702          MOV KPTDEN,R2        ;R2 <-- DIVISOR (DIVIDEND IS LAST PRODUCT)
           000000G
65 000144   004767          JSR PC,DIVIDE        ;R0 <-- QUOTIENT (IGNORE REMAINDER IN R1)
           000000G
66 000150   010003          MOV R0,R3            ;INTERMEDIATE VALUE
67                   ;
68 000152   026727          CMP NEGFLG,#TRUE     ;IF NEGATE FLAG IS TRUE, NEGATE
           000514
           000001
69 000160   001004          BNE CC2              ;BRANCH => DO NOT NEGATE
70 000162   005403          NEG R3               ;TWO'S COMPLEMENT
71 000164   012767          MOV #FALSE,NEGFLG    ;RESET NEGATE FLAG
           000000
           000500
72                   ;
73 000172   016700   CC2: MOV RTN,R0
           000000G
74 000176   166700          SUB CTN,R0           ;R0 <-- (RTN-CTN) WHICH IS MULTIPLICAND
           000444
75                   ;
76 000202   005700          TST R0
77 000204   002004          BGE CC3
78 000206   012767          MOV #TRUE,NEGFLG
           000001
           000456
79 000214   005400          NEG R0
80                   ;
81 000216   016702   CC3: MOV KITNUM,R2          ;R2 <-- MULTIPLIER
           000000G
82 000222   004767          JSR PC,MULT          ;R0 AND R1 <-- PRODUCT
           000000G
83                   ;
84 000226   016702          MOV KITDEN,R2        ;R2 <-- DIVISOR
           000000G
85 000232   004767          JSR PC,DIVIDE        ;R0 <-- QUOTIENT
           000000G
86                   ;
87 000236   026727          CMP NEGFLG,#TRUE
           000430
           000001
88 000244   001004          BNE CC4
89 000246   012767          MOV #FALSE,NEGFLG
           000000
           000416
90 000254   005400          NEG R0
91                   ;
92 000256   060003   CC4: ADD R0,R3              ;R3 <-- DELMT
93 000260   010367          MOV R3,DELMT         ;FOR LIST ROUTINE
           000402
94                   ;
```

```
 95                    ; NOW CALCULATE DELTA MF AS:
 96                    ;
 97                    ; DELMF=[KPFNUM*(CFNM1-CFN)/KPFDEN] + [KIFNUM*(RFN-CFN)/KIFDEN]
 98                    ;
 99 000264  016700            MOV  CFNM1,R0              ;AS FOR DELMT
            000364
100 000270  166700            SUB  CFN,R0
            000356
101                    ;
102 000274  005700            TST  R0
103 000276  002004            BGE  CC5
104 000300  012767            MOV  #TRUE,NEGFLG
            000001
            000364
105 000306  005400            NEG  R0
106                    ;
107 000310  016702  CC5:  MOV  KPFNUM,R2
            000000G
108 000314  004767            JSR  PC,MULT
            000000G
109                    ;
110 000320  016702            MOV  KPFDEN,R2
            000000G
111 000324  004767            JSR  PC,DIVIDE
            000000G
112                    ;
113 000330  026727            CMP  NEGFLG,#TRUE
            000336
            000001
114 000336  001004            BNE  CC6
115 000340  012767            MOV  #FALSE,NEGFLG
            000000
            000324
116 000346  005400            NEG  R0
117                    ;
118 000350  010004  CC6:  MOV  R0,R4                  ;INTERMEDIATE RESULT
119                    ;
120 000352  016700            MOV  RFN,R0
            000000G
121 000356  166700            SUB  CFN,R0
            000270
122                    ;
123 000362  005700            TST  R0
124 000364  002004            BGE  CC7
125 000366  012767            MOV  #TRUE,NEGFLG
            000001
            000276
126 000374  005400            NEG  R0
127                    ;
128 000376  016702  CC7:  MOV  KIFNUM,R2
            000000G
129 000402  004767            JSR  PC,MULT
            000000G
130                    ;
131 000406  016702            MOV  KIFDEN,R2
            000000G
132 000412  004767            JSR  PC,DIVIDE
            000000G
133                    ;
134 000416  026727            CMP  NEGFLG,#TRUE
            000250
            000001
135 000424  001004            BNE  CC8
136 000426  012767            MOV  #FALSE,NEGFLG
            000000
```

```
              000236
137 000434    005400              NEG R0
138                         ;
139 000436    060004     CC8:    ADD R0,R4           ;R4 <-- DELMF
140 000440    010467            MOV R4,DELMF         ;FOR LIST ROUTINE
              000224
141                         ;
142                         ; NOW UPDATE MANIPULATED AND CONTROL VARIABLES
143                         ;
144 000444    016767            MOV MHN,MHNM1        ;MH(N-1) <-- MH(N)
              000206
              000206
145 000452    016767            MOV MCN,MCNM1        ;MC(N-1) <-- MC(N)
              000204
              000204
146                         ;
147 000460    010400            MOV R4,R0            ;R0 <-- DELTA MF
148 000462    060300            ADD R3,R0            ;R0 <-- (DELTA MF) + (DELTA MT)
149 000464    060067            ADD R0,MHN           ;MHN <-- MH(N-1)+(DELTA MF)+(DELTA MT)
              000166
150                         ;
151 000470    026727            CMP MHN,#DAMAX       ;GREATER THAN ALLOWED?
              000162
              003777
152 000476    002403            BLT C3
153 000500    012767            MOV #DAMAX,MHN       ;LIMIT OUTPUT
              003777
              000150
154                         ;
155 000506    026727     C3:    CMP MHN,#DAMIN       ;LESS THAN ALLOWED?
              000144
              174000
156 000514    003003            BGT C4
157 000516    012767            MOV #DAMIN,MHN       ;LIMIT OUTPUT
              174000
              000132
158                         ;
159 000524    160304     C4:    SUB R3,R4            ;R4 <-- (DELTA MF) - (DELTA MT)
160 000526    060467            ADD R4,MCN           ;MCN <-- MC(N-1)+(DELTA MF)-(DELTA MT)
              000130
161                         ;
162 000532    026727            CMP MCN,#DAMAX       ;GREATER THAN ALLOWED?
              000124
              003777
163 000540    002403            BLT C5
164 000542    012767            MOV #DAMAX,MCN       ;LIMIT OUTPUT
              003777
              000112
165                         ;
166 000550    026727     C5:    CMP MCN,#DAMIN       ;LESS THAN ALLOWED?
              000106
              174000
167 000556    003003            BGT C6
168 000560    012767            MOV #DAMIN,MCN       ;LIMIT OUTPUT
              174000
              000074
169                         ;
170 000566    016767     C6:    MOV CTN,CTNM1        ;CT(N-1) <-- CTN
              000054
              000054
171 000574    016767            MOV CFN,CFNM1        ;CF(N-1) <-- CFN
              000052
              000052
172                         ;
173                         ; NOW, COPY MANIPULATED VARIABLES TO D/A
174                         ;
```

```
175 000602 016700         MOV MHN,R0
           000050
176 000606 062700         ADD #2048.,R0           ;D/A OFFSET
           004000
177 000612 010037         MOV R0,@#DTOA1          ;ACTUATION SIGNAL FOR HOT PUMP
           170440
178                  ;
179 000616 016700         MOV MCN,R0
           000040
180 000622 062700         ADD #2048.,R0           ;D/A OFFSET
           004000
181 000626 010037         MOV R0,@#DTOA2          ;ACTUATION SIGNAL FOR COLD PUMP
           170442
182                  ;
183 000632 012604         MOV (SP)+,R4            ;RESTORE STATE OF MACHINE
184 000634 012603         MOV (SP)+,R3
185 000636 012602         MOV (SP)+,R2
186 000640 012601         MOV (SP)+,R1
187 000642 012600         MOV (SP)+,R0
188                  ;
189 000644 000002         RTI                     ;EXIT
190                  ;
191                  ;
192 000646 000000 CTN:    .WORD 0                 ;SAMPLED VALUE, TEMPERATURE
193 000650 000000 CTNM1:  .WORD 0                 ;CT(N-1)
194 000652 000000 CFN:    .WORD 0                 ;SAMPLED VALUE, FLOW
195 000654 000000 CFNM1:  .WORD 0                 ;CF(N-1)
196 000656 000000 MHN:    .WORD 0                 ;MANIPULATED VARIABLE, HOT
197 000660 000000 MHNM1:  .WORD 0                 ;MH(N-1)
198 000662 000000 MCN:    .WORD 0                 ;MANIPULATED VARIABLE, COLD
199 000664 000000 MCNM1:  .WORD 0                 ;MC(N-1)
200 000666 000000 DELMT:  .WORD 0                 ;DELTA TEMPERATURE MANIP. VAR.
201 000670 000000 DELMF:  .WORD 0                 ;DELTA FLOW MANIP. VAR.
202 000672 000000 NEGFLG: .WORD 0                 ;NEGATE FLAG
203                  ;
204                  ; END OF CLOCK INTERRUPT ROUTINE
205                  ;
206        000001         .END
ERRORS DETECTED:  0

VIRTUAL MEMORY USED:  8192 WORDS  ( 32 PAGES)
DYNAMIC MEMORY AVAILABLE FOR  66 PAGES
C43,C43.L/N:SYM/L:TTM=C43
```

B26   Terminal Input Interrupt Program

```
1           ;                TERMINAL INPUT INTERRUPT PROGRAM
2           ;
3                   .TITLE C41
4                   .GLOBL  BF1STT,BF2STT,DISBUF,DISCSR,INBF1,INBF2,INPOINT,LFED
5                   .GLOBL KINT
6           ;
7           ; THIS INTERRUPT PROGRAM IS USED IN THE FINAL PROGRAM OF
8           ; CHAPTER 6.  THIS ROUTINE FILLS THE CURRENT BUSY BUFFER
9           ; AND MARKS IT READY WHEN A RETURN IS ENTERED.  TWO BUFFER
10          ; MODIFICATION CHARACTERS, DELETE (RUBOUT) AND CONTROL-U
11          ; ARE RECOGNIZED.
12          ;
13   000177 DEL=177          ;ASCII CODE FOR DELETE (RUBOUT)
14   000025 CNTRLU=21.       ;ASCII CODE FOR CONTROL-U
15          ;
16   000001 TRUE=1           ;LOGICAL FLAG
17   000000 FALSE=0          ;LOGICAL FLAG
18          ;
19   000000 VACANT=0
```

```
20              000001    BUSY=1
21              000002    READY=2        ;BUFFER STATUS FLAGS
22                        ;
23              000015    CR=15          ;ASCII CODE FOR CARRIAGE RETURN
24              000012    LF=12          ;ASCII CODE FOR LINE FEED
25                        ;
26              177560    KBCSR=177560
27              177562    KBBUF=177562
28              177564    DISCSR=177564
29              177566    DISBUF=177566;CONSOLE DISPLAY AND KEYBOARD STATUS AND DATA REGISTERS
30                        ;
31                        ;
32                        ; NOTE: THIS ROUTINE USES NO REGISTERS
33                        ;
34 000000      113777    KINT:   MOVB @#KBBUF,@INPOINT   ;STORE CHARACTER IN BUFFER
             177562
             000000G
35 000006      142777            BICB #200,@INPOINT      ;STRIP PARITY
             000200
             000000G
36                        ;
37 000014      122777            CMPB #CR,@INPOINT       ;IS CHARACTER A RETURN?
             000015
             000000G
38 000022      001043            BNE K1
39                                                       ;TO HERE, CHARACTER IS A RETURN
40                                                       ;THUS, SWITCH BUFFERS
41 000024      012767            MOV #TRUE,LFED          ;LINEFEED FLAG <-- TRUE
             000001
             000274
42 000032      117737            MOVB @INPOINT,@#DISBUF  ;ECHO CHARACTER
             000000G
             177566
43 000040      052737            BIS #100,@#DISCSR       ;ENABLE TERMINAL OUTPUT INTERRUPTS
             000100
             177564
44                        ;
45                                                       ;NOW, SWITCH BUFFERS
46 000046      026727            CMP BF1STT,#BUSY        ;WHICH BUFFER IS CURRENTLY BUSY?
             000000G
             000001
47 000054      001013            BNE K2
48                                                       ;TO HERE, BUFFER#1 IS BUSY
49 000056      012767            MOV #BUSY,BF2STT        ;BUFFER#2 <-- BUSY
             000001
             000000G
50 000064      012767            MOV #READY,BF1STT       ;BUFFER#1 <-- READY
             000002
             000000G
51 000072      012767            MOV #INBF2,INPOINT      ;INITIALIZE INPUT POINTER
             000000G
             000000G
52 000100      000167            JMP XIT                 ;EXIT
             000220
53                        ;  .
54                                                       ;TO HERE, BUFFER#2 IS BUSY
55 000104      012767    K2:     MOV #BUSY,BF1STT        ;BUFFER#1 <-- BUSY
             000001
             000000G
56 000112      012767            MOV #READY,BF2STT       ;BUFFER#2 <-- READY
             000002
             000000G
57 000120      012767            MOV #INBF1,INPOINT      ;INITIALIZE INPUT POINTER
             000000G
             000000G
```

```
58 000126  000167          JMP XIT
           000172
59                    ;
60                                               ;TO HERE, CHARACTER IS NOT A RETURN
61                    ;
62 000132  122777  K1:  CMPB #DEL,@INPOINT   ;IS CHARACTER A DELETE (RUBOUT)?
           000177
           000000G
63 000140  001027          BNE K3
64                    ;
65 000142  022767          CMP #INBF1,INPOINT   ;IS BUFFER#1 EMPTY?
           000000G
           000000G
66 000150  001404          BEQ K4              ;BRANCH => EMPTY
67 000152  022767          CMP #INBF2,INPOINT   ;IS BUFFER#2 EMPTY?
           000000G
           000000G
68 000160  001005          BNE K5              ;BRANCH => NOT EMPTY
69                    ;
70                                               ;TO HERE, WE'VE RECEIVED A DELETE
71                                               ;BUT THE BUFFER IS EMPTY, THUS EXIT
72 000162  042737  K4:  BIC #100,@#DISCSR    ;DISABLE TERMINAL OUTPUT INTERRUPTS
           000100
           177564
73 000170  000167          JMP XIT             ;EXIT
           000130
74                    ;
75                                               ;TO HERE, A DELETE WAS RECEIVED AND
76                                               ;BUFFER IS NOT EMPTY, THUS REMOVE.
77 000174  005367  K5:  DEC INPOINT          ;REMOVE CHARACTER FROM BUFFER
           000000G
78 000200  117737          MOVB @INPOINT,@#DISBUF;ECHO CHARACTER DELETED
           000000G
           177566
79 000206  042737          BIC #100,@#DISCSR    ;DISABLE TERMINAL OUTPUT INTERRUPTS
           000100
           177564
80 000214  000167          JMP XIT             ;EXIT
           000104
81                    ;
82 000220  122777  K3:  CMPB #CNTRLU,@INPOINT ;IS CHARACTER A CONTROL-U?
           000025
           000000G
83 000226  001026          BNE K6
84                                               ;TO HERE, A CONTROL-U WAS TYPED
85 000230  112737          MOVB #CR,@#DISBUF    ;SEND RETURN TO DISPLAY
           000015
           177566
86 000236  012767          MOV #TRUE,LFED       ;LINEFEED <-- TRUE
           000001
           000062
87 000244  052737          BIS #100,@#DISCSR    ;ENABLE TERMINAL OUTPUT INTERRUPTS
           000100
           177564
88                    ;
89                                               ;NOW, RESET CURRENT BUFFER POINTER
90 000252  026727          CMP BF1STT,#BUSY     ;ARE WE FILLING BUFFER#1?
           000000G
           000001
91 000260  001004          BNE K7
92 000262  012767          MOV #INBF1,INPOINT   ;RESET BUFFER#1
           000000G
           000000G
93 000270  000403          BR K8
94                    ;
```

```
 95 000272  012767  K7:  MOV #INBF2,INPOINT     ;RESET BUFFER#2
            000000G
            000000G
 96                   ;
 97 000300  000167  K8:  JMP XIT
            000020
 98                   ;
 99                                             ;TO HERE, CHARACTER IS NOT A RETURN,
100                                             ;DELETE, OR CONTROL-U.  THUS, PLACE
101                                             ;IN BUFFER AND ECHO.
102 000304  117737  K6:  MOVB @INPOINT,@#DISBUF ;ECHO CHARACTER
            000000G
            177566
103 000312  005267       INC INPOINT            ;INCREMENT POINTER
            000000G
104 000316  042737       BIC #100,@#DISCSR       ;DISABLE TERMINAL OUTPUT INTERRUPTS
            000100
            177564
105 000324  000002  XIT: RTI                    ;EXIT
106                   ;
107 000326  000000  LFED: .WORD 0               ;LOGICAL FLAG
108                   ;
109                   ; END OF TERMINAL INPUT INTERRUPT ROUTINE
110                   ;
111         000001       .END
ERRORS DETECTED:  0

VIRTUAL MEMORY USED:  8192 WORDS  ( 32 PAGES)
DYNAMIC MEMORY AVAILABLE FOR  66 PAGES
C41,DY0:C41.L/N:SYM/L:TTM=C41
```

B27   Terminal Output Interrupt Program

```
  1                   ;                    TERMINAL OUTPUT INTERRUPT PROGRAM
  2                   ;
  3                        .TITLE C42
  4                        .GLOBL  DISBUF,DISCSR,LFED,OUTPNT,DINT,BUF
  5                   ;
  6                   ; THIS INTERRUPT PROGRAM IS USED IN THE FINAL PROGRAM OF
  7                   ; CHAPTER 6.  THIS ROUTINE SENDS A LINEFEED OR BUFFER TO DISPLAY
  8                   ;
  9         000001  TRUE=1          ;LOGICAL FLAG
 10         000000  FALSE=0         ;LOGICAL FLAG
 11                   ;
 12         000015  CR=15           ;ASCII CODE FOR CARRIAGE RETURN
 13         000012  LF=12           ;ASCII CODE FOR LINE FEED
 14                   ;
 15                   ;
 16 000000  026727  DINT: CMP LFED,#TRUE        ;IS VARIABLE LINEFEED TRUE?
            000000G
            000001
 17 000006  001007       BNE D1
 18                   ;
 19 000010  112737       MOVB #LF,@#DISBUF       ;SEND LINEFEED TO TERMINAL DISPLAY
            000012
            000000G
 20 000016  012767       MOV #FALSE,LFED         ;LINEFEED <-- FALSE
            000000
            000000G
 21                   ;
 22 000024  000433       BR XIT                  ;EXIT
 23                   ;
 24 000026  026727  D1:  CMP BUF,#TRUE           ;EXIST A BUFFER TO SEND?
            000000G
            000001
```

```
25 000034  001404        BEQ D4                ;BRANCH => YES
26 000036  042737        BIC #100,@#DISCSR     ;NO => DISABLE AND EXIT
           000100
           000000G
27 000044  000423        BR XIT
28                   ;
29 000046  117737   D4:  MOVB @OUTPNT,@#DISBUF ;SEND CHARACTER POINTED TO BY
           000000G
           000000G
30                                             ;OUTPUT POINTER
31 000054  127727        CMPB @OUTPNT,#CR      ;WAS CHARACTER SENT A RETURN?
           000000G
           000015
32 000062  001007        BNE D2
33                   ;
34 000064  012767        MOV #FALSE,BUF        ;BUFFER <-- FALSE
           000000
           000000G
35                   ;
36 000072  012767        MOV #TRUE,LFED        ;LINEFEED <-- TRUE
           000001
           000000G
37 000100  000402        BR D3
38                   ;
39 000102  005267   D2:  INC OUTPNT            ;POINT TO NEXT CHARACTER
           000000G
40 000106  052737   D3:  BIS #100,@#DISCSR     ;ENABLE (OR LEAVE ENABLED) OUTPUT
           000100
           000000G
41                                             ;INTERRUPT
42 000114  000002   XIT: RTI                   ;EXIT
43                   ;
44                   ; END OF TERMINAL OUTPUT INTERRUPT ROUTINE
45                   ;
46         000001        .END
ERRORS DETECTED:  0

VIRTUAL MEMORY USED:  8192 WORDS  ( 32 PAGES)
DYNAMIC MEMORY AVAILABLE FOR  66 PAGES
C42,DY0:C42.L/N:SYM/L:TTM=C42
```

B28   Blending Program

```
 1              ;                FLOW CONTROL PROGRAM
 2              ;
 3                      .TITLE C44
 4 000000              .CSECT FLOW
 5                      .GLOBL  DISCSR,CLKINT,DINT,DIVIDE,KINT,MULT
 6                      .GLOBL  OUTPNT,BF1STT,BF2STT,INBF1,INBF2,INPOINT
 7                      .GLOBL  KIFNUM,KIFDEN,KITNUM,KITDEN,KPFNUM,KPFDEN,KPTNUM,
                                KPTDEN
 8                      .GLOBL RTN,RFN,BUF,CTN,CFN,MCN,MHN,DELMT,DELMF
 9
10              ;
11              ; THIS IS THE FINAL PROGRAM OF CHAPTER 6.  IT
12              ; INCORPORATES TERMINAL INPUT AND OUTPUT INTERRUPT
13              ; ROUTINES AND A CLOCK INTERRUPT ROUTINE.
14              ;
15      170440  DTOA1=170440    ;ADDRESS OF FIRST D/A
16      170442  DTOA2=170442    ;ADDRESS OF SECOND D/A
17              ;
18      000060  KVEK=60         ;ADDRESS OF KEYBOARD VECTOR
19      000064  DVEK=64         ;ADDRESS OF DISPLAY VECTOR
20      000100  CLKVEK=100      ;ADDRESS OF CLOCK VECTOR
21              ;
```

```
22            000000  VACANT=0           ;BUFFER STATUS FLAG FOR UNUSED BUFFER
23            000001  BUSY=1             ;BUFFER BUSY
24            000002  READY=2            ;BUFFER READY FOR PROCESSING
25                    ;
26            000015  CR=15              ;ASCII CODE FOR CARRIAGE RETURN
27                    ;
28            000001  TRUE=1             ;LOGICAL VALUE
29            000000  FALSE=0            ;LOGICAL VALUE
30                    ;
31                    ;
32 000000     012767  MAIN:   MOV #INBF1,INPOINT     ;INITIALIZE INPUT BUFFER POINTER
              001142'
              001410
33 000006     012767          MOV #BUSY,BF1STT       ;STATUS OF INPUT BUFFER#1 <-- BUSY
              000001
              001122
34 000014     012767          MOV #VACANT,BF2STT     ;STATUS OF INPUT BUFFER#2 <-- VACANT
              000000
              001116
35                    ;
36 000022     012737          MOV #2047.,@#DTOA1     ;TURN OFF PUMP#1
              003777
              170440
37 000030     012737          MOV #2047.,@#DTOA2     ;TURN OFF PUMP#2
              003777
              170442
38                    ;
39 000036     013767          MOV @#DVEK,DSAVE                   ;SAVE DISPLAY VECTOR
              000064
              001336
40 000044     013767          MOV @#<DVEK+2>,<DSAVE+2>           ;SAVE DISPLAY PSW
              000066
              001332
41 000052     013767          MOV @#KVEK,KSAVE                   ;SAVE KEYBOARD VECTOR
              000060
              001326
42 000060     013767          MOV @#<KVEK+2>,<KSAVE+2>           ;SAVE DISPLAY PSW
              000062
              001322
43 000066     013767          MOV @#CLKVEK,CLKSAV                ;SAVE CLOCK VECTOR
              000100
              001316
44 000074     013767          MOV @#<CLKVEK+2>,<CLKSAV+2>        ;SAVE CLOCK PSW
              000102
              001312
45                    ;
46 000102     012737          MOV #200,@#<DVEK+2>    ;DISABLE INTERRUPTS DURING
              000200
              000066
47                                                   ;THE DISPLAY INTERRUPT ROUTINE
48 000110     012737          MOV #DINT,@#DVEK       ;NEW DISPLAY VECTOR
              `00000G
              000064
49 000116     012737          MOV #200,@#<KVEK+2>    ;DISABLE INTERRUPTS DURING
              000200
              000062
50                                                   ;THE KEYBOARD INTERRUPT ROUTINE
51 000124     012737          MOV #KINT,@#KVEK       ;NEW KEYBOARD VECTOR
              000000G
              000060
52                    ;
53 000132     026727  M1:     CMP BF1STT,#READY      ;IS BUFFER#1 READY?
              001000
              000002
54 000140     001004          BNE M2                 ;BRANCH => BUFFER#1 NOT READY
```

```
55 000142  012767        MOV #INBF1,MPOINT      ;INITIALIZE MESSAGE POINTER
           001142'
           001456
56 000150  000407        BR M3
57                    ;
58 000152  026727  M2:   CMP BF2STT,#READY      ;IS BUFFER#2 READY?
           000762
           000002
59 000160  001364        BNE M1                 ;BRANCH => BUFFER#2 NOT READY
60 000162  012767        MOV #INBF2,MPOINT      ;INITIALIZE MESSAGE POINTER
           001262'
           001436
61                    ;
62                    ; TO HERE, A MESSAGE EXISTS FROM OPERATOR
63                    ; POSSIBLE MESSAGES ARE: E=EXIT TO MONITOR, S=STOP PUMPS,
64                    ; G=BEGIN CONTROL (GO), L=LIST VARIABLES, T=SETPOINT (TEMP),
65                    ; F=SETPOINT (FLOW), K=GAINS (FOUR POSSIBLE GAINS).
66                    ;
67 000170  127727  M3:   CMPB @MPOINT,#'E       ;COMMAND=EXIT?
           001432
           000105
68 000176  001044        BNE M4
69                    ;
70                    ; EXIT => STOP PUMPS, DISARM INTERRUPTS, RETURN TO MONITOR
71                    ;
72 000200  016737        MOV DSAVE,@#DVEK       ;RESTORE VECTORS
           001176
           000064
73 000206  016737        MOV <DSAVE+2>,@#<DVEK+2>
           001172
           000066
74 000214  016737        MOV KSAVE,@#KVEK
           001166
           000060
75 000222  016737        MOV <KSAVE+2>,@#<KVEK+2>
           001162
           000062
76 000230  016737        MOV CLKSAV,@#CLKVEK
           001156
           000100
77 000236  016737        MOV <CLKSAV+2>,@#<CLKVEK+2>
           001152
           000102
78                    ;
79 000244  012737        MOV #2047.,@#DTOA1     ;TURN OFF PUMP#1
           003777
           170440
80 000252  012737        MOV #2047.,@#DTOA2     ;TURN OFF PUMP#2
           003777
           170442
81                    ;
82 000260  026727        CMP BF1STT,#READY      ;NOW, VACATE BUFFER WHICH CONTAINED
           000652
           000002
83                                              ;EXIT COMMAND
84 000266  001004        BNE B1
85 000270  012767        MOV #VACANT,BF1STT
           000000
           000640
86 000276  000403        BR B2
87 000300  012767  B1:   MOV #VACANT,BF2STT
           000000
           000632
88 000306  000003  B2:   BPT                    ;RETURN TO MONITOR
89                    ;
```

```
 90 000310  127727  M4:    CMPB  @MPOINT,#'S          ;COMMAND=STOP?
            001312
            000123
 91 000316  001027         BNE   M5
 92                 ;
 93                 ; STOP => DISARM CLOCK INTERRUPT, STOP PUMPS, PRINT "STOPPED"
 94                 ;
 95 000320  016737         MOV   CLKSAV,@#CLKVEK      ;RESTORE OLD CLOCK VECTOR
            001066
            000100
 96 000326  016737         MOV   <CLKSAV+2>,@#<CLKVEK+2>    ;RESTORE OLD CLOCK PSW
            001062
            000102
 97                 ;
 98 000334  012737         MOV   #2047.,@#DTOA1       ;TURN OFF PUMP#1
            003777
            170440
 99 000342  012737         MOV   #2047.,@#DTOA2       ;TURN OFF PUMP#2
            003777
            170442
100                 ;
101 000350  012767         MOV   #SBUF,OUTPNT         ;INITIALIZE OUTPUT BUFFER POINTER
            001632'
            001042
102 000356  012767         MOV   #TRUE,BUF
            000001
            001244
103 000364  052737         BIS   #100,@#DISCSR        ;ENABLE OUTPUT INTERRUPTS TO
            000100
            000000G
104                                                   ;PRINT "STOPPED"
105 000372  000167         JMP   VACAT                ;VACATE READY BUFFER
            000460
106                 ;
107 000376  127727  M5:    CMPB  @MPOINT,#'G          ;COMMAND=GO?
            001224
            000107
108 000404  001020         BNE   M6
109                 ;
110                 ; GO => ARM CLOCK INTERRUPT, PRINT "RUNNING"
111                 ;
112 000406  005037         CLR   @#<CLKVEK+2>         ;NEW CLOCK INTERRUPT ROUTINE PSW
            000102
113 000412  012737         MOV   #CLKINT,@#CLKVEK     ;PLACE ADDRESS OF CLOCK INTERRUPT
            000000G
            000100
114                                                   ;ROUTINE AT VECTOR ADDRESS
115 000420  012767         MOV   #GOBUF,OUTPNT        ;INITIALIZE OUTPUT BUFFER POINTER
            001637'
            000772
116 000426  012767         MOV   #TRUE,BUF
            000001
            001174
117 000434  052737         BIS   #100,@#DISCSR        ;ENABLE OUTPUT INTERRUPTS
            000100
            000000G
118                                                   ;TO PRINT "RUNNING"
119 000442  000167         JMP   VACAT                ;VACATE READY BUFFER
            000410
120                 ;
121 000446  127727  M6:    CMPB  @MPOINT,#'T          ;COMMAND=TEMPERATURE SETPOINT?
            001154
            000124
122 000454  001013         BNE   M7
123                 ;
```

```
124                           ; SETPOINT => UPDATE VARIABLE  WITH VALUE OF THREE DECIMAL DIGITS
125                           ;
126 000456   005267          INC MPOINT              ;PONT TO FIRST NUMBER
            001144
127 000462   004767          JSR PC,VALUE            ;VALUE RETURNS BINARY NUMBER IN R0
            001420
128 000466   103404          BCS ER1                 ;CARRY SET => ERROR ON CONVERT
129                           ;
130 000470   010067          MOV R0,RTN              ;UPDATE TEMPERATURE SETPOINT
            001366
131 000474   000167          JMP VACAT               ;VACATE BUFFER
            000356
132 000500   000167   ER1:   JMP ERR                 ;EXTEND BRANCH
            000404
133                           ;
134 000504   127727   M7:    CMPB @MPOINT,#'F        ;FLOW SETPOINT?
            001116
            000106
135 000512   001011          BNE M8
136 000514   005267          INC MPOINT              ;POINT TO FIRST NUMBER
            001106
137 000520   004767          JSR PC,VALUE            ;VALUE RETURNS BINARY VALUE IN R0
            001362
138 000524   103571          BCS ERR
139 000526   010067          MOV R0,RFN              ;UPDATE FLOW SETPOINT
            001332
140 000532   000167          JMP VACAT               ;VACATE BUFFER
            000320
141                           ;
142 000536   127727   M8:    CMPB @MPOINT,#'K        ;GAIN UPDATE COMMAND?
            001064
            000113
143 000544   001077          BNE M12
144                           ;
145                           ; GAIN UPDATE MAY BE ONE OF FOUR (KPF,KPT,KIF,KIT)
146                           ;
147 000546   062767          ADD #3,MPOINT           ;POINT TO FIRST NUMERIC VALUE
            000003
            001052
148 000554   004767          JSR PC,VALUE
            001326
149 000560   103553          BCS ERR
150 000562   010001          MOV R0,R1               ;R1 <-- KNUM
151 000564   062767          ADD #4,MPOINT           ;POINT TO KDEN
            000004
            001034
152 000572   004767          JSR PC,VALUE
            001310
153 000576   103544          BCS ERR
154                           ;
155                           ; NOW PLACE NUMERATOR AND DENOMINATOR IN CORRECT VARIABLE
156                           ;
157 000600   016703          MOV MPOINT,R3
            001022
158 000604   126327          CMPB -6(R3),#'P         ;PROPORTIONAL GAIN?
            177772
            000120
159 000612   001024          BNE M9
160 000614   126327          CMPB -5(R3),#'F         ;FLOW?
            177773
            000106
161 000622   001006          BNE M10
162 000624   010167          MOV R1,KPFNUM           ;NUMERATOR OF PROPORTIONAL FLOW
            001246
163 000630   010067          MOV R0,KPFDEN
```

```
                001244
164 000634      000167          JMP VACAT               ;VACATE BUFFER
                000216
165                         ;
166 000640      126327      M10: CMPB -5(R3),#'T
                177773
                000124
167 000646      001120          BNE ERR
168 000650      010167          MOV R1,KPTNUM           ;NUMERATOR OF PROPORTIONAL TEMPERATURE GAIN
                001226
169 000654      010067          MOV R0,KPTDEN           ;UPDATE VALUE
                001224
170 000660      000167          JMP VACAT
                000172
171                         ;
172 000664      126327      M9:  CMPB -6(R3),#'I        ;IF NOT P, MUST BE I
                177772
                000111
173 000672      001106          BNE ERR
174 000674      126327          CMPB -5(R3),#'F         ;FLOW?
                177773
                000106
175 000702      001006          BNE M11
176 000704      010167          MOV R1,KIFNUM           ;NUMERATOR OF INTEGRAL FLOW GAIN
                001156
177 000710      010067          MOV R0,KIFDEN
                001154
178 000714      000167          JMP VACAT
                000136
179                         ;
180 000720      126327      M11: CMPB -5(R3),#'T        ;MUST BE TEMPERATURE
                177773
                000124
181 000726      001070          BNE ERR
182 000730      010167          MOV R1,KITNUM           ;NUMERATOR OF INTEGRAL TEMPERATURE
                001136
183 000734      010067          MOV R0,KITDEN
                001134
184 000740      000167          JMP VACAT
                000112
185                         ;
186 000744      127727      M12: CMPB @MPOINT,#'L       ;LIST COMMAND?
                000656
                000114
187 000752      001056          BNE ERR                 ;NO MORE VALID COMMANDS
188                         ;
189 000754      005367          DEC HEDCNT              ;PRINT HEADER EVERY 10 TIMES
                001100
190 000760      003007          BGT MM12
191 000762      012767          MOV #10.,HEDCNT         ;RESET COUNTER
                000012
                001070
192 000770      012767          MOV #HEAD,OUTPNT        ;PREPARE TO PRINT HEADER
                001720'
                000422
193 000776      000421          BR MM13
194                         ;
195 001000      012767      MM12:MOV #OUTBUF,OUTPNT ;INITIALIZE PRINT BUFFER
                001422'
                000412
196 001006      012700          MOV #LIST,R0            ;R0 <-- START OF LIST OF VALUES TO PRINT
                001656'
197 001012      004767      M13: JSR PC,FORMAT          ;FORMAT CONVERTS @(R0) TO ASCII AND
                001250
198                                                     ;PLACES INOUTBUFFER AT OUTPNT
```

```
199 001016   062700          ADD #2,R0           ;POINT TO NEXT LIST ELEMENT
             000002
200 001022   005710          TST (R0)            ;VALUE NULL?
201 001024   001372          BNE M13             ;LOOP FOR LENGTH OF LIST
202                  ;
203 001026   112777          MOVB #CR,@OUTPNT     ;TERMINATE WITH RETURN
             000015
             000364
204 001034   012767          MOV #OUTBUF,OUTPNT   ;RESET BUFFER POINTER
             001422'
             000356
205 001042   012767   MM13:  MOV #TRUE,BUF
             000001
             000560
206 001050   052737          BIS #100,@#DISCSR    ;ENABLE OUTPUT INTERRUPTS
             000100
             000000G
207                                               ;IN ORDER TO PRINT MESSAGE
208                  ;
209 001056   026727   VACAT: CMP BF1STT,#READY    ;IS BUFFER#1 READY?
             000054
             000002
210 001064   001004          BNE V1
211 001066   012767          MOV #VACANT,BF1STT   ;VACATE BUFFER#1
             000000
             000042
212 001074   000403          BR V2
213 001076   012767   V1:    MOV #VACANT,BF2STT
             000000
             000034
214 001104   000167   V2:    JMP M1              ;BACK FOR NEXT PACKET
             177022
215                  ;
216 001110   012767   ERR:   MOV #ERRBUF,OUTPNT   ;INITIALIZE OUTPUT BUFFER POINTER
             001647'
             000302
217                                               ;TO START OF BUFFER WHICH SAYS "ERROR"
218 001116   012767          MOV #TRUE,BUF
             000001
             000504
219 001124   052737          BIS #100,@#DISCSR    ;ENABLE OUTPUT INTERRUPTS TO  RINT
             000100
             000000G
220                                               ;MESSAGE
221 001132   000167          JMP VACAT           ;VACATE BUFFER
             177720
222                  ;
223                  ;
224 001136   000000   BF1STT: .WORD 0             ;STATUS OF BUFFER#1
225 001140   000000   BF2STT: .WORD 0             ;STATUS OF BUFFER#2
226 001142            INBF1:  .BLKB 80.           ;INPUT BUFFER#1
227 001262            INBF2:  .BLKB 80.           ;INPUT BUFFER#2
228                  ;
229 001402            DSAVE:  .BLKW 2             ;DISPLAY VECTOR AND PSW SAVED HERE
230 001406            KSAVE:  .BLKW 2             ;KEYBOARD VECTOR AND PSW SAVED HERE
231 001412            CLKSAV: .BLKW 2             ;CLOCK VECTOR AND PSW SAVED HERE
232                  ;
233 001416   000000   INPOIN: .WORD 0             ;POINTER TO INPUT BUFFER
234                  ;
235 001420   000000   OUTPNT: .WORD 0             ;POINTER TO OUTPUT BUFFER
236 001422            OUTBUF: .BLKB 132.          ;OUTPUT BUFFER
237                  ;
238 001626   000000   MPOINT: .WORD 0             ;POINTER TO CURRENT MESSAGE BUFFER
239 001630   000000   BUF:    .WORD 0             ;LOGICAL FLAG USED TO PRINT BUFFER
240                  ;
```

```
241 001632      123   SBUF:   .ASCII/STOP/
    001633      124
    001634      117
    001635      120
242 001636      015           .BYTE 15        ;RETURN
243                   ;
244 001637      122   GOBUF:  .ASCII/RUNNING/
    001640      125
    001641      116
    001642      116
    001643      111
    001644      116
    001645      107
245 001646      015           .BYTE 15
246                   ;
247 001647      105   ERRBUF: .ASCII/ERROR/
    001650      122
    001651      122
    001652      117
    001653      122
248 001654      015           .BYTE 15
249                   ;
250                   .EVEN       ;INSURE THAT FOLLOWING WORDS BEGIN ON EVEN ADDRESSES
251                   ;
252 001656   002062'  LIST:   .WORD RTN,RFN,KIFNUM,KIFDEN,KITNUM,KITDEN,KPFNUM,KPFDEN
    001660   002064'
    001662   002066'
    001664   002070'
    001666   002072'
    001670   002074'
    001672   002076'
    001674   002100'
253 001676   002102'          .WORD KPTNUM,KPTDEN,CTN,CFN,MCN,MHN,DELMT,DELMF,0
    001700   002104'
    001702   000000G
    001704   000000G
    001706   000000G
    001710   000000G
    001712   000000G
    001714   000000G
    001716   000000
254                   ;
255 001720      040   HEAD:   .ASCII/ RTN    RFN    KIFN  KIFD  KITN  KITD /
    001721      122
    001722      124
    001723      116
    001724      040
    001725      040
    001726      040
    001727      122
    001730      106
    001731      116
    001732      040
    001733      040
    001734      040
    001735      113
    001736      111
    001737      106
    001740      116
    001741      040
    001742      040
    001743      113
    001744      111
    001745      106
    001746      104
```

```
         001747        040
         001750        040
         001751        113
         001752        111
         001753        124
         001754        116
         001755        040
         001756        040
         001757        113
         001760        111
         001761        124
         001762        104
         001763        040
256      001764        040          .ASCII/ KPFN   KPFD   KPTN   KPTD   CTN    CFN    /
         001765        113
         001766        120
         001767        106
         001770        116
         001771        040
         001772        040
         001773        113
         001774        120
         001775        106
         001776        104
         001777        040
         002000        040
         002001        113
         002002        120
         002003        124
         002004        116
         002005        040
         002006        040
         002007        113
         002010        120
         002011        124
         002012        104
         002013        040
         002014        040
         002015        103
         002016        124
         002017        116
         002020        040
         002021        040
         002022        040
         002023        103
         002024        106
         002025        116
         002026        040
         002027        040
257      002030        040          .ASCII/ MCH    MHN    DELT   DELF/
         002031        115
         002032        103
         002033        110
         002034        040
         002035        040
         002036        040
         002037        115
         002040        110
         002041        116
         002042        040
         002043        040
         002044        040
         002045        104
         002046        105
         002047        114
```

```
        002050    124
        002051    040
        002052    040
        002053    104
        002054    105
        002055    114
        002056    106
258     002057    015              .BYTE 15
259                               .EVEN
260                         ;
261     002060    000000  HEDCNT: .WORD 0         ;PRINT HEADER FLAG
262                         ;
263     002062    000000  RTN:    .WORD 0         ;TEMPERATURE SET POINT
264     002064    000000  RFN:    .WORD 0         ;FLOW SET POINT
265     002066    000000  KIFNUM: .WORD 0         ;NUMERATOR OF INTEGRAL FLOW GAIN
266     002070    000000  KIFDEN: .WORD 0
267     002072    000000  KITNUM: .WORD 0         ;NUMERATOR OF INTEGRAL TEMPERATURE GAIN
268     002074    000000  KITDEN: .WORD 0
269     002076    000000  KPFNUM: .WORD 0         ;NUMERATOR OF PROPORTIONAL FLOW GAIN
270     002100    000000  KPFDEN: .WORD 0
271     002102    000000  KPTNUM: .WORD 0         ;NUMERATOR OF PROPORTIONAL TEMPERATURE GAIN
272     002104    000000  KPTDEN: .WORD 0
273                         ;
274                         ;
275                         ; END OF MAIN PROGRAM
276                         ;
277                         ; SUBROUTINES FOLLOW
278                         ;
279                         ; SUBROUTINE VALUE RETURNS, IN R0, BINARY VALUE OF THREE ASCII
280                         ; CHARACTERS THE MOST SIGNIFICANT OF WHICH IS POINTED TO BY
281                         ; MPOINT.  MPOINT IS RETURNED UNAFFECTED.  IF ALL THREE CHARACTERS
282                         ; ARE NOT 0-9, THE CARRY IS SET AND NO VALUE IS RETURNED.
283                         ; NO REGISTERS ARE CHANGED OVER CALL.
284                         ;
285     002106    010146  VALUE:  MOV R1,-(SP)   ;SAVE R1 -- R4
286     002110    010246          MOV R2,-(SP)
287     002112    010346          MOV R3,-(SP)
288     002114    010446          MOV R4,-(SP)
289                         ;
290     002116    016703          MOV MPOINT,R3  ;R3 NOW POINTS TO FIRST (MSD)
                  177504
291     002122    112300          MOVB (R3)+,R0  ;R0 <-- CHARACTER, INCREMENT POINTER
292                                              ;TEST FOR VALID NUMBER (NOTE: PARITY WAS
                                                                                 CLEARED)
293     002124    120027          CMPB R0,#'0    ;LESS THAN ZERO?
                  000060
294     002130    002450          BLT EOUT       ;YES => ERROR EXIT
295     002132    120027          CMPB R0,#'9    ;GREATER THAN NINE?
                  000071
296     002136    003045          BGT EOUT       ;YES => ERROR EXIT
297                         ;
298     002140    162700          SUB #'0,R0     ;MAKE BINARY
                  000060
299     002144    012702          MOV #100.,R2   ;MULTIPLIER
                  000144
300     002150    004767          JSR PC,MULT    ;R1 <-- CHARACTER#1 * 100
                  000000G
301     002154    010104          MOV R1,R4      ;R4 <-- INTERMEDIATE RESULT
302                         ;
303     002156    112300          MOVB (R3)+,R0  ;R0 <-- MIDDLE CHARACTER
304     002160    120027          CMPB R0,#'0    ;AS ABOVE, TEST FOR VALID CHARACTER
                  000060
```

```
305 002164  002432           BLT EOUT
306 002166  120027           CMPB R0,#'9
            000071
307 002172  003027           BGT EOUT
308                   ;
309 002174  162700           SUB #'0,R0      ;MAKE BINARY
            000060
310 002200  012702           MOV #10.,R2     ;MULTIPLIER
            000012
311 002204  004767           JSR PC,MULT     ;R1 <-- CHARACTER#2 * 10
            000000G
312 002210  060104           ADD R1,R4       ;UPDATE INTERMEDIATE RESULT
313                   ;
314 002212  111300           MOVB (R3),R0    ;R0 <-- LEAST SIGNIFICANT DIGIT
315 002214  120027           CMPB R0,#'0     ;TEST FOR VALID CHARACTER
            000060
316 002220  002414           BLT EOUT
317 002222  120027           CMPB R0,#'9
            000071
318 002226  003011           BGT EOUT
319                   ;
320 002230  162700           SUB #'0,R0      ;MAKE BINARY
            000060
321 002234  060400           ADD R4,R0       ;R0 <-- FINAL RESULT
322                   ;
323 002236  012604           MOV (SP)+,R4    ;RESTORE REGISTERS
324 002240  012603           MOV (SP)+,R3
325 002242  012602           MOV (SP)+,R2
326 002244  012601           MOV (SP)+,R1
327                   ;
328 002246  000241           CLC             ;CLEAR CARRY
329 002250  000207           RTS PC
330                   ;
331 002252  012604   EOUT:    MOV (SP)+,R4    ;RESTORE REGISTERS
332 002254  012603           MOV (SP)+,R3
333 002256  012602           MOV (SP)+,R2
334 002260  012601           MOV (SP)+,R1
335                   ;
336 002262  000261           SEC             ;SET CARRY FOR ERROR EXIT
337 002264  000207           RTS PC
338                   ;
339                   ; END OF VALUE SUBROUTINE
340                   ;
341                   ;
342                   ;
343                   ; SUBROUTINE FORMAT TAKES A BINARY VALUE WHOSE ADDRESS'S
344                   ; ADDRESS IS IN R0 AND CONVERTS IT INTO SIX ASCII CHARACTERS
345                   ; (MAXIMUM VALUE 2**15-1) PRECEEDED BY A SIGN (+ OR -) AND
346                   ; FOLLOWED BY TWO ASCII SPACES.  THE RESULTING STRING IS
347                   ; PLACED IN THE BUFFER POINTED TO BY OUTPNT.  REGISTERS
348                   ; R1, R2, AND R3 ARE CHANGED.
349                   ;
350 002266  010046   FORMAT: MOV R0,-(SP)            ;SAVE POINTER IN R0
351                   ;
352 002270  011000           MOV (R0),R0            ;R0 <-- ADDRESS OF BINARY VALUE
353 002272  011000           MOV (R0),R0            ;R0 <-- BINARY VALUE
354 002274  005700           TST R0                 ;IS VALUE NEGATIVE?
355 002276  002404           BLT F1
356 002300  112777           MOVB #'+,@OUTPNT       ;VALUE IS POSITIVE
            000053
            177112
357 002306  000404           BR F2
358                   ;
359 002310  005400   F1:      NEG R0                 ;R0 <-- TWO'S COMPLEMENT
360 002312  112777           MOVB #'-,@OUTPNT       ;VALUE IS NEGATIVE
```

```
            000055
            177100
 361 002320 005267  F2:  INC OUTPNT       ;INCREMENT POINTER
            177074
 362                     ;
 363 002324 062767       ADD #4,OUTPNT    ;BUFFER WILL BE FILLED BACKWARDS
            000004
            177066
 364                                      ;FOR EACH BINARY VALUE
 365 002332 012703       MOV #4,R3        ;ITERATION COUNT FOR 6 DIGITS
            000004
 366                     ;
 367 002336 010001  FLOP:MOV R0,R1        ;SET UP FOR DIVIDE
 368 002340 005000       CLR R0           ;CLEAR HIGH ORDER
 369 002342 012702       MOV #10.,R2      ;DIVIDE BY 10
            000012
 370 002346 004767       JSR PC,DIVIDE
            000000G
 371 002352 062701       ADD #'0,R1       ;MAKE RESULT ASCII
            000060
 372 002356 005367       DEC OUTPNT       ;PREDECREMENT BUFFER POINTER
            177036
 373 002362 110177       MOVB R1,@OUTPNT  ;STORE CHARACTER
            177032
 374 002366 005303       DEC R3           ;ITERATION COUNT
 375 002370 003362       BGT FLOP         ;LOOP FOR SIX DIGITS
 376                     ;
 377 002372 062767       ADD #4,OUTPNT    ;SKIP TO END OF STRING
            000004
            177020
 378 002400 112777       MOVB #' ,@OUTPNT ;PLACE FIRST SPACE
            000040
            177012
 379 002406 005267       INC OUTPNT       ;LEAVE POINTER POINTING TO NEXT LOCATION
            177006
 380                     ;
 381 002412 012600       MOV (SP)+,R0     ;RESTORE POINTER
 382                     ;
 383 002414 000207       RTS PC
 384                     ;
 385                     ; END OF FORMAT SUBROUTINE
 386                     ;
 387                     ; END OF CONTROL PROGRAM
 388                     ;
 389        000001           .END
ERRORS DETECTED:   0

VIRTUAL MEMORY USED:  8192 WORDS  ( 32 PAGES)
DYNAMIC MEMORY AVAILABLE FOR  66 PAGES
C44,DY0:C44.L[60]/N:SYM/L:TTM=C44
```

AUTOMATED WEIGHING PROGRAMS IN FORTRAN

The automated weighing programs use a mixture of high-level language and assembly language to optimize programming and debugging efficiency without losing computer capabilities that can only be implemented in assembly language. At a minimum, assembly language must be used to save and restore registers and return from the interrupt. RT-11 FORTRAN is not re-entrant, so assembly language must also be used for the sampling and graphic refresh portions of the program. The transition diagram for processing the scale data, Figure 7.6, is completely implemented in

FORTRAN as the background program. The states in the transition diagram have been associated with statement numbers by using ASSIGN statements so that the transitions between states can be done by name. Otherwise, the structure of the FORTRAN portion of the program, Listing B29, is very similar to the structure used for the DC motor test programs. The assembly language portion of the program appears in Listing B30.

The first instance of communication between FORTRAN and assembly language occurs when the clock interrupt must be activated. This is done by the FORTRAN statement CALL CLKON. The assembly language subroutine CLKON must be identified for the linker by declaring its name to be global with a GLOBL statement. CLKON sets up the interrupt vectors for the line-time clock (LTC), the same clock used in the blending control programs. By setting the priority portion of the processor status word (PSW) to zero, the interrupt service routine will run at lowest priority and will therefore be interruptable. The return to FORTRAN is accomplished with an RTS PC statement.

When the clock interrupts, control transfers to the assembly language routine CLK. If CLK determines that this moment is a time to sample, it takes a data sample from the A/D converter. It must then communicate both the value of the sample itself (IADDAT) and the fact that a new sample is ready (the variable DR). In RT-11 FORTRAN, this is most easily accomplished with the use of a labelled COMMON in the FORTRAN portion of the program and an appropriately labelled .PSECT in the assembly language. The PSECT name must match the name used for the labelled COMMON, and its attributes must be RW (for Read/Write), D (for Data), OVR (for Overlay, so all blocks with the same name overlay each other rather than occupy distinct areas of memory), and GBL (for Global).

Since variables in corresponding positions in their respective blocks access the same memory locations, the new value can be accessed in the FORTRAN program when the variable DR is changed in the assembly routine CLK. There is no requirement that the same names be used for the variables in both places; however, in this case, using the same names makes the program more understandable.

The last form of interaction between FORTRAN and assembly language is used in the call from FORTRAN to the assembly language subroutine LED. LED is used to shift the digits used for the LED display into their correct positions. This is an operation that is done much more conveniently in assembly language than in FORTRAN. Since the digits are passed to LED as arguments, the assembly language routine must mimic the procedure FORTRAN uses to pick up arguments in subroutines. The information concerning the arguments is put in a table in memory.

The first word of the table contains the number of arguments in its lower order byte (nothing in the higher order byte). Subsequent words in the argument block contain the addresses of each of the arguments. Register 5 (R5) is set up as a pointer to the argument block by the calling program. For integer arguments, the values can be accessed most easily in assembly language by using the offset deferred mode of addressing. For example, the value of the first argument can be accessed with an @2(R5) (the offset of 2 is because the first word of the argument block contains the number of arguments, while the address of the first argument is in the second word).

B29   Background Program In FORTRAN

```
C AUTOMATIC WEIGHING SYSTEM -- MAIN PROGRAM
        LOGICAL DR,POS,MC,ERROR
        COMMON/INTRPT/DR,ITCNT,ITSAMP,IADDAT,ERROR
        DIMENSION ISCALE(200)
        INTEGER DRFALS,DATAWT,FILTER,CHKUP,CHKLOW
        INTEGER CHKSET,MCFALS,COMPLT

C READ IN PARAMETER VALUES
        TYPE 99
99      FORMAT(' TYPE VALUES FOR ILTH,IUTH,ITSAMP,IPCMAX ')
        ACCEPT 98,ILTH,IUTH,ITSAMP,IPCMAX
        TYPE 97
97      FORMAT(' TYPE VALUES FOR CFILT,LSETL,ITOL')
98      FORMAT(I5)
        ACCEPT 96,CFILT,LSETL,ITOL
96      FORMAT(F10.3/(I5))
C ASSIGN MODULE STATEMENT LABELS NAMES SO PROGRAM WILL BE
C MORE READABLE.
        ASSIGN 200 TO DRFALS
        ASSIGN 300 TO DATAWT
        ASSIGN 400 TO FILTER
        ASSIGN 500 TO CHKUP
        ASSIGN 600 TO CHKLOW
        ASSIGN 700 TO CHKSET
        ASSIGN 900 TO MCFALS
        ASSIGN 1000 TO COMPLT
C INITIALIZATION SECTION
        POS=.FALSE.
        IPC=IPCMAX
        MC=.FALSE.
        ITCNT=ITSAMP
C ITCNT IS THE COUNTER USED IN THE CLOCK INTERRUPT ROUTINE
C TO FIGURE OUT WHEN A SAMPLE SHOULD BE TAKEN.
        IFILT=0
        ITW=0
C SET SCALE OUTPUT VOLTAGE RING BUFFER TO ZERO
        DO 100 I=1,LSETL
100     ISCALE(I)=0
C MSC IS POINTER FOR SCALE DATA RING BUFFER
        MSC=1
C CALL CLKON, AN ASSEMBLY LANGUAGE ROUTINE TO SET UP INTERRUPTS
        CALL CLKON
C ***
C DRFALS MODULE
C ***
200     DR=.FALSE.
C ***
C DATA-WAIT MODULE
C ***
300     CONTINUE
        IF(.NOT.DR)GO TO 300
C MAKE SURE NO ERROR HAS OCCURRED.
        IF(.NOT.ERROR)GO TO FILTER
C IF THERE IS AN ERROR, TURN OFF INTERRUPTS USING CLKOFF
C AND TYPE ERROR MESSAGE ON CONSOLE.
        CALL CLKOFF
        TYPE 399
399     FORMAT(' ERROR IN DATA-WAIT')
        STOP
C ***
C FILTER MODULE
C ***
400     CONTINUE
```

```
          ITW=ITW+1
C ITW IS A VARIABLE THAT TELLS HOW MANY SAMPLES WERE REQUIRED
C TO COMPLETE THE MEASUREMENT.  IT CN BE USED TO TUNE THE
C FILTER AND SAMPLE TIME.
C
C USE FLOATING POINT IN THE FILTER TO AVOID INTEGER OVERFLOW
C AND ROUNDOFF PROBLEMS.  THIS TAKES MORE COMPUTER TIME BUT
C SIMPLIFIES PROGRAMMING.
          IFILT=CFILT*IFILT+(1.0-CFILT)*IADDAT +0.5
C 0.5 IS ADDED TO ROUND OFF RESULT INSTEAD OF TRUNCATE IT.
C
C UPDATE RINGG BUFFER
          ISCALE(MSC)=IFILT
          MSC=MSC+1
          IF(MSC.GT.LSETL)MSC=1
          IF(POS)GO TO CHKLOW
          GO TO CHKUP
C ***
C CHECK-UPPER MODULE
C ***
500       CONTINUE
          IF(IFILT.GT.IUTH)POS=.TRUE.
          IF(.NOT.POS)GO TO DRFALS
C NEW PART IS ON SCALE
          MC=.FALSE.
          ITW=0
          GO TO DRFALS
C ***
C CHECK-LOWER MODULE
C ***
600       CONTINUE
          IF(IFILT.LT.ILTH)POS=.FALSE.
          IF((POS.AND.MC).OR.(.NOT.POS.AND..NOT.MC))GO TO DRFALS
          IF(POS.AND..NOT.MC)GO TO CHKSET
          IF((.NOT.POS).AND.MC)GO TO MCFALS
C ***
C CHECK-SETTLING MODULE
C ***
700       CONTINUE
C COMPUTE AVERAGE USING FLOATING POINT TO AVOID INTEGER OVERFLOW.
          SUM=0.0
          DO 750 I=1,LSETL
750       SUM=SUM+ISCALE(I)
          ISUM=SUM/LSETL+0.5
C NOW CHECK TO SEE IF ALL SAMPLES ARE WITHIN TOLERANCE OF THE
C AVERAGE.
          DO 800 I=1,LSETL
          IF(IABS(ISCALE(I)-ISUM).GT.ITOL)GO TO 850
800       CONTINUE

C NORMAL EXIT FROM THE LOOP MEANS ALL SAMPLES PASSED SO
C THAT THE WEIGHING IS COMPLETE.
          MC=.TRUE.
          GO TO COMPLT
850       MC=.FALSE.
          GO TO DRFALS
C ***
C MC-FALSE MODULE
C ***
900       MC=.FALSE.
          GO TO DRFALS
C ***
C WEIGHING-COMPLETE MODULE
1000      CONTINUE
C DISPLAY RESULT ON CONSOLE TERMINAL
```

```
          TYPE 1099,ITW*ITSAMP,ISUM
1099      FORMAT(' TIME,WEIGHT = ',2I6)
          IPC=IPC-1
          IF(IPC.NE.0)GO TO DRFALS
C CLKOFF TURNS OFF INTERRUPTS
          CALL CLKOFF
          STOP
          END
```

B30   Assembly Language Interrupt Routine

```
;ASSEMBLY LANGUAGE ROUTINES FOR AUTOMATIC WEIGHING.
;
;CLKON INITIATES INTERRUPTS; CLKOFF TERMINATES THEM.
;
          .GLOBL CLKON,CLKOFF
;
CLVECT=100
;
CLKON:    MOV @#CLVECT,VCSAVE       ;SAVE RT-11'S VECTOR
          MOV @#CLVECT+2,VCSAVE+2
          MOV #CLK,@#CLVECT         ;PUT ADDRESS OF CLOCK INTERRUPT
                                    ;ROUTINE IN VECTOR LOCATION.
          MOV #0,@#CLVECT+2         ;SET PRIORITY LOW -- I.E.,
                                    ;DON'T LOCK OUT OTHER INTERRUPTS.
          RTS PC                    ;RETURN
CLKOFF:   MOV VCSAVE+2,@#CLVECT+2   ;RESTORE RT-11 BEFORE RETURNING
          MOV VCSAVE,@#CLVECT
          RTS PC                    ;RETURN
;
VCSAVE:   .WORD 0,0
;
; CLOCK INTERRUPT ROUTINE
;
TRUE=177777
FALSE=0
ADCSR=170400
ADBUF=170402
;
; NO REGISTERS ARE USED SO NONE NEED BE SAVED
;
CLK:      DEC ITCNT
          BEQ 1$                    ;1$ IS A LOCAL SYMBOL
          RTI                       ;IF NOT TIME FOR A SAMPLE, RETURN.
1$:       CMP DR,#TRUE              ;HAS PREVIOUS DATA BEEN PROCESSED?
          BNE 2$
          MOV #TRUE,ERROR           ;YES..SET ERROR TO TRUE
          MOV #TRUE,ERROR+1         ;RT-11 FORTRAN USES TWO
                                    ;WORDS FOR LOGICAL VARIABLES.
2$:       MOV #1,@#ADCSR            ;START A/D ON CHANNEL 0
3$:       BIT #200,@#ADCSR          ;CHECK FOR DONE
          BEQ 3$
          MOV @#ADBUF,IADDAT        ;GET A/D DATA
          MOV #TRUE,DR              ;SET DATA-READY FLAG
          MOV #TRUE,DR+1            ;SET SECOND WORD
          MOV ITSAMP,ITCNT          ;RESET CLOCK COUNTER.
          RTI                       ;RETURN
;
          .PSECT INTRPT RW,D,OVR,GBL
;
; THE PSECT DIRECTIVE IS USED TO SET UP THE COMMON BLOCK
; INTRPT.  RW,D.... ARE BLOCK ATTRIBUTES APPROPRIATE TO
; A NAMED COMMON BLOCK.
;
DR:       .BLKW 2                   ;BLKW IS USED SO THE BLOCK CAN
```

```
                    ;BE INITIALIZED WITH FORTRAN DATA
                    ;STATEMENTS WITHOUT DANGER OF
                    ;OVERWRITING THE DATA HERE.
                    ;RT-11 USES TWO WORDS FOR LOGICAL
                    ;VARIABLES, DR AND ERROR.
ITCNT:   .BLKW 1
ITSAMP:  .BLKW 1
IADDAT:  .BLKW 1
ERROR:   .BLKW 2
;
         .END
```

AUTOMATED WEIGHING PROGRAMS IN C

The automated weighing programs use a mixture of high-level language and assembly language to optimize programming and debugging efficiency without losing computer capabilities that can only be implemented in assembly language. At a minimum, assembly language must be used to save and restore registers and return from the interrupt. Because Whitesmith's C, which is used here, is completely re-entrant, both interrupt level tasks and background tasks can be done in C. Furthermore, since pointer variables in C can be used to access absolute computer memory locations, and since PDP-11 I/O is all memory mapped, all I/O operations and interrupt set-up procedures can also be done in C.

Thus, the only assembly language programming that must be used is an interrupt service routine that saves the registers, calls a C function, and, on return from the C function, restores the registers and returns from the interrupt. The C interrupt routine can communicate with the background portion of the C program through the use of globally defined variables. The C program appears in Listing B31 and the assembly language program is given in Listing B32.

The clock interrupt is set up by the function clkset. The assembly language interrupt service routine's name (CLOCK), which must be declared global (GLOBAL) in the assembly language portion, is stored in the interrupt vector by using a pointer variable set to point at location 100Q, the clock's vector address. When an interrupt occurs, CLOCK first saves the registers, then calls the C function CLKINT by using a JSR PC,CLKINT. Throughout the C program, pointer variables are also used to access arrays in order to minimize computing time.

B31   C Programs

```
/* automated weighing program */
#include <std.h>
#define FALSE 0
#define TRUE  1

BOOL dr=FALSE,error=FALSE, errorg=FALSE;
int tsamp=100, tcount=100, data=0;
int *grf=0, gcount=100, tgr=100, npoint=0, dx=0;        /* graphics variables */

/* The above variables must be global for communication with
   the interrupt routines.  */

COUNT _main()
{
extern int tsamp,tcount,data;
```

```
extern BOOL dr;
int stdout,ir;

/* Initialization Section  */

#define MAXSC 100

int lowth,highth,*psctop,filt,itw,weight,pc;
int scalv[MAXSC];
int *psc;
BOOL pos,mc,error;
float cfilt;
int lset1,tol,nv,*pscset;
long sum;

/* The following variables are used in the calculation of the distribution
and in the graphics.  */

#define PAROUT 0167772
int *par=PAROUT;        /* Parallel interface pointer for LED display */
int dis[50],graph[50],wring[100];       /* distribution, graph and ring
                                           buffer arrays  */
static int dsplay[10] = {0,1,2,3,4,5,6,7,8,9};  /* LED display codes  */
BOOL first=TRUE;        /* flags partially full ring buffer  */
int dmin,dmax,ddel,npast,gsc,num,i;     /* distribution, graph parameters */
int *g,*wr,*wrtop,*ww,*gg,*wend,*distop,*dd;    /* array pointers */


        pos=FALSE;      /* part-on-scale indicator */
        mc=FALSE;       /* measurement-complete indicator  */
        filt=0;         /* filter output */
        itw=0;          /* counter for number of data points required
                        for settling */

/* Initial data input ... */
        putfmt("type: tsamp,part count\n");
        getfmt("%i%i",&tsamp,&pc);
        tcount = tsamp;         /* initialize clock counter  */
        putfmt("type: lowth,highth\n");
        getfmt("%i%i",&lowth,&highth);
        putfmt("type: cfilt,lset1,tol\n");
        getfmt("%f%i%i",&cfilt,&lset1,&tol);
        putfmt("dmin,dmax,ddel,npast,gsc,tgr\n");       /* graphics input */
        getfmt("%i%i%i%i%i%i",&dmin,&dmax,&ddel,&npast,&gsc,&tgr);
        npoint = (dmax - dmin)/ddel;    /* number of distribution points */
        dx = 2048/npoint;               /* x increment on graph */
        grf = graph;                    /* pointer to graph array */
        wr = wring;                     /* pointer to weight ring buffer */
        wrtop = wring + npast -1;       /* pointer to end of buffer */
        distop = dis + npoint -1;       /* pointer to end of distribution */
        gcount = tgr;                   /* initialize graphics timer */

/* Now initialize the scale data array */
        psctop= scalv + lset1 - 1;      /*address of top of ring buffer */
        for(psc=scalv; psc <= psctop;)*psc++ = 0;
        psc = scalv;    /* Initialize psc for processing scale data */
        clkset(0);      /* set up clock interrupt   */

/* DR-False Module */
drfals:
        dr = FALSE;

/* Data-Wait Module */
datawt:
        while(dr == FALSE) ;    /* Wait for data-ready  */
```

```
                if(error == TRUE)
                        { putfmt("e\n");
                          error = FALSE;
                        }
                if(errorg == TRUE)
                        { putfmt("eg\n");
                          errorg = FALSE;
                        }
                goto filter;

/* Filter Module */
filter:
                itw++;
/* Filter calculation should be done as either long integer or
float to avoid overflow problems */
                filt=cfilt*filt+(1.0-cfilt)*data+0.5;
                *psc++ = filt;
                if(psc>psctop)psc = scalv;        /* update ring buffer */
                if(pos)goto chklow;
                else goto chkup;

/* Check-Upper Module */
chkup:
                if(filt <= highth)goto drfals;
                pos=TRUE;
                mc=FALSE;
                itw=0;
                goto drfals;

/* Check-Lower Module */
chklow:
                pos=filt >= lowth;
                if((pos && mc)|| (!pos && !mc))goto drfals;
                if(pos && !mc)goto chkset;
                if(!pos && mc)goto mcfals;

/* Check-Settling Module */
chkset:
/* use long integer to avoid overflow in summation */
                sum=0;
                for(pscset=scalv; pscset <= psctop;) sum += *pscset++;
                weight = sum/lsetl;      /* weight is the average of buffer
                                   now compare all values to average to check
                                   for settling */
                for(pscset=scalv;pscset <= psctop;)
                {
                if(abs((*pscset++) - weight) >= tol)
                        { mc = FALSE;
                          goto drfals;
                        }
                }
/* The above statements check all values against the average */
                mc = TRUE;
                goto complt;

/* MC-False Module */
mcfals:
                mc = FALSE;
                *par = 0;         /* Zero LED display.  */
                goto drfals;
/* Weighing-Complete Module */
complt:
                putfmt(" itw=%i weight=%i\n",itw,weight);
                *wr++ = weight;          /* Update weight ring buffer  */
                if(wr > wrtop)
```

```
                { wr = wring;    /* Reset pointer  */
                  first = FALSE;         /* Ring buffer now full */
                }
        if(first == TRUE)        /* Number of data points in distribution
                                   depends on whether or not the buffer is
                                   full, signalled by first.  */
                wend = wr;
        else
                wend = wrtop;

        for (dd=dis; dd <= distop; )*dd++ = 0;   /* Zero distribution  */
        for (ww=wring; ww <= wend; ww++)
                dis[(*ww - dmin)/ddel]++ ;       /* Increment distribution
                                                  /* counter.  */
        for (gg=graph,dd=dis; dd <= distop; )
                *gg++ = (*dd++) * gsc;            /* Scale graph.  */

        num = weight;                    /* Now set up output to LED display */
        *par = 0;                        /* Make sure display is zeroed. */
        for (i=1; i <= 4; i++)
                { *par |= dsplay[num % 10] << (i-1)*4;
                                        /* Break out decimal digits
                                           and code them for display.  */
                  num /= 10;                    /* Get next digit.  */
                }

        if(--pc == 0)goto stop;
        goto drfals;
/* Stop execution; reset clock interrupt, exit  */
stop:
        clkset(1);
        exit(YES);

}


clkset(i)
int i;
/* This routine sets up and turns off the real-time clock.  Its
details are system dependent.
 This version supports the PDP-11 line-time-clock.
*/
{
#define CLKADR 0100
static int sv1,sv2;     /* Space to save the old clock vector */
int CLOCK(),*clp1 = CLKADR,*clp2 = CLKADR + 2;
                    /* CLOCK is the assembly language
                       clock interrupt routine.  clp1 and clp2 are used
                       as pointers to the clock vector. */
        if(i == 0)
                {
                sv1 = *clp1;
                sv2 = *clp2;            /* Save current vector. */
                *clp2 = 0;              /* Set clock interrupt
                                         priority to 0 */
                *clp1 = CLOCK;          /* Vector to interrupt routine */
                return;
                }
        else
                {
                /* Restore the clock vector to its previous contents. */
                *clp1 = sv1;
                *clp2 = sv2;
                return;
                }
```

```
CLKINT()          /* This routine is called by the clock interrupt routine */
{
extern int tsamp,tcount,data;
int *adcsr=0170400, *adbuf=0170402, dmask=0200;
extern BOOL dr,error,errorg;
/* Now define graphics variables.. */
#define DA 0170440
static int grflag = FALSE;        /* Flag to check for too fast refresh.  */
int *da0 = DA,*da1 = DA + 2,*da2 = DA + 4;     /* Pointer to D/A converters */
int inten = 07777,deten = 04000;              /* Intensify parameters  */
extern int *grf,npoint,gcount,tgr,dx;
int *g,i,j,x;

        if(--tcount == 0)
                {
                tcount = tsamp;
                if(dr == TRUE)error = TRUE;       /* Make sure that
                                                  /* processing is done */
                *adcsr = 1;               /* Start A/D conversion  */
                while((*adcsr & dmask) == 0) ;  /* Wait for conversion
                                                  to finish */
                data = *adbuf;
                dr = TRUE;                        /* Set data-ready flag  */
                }
        if(--gcount != 0)return;          /* No graph refresh this time.  */
        gcount = tgr;
        if(grflag != FALSE)
                { errorg = TRUE;          /* Refresh rate too fast!  */
                  return;
                }
        grflag = TRUE;                    /* Refresh in progress.   */
/* Refresh graph... */
        g = grf;                          /* Initialize pointer to graph. */
        for(i = 1; i <= npoint; i++)
                {
                *da0 = x;                 /* X-value to D/A  */
                x += dx;                  /* Increment x   */
                *da1 = *g++;              /* Y-value to D/A   */
                *da2 = inten;             /* Intensify point.   */
                for (j=1; j <= 10; j++) ;    /* Wait.... */
                *da2 = deten;             /* De-intensify  */
                *da1 = 0;                 /* Graph zero Y-value. */
                *da2 = inten;             /* Repeat intensify cycle.   */
                for (j=1; j <= 10; j++) ;
                *da2 = deten;
                }
        grflag = FALSE;                   /* Refresh cycle done.  */
        return;
}
```

B32   Assembly Language Routine

```
        .enable lc
        .title c62
;
; This is the interrupt service routine for the automated
; weighing program of Chapter 7.
;
        .globl clock,clkint
;
clock:  mov r0,-(sp)                 ;preserve machine state
        mov r1,-(sp)
        mov r2,-(sp)
        mov r3,-(sp)
```

```
        mov r4,-(sp)
        mov r5,-(sp)
;
        jsr pc,clkint           ;execute C clock interrupt routine
;
        mov (sp)+,r5            ;restore machine state
        mov (sp)+,r4
        mov (sp)+,r3
        mov (sp)+,r2
        mov (sp)+,r1
        mov (sp)+,r0
;
        rti                     ;return from interrupt
;
        .end
```

POLAR PLOTTER PROGRAMS IN FORTRAN

The polar plotter programs use a mixture of high-level language and assembly language to allow rapid development of an algorithm which is independent of timing constraints of the motor systems. The FORTRAN subroutine (Listing B33) communicates with the assembly language routine (Listing B35) through a common block containing flags which indicate that either radial, angular, or both steps are needed. The assembly language routine keeps track of the need to introduce delays when the pen is not in the proper vertical position. The pen delay is needed since the time required for the pen to drop and settle or lift from the plotting surface is large compared to the rate of motor stepping.

The subroutine vdraw is passed three values. The Cartesian coordinates of the end point of the desired vector are passed as 16-bit integers, while a floating point value called radst is passed, which is the number of radians per angular step. This value must be adjusted for the plotting mechanism (gearing) if straight lines are to be drawn. The value radst is varied until the optimum value is found and then not changed again.

Several checks must be made of the values calculated in the trigonometric library functions. Although the sine of an angle should not be greater than one, a result which is any amount greater than one will produce a negative value when subtracted from one. Since the square root of this value is desired, a run-time error will occur. To avoid this problem, an explicit limit is placed on the value of the sine of alpha. Similar tests are made on function returns to avoid dividing by zero. Because the angles used in the polar plotting subroutine range from 0 to 90 degrees, all possible values of the sine must be dealt with.

The assembly language routine hafset (Listing B34) is called by the main program to place the address of the stepping motor driver at the address of the LSI-11 line time clock (LTC). Every 10 milliseconds (for our 100Hz clock) the interrupt routine hafstp is entered. If no steps are to be made, it merely exits. If either an angular or radial step exists to be made, then hafstp indexes through a table of stepping motor actuation sequences in the direction requested by the subroutine vdraw, and writes the new actuation to a parallel output port. The assembly language routine then clears a software latch which allows the high-level language program to proceed.

This latch scheme is used to free the

algorithm designer from any concern for how fast the high-level language executes the various sections of code. As the text states, a performance improvement would be achieved by carefully reworking and rescaling the calculations once the combination of software and mechanism was shown to function properly.

B33   Vector Generation Subroutine

```
        Subroutine vdraw(ix2,iy2,radst)
c
c This routine drives a radial arm (polar) plotter and
c causes a vector to be drawn between the present pen
c position and the point described by the rectangular
c coordinates (ix2,iy2).  A coordinate transformation
c is first made and then the vector is drawn.
c
c
        COMMON/STEP/ISTEPR,ISTEPT,ISTEP,ILAST,IRDIRC,ITDIRC
c
        data irc,irc2,ix1,iy1,irl,thetal/
     $430,680,430,680,792,0.920/
c
c radst is the number of radians per angular step.
c
c state initial
c
        itmp=ix2
        ix2=iy2+irc
        iy2=-(itmp-irc2)
c
c coordinate transformation
c
        ir2=sqrt(float(ix2)**2+float(iy2)**2)
c
c ir2 is radial distance to endpoint of vector
c
        alenth=sqrt(float(ix2-ix1)**2+float(iy2-iy1)**2)
c
c alenth is length of vector.
c
        theta2=atan(float(iy2)/float(ix2))
c
c theta2 is polar angle to end point of vector (IN RADIANS).
c
        cosalp=(float(irl)**2+alenth**2-float(ir2)**2)
     $/(2.*float(irl)*alenth)
        sinalp=cosalp**2
        if(sinalp.gt.1.)sinalp=1.
        sinalp=sqrt(1.-sinalp)
        if(sinalp.lt.0.1e-11)sinalp=0.1e-11
        tanalp=sinalp/cosalp
        alpha=atan(tanalp)
        if(tanalp.lt.0.)alpha=alpha+3.14159
c
c Alpha is the suplement of the angle between the radius
c irl and the vector (in radians).
c
        cl=abs(float(irl)*sin(alpha))
c
        c2=3.14159-alpha
c
c cl and c2 are constants used in finding the
c radial distance "iri".
c c2 is the angle in radians which the radius to the
```

```
c starting point of the vector makes with the radius to
c the current end point of the vector (point "i").
c
        thstp=-radst
        itdirc=0
        if(theta1.ge.theta2)go to 100
        thstp=radst
        itdirc=1
c
c determine angular direction for plot.
c
c end state initial
c
100     continue
c
c determine next state
c
        if(abs(theta2-theta1).gt.radst/1.2)go to 200
c
c to here, theta is at goal, check radial value.
c
110     continue
c
        if(iabs(ir2-ir1).gt.1)go to 120
c
c state exit
c
c to here, plot is finished.  Now, update values
c before exit.
c
        ix1=ix2
        iy1=iy2
c
        return
c subroutine exit point.
c
c end state exit
c
120     continue
c
c determine next state
c
c to here, a radial step exists to be taken.
c
        if(ilast.eq.0)go to 120
c
c wait for last step to take place.
c
        ilast=0
        irdirc=0
        if(ir2.gt.ir1)irdirc=1
c
c set step direction.
c
        istepr=1
        istept=0
        istep=1
c
        ir1=ir1+2
        if(irdirc.eq.0)ir1=ir1-4
c
        go to 110
c
c
200     continue
```

```
c
c state angular step
c
c to here, exists an angular step to make.
c
         c2=c2-radst
c
         iri=cl/sin(c2)
c
         ilatch=1
c
c we must take only one step in angular direction
c but perhaps many in radial.
c
c end state angular step
c
210      continue
c
c state radial step
c
         if(ilast.eq.0)go to 210
c
c wait for last step
c
         if(iri.LE.irl)go to 250
c
c to here, we must take a step in the positive
c radial direction.
c
         istept=ilatch
         ilatch=0
         if(istept.eq.1)thetal=thetal+thstp
         ilast=0
         irdirc=1
         istepr=1
         istep=1
         irl=irl+2
         go to 210
c
250      continue
c
         if(irl-iri.le.1)go to 300
c
c to here, we must take a step in the negative radial direction.
c
         istept=ilatch
         ilatch=0
         if(istept.eq.1)thetal=thetal+thstp
         ilast=0
         irdirc=0
         istepr=1
         istep=1
         irl=irl-2
         go to 210
c
300      continue
c
         istept=ilatch
         ilatch=0
         if(istept.eq.0)go to 100
c
c end state radial step
c
c
c state angular step
```

```
c
c to here, we need to take an angular step
c
        ilast=0
        istepr=0
        istep=1
        thetal=thetal+thstp
        go to 100
c
c end state angular step
c
        end
```

B34   Assembly Language Subroutine to Initialize Interrupts

```
        .TITLE HAFSET
        .GLOBL HAFSET,HAFSTP,RTSAV
;
; THIS ROUTINE ARMS INTERRUPTS FOR VDRAW ROUTINE
;
;
HAFSET: MOV @#100,RTSAV
        MOV @#102,RTSAV+2
        MOV #0,@#102
        MOV #HAFSTP,@#100
        RTS PC
;
        .END
```

B35   Assembly Language Subroutines for Sequencing Stepping Motors

```
        .TITLE HAFSTP
        .GLOBL HAFSTP,PENUP,PENDWN
;
; THIS CLOCK-DRIVEN INTERRUPT ROUTINE DRIVES TWO
; STEPPING MOTORS.
;
PAROUT=167772   ;PARALLEL OUTPUT PORT ADDRESS
;
;
HAFSTP: TST ISTEP
        BNE INT1
        MOV #1,ILAST
        RTI
;
INT1:   TST ISTEPR                  ;EXIST RADIAL STEP TO TAKE?
        BEQ INT2
;
                ;TO HERE, TAKE RADIAL STEP
;
        TST IRDIRC                  ;WHICH DIRECTION?
        BNE INT3
        INC RADPNT                  ;POINTER <-- POINTER+1
        CMP RADPNT,#RADTAB+LTABR    ;PAST END OF TABLE?
        BLT STEPR
        MOV #RADTAB,RADPNT          ;RESET POINTER TO START OF TABLE
        BR STEPR
;
INT3:   DEC RADPNT                  ;POINTER <-- POINTER-1
        CMP RADPNT,#RADTAB          ;PAST END OF TABLE?
        BGE STEPR
        MOV #RADTAB+LTABR-1,RADPNT  ;RESET POINTER TO END OF TABLE
;
STEPR:  MOVB @RADPNT,@#PAROUT       ;STEP RADIAL MOTOR
```

```
        CMP IPEN,#1                     ;PEN DOWN?
        BNE INT2
        BIS #200,@#PAROUT               ;SET PEN
;
;
INT2:   TST ISTEPT                      ;EXIST ANGULAR STEP TO TAKE?
        BEQ XIT
;
                    ;TO HERE, TAKE ANGULAR STEP
;
        TST ITDIRC                      ;WHICH DIRECTION?
        BNE INT4
        INC THEPNT                      ;THETA POINTER <-- POINTER+1
        CMP THEPNT,#THETAB+LTABT        ;POINTER PAST END OF TABLE?
        BLT STEPT
        MOV #THETAB,THEPNT              ;RESET POINTER
        BR STEPT
;
INT4:   DEC THEPNT                      ;THETA POINTER <-- POINTER+1
        CMP THEPNT,#THETAB              ;POINTER PAST END OF TABLE?
        BGE STEPT
        MOV #THETAB+LTABT-1,THEPNT      ;RESET POINTER TO END OF TABLE
;
STEPT:  MOVB @THEPNT,@#PAROUT+1         ;STEP ANGULAR MOTOR
        CLR ISTEPT
;
XIT:    CLR ISTEP                       ;ISTEP <-- FALSE
        MOV #1,ILAST                    ;LAST STEP <-- TRUE
        RTI
;
;
PENUP:  CMP IPEN,#0             ;0 => PEN IS UP
        BNE 1$
        RTS PC                          ;PEN IS ALREADY UP
;
1$:     BIC #200,@#PAROUT      ;RAISE PEN
        CLR IPEN               ;IPEN <-- UP
        MOV #15000.,R0
2$:     DEC R0
        BNE 2$                 ;PEN DELAY
        RTS PC
;
PENDWN: CMP IPEN,#1            ;1 => PEN IS DOWN
        BNE 1$
        RTS PC                          ;PEN IS ALREADY DOWN
;
1$:     BIS #200,@#PAROUT      ;LOWER PEN
        MOV #1,IPEN            ;IPEN <-- DOWN
        MOV #15000.,R0
2$:     DEC R0
        BNE 2$
        RTS PC
;
;
;
RADPNT: .WORD RADTAB                    ;POINTER INTO RADIAL STEP SEQUENCE
                                        ;TABLE
RADTAB: .BYTE 10.,8.,9.,1,5,4,6,2
LTABR=.-RADTAB
;
;
THEPNT: .WORD THETAB                    ;POINTER INTO THETA STEP SEQUENCE TABLE
THETAB: .BYTE 10.,8.,9.,1,5,4,6,2
LTABT=.-THETAB
;
```

```
;
        .PSECT STEP RW,D,OVR,GBL
;
ISTEPR: .WORD 0
ISTEPT: .WORD 0
ISTEP:  .WORD 0
ILAST:  .WORD 0
IRDIRC: .WORD 0
ITDIRC: .WORD 0
IPEN:   .WORD 0
;
        .END
```

INDEX

David Auslander has presented papers and published articles in a number of engineering and scholarly journals on such subjects as: the design and analysis of dynamic systems, computer simulation and modeling, real time computing for mini- and microcomputers, population dynamics, and automatic control systems. He is a frequent contributor to the *American Society of Mechanical Engineers Journal of Dynamic Systems, Measurement and Control* and regularly presents papers before the ASME. He has co-authored four books, including *Case Studies in Computer Control* and *Introducing Systems and Control.*

The material in this book is based on courses he has taught and developed in the Department of Mechanical Engineering at the University of California, Berkeley. Previously, Professor Auslander accepted invitations to teach in the Electrical Engineering departments of the University of Tokyo and the National Polytechnical Institute of Mexico City. His publications have been translated into Polish, Japanese, and Spanish.

He is a member of ASME and the Society for Computer Simulation. In 1973 and 1976 the Franklin Institute awarded him the Louis E. Levy Medal for outstanding papers.

Professor Auslander received a Bachelors in Mechanical Engineering from The Cooper Union, and a Masters and Doctorate of Science from the Massachusetts Institute of Technology.

Paul Sagues is president of Berkeley Process Control, Inc. He has designed automated inspection equipment for the semiconductor industry, a network data acquisition system for the food processing industry, and analog and discrete-logic control systems. He has worked with speech recognition and dynamic control systems and has performed modeling of dynamic systems. He has also worked in the field of automotive control.

Mr. Sagues received a Bachelor of Science in Biology from Stanford University and a Master of Science in Mechanical Engineering, specializing in dynamic systems and control, from the University of California, Berkeley. He has presented papers before the Joint Automatic Control Conference, the American Society of Mechanical Engineers and the National Computer Conference.